The Anti-Federalist

The
Anti-Federalist

An Abridgment, by Murray Dry, of
The Complete Anti-Federalist
Edited, with Commentary and Notes, by

Herbert J. Storing

The University of Chicago Press
Chicago and London

The University of Chicago Press, Chicago 60637
The University of Chicago Press, Ltd., London

ISBN: 0-226-77563-1 (cloth); 0-226-77565-8 (paper)

Library of Congress Cataloging in Publication Data
Complete Anti-Federalist. Selections.
    The Anti-Federalist.

    Bibliography: p.
    Includes index.
        1. United States—Constitutional history—
Sources.   2. Political science—United States—
History—Sources.   3. United States—Constitutional
law.   I. Dry, Murray.   II. Storing, Herbert J.,
1928–77.   III. Title.
JK155.C6525   1985   342.73'029   84-16207
                           347.30229

Contents

Contents

VIRGINIA

NEW YORK

Preface

The purpose of this abridgment of Herbert J. Storing's *The Complete Anti-Federalist* is to provide students of American political thought, especially those concerned with the American founding, with a one-volume companion to *The Federalist*. The writings and speeches have been chosen on the basis of the importance of their arguments and their prominence in the ratification campaign.

In making the selections I have followed my late teacher's suggestions as implicit in his commentary to the entries in the complete work and in his extended essay *What the Anti-Federalists Were For* (see bibliography). The first chapter of that essay forms the introduction to the present book.

Storing's manner of presenting the Anti-Federalists was to begin with the non-signers' objections and the first major essays, moving to a geographical order that follows the chronology of the ratification—Pennsylvania, Massachusetts and New England, Virginia and the South, and New York. My abridgment adopts the same order, with material from each area. The most substantial selections are the letters of Brutus (complete) and those of The Federal Farmer (abridged). These are the ablest and most influential of the Anti-Federalist writings and offer an alternative to *The Federalist* on such subjects as federalism, republicanism, judicial review, and a Bill of Rights.

Much of the editorial apparatus of *The Complete Anti-Federalist* has been retained—Storing's introductions to each part of the ratification campaign and to each selection included here; the notes with their extensive cross references; and the marginal paragraph numbers. (The three-part number system was devised for convenient cross reference; the first number denotes the volume of *The Complete Anti-Federalist*, the second the position of the essay within that volume, and the third the paragraph.) Where omissions have been made within a selection, the original paragraph and note numbers remain unchanged. Some numbers are therefore nonconsecutive, and Storing's introductions in some instances refer to passages not included in this abridgment. The reader wishing to consult the complete edition should have little trouble locating particular passages there. (A table of contents of *The Complete Anti-Federalist* may be found in the Appendix to the paperback *What the Anti-Federalists Were For*.)

The bibliography for this abridgment consists of two parts. To the list of works frequently cited by Storing, with the abbreviations he uses in the notes, I have added a number of books and articles—some cited by or known to Storing and others published since his death in 1977.

I have sought to keep the one-volume edition faithful to the high quality and thoroughness of Storing's original work.

MURRAY DRY

Introduction

The Constitution of the United States was viewed by the founding generation as distinctive, even unique, in the extent to which it was the product of deliberation. Most previous foundings seemed to have been the result of chance or the edict of one all-powerful man. But the United States Constitution was framed by a numerous and diverse body of statesmen, sitting for over three months; it was widely, fully, and vigorously debated in the country at large; and it was adopted by (all things considered) a remarkably open and representative procedure. Viewed in this light, those who opposed the Constitution must be seen as playing an indispensable if subordinate part in the founding process. They contributed to the dialogue of the American founding. To take only the most obvious case, the Constitution that came out of the deliberations of 1787 and 1788 was not the same Constitution that went in; for it was accepted subject to the understanding that it would be amended immediately to provide for a bill of rights. Moreover, the founding of a nation does not end with the making of a constitution. The Constitution *did* settle many questions, and it established a lasting structure of rules and principles—we do not adopt the current cant that fundamental law is shapeless stuff to be formed at will by future generations. But it did not settle *everything;* it did not finish the task of making the American polity. The political life of the community continues to be a dialogue, in which the Anti-Federalist concerns and principles still play an important part.

The Anti-Federalists are entitled, then, to be counted among the Founding Fathers, in what is admittedly a somewhat paradoxical sense, and to share in the honor and the study devoted to the founding. In general, however, they have not enjoyed such a position. Champions of a negative and losing cause, they have found only a cramped place in the shadow of the great constitutional accomplishment of 1787. They have often been presented as narrow-minded local politicians, unwilling to face the utter inadequacy of the Articles of Confederation or incapable of seeing beyond the boundaries of their own states or localities. They have been described as men without principle, willing to use any argument to drag down the Constitution, yet willing, many of them, when the Constitution was adopted, to change their colors and become enthusiastic Federalists.[1] It is true that with the rise of the Beardian critique of the Constitution and its framers, the Anti-Federalists have been viewed with a more friendly eye. Merrill Jensen

I

has taught us to take seriously the possibility that the Anti-Federalists were right about the need for only modest changes in the Articles of Confederation and about the departure of the Constitution from the principles of the Revolution. He has inspired a full historical account of the Anti-Federal movement, and he has pointed to the need to take up the serious study of Anti-Federal thought. At the same time, the harsh edges of Beardian analysis have been worn away, and we are now in a position to consider afresh the class differences involved in the constitutional controversy, freed of many of the Beardian excesses.[2] Yet valuable as all of this has been, the corrected Beardian eye betrays still its original squint. It tends to see simple democratic agrarians among the Anti-Federalists as it tends to see self-seeking commercial oligarchs among the Federalists.[3] There is some basis for these views, but the picture is thin and distorted. Indeed, one of the few substantial accounts of Anti-Federal thought is a persuasive refutation of the Beardian thesis as applied to the Anti-Federalists and an attempt to show that the Anti-Federalists were in fact "men of little faith" in American national self-government.[4] Gordon Wood has added greatly to our understanding of the Anti-Federalists in his rich and encyclopedic account of the American founding and the way the Americans gradually blundered into a new political theory. Deep and lucid as his insights often are, however, Wood is finally less interested in understanding the Anti-Federalists (or the Federalists) as they understood themselves than in exposing the deeper social forces from which the whole sphere of "ideology," to use Bailyn's term, is derivative. Thus a debate that was for the Anti-Federalists fundamentally political becomes for Wood fundamentally sociological.[5]

There has been no sustained, comprehensive attempt to examine the thought, the principles, the argument of the Anti-Federalists, as they were understood by the Anti-Federalists themselves and by the other men of that time. Such an examination will be undertaken here. The aim will not be a history of the Anti-Federal movement or an analysis of its economic, sociological, or psychological underpinnings. We shall try to avoid presupposing some external set of questions or framework of analysis. Rather, we shall try to proceed from inside Anti-Federal thought, seeing the questions as they saw them, following the arguments as they made them. We shall explore the different levels of Anti-Federal theorizing, working our way critically through and if necessary beyond them, but always with the idea that the Anti-Federalists may have something to teach. Because the American founding took the form of a debate or dialogue, Anti-Federal thought is best examined within the movement and different levels of that dialogue. For this reason it will be necessary to take some note of the Federalist as well as the Anti-Federalist side of the debate, but the purpose is to present only so much of what the Anti-Federalists were against as is necessary to understand what they were for.

In beginning with the question of what the Anti-Federalists were *for*, we are not, it must be admitted, adhering to the aim of presenting the Anti-Federalist argument as it presented itself. The Anti-Federalists were primarily *against* the Constitution. We do remain true to our aim in a deeper and more significant sense, however, because the Anti-Federalists themselves understood their negative conclusions about the Constitution to be derived from a positive political theory or set of political principles. [6] The aim, then, will be to give a sympathetic, critical, and full account of the fundamental Anti-Federal position.

Was there, however, a single Anti-Federal position? In the most obvious sense there surely was not. The Federalists claimed that the opposers of the Constitution could not agree among themselves, that they shared no common principles, that their arguments canceled each other out. This is an exaggeration, for there was more agreement about many points of opposition to the Constitution than might appear at first glance.[7] Yet it is not possible to read far among the Anti-Federal writings without being struck by an extraordinary heterogeneity. It would be difficult to find a single point about which *all* of the Anti-Federalists agreed. They did not, finally, even agree unanimously in opposing the adoption of the Constitution. Many favored adoption if amendments could be secured; and others finally accepted the Constitution, even without a guarantee of amendment, as the best of the available choices. There is in fact no hard and fast way of even identifying "Anti-Federalists." Some men, notably Edmund Randolph, were Federalist and Anti-Federalist at different times. Moderate or lukewarm adherents to either side were often almost indistinguishable from one another. Moreover, the specific points of disagreement and the reasons given by the Anti-Federalists were various and even contradictory. This is not to say that the Federalists were in much better condition. There is an impression of greater unity here because the Federalists were (in general) unified in supporting the Constitution, although some Federal reservations are scarcely distinguishable from Anti-Federal objections. That impression has been strengthened by the Federalists' victory and by the massive impact on later generations of *The Federalist* papers, which have tended to occupy the Federalist stage and lend their unity to the whole group supporting the Constitution. [8] There were in fact diverse and contradictory opinions among the Federalists just as there were among their opponents.

If the Federalists and Anti-Federalists were divided among themselves, they were, at a deeper level, united with one another. Their disagreements were not based on different premises about the nature of man or the ends of political life. They were not the deep cleavages of contending regimes. They were the much less sharp and clear-cut differences within the family, as it were, of men agreed that the purpose of government is the regulation and thereby the protection of individual rights and that the best instrument for this purpose is some form of limited, republican government. It is their common ground that explains, to a large extent, the relatively unclear line between the two camps and the diversity within each of them. This is not to say that the differences are negligible, as those would argue who claim that there is no basic political controversy or political theorizing in the United States.[9] The differences are limited, but they are nevertheless substantial and well formed. The nation was born in consensus but it lives in controversy, and the main lines of that controversy are well-worn paths leading back to the founding debate.

In searching for the underlying unity in the Anti-Federal position we are not tabulating the frequency of different arguments. We are looking not for what is *common* so much as for what is *fundamental*. We might well find the foundations laid in a very few writings, even a single one. Thus, on the Federalist side, a James Madison is more important in this kind of quest than a Tench Coxe, not because he is more typical or more influential in a direct sense but because he sees farther or better. He can *explain* more. The same is true on the Anti-Federal side of The Federal Farmer, Brutus, and such little known writers as A [Maryland] Farmer and The Impartial Examiner. Not all of these men were widely read, and some of them made arguments that were uncommon; but they explored or at least exposed the theoretical ground that most other Anti-Federalists took for granted.

Proceeding in this way, clearing our path through the superficial tangle, dealing as well as we can with the patches of obscurity and looseness we find in even the best Anti-Federal thinkers, we shall discover a set of principles that is a good deal clearer and more coherent, and also more relevant to an understanding of the American founding and the American polity, than has usually been supposed. But we shall also find, at the very heart of the Anti-Federal position, a dilemma or a tension. This is the critical weakness of Anti-Federalist thought and at the same time its strength and even its glory. For the Anti-Federalists could neither fully reject nor fully accept the leading principles of the Constitution. They were indeed open to Hamilton's scornful charge of trying to reconcile contradictions.[10] This is the element of truth in Cecelia Kenyon's characterization of them as men of little faith. They did not fail to *see* the opportunity for American nationhood that the Federalists seized so gloriously, but they could not join in grasping it. They doubted; they held back; they urged second thoughts. This was, however, not a mere failure of will or lack of courage. They had *reasons,* and the reasons have weight. They thought—and it cannot easily be denied—that this great national opportunity was profoundly problematical, that it could be neither grasped nor let alone without risking everything. The Anti-Federalists were committed to both union and the states; to both the great American republic and the small, self-governing community; to both commerce and civic virtue; to both private gain and public good. At its best, Anti-Federal thought explores these tensions and points to the need for any significant American political thought to confront them; for they were not resolved by the Constitution but are inherent in the principles and traditions of American political life.

4

1. See John Fiske, *The Critical Period of American History, 1783–1789* (Boston 1888) ch. 7; George Bancroft, *History of the Formation of the Constitution of the United States of America* (New York 1882) II, book 4 passim; George Ticknor Curtis, *Constitutional History of the United States: From Their Declaration of Independence to the Close of the Civil War* (New York 1889) I, 626; Andrew McLaughlin, *The Confederation and the Constitution, 1783–1789* (New York 1905) ch. 17; Forrest McDonald, *E Pluribus Unum* (Boston 1965) 208.

2. Charles A. Beard, *An Economic Interpretation of the Constitution* (New York 1913, 1935); Merrill Jensen, *The Articles of Confederation* (Madison, Wisc., 1940); Jensen, *The New Nation* (New York 1950); Jackson Turner Main, *The Antifederalists: Critics of the Constitution* (Chapel Hill, N.C., 1960); Forrest McDonald, *We the People: The Economic Origins of the Constitution* (Chicago 1958); Robert E. Brown, *Charles Beard and the Constitution: A Critical Analysis of "An Economic Interpretation of the Constitution"* (Princeton 1956); Jackson Turner Main, "Charles A. Beard and the Constitution: A Critical Review of Forrest McDonald's *We the People*," *William and Mary Quarterly* January 1960, 88–102, with a rebuttal by Forrest McDonald, ibid. 102–10.

3. See, e.g., Main, *Antifederalists* 280–81.

4. Cecelia Kenyon, "Men of Little Faith: The Anti-Federalists on the Nature of Representative Government," *William and Mary Quarterly* January 1955; Kenyon, "Introduction," *The Anti-Federalists* (Indianapolis 1966).

5. Gordon Wood, *The Creation of the American Republic, 1776–1787* (Chapel Hill, N.C., 1969) ch. 12. See Bernard Bailyn, *The Ideological Origins of the American Revolution* (Cambridge, Mass., 1967).

6. For this reason "Anti-Federalist" seems the best rendering of the name. There was no consistent usage at the time and there has been none since. "Anti-Federalist" balances the positive and negative sides by giving the group (or the position) a proper name, while still emphasizing its character as opposition. The typographically convenient "Antifederalist," now generally in favor, suggests more cohesion than actually existed, while "anti-Federalist" suggests a merely negative, dependent unity. Forrest McDonald, apparently the only other writer to consider this little question in print, agrees about the implications of the main forms. He adopts "anti-Federalist" as "the more neutral term"; and while it is not neutral, it does accurately reflect his opinion, contrary to the conclusion here, that there was no significant theoretical coherence in the Anti-Federalist arguments or principles. Forrest McDonald, "The anti-Federalists, 1781–1789," *Wisconsin Magazine of History* Spring 1963, 206n.

7. Plebeian 6.11 and others.

8. The fundamental unity of *The Federalist* can be disputed. See Douglass Adair, "The Authorship of the Disputed Federalist Papers" part 2, *William and Mary Quarterly* April and July 1944; repr. in Adair, *Fame and the Founding Fathers*, ed. H. Trevor Colbourn (New York 1974) 27–74. Alpheus Mason, "The Federalist—a Split Personality," *American Historical Review* LVII, no. 3 (1952). Gottfried Dietze, *The Federalist* (Baltimore 1960).

9. See Daniel Boorstin, *The Genius of American Politics* (Chicago 1953).

10. *The Federalist* no. 23, 151.

Centinel, Letter I

(PHILADELPHIA) INDEPENDENT GAZETTEER
and
(PHILADELPHIA) FREEMAN'S JOURNAL
October 1787

The most prolific and one of the best known of the Anti-Federalist essayists was the Centinel, whose essays appeared in the Philadelphia *Independent Gazetteer* and the Philadelphia *Freeman's Journal* and were widely reprinted, although not in their entirety.[1] The first two numbers were printed in numerous newspapers and also appeared separately as broadsides.[2] The first nine letters were reprinted in an Anti-Federalist collection, issued in New York in 1788.[3]

There are three groups of Centinel essays. The first eighteen numbers, published between 5 October 1787 and 9 April 1788, discuss the principles of the new Constitution and of its advocates. Papers XIX to XXIV, published in October and November 1788, were aimed at influencing the election of representatives to the new Congress, the Constitution having been adopted; they are concerned chiefly with party politics in Pennsylvania, past and present, and with the financial affairs of Robert Morris and his associates. Finally, in the autumn of 1789, there appeared another dozen essays under the heading "Centinel Revived," which deal with the proposed amendments to the federal Constitution and with the state constitution and state political affairs. Only the first group is reprinted here.

The Centinel letters were generally attributed at the time to Judge George Bryan, a prominent Pennsylvania legislator and judge, who was the principal leader of the Anti-Federalists in his state. However, Judge Bryan's son, Samuel, claimed to be the author in several private letters;[4] and it is now generally thought that he was the author, although reflecting the views of and no doubt working in close collaboration with his father.[5]

Centinel does not present systematic arrangement and development of argument, like, say, the letters of The Federal Farmer, or the essays of Cato or Brutus; his essays are rather like a series of partially spontaneous speeches made over a period of time to a shifting and somewhat inattentive audience. Variations on a set of themes rather than a schematic development of themes is Centinel's style. Typically he starts an essay by going over some of the ground of the last one, sometimes moving on to new matters, sometimes developing themes barely mentioned before, sometimes substantially repeating earlier arguments. Centinel tends to lay his heaviest emphasis on rather shallow statements of certain standard themes—the importance of resisting the influence of great names, the critical position of the press and the attempts by Federalists to stifle it, the various nefarious practices indulged in by the friends of the Constitution, etc. The more significant and substantial arguments typically spin out from these primary themes.

Except for their length and their notoriety, it can hardly be maintained, as Konkle attempts to do, that "these papers at once took rank, on their side, with *The Federalist* papers on the other."[6] There are substantial and important arguments, in addition to information of a historical interest, scattered throughout the papers; but the papers do not, taken as a whole, compare in quality with the best Anti-Federalist writing, to say nothing of *The Federalist*. The first essay is indeed of major importance in the corpus of Anti-Federalist writings; the second essay is important; the fourth, fifth, sixth, and eleventh contain material of interest to the student of Anti-Federalist ideas; the remaining essays will properly be passed over by most nonspecialist readers. There follows a brief description of the content of each essay.

In his first essay, Centinel, after urging the need for dispassionate and deliberate examination, turns to a discussion of John Adams' principle of balanced government. Centinel objects that, first, there is not human wisdom enough to construct such a government; second, it would not last; third, it would not, in any case, answer the purpose of preserving liberty. The correct principle of free government is responsibility of the government to the people where the people are virtuous and property is pretty equally distributed. Thus the best government has a simple structure, short terms of office, rotation, etc. The proposed Constitution is *neither* balanced, as Adams wants, *nor* responsible, as Centinel thinks best. Centinel next turns to the powers of the Congress under the new Constitution, concluding with the warning that it is the opinion of all writers that a very extensive country cannot be governed on democratic principles except by a confederation of a number of smaller republics (2.7.11–19). He then discusses the structure of the new government, concluding that the Senate will be the great efficient body and that the government will be in practice an irresponsible aristocracy. Finally Centinel objects that no provision has been made for the liberty of the press or for jury trial.

Repeating the need for fundamental and free discussion, free of the "splendor of names," Centinel turns in his second essay to a point-by-point refutation of one of the most influential Federalist statements, James Wilson's brief address to the citizens of Philadelphia on 6 October.[7] Centinel argues that the powers of the federal government, particularly in the area of taxation and the judiciary, will destroy the states and endanger the freedom of the press and personal liberty, which are unprotected by a bill of rights.

He argues that no standing army should be permitted in time of peace except with the vote of two-thirds of the legislature, that the Senate will become the nucleus of a permanent aristocracy, that the provisions for amendment are illusory, and that the opposition to the Constitution, far from consisting of interested men, includes the respectable yeomen, a number of the members of the Philadelphia Convention, and the majority of the Congress.

The third essay begins with repetition of earlier arguments about the importance of the decision to be made, the need for fundamental investigation, and the dubious motives of the Federalists. Centinel describes the events leading to the Constitution and its ratification in Pennsylvania, which show an intention to establish a new permanent aristocracy, hidden by the old forms. He goes on to criticize the power given to the Congress to alter state regulations regarding the times, places, and manner of holding elections for the federal congress, for calling forth the militia, and for protecting the slave trade for a period of twenty years—this last being the only significant contribution of this paper (2.7.76). He concludes with an expression of surprise at Quaker support of the Constitution and a reference to Brutus' discussion of the impracticability of maintaining a free government over so extensive a territory.

The fourth essay is more substantial. Here Centinel contends that the present difficulties of the United States are due to the enormous demands of financing the Revolution rather than to intrinsic deficiencies in the Articles of Confederation. Warning against the danger of governing overmuch and thus weakening the people's sense of obligation and duty, so important in free government, Centinel argues that the only amendment necessary is one giving Congress the power to lay an impost on commerce and to regulate trade. He concludes by yet again discoursing on the secrecy with which the Constitution was formulated, the stifling of discussion, the reliance on great names, the exaggeration of present distresses, the attempt to represent the new government as the only alternative, the weight of the opposition, and the need for reconsideration.

The fifth essay is cast in the form of a reply to a remark by James Wilson in the Pennsylvania ratifying convention that a consolidation of the United States would be improper. It is largely a repetition of arguments made in numbers I and II about the extensive powers of the general government under the new Constitution, but Centinel discusses the "necessary and proper" clause for the first time and rebuts Wilson's argument that the Constitution requires the preservation of the states by showing that the states might become mere boards of election and eventually (by means of Congress's ultimate power to provide for elections) be eliminated altogether. This paper contains brief but interesting remarks on dual sovereignty (2.7.99–100) and on the object of government being to check and control the ambitious and designing (2.7.101).

Commenting on the "incredible transition" of a people once full of zest for liberty now about to sacrifice it, ignoring acknowledged danger in the new Constitution "in order to reap the golden harvest of regulated commerce," Centinel expatiates in his sixth essay on the lust of dominion and the need to guard against it in establishing political systems: "the great end of civil government is to protect the weak from the oppression of the powerful to put every man upon the level of equal liberty. . . ." (2.7.107).

The seventh essay contains nothing of substance. Centinel goes beyond his earlier remarks only in the strength of his denunciation of the Pennsylvania Federalists and in his suggestion that, despite the favorable action of the Pennsylvania convention, the people, aroused by "the enlightened pen of patriotism," will "assert their liberty, if necessary, by the sword" (2.7.116). He ends by calling for a second convention.

The eighth essay contains further reflections on the benefits of freedom, the dangers of the new Constitution, the corrupt character and treasonable activities of the advocates of the Constitution, concealed behind such respected names as Washington. The essay adds little to previous discussions except violence of language and a remark on the character of the merchant who, immersed in his narrow schemes of wealth, is the last to see a threat to public liberty (2.7.126).

Essay IX opens with praise of the Pennsylvania constitution as the triumph of patriotism over ambition, a victory which the well-born few seek to overturn. The Constitution contains a mere pretense of reservations in favor of liberty and is in fact a surrender at will and pleasure to our rulers. The illicit activities of the Federalists are further traced.

The tenth essay describes the success of the press in rousing the people to the dangers of the Constitution and the reaction of James Wilson and the Federalists in establishing a committee to collect funds to increase the stream of Federalist propaganda and to prepare for the use of force if necessary.

In his eleventh essay Centinel returns to more systematic argument. There are three arguments chiefly relied upon by the advocates of the Constitution: (1) the distresses of the community, (2) the evils of anarchy, (3) and the horrible consequences of the dissolution of the Union. The first having been treated in previous papers, Centinel here discusses the second and third, arguing that even anarchy is preferable to certain despotism because good government may grow out of it, that in any case anarchy is more likely if the Constitution is adopted than if it is not, that the event of separate confederacies is improbable—is in fact a hobgoblin sprung from the brain of the author of *The Federalist*—and that, even admitting that disunion would be the result of rejection of the Constitution, occasional wars are preferable to despotism. Centinel closes with a complaint about the Post Office suppression of the circulation of newspapers from state to state.

In the twelfth essay Centinel defends his contention that the activities of the proponents of the Constitution constitute a conspiracy, by exposing their sensitiveness to the charge, their reliance on the authority of names, their precipitation in such places as Massachusetts, and their attempt to shackle the press, particularly in Pennsylvania.

The thirteenth essay contains further denunciations of the activity of the "conspirators," ending with a call for the establishment of local societies by and communication among the "patriots" to "frustrate the machinations of an ambitious junto" (2.7.160).

In his fourteenth essay *Centinel* presents extensive extracts from Luther Martin's Genuine Information to prove that the new Constitution does not and was not intended to establish a federal government but provides instead for a consolidation. He ends with further discussion of the suppression of the circulation of Anti-Federalist newspapers.

Returning to the theme of the first essay, Centinel observes in his fifteenth paper that, the science of government being most difficult and abstruse, men are likely to be imposed on by the artful and designing, particularly at times like the present, when the healthy distrust of innovation has been lost. The bulk of the paper is devoted to a consideration of the Massachusetts ratification, showing that circumstances in Massachusetts led many men of property to join the Federalist conspiracy, that the elections were held in the heat of enthusiasm, and that few able Anti-Federalists were elected, and that even so, the Constitution was ratified by a bare majority and with qualifying amendments.

In his sixteenth essay Centinel argues that the ex post facto provision precludes the new Congress from taking measures to compel public defaulters to render an account. If Congress should desire nevertheless to secure the money for the government, the members would be precluded by their oath to support the Constitution; and if they proceeded nevertheless, they would be restrained by the Supreme Court, which (Centinel argues here) will have the power to construe the Constitution in last resort. The failure to secure the old debts due to the United States would also be unjust to certain states, like Pennsylvania, which had made unusual exertions to meet their obligations, and would give unfair advantage to the delinquent states.

Centinel devotes the first part of his seventeenth essay to a continuation of his argument that the Constitution was intended to screen public defaulters, discussing particularly the financial affairs of Robert Morris and of General Thomas Mifflin, the quartermaster general. He alludes again to the Post Office "suppression" of "patriotic" newspapers and concludes with a defense of Anti-Federalist writer, Benjamin Workman, against the attack of Francis Hopkinson.

The eighteenth and last essay contains further discussion of the insidious measures taken to promote the establishment of the Constitution, particularly the propagation of false information of unanimous Federalist sentiment in various parts of the country and the muzzling of the press. The strength of

Anti-Federalist sentiment in Pennsylvania is described. The Centinel retains his anonymity in order to avoid mere personal attacks, which would deflect attention from the proper object.

1. With the exception of the second essay, the essays appeared first in the *Independent Gazetteer*. Most but not all were printed shortly thereafter in the *Freeman's Journal*.

2. It was these broadsides, presumably, that were distributed by the New York Federal Republican Committee. See Main, *Antifederalists* 235.

3. *Observations on the Proposed Constitution for the United States of America, Clearly Shewing It To Be a Complete System of Aristocracy and Tyranny and Destructive of the Rights and Liberties of the People* (New York 1788. Contains, in addition to the Centinel essays, the Address and Reasons of Dissent of the Minority of the Pennsylvania Convention [below, 3.11], Edmund Randolph's letter of 10 October 1787 to the Speaker of the Virginia House of Delegates [above, 2.5] and the proposed Constitution).

4. According to McMaster and Stone, whose source is a private communication from the historian Paul Leicester Ford, Samuel Bryan wrote to George Clinton, saying, "I have not the honor of being personally known to your Excellency, but . . . I flatter myself that in the character of Centinel I have been honored with your approbation and esteem." McMaster and Stone 6–7n. Burton Konkle's version of the letter is significantly different: ". . . I flatter myself that in the character of Centinel I, I have been honored with your approbation and esteem." Burton Alva Konkle, *George Bryan and the Constitution of Pennsylvania, 1731–1791* (Philadelphia 1922) 309. The correct version is probably McMaster and Stone's, which Konkle seems to have misread. The original letter has been lost. Samuel Bryan also claimed authorship of Centinel in letters to Thomas Jefferson, 27 February 1801 and 24 July 1807, and to Albert Gallatin, 18 December 1790. Files of Ratification of the Constitution Project, National Archives. See Pennsylvania Convention Minority 3.11.2 n. 2.

5. McMaster and Stone 6–7. A contemporary critic referred to "the author (I should have said authors) of illiberal and scandalous performance. . . ." A Federalist, *Independent Gazetteer* 25 October 1787, McMaster and Stone 166.

Konkle reflects all the uncertainties involved. First he contends that "there can be as little doubt that Samuel Bryan was the author of them all, as that they expressed in fullness and accuracy the sentiments and convictions of Justice Bryan." *George Bryan* 309. Or perhaps the father wrote them: "No one familiar with Justice Bryan's writing but can see the Bryanesque ear-marks in both style and verbal expression in this paper [I], as well as the rest." Ibid. 310–11; cf. 320. The father must have written one of them: "There is a wealth of legal knowledge in this paper [II] that sounds very much like Justice Bryan, rather than the son, so that one is inclined to feel that, even though the son wrote 'No. I,' the father must have written 'No. II.' " Ibid. 313.

6. Ibid. 309.

7. See below, 2.7.35 n. 14. Konkle suggests, "It would seem as though Mr. Wilson's speech of the 6th had *Centinel*'s paper of the 5th in contemplation, as *Centinel No. II* did his of the 6th of October." Ibid. p. 313. But the supposition is unlikely. Wilson would barely have had time to read the first number of Centinel and formulate his reply, and according to his biographer, Wilson spent much time and thought in preparing the address. Charles Page Smith, *James Wilson, Founding Father, 1742–1798* (Chapel Hill 1956) 264–65. Moreover, Wilson does not reply to the most interesting part of Centinel's argument, that dealing with responsibility, and he does not follow Centinel's more detailed argument. It is more likely that Wilson was replying to arguments made in the legislature, at the early sessions of the state ratifying convention, and particularly by the sixteen seceders from the Pennsylvania Assembly. See below, 3.2.

I

Mr. Oswald,

As the Independent Gazetteer seems free for the discussion of all public matters, I expect you will give the following a place in your next.

To the Freemen of Pennsylvania.

Friends, Countrymen and Fellow Citizens,

Permit one of yourselves to put you in mind of certain *liberties* and *privileges* secured to you by the constitution of this commonwealth, and to beg your serious attention to his uninterested opinion upon the plan of federal government submitted to your consideration, before you surrender these great and valuable privileges up forever. Your present frame of government, secures to you a right to hold yourselves, houses, papers and possessions free from search and seizure, and therefore warrants granted without oaths or affirmations first made, affording sufficient foundation for them, whereby any officer or messenger may be commanded or required to search your houses or seize your persons or property, not particularly described in such warrant, shall not be granted. Your constitution further provides "that in controversies respecting property, and in suits between man and man, the parties have a right *to trial by jury, which ought to be held sacred.*" It also provides and declares, "*that the people have a right of* FREEDOM OF SPEECH, *and of* WRITING *and* PUBLISHING *their sentiments, therefore* THE FREEDOM OF THE PRESS OUGHT NOT TO BE RESTRAINED."[1] The constitution of Pennsylvania is *yet* in existence, *as yet* you have the right to *freedom of speech*, and of *publishing your sentiments*. How long those rights will appertain to you, you yourselves are called upon to say, whether your *houses* shall continue to be your *castles;* whether your *papers*, your *persons* and your *property*, are to be held sacred and free from *general warrants*, you are now to determine. Whether the *trial by jury* is to continue as your birth-right, the freemen of Pennsylvania, nay, of all America, are now called upon to declare.

Without presuming upon my own judgement, I cannot think it an unwarrantable presumption to offer my private opinion, and call upon others for their's; and if I use my pen with the boldness of a freeman, it is because I know that *the liberty of the press yet remains unviolated*, and *juries yet are judges*.

The late Convention have submitted to your consideration a plan of a new federal government—The subject is highly interesting to your future welfare—Whether it be calculated to promote the great ends of civil society, *viz.* the happiness and prosperity of the community; it behoves you well to consider, uninfluenced by the authority of names. Instead of that frenzy of

2.7.1

2.7.2

2.7.3

13

enthusiasm, that has actuated the citizens of Philadelphia, in their approbation of the proposed plan, before it was possible that it could be the result of a rational investigation into its principles; it ought to be dispassionately and deliberately examined, and its own intrinsic merit the only criterion of your patronage. If ever free and unbiassed discussion was proper or necessary, it is on such an occasion.—All the blessings of liberty and the dearest privileges of freemen, are now at stake and dependent on your present conduct. Those who are competent to the task of developing the principles of government, ought to be encouraged to come forward, and thereby the better enable the people to make a proper judgment; for the science of government is so abstruse, that few are able to judge for themselves; without such assistance the people are too apt to yield an implicit assent to the opinions of those characters, whose abilities are held in the highest esteem, and to those in whose integrity and patriotism they can confide; not considering that the love of domination is generally in proportion to talents, abilities, and superior acquirements; and that the men of the greatest purity of intention may be made instruments of despotism in the hands of the *artful and designing*. If it were not for the stability and attachment which time and habit gives to forms of government, it would be in the power of the enlightened and aspiring few, if they should combine, at any time to destroy the best establishments, and even make the people the instruments of their own subjugation.

2.7.4 The late revolution having effaced in a great measure all former habits, and the present institutions are so recent, that there exists not that great reluctance to innovation, so remarkable in old communities, and which accords with reason, for the most comprehensive mind cannot foresee the full operation of material changes on civil polity; it is the genius of the common law to resist innovation.

2.7.5 The wealthy and ambitious, who in every community think they have a right to lord it over their fellow creatures, have availed themselves, very successfully, of this favorable disposition; for the people thus unsettled in their sentiments, have been prepared to accede to any extreme of government; all the distresses and difficulties they experience, proceeding from various causes, have been ascribed to the impotency of the present confederation, and thence they have been led to expect full relief from the adoption of the proposed system of government; and in the other event, immediately ruin and annihilation as a nation. These characters flatter themselves that they have lulled all distrust and jealousy of their new plan, by gaining the concurrence of the two men in whom America has the highest confidence, and now triumphantly exult in the completion of their long meditated schemes of power and aggrandisement. I would be very far from insinuating that the two illustrious personages alluded to, have not the welfare of their country at heart; but that the unsuspecting goodness and zeal of the one, has been imposed on, in a subject of which he must be necessarily inexperienced, from his other arduous engagements; and that the weakness and indecision attendant on old age, has been practised on in the other.[2]

I am fearful that the principles of government inculcated in Mr. Adams's treatise,[3] and enforced in the numerous essays and paragraphs in the newspapers, have misled some well designing members of the late Convention.—But it will appear in the sequel, that the construction of the proposed plan of government is infinitely more extravagant.

2.7.6

I have been anxiously expecting that some enlightened patriot would, ere this, have taken up the pen to expose the futility, and counteract the baneful tendency of such principles. Mr. Adams's *sine qua non* of a good government is three balancing powers, whose repelling qualities are to produce an equilibrium of interests, and thereby promote the happiness of the whole community. He asserts that the administrators of every government, will ever be actuated by views of private interest and ambition, to the prejudice of the public good; that therefore the only effectual method to secure the rights of the people and promote their welfare, is to create an opposition of interests betweeen the members of two distinct bodies, in the exercise of the powers of government, and balanced by those of a third.[4] This hypothesis supposes human wisdom competent to the task of instituting three co-equal orders in government, and a corresponding weight in the community to enable them respectively to exercise their several parts, and whose views and interests should be so distinct as to prevent a coalition of any two of them for the destruction of the third. Mr. Adams, although he has traced the constitution of every form of government that ever existed, as far as history affords materials, has not been able to adduce a single instance of such a government; he indeed says that the British constitution is such in theory, but this is rather a confirmation that his principles are chimerical and not to be reduced to practice. If such an organization of power were practicable, how long would it continue? not a day—for there is so great a disparity in the talents, wisdom and industry of mankind, that the scale would presently preponderate to one or the other body, and with every accession of power the means of further increase would be greatly extended. The state of society in England is much more favorable to such a scheme of government than that of America. There they have a powerful hereditary nobility, and real distinctions of rank and interests; but even there, for want of that perfect equallity of power and distinction of interests, in the three orders of government, they exist but in name; the only operative and efficient check, upon the conduct of administration, is the sense of the people at large.

2.7.7

Suppose a government could be formed and supported on such principles, would it answer the great purposes of civil society; if the administrators of every government are actuated by views of private interest and ambition, how is the welfare and happiness of the community to be the result of such jarring adverse interests?

2.7.8

Therefore, as different orders in government will not produce the good of

2.7.9

the whole, we must recur to other principles. I believe it will be found that the form of government, which holds those entrusted with power, in the greatest responsibility to their constitutents, the best calculated for freemen.[5] A republican, or free government, can only exist where the body of the people are virtuous, and where property is pretty equally divided[;] in such a government the people are the sovereign and their sense or opinion is the criterion of every public measure; for when this ceases to be the case, the nature of the government is changed, and an aristocracy, monarchy or despotism will rise on its ruin. The highest responsibility is to be attained, in a simple structure of government, for the great body of the people never steadily attend to the operations of government, and for want of due information are liable to be imposed on—If you complicate the plan by various orders, the people will be perplexed and divided in their sentiments about the source of abuses or misconduct, some will impute it to the senate, others to the house of representatives, and so on, that the interposition of the people may be rendered imperfect or perhaps wholly abortive. But if, imitating the constitution of Pennsylvania, you vest all the legislative power in one body of men (separating the executive and judicial) elected for a short period, and necessarily excluded by rotation from permanency, and guarded from precipitancy and surprise by delays imposed on its proceedings, you will create the most perfect responsibility for then, whenever the people feel a grievance they cannot mistake the authors, and will apply the remedy with certainty and effect, discarding them at the next election. This tie of responsibility will obviate all the dangers apprehended from a single legislature, and will the best secure the rights of the people.

2.7.10   Having premised this much, I shall now proceed to the examination of the proposed plan of government, and I trust, shall make it appear to the meanest capacity, that it has none of the essential requisites of a free government; that it is neither founded on those balancing restraining powers, recommended by Mr. Adams and attempted in the British constitution, or possessed of that responsibility to its constituents, which, in my opinion, is the only effectual security for the liberties and happiness of the people; but on the contrary, that it is a most daring attempt to establish a despotic aristocracy among freemen, that the world has ever witnessed.

2.7.11   I shall previously consider the extent of the powers intended to be vested in Congress, before I examine the construction of the general government. It will not be controverted that the legislative is the highest delegated power in government, and that all others are subordinate to it. The celebrated *Montesquieu* establishes it as a maxim, that legislation necessarily follows the power of taxation.[6] By sect. 8, of the first article of the proposed plan of government, "the Congress are to have power to lay and collect taxes, duties, imposts and excises, to pay the debts and provide for the common defence and *general welfare* of the United States; but all duties, imposts and excises, shall be uniform throughout the United States." Now what can be more comprehensive than these words; not content by other sections of this plan, to grant all the great executive powers of a confederation, and a STANDING ARMY IN TIME OF PEACE, that grand engine of oppression, and moreover the absolute controul over the commerce of the United States and all external objects of revenue, such as unlimited imposts upon imports, etc.—they are to be vested with every species of *internal* taxation; —whatever taxes, duties and excises that they may deem requisite for the *general welfare,* may be imposed on the citizens of these states, levied by the officers of Congress, distributed through every district in America; and the collection would be enforced by the standing army, however grievous or improper they may be. The Congress may construe every purpose for which the state legislatures now lay taxes, to be for the *general welfare,* and thereby seize upon every object of revenue.

The judicial power by 1st sect. of article 3 ["]shall extend to all cases, in law and equity, arising under this constitution, the laws of the United States, and treaties made or which shall be made under their authority; to all cases affecting ambassadors, other public ministers and consuls; to all cases of admirality and maritime jurisdiction, to controversies to which the United States shall be a party, to controversies between two or more states, between a state and citizens of another state, between citizens of different states, between citizens of the same state claiming lands under grants of different states, and between a state, or the citizens thereof, and foreign states, citizens or subjects." 2.7.12

The judicial power to be vested in one Supreme Court, and in such Inferior Courts as the Congress may from time to time ordain and establish. 2.7.13

The objects of jurisdiction recited above, are so numerous, and the shades of distinction between civil causes are oftentimes so slight, that it is more than probable that the state judicatories would be wholly superceded; for in contests about jurisdiction, the federal court, as the most powerful, would ever prevail. Every person acquainted with the history of the courts in England, knows by what ingenious sophisms they have, at different periods, extended the sphere of their jurisdiction over objects out of the line of their institution, and contrary to their very nature; courts of a criminal jurisdiction obtaining cognizance in civil causes. 2.7.14

To put the omnipotency of Congress over the state government and judicatories out of all doubt, the 6th article ordains that "this constitution and the laws of the United States which shall be made in pursuance thereof, and all treaties made, or which shall be made under the authority of the United States, shall be the *supreme law of the land,* and the judges in every state shall be bound thereby, any thing in the constitution or laws of any state to the contrary notwithstanding." 2.7.15

By these sections the all-prevailing power of taxation, and such extensive legislative and judicial powers are vested in the general government, as must in their operation, necessarily absorb the state legislatures and judicatories; and that such was in the contemplation of the framers of it, will appear from 2.7.16

the provision made for such event, in another part of it; (but that, fearful of alarming the people by so great an innovation, they have suffered the forms of the separate governments to remain, as a blind.) By sect. 4th of the 1st article, "the times, places and manner of holding elections for senators and representatives, shall be prescribed in each state by the legislature thereof; *but the Congress may at any time, by law, make or alter such regulations, except as to the place of chusing senators.*" The plain construction of which is, that when the state legislatures drop out of sight, from the necessary operation of this government, then Congress are to provide for the election and appointment of representatives and senators.

2.7.17   If the foregoing be a just comment—if the United States are to be melted down into one empire, it becomes you to consider, whether such a government, however constructed, would be eligible in so extended a territory; and whether it would be practicable, consistent with freedom? It is the opinion of the greatest writers, that a very extensive country cannot be governed on democratical principles, on any other plan, than a confederation of a number of small republics, possessing all the powers of internal government, but united in the management of their foreign and general concerns.

2.7.18   It would not be difficult to prove, that any thing short of despotism, could not bind so great a country under one government; and that whatever plan you might, at the first setting out, establish, it would issue in a depotism.

2.7.19   If one general government could be instituted and maintained on principles of freedom, it would not be so competent to attend to the various local concerns and wants, of every particular district[,] as well as the peculiar governments, who are nearer the scene, and possessed of superior means of information[;] besides, if the business of the *whole* union is to be managed by one government, there would not be time. Do we not already see, that the inhabitants in a number of larger states, who are remote from the seat of government, are loudly complaining of the inconveniencies and disadvantages they are subjected to on this account, and that, to enjoy the comforts of local government, they are separating into smaller divisions.[7]

2.7.20   Having taken a review of the powers, I shall now examine the construction of the proposed general government.

Art. 1. sect. 1. "All legislative powers herein granted shall be vested in a Congress of the United States, which shall consist of a senate and house of representatives." By another section, the president (the principal executive officer) has a conditional controul over their proceedings.

Sect. 2. "The house of representatives shall be composed of members chosen every second year, by the people of the several states. The number of representatives shall not exceed one for every 30,000 inhabitants."

The senate, the other constituent branch of the legislature, is formed by the legislature of each state appointing two senators, for the term of six years.

2.7.21   The executive power by Art. 2, sec. 1. is to be vested in a president of the United States of America, elected for four years: Sec. 2. gives him "power, by and with the consent of the senate to make treaties, provided two thirds of the senators present concur; and he shall nominate, and by and with the advice and consent of the senate, shall appoint ambassadors, other public ministers and consuls, judges of the Supreme Court, and all other officers of the United States, whose appointments are not herein otherwise provided for, and which shall be established by law, etc. And by another section he has the absolute power of granting reprieves and pardons for treason and all other high crimes and misdemeanors, except in case of impeachment.

The foregoing are the outlines of the plan.

Thus we see, the house of representatives, are on the part of the people to balance the senate, who I suppose will be composed of the *better sort*, the *well born*, etc. The number of the representatives (being only one for every 30,000 inhabitants) appears to be too few, either to communicate the requisite information, of the wants, local circumstances and sentiments of so extensive an empire, or to prevent corruption and undue influence, in the exercise of such great powers; the term for which they are to be chosen, too long to preserve a due dependence and accountability to their constituents; and the mode and places of their election not sufficiently ascertained, for as Congress have the controul over both, they may govern the choice, by ordering the *representatives* of a *whole* state, to be *elected* in *one* place, and that too may be the most *inconvenient*. 2.7.22

The senate, the great efficient body in this plan of government, is constituted on the most unequal principles. The smallest state in the union has equal weight with the great states of Virginia, Massachusetts, or Pennsylvania—The Senate, besides its legislative functions, has a very considerable share in the Executive; none of the principal appointments to office can be made without its advice and consent. The term and mode of its appointment, will lead to permanency; the members are chosen for six years, the mode is under the controul of Congress, and as there is no exclusion by rotation, they may be continued for life, which, from their extensive means of influence, would follow of course. The President, who would be a mere pageant of state, unless he coincides with the views of the Senate, would either become the head of the aristocratic junto in that body, or its minion; besides, their influence being the most predominant, could the best secure his re-election to office. And from his power of granting pardons, he might skreen from punishment the most treasonable attempts on the liberties of the people, when instigated by the Senate. 2.7.23

From this investigation into the organization of this government, it appears that it is devoid of all responsibility or accountability to the great body of the people, and that so far from being a regular balanced government, it would be in practice a *permanent* ARISTOCRACY. 2.7.24

The framers of it[,] actuated by the true spirit of such a government, which ever abominates and suppresses all free enquiry and discussion, have made no provision for the *liberty of the press*, that grand *palladium of freedom*, and *scourge of tyrants;* but observed a total silence on that head. It 2.7.25

is the opinion of some great writers, that if the liberty of the press, by an institution of religion, or otherwise, could be rendered *sacred,* even in *Turkey,* that despotism would fly before it.[8] And it is worthy of remark, that there is no declaration of personal rights, premised in most free constitutions; and that trial by *jury* in *civil* cases is taken away; for what other construction can be put·on the following, viz. Article III. Sect. 2d. "In all cases affecting ambassadors, other public ministers and consuls, and those in which a State shall be party, the Supreme Court shall have *original* jurisdiction. In all the other cases above mentioned, the Supreme Court shall have *appellate* jurisdiction, both as to *law and fact?*" It would be a novelty in jurisprudence, as well as evidently improper to allow an appeal from the verdict of a jury, on the matter of fact; therefore, it implies and allows of a dismission of the jury in civil cases, and especially when it is considered, that jury trial in criminal cases is expresly stipulated for, but not in civil cases.

2.7.26   But our situation is represented to be so *critically* dreadful, that, however reprehensible and exceptionable the proposed plan of government may be, there is no alternative, between the adoption of it and absolute ruin.—My fellow citizens, things are not at that crisis, it is the argument of tyrants; the present distracted state of Europe secures us from injury on that quarter, and as to domestic dissentions, we have not so much to fear from them, as to precipitate us into this form of government, without it is a safe and a proper one. For remember, of all *possible* evils, that of *despotism* is the *worst* and the most to be *dreaded.*

2.7.27   Besides, it cannot be supposed, that the first essay on so difficult a subject, is so well digested, as it ought to be,—if the proposed plan, after a mature deliberation, should meet the approbation of the respective States, the matter will end; but if it should be found to be fraught with dangers and inconveniencies, a future general Convention being in possession of the objections, will be the better enabled to plan a suitable government.

> *Who's here so base, that would a bondman be?*
> *If any, speak; for him have I offended.*
> *Who's here so vile, that will not love his country?*
> *If any, speak; for him have I offended.*[9]

Centinel.

Letter I

1. Pennsylvania Constitution of 1776, Declaration of Rights, arts. 10, 11, 12.

2. Centinel goes further here in his criticism of Washington and Franklin than most Anti-Federalists thought prudent, and he was strongly criticized on this account. Cf. A Federalist, in the Philadelphia *Independent Gazetteer*, 25 October 1787 (McMaster and Stone 168). Resisting the weight of these venerable statesmen provided one of the Anti-Federalists' major rhetorical problems. The following Federalist appeal, exaggerated in style but characteristic in substance, was made by One of the Four Thousand, writing in the *Independent Gazetteer* 15 October 1787 (McMaster and Stone 117–18): "Freemen of Pennsylvania, consider the character and services of the men who made this government. Behold the venerable FRANKLIN, in the 70th year of his age, cooped up in the cabin of a small vessel, and exposing himself to the dangers of a passage on the ocean, crowded with British cruisers, in a winter month, in order to solicit from the court of France that aid, which finally enabled America to close the war with so much success and glory—and then say, is it possible that this man would set his hand to a constitution that would endanger your liberties? From this aged servant of the public, turn your eyes to the illustrious American hero, whose name has ennobled human nature—I mean our beloved WASHINGTON. Behold him, in the year 1775, taking leave of his happy family and peaceful retreat, and flying to the relief of a distant, and at that time an unknown part of the American continent. See him uniting and cementing an army, composed of the citizens of thirteen states, into a band of brothers. Follow him into the field of battle, and behold him the *first* in danger, and the *last* out of it. Follow him into his winter quarters, and see him sharing in the hunger, cold and fatigues of every soldier in his army. Behold his fortitude in adversity, his moderation in victory, and his tenderness and respect upon all occasions for the civil power of his country. But above all, turn your eyes to that illustrious scene he exhibited at Annapolis in 1782, when he resigned his commission, and laid his sword at the feet of Congress, and afterwards resumed the toils of an American farmer on the banks of the Potomac. Survey, my countrymen, these illustrious exploits of patriotism and virtue, and then say, is it possible that the deliverer of our country would have recommended an unsafe form of government for that liberty, for which he had for eight long years contended with such unexampled firmness, constancy and magnanimity." For other Federalists who stress the respectability of the framers, and particularly Washington and Franklin, see McMaster and Stone 117, 129, 136, 168; Ford, *Essays* 23, 26; Ford, *Pamphlets* 64, 74, 221, 245–47. See Federal Republican 3.6.5 n. 4. The Anti-Federalists frequently shared their opponents' high opinion of the framers. The Federal Farmer (V. 2.8.62) thought that "America probably never will be an assembly of men of a like number, more respectable." There were, however, frequent criticisms. See Martin 2.4.13, 19–20; Cato I, 2.6.5–6; Brutus I, 2.9.1–3; Old Whig VII, 3.3.41–42; Aristocrotis 3.16.1–3; Yeomanry of Massachusetts 4.19.1–3; American 4.20.1–3; Countryman from Dutchess County 6.6.2–4.

3. John Adams, *Defence of the Constitutions of Government of the United States*. The first volume of the *Defence* was published in England in 1787, arriving in the United States "in the midst of the agitation caused by the assembling of the convention to form the federal constitution." Editorial note, John Adams, *Works* IV, 275–76. Two more volumes of the *Defence* followed in 1788.

4. See the "Preface" of the first volume of Adams' *Defence (Works* IV, 283ff.); Letters V, XXIII (ibid. 284, 322, 380–82); Conclusion (ibid. 579 ff.); and *Thoughts on Government* (1776) (ibid. 193 ff.). While some Anti-Federalists join *Centinel* in his opposition to balanced government (see Brutus XVI, 2.9.202; [Maryland] Farmer V, 5.1.71–72; Lowndes 5.12.4; Impartial Examiner 5.14.35–40; Republicus 5.13.7; Monroe 5.21.19–28), others display views very similar to Adams' (see *Federal Farmer* VII, 2.8.97 n. 60). Note that Centinel, while opposing a balancing of orders, emphatically supports the principle of separation of powers. See II, 2.7.50 and n. 29.

5. A Federalist writer replied: "The Centinel asserts, that responsibility in the rulers is the best security the people can have of their rights. Now were this true, every discerning person will see that there is as great a responsibility in this plan as if all the powers of government were blended in one body of men. But the assertion is false. Interest is the greatest tie that one man can have on another, I mean taking mankind in general. And for the truth of this I appeal to your own experience and

observation. The thief, the robber knows that he is responsible to the state, and in danger of the halter or the wheel-barrow, yet this does not influence his conduct; but convince him in any particular instance that it is more for his interest to forbear this practice, and he will, for that time, be honest. According to the proposed plan, the interest of the rulers and the ruled are the same; they never can be separated, for they are all one mass, having no difference of rights or privileges; or, as I said before, it is the people governing themselves; and therefore their rights will be secure." A Citizen, *Carlisle* [Pennsylvania] *Gazette* 24 October 1787.

6. The argument in this section is repeated and somewhat elaborated in V, 2.7.96. Cf. also II, 2.7.40.

7. See Cato III, 2.6.16 n. 11.

8. See [Gordon and Trenchard], *Cato's Letters* III, no. 71: "In Turky, Printing is forbid, lest by its Means common Sense might get the better of Violence, and be too hard for the Imperial Butcher."

9. Shakespeare, *Julius Caesar* act 3, sc. 2.

Observations
Leading to a Fair Examination of the System
Of Government
Proposed by the Late Convention;
And to Several Essential and Necessary
Alterations in It.
In a Number of Letters from the
Federal Farmer to the Republican

1787

and
An Additional Number of Letters
From the Federal Farmer to the Republican
Leading to a Fair Examination of the System of Government
Proposed by the Late Convention;
To Several Essential and Necessary Alterations in It;
And Calculated to Illustrate and Support the Principles
And Positions Laid Down in the Preceding Letters

1788

Letters I–VII and XVI–XVII

The Observations of The Federal Farmer are generally, and correctly, considered to be one of the ablest Anti-Federalist pieces; they deserve to be read fully and carefully by any student of Anti-Federalist thought. Contrary to a common impression, the letters were surprisingly little reprinted in the newspapers, apparently only the Poughkeepsie *Country Journal* printing the whole series. But they enjoyed wide popularity in pamphlet form.[1] Four editions totaling, according to the publisher, several thousands of the pamphlet were sold in a few months; and in January 1788 the author published An Additional Number of Letters, which, being longer and more diffuse, apparently enjoyed less success. The texts of the original pamphlets are followed here.[2] Paul Leicester Ford printed only the original five letters, finding the Additional Letters largely repetitious. Forrest McDonald generally agreed and printed only four of the Additional Letters in his 1962 paperback edition.[3] There is no doubt that there *is* much repetition and that the Additional Letters are somewhat loosely constructed; but there is scarcely a letter that does not contain material of the first importance, and it is a mistake to confine one's study of The Federal Farmer's arguments to the first five letters. One of the best criticisms of these letters was made by Timothy Pickering in a letter to Charles Tillinghast dated 24 December 1787. They were also reviewed in Noah Webster's *American Museum.*[4]

The Federal Farmer is generally supposed to have been Richard Henry Lee, but this was unequivocally denied by William W. Crosskey in his *Politics and the Constitution.*[5] Crosskey promised to discuss the matter in a later volume, which, unfortunately, was never published.[6] While Crosskey's case against Lee's authorship does not appear to have been very strong, neither, it turns out, is the case to support the usual view. The present editor's review of the evidence was at an advanced stage when he was pleased to discover that Gordon Wood's independent and often parallel investigation, also stimulated by Crosskey's remark, had led him too to doubt the solidity of the usual attribution.[7]

Wood makes a powerful and substantial rebuttal to the usual assumption that Lee's thought and style are evident in The Federal Farmer. The reader may make his own comparison of The Federal Farmer and Lee's letter to Governor Randolph, also printed here.[8] The yield of such a comparison seems to be, generally speaking, many differences but none that are flatly contradictory, and many similarities, but none that were not shared with many other Anti-Federal writers. Perhaps most telling against the case for Lee's authorship is the fact that the primary concern of The Federal Farmer is the question of consolidation and the destruction of the states, about which Lee's letter says nothing. This is a puzzling difference, and it seems to have been the source of Crosskey's doubt. Of course to attempt to deny, and especially to establish, authorship on such grounds is an extremely treacherous business. Lee's private letters during the fall of 1787 and the first half of 1788 show many points of similarity with The Federal Farmer (though no more, perhaps, than with several other Anti-Federal writers), and they demonstrate in particular that Lee, like The Federal Farmer, was concerned with the issue of consolidation and doubtful that a single government could extend over the whole United States.[9] Crosskey's contention that Lee's opinion changed shortly before the Virginia ratifying convention, while not without some foundation, is not very persuasive.[10] Yet it *is* striking that Lee does not in his official letter of opposition give any attention to the argument that is most prominent in the Observations.

Lee is positively identified as The Federal Farmer in a piece by New England published in the *Connecticut Courant* on 24 December 1787. This piece was quite widely reprinted and seems to have given rise to a handful of essays in Massachusetts in which Lee is named as The Federal Farmer.[11]

This is probably also the source of George Cabot's penciled note, in his copy of the Additional Letters, of Lee's "supposed" authorship. This copy of the Additional Letters was given to the Boston Athenaeum and was, as Wood shows, apparently the authority for the attribution of The Federal Farmer to Lee in the *Athenaeum Catalogue* published in 1874, thence to Sabin's *Dictionary of Books Relating to America*, and thence to Bancroft, Ford, and American historians generally.[12] This is a slim basis for attribution, but the evidence in these matters is usually slim, and it would hardly have been contradicted, even given the discrepancies in tone and argument between The Federal Farmer and Lee's letter, but for silence or ignorance among contemporaries who might be expected to know of Lee's authorship.[13]

Webster and Pickering, in their reviews of the essays, gave no evidence of knowing the author.[14] Virginian Edward Carrington sent The Federal Farmer's two volumes to Jefferson, describing them as reputedly "the best of anything that has been written in the opposition," but reporting that "the author is not known."[15] There is no evidence of authorship in Lee's correspondence or in the Lee family papers.[16] Moreover, while Lee's grandson and early biographer refers to "the objections of Mr. Lee to the constitution, and his arguments in support of them, [which] may be seen by the reader in eloquent and powerful detail, in his letters in the body of correspondence written during the years 1787 and 1788," he makes no reference to The Federal Farmer, as he surely would have done had he thought Lee was the author.[17] Considering the success and reputation of The Federal Farmer, it is strange that Lee never acknowledged authorship if they were his—yet the same could be said of just about any other possible author. The case against Lee's authorship remains inconclusive. But if, as seems probable, the only solid positive evidence is the essay of New England and its derivatives, the case for Lee's authorship is surely a good deal weaker than has usually been assumed.

Why is there so little extant evidence about a pamphlet so widely known and respected? Part of the reason, at least, is that these eighteenth-century Americans, while sharing with the rest of humankind a curiosity and disposition to gossip about personalities, really did think that what counts most (or at least what ought to count most) in political debate is what is said rather than who said it.[18] The Observations fall into four parts: first, a preface dealing with the way in which the Constitution ought to be considered (I, 2.8.1–8); second, an examination of the feasibility of a consolidation of the United States into one government on free principles (I, 2.8.9–14; II, 2.8.15–23); third, an examination of the organization and powers of the proposed government (III, 2.8.24–43; IV, 2.8.44–58); fourth, a conclusion (V, 2.8.59–66). Of particular importance are the excellent discussions of representation and the jury trial that run throughout these and the Additional Letters. The Additional Letters, which are taken up largely with an examination of the organization of the three branches of the government, also contain especially important discussions of federalism (VI, 2.8.72–73), the federal republic (VI, 2.8.75–80; XVII, 2.8.204–13), and bills of rights (XVI, 2.8.196–203). What follows is an extended outline of the argument of the essays.

OBSERVATIONS

I. *Preface* (I, 2.8.1–8).

There is no reason for hasty or ill-considered adoption.

While the plan proposed appears to be partly federal, it is principally calculated to make the states one consolidated government, as is seen by examining the plan, its history, and the politics of its friends.

II. *The states cannot be consolidated into one entire government on free principles* (I, 2.8.9–14; II, 2.8.15–23; III, 2.8.24).

A. A consideration of the several forms on which the United States might exist as one nation (I, 2.8.10–13).

B. Impracticability of free and equal government extending over large and heterogeneous territory (I, 2.8.14).

C. The Constitution does not, and cannot, provide the two essential parts of free government, a substantial representation of the people in the legislature (II, 2.8.15) and the jury trial of the vicinage (II, 2.8.16).

D. Other considerations:

1. The center and the extremes will not share benefits; and, because of the limited operation of the laws of a free government, the law will have to be enforced at the extremes by fear and fraud (II, 2.8.17–18).

2. It is difficult, though not impossible, to frame a Bill of Rights for such a varied country (II, 2.8.19–21).

E. The Constitution lodges very extensive powers in an inherently defective government, with the result either of neglected laws or military enforcement leading, in either case, to despotism (II, 2.8.22–23).

III. *Organization and powers of the new government* (III, 2.8.25–43, IV, 2.8.44–58).

A. Organization (III, 2.8.25–34):

Each part of the government briefly examined and criticized (III, 2.8.25–30). The deficiencies, particularly the smallness of the House of Representatives, the compromise basis of the Senate, and the blending of powers, are admittedly the inevitable result of our situation, which reinforces the conclusion that it is not possible to consolidate the states on proper principles (III, 2.8.31–34).

B. Powers improperly or prematurely lodged (III, 2.8.35–43; IV, 2.8.44):
  1. Powers regarding external objects and some regarding internal objects ought to be lodged in the general government, but unlimited power to lay taxes and extensive control of military strength of the country are dangerous; power in these critical areas should be granted extremely cautiously so long as the federal government is so defective especially regarding representation (which is further discussed here) (III, 2.8.35–40).
  2. The extensive jurisdiction given to federal judiciary is examined and shown, in many points, to be unnecessary and dangerous. Jury trial of the vicinage is not secured (III, 2.8.41–43; IV, 2.8.44).
C. Undefined powers (IV 2.8.44–45): Provisions regarding direct taxes, regarding qualifications of the vice president, regarding appointment of inferior officers, regarding congressional control over the appellate jurisdiction of the Supreme Court.
D. Powers the exercise of which is unsecured (IV, 2.8.46–58):
  1. Supremacy clause—no provision that treaties shall be made in pursuance of Constitution.
  2. Necessary and proper clause—power of Congress not restricted to a few national objects.
  3. No Bill of Rights with reservations for states and individuals: (a) religion, (b) trial by jury, (c) press.
  4. Provision for amendment—Constitution will transfer power from the many to the few, who will resist further change.

IV. *Conclusion* (V, 2.8.59–66).
Government ought to preserve, not undermine, the equal division of our land and the free and manly habits of our people.

We need improved federal government, and there are many good things here, but the value is lessened by the want of a representation of the people.

Extreme partisans favoring and opposing the Constitution—examination of activities of partisans for the Constitution.

Constitution should be considered freely and carefully and amendments proposed.

ADDITIONAL LETTERS

I. *General and introductory* (VI, 2.8.67–92).
A. Character of Federalist and Anti-Federalist partisans (VI, 2.8.71–73):

This is a continuation of the preface in letter I and of discussion in V, with important discussion of "honest" federalists, "pretended" federalists, "true" federalists, and of misleading terms, "federalist" and "anti-federalist."

B. General positions and principles (VI, 2.8.74–80):
A (rather miscellaneous) brief restatement of earlier points about the need for a more efficient government, the necessity of a federal republic in such an extensive territory, the importance of a substantial representation and jury trial. A distinction is drawn between natural, constitutional, and common or legal rights.

C. Leading features of the Articles of Confederation (VI, 2.8.81–86).

D. Organization of state governments (VI, 2.8.87–92).

II. *Legislative branch* (VII–XII, 2.8.93–165).
A. Introduction (VII, 2.8.93–96):
Must have government—aim is to have one operating by *persuasion*, or it will operate by *force*.

Criteria of fair and equal representation: same interests, feelings, opinions, and views as people at large.

B. Representation is insubstantial and ought to be increased (VII–X, 2.8.97–142).
1. Substantial representation should contain representatives of all orders of society to maintain balance. Two major classes, aristocracy and democracy; their subordinate classes, their characteristics; and subsidiary interests and parties. (An important discussion.) The representation in the House of Representatives is too small to reflect these classes and interests and will be drawn largely from the aristocracy (VII, 2.8.97–100).

Observations in defense of representation as provided in the Constitution listed (VII, 2.8.101).

2. England as a genuine balance among the several orders (VIII, 2.8.102–10):
Contrast to Rome—the differences lie in substantial representation in England. (Secondary discussion but still important on question of representation.)

3. Observations of advocates answered (IX–X, 2.8.111–42):
People will elect good men (important on representation) (X, 2.8.111–18).

Members of Congress must return home and bear the burdens they impose on others (IX, 2.8.119–26).

People have a strong arm to check their rulers (X, 2.8.127).

States are part of the system and will balance the general government (but states have no *constitutional* check) (X, 2.8.128).

Objects of Congress are few and national (X, 2.8.130–32).

House of Representatives will increase in size in time (X, 2.8.133–34).

Difficulty of assembling many men without making them a mob (X, 2.8.136).

Congress will have no temptation to do wrong (X, 2.8.138).

People will be free as long as they possess habits of free men (X, 2.8.139).

4. Organization, appointment, powers of Senate (XI, 2.8.143–47): Cannot have genuine representation of aristocracy in the United States; so Senate will contain generally same kind of men as high posts of House of Representatives; checks will be only those limited ones derived from different modes of appointment, different terms of office, mere fact of a second branch, etc.

While Senate is useful, some revisions should be made: terms of office should be shortened, senators should be recallable, and provisions should be made for rotation. Treaty power might be dangerous, but whole Congress has power to make commercial regulations.

C. The elections ought to be better secured (XII, 2.8.148–65): All general principles regarding electors and elected, mode of election (which should be by majority vote in districts, etc.), should be laid down in Constitution. Any necessary discretion should reside in state legislatures, closest to the people.

III. *Executive branch* (XIII–XIV, 2.8.166–82).
   A. Appointments (XIII, 2.8.166–72; XIV, 2.8.173–76): Executive necessary but dangerous—need to keep it balanced by distributing appointments.

   Various methods of appointment sketched and discussed—in selecting from among these the aims are to keep balance in government and to prevent legislature from becoming infected by the spirit of office-men.

   B. Election and powers of President (XIV, 2.8.177–82): Unity in executive; general need for "first man."

Must be given ample powers; chief concern should be to avoid *perpetuation* of power in any man or family. Thus should not be reeligible.

Veto power—combination of executive and judges is best.

IV. *Judicial branch* (XV, 2.8.183–95).
Peculiar character of judicial branch and its dangerous tendency in popular government (2.8.183–84).

Organization of judiciary (2.8.185–88).

Supreme Court appellate jurisdiction over fact and law (2.8.189).

Importance of trial by jury (2.8.190–94).

Law and equity (2.8.195).

V. *Powers of new government* (XVI–XVIII, 2.8.196–230).
A. Bill of Rights (XVI, 2.8.196–203).
  1. Basic purpose of Bill of Rights in limited government (XVI, 2.8.196–98).
  2. Specific protections needed, relating to trial by jury, ex post facto laws, habeas corpus, judicial procedure, quartering of soldiers, and freedom of press (XVI, 2.8.199–203).

B. Need for federal republic to preserve free and mild government in the United States (XVII, 204–13; XVIII, 214–30).
  1. Description of federal republic (XVII, 2.8.204–13).

  Essential characteristics of federal republic (2.8.204–5).

  Additional powers needed but checks of federal system must be maintained (2.8.206–9).

  Additional federal checks that may be desirable (2.8.210).

  Enlightened and spirited character of the people will not be sufficient if state governments possess no real power (2.8.211–13).

  2. Discussion of powers granted to new government (XVIII, 2.8.214–29).
  3. The true bond of the American union must be formed of pure federal principles (XVIII, 2.8.230).

1. See J. Wadsworth to R. King, 16 December 1787, *The Life and Correspondence of Rufus King* X, 264; DePauw, *The Eleventh Pillar* 104, 113; Samuel Bannister

Harding, *The Contest over the Ratification of the Federal Constitution in the State of Massachusetts* (Cambridge, Mass., 1896) 17. Robert Rutland mistakenly says that the letters of The Federal Farmer were published in the *New York Journal;* they were in fact published in the Poughkeepsie *Country Journal,* November 1787 through January 1788, as Rutland later correctly notes; *The Ordeal of the Constitution* 22.

2. Both the Observations and the Additional Letters were printed in New York by Thomas Greenleaf.

3. Ford, *Pamphlets* 277 ff.; *Empire and Nation,* ed. McDonald. The text of the McDonald edition is extremely unreliable, containing numerous alterations of spelling and punctuation which the reader is not led to expect and, more seriously, a substantial number of misreadings, misprints, omitted lines, etc. A copy of the original edition of the Additional Letters was brought out by Quadrangle Books, Chicago, in 1962, but it is now out of print.

4. Octavius Pickering and Charles Upham, *The Life of Timothy Pickering* (Boston 1873) II, 352–68; *American Museum* May 1788, 422–33.

5. (Chicago 1953) II, 1299–1300.

6. [A third volume was completed by Crosskey's literary executor, William Jeffrey, Jr., and published in 1980 under the title *The Political Background of the Federal Convention,* but, since it covers events through 22 May 1788 only, it does not include the Federal Farmer discussion.—M.D.] I am informed by Professor Jeffrey that Crosskey's opinion was based on the following grounds. First, Crosskey reportedly discovered in the John Lamb papers a letter from Lee to Lamb saying that he "would be interested in seeing the Letters of a Federal Farmer." There being no reason why he should conceal his authorship from Lamb, this would strongly suggest that he was not the author. But I find no such letter in the Lamb papers. Lamb's committee did distribute, among other materials, the Observations of The Federal Farmer; and Lee did thank Lamb for sending him some Anti-Federal materials, promising to read them with pleasure; but there is no evidence that The Federal Farmer was included in the packet sent to Lee. See Letter of Joshua Atherton, 23 June 1788, John Lamb Papers, box 5, no. 25, New-York Historical Society; letter of Richard Henry Lee to John Lamb, 27 June 1788, in Leake, *Memoir of the Life and Times of General John Lamb* 309–10. [On reconsidering this question, Professor Jeffrey reports that he may have misled Storing about this ground for Crosskey's opinion. Jeffrey believes that Lamb's letter to Lee, and Lee's response acknowledging receipt of the Anti-Federal materials, including The Federal Farmer, persuaded Crosskey that Lee was not the author.—M.D.] Crosskey's second ground was the fact that Lee published over his own name his objections to the Constitution in his letter to Governor Randolph of 16 October 1787 (see below, 5.6), and would therefore, Crosskey reasoned, have had no motive for concealing his opposition by assuming a pseudonym for the longer pamphlet. But a pseudonym was used not merely or even mainly to enable the author to conceal his opinion or to protect himself; it was a convention aimed at directing attention at the arguments rather than at personalities. A public figure might well declare his own position in a speech or letter and go on to publish a longer, more analytical piece over a pseudonym. Many of the prominent figures in the debate over the Constitution did precisely that.

7. Gordon S. Wood, "The Authorship of *The Letters from the Federal Farmer,*" *William and Mary Quarterly* April 1974.

8. See below, 5.6.

9. Lee, *Letters* II, 433–76.

10. Crosskey, *Politics and the Constitution* II, 1300.

11. New England was reprinted in the *New Hampshire Mercury* 2 January 1788; New York *Daily Advertiser* 4 January; *Massachusetts Centinel* 5 January; *Gazette of the State of Georgia* 21 February; Charleston *City Gazette* 7 April 1788; Charleston *Columbian Herald* 14 April. Subsequent items identifying Lee as The Federal Farmer (and not mentioned by Wood) appeared in the *Massachusetts Gazette* 1 January (and was reprinted in New York and Pennsylvania papers); *Massachusetts Centinel* 2 January; and Boston *American Herald* 7 January. I am indebted for most of this

information to Steven R. Boyd, University of Texas, San Antonio, who finds here a widespread assumption among contemporaries that Lee was the author.

12. Wood, *William and Mary Quarterly* April 1974, 304–7. See Bancroft, *History of the Formation of the Constitution* II, 230; see also 451–52; Ford, *Pamphlets* 277.

13. One further shred of evidence is provided by the title page of the copy of the Observations of The Federal Farmer in the American Antiquarian Society, which bears a notation, "Richard Henry Lee." The handwriting does not, however, appear to be contemporaneous with the publication of the pamphlet.

14. See above, note 4.

15. 9 June 1788. *Proceedings of the Massachusetts Historical Society* 2d series, XVII (1903), 501. Oliver Ellsworth (as A Landholder) contended that Lee had revised Mason's and Gerry's statements of their objections and was "supposed to be the author of most of the scurrility poured out in the New York papers against the new constitution," but he did not mention The Federal Farmer specifically. Ford, *Essays* 161. See letter from J. Wadsworth to Rufus King, 16 December 1787 (above, n. 1), describing the distribution of the Letters, without identifying the author. One of John Lamb's correspondents, Hugh Ledlie, writing from Hartford, reported insinuations made in the Connecticut convention "that out of the impost £8,000 was paid by this State annually to the State of New York out of which you recd. upwards of £900 which enabled you & others to write the foederal farmer and other false Libels and send them into this & the Neighbouring States to poison the minds of the good people against the good C——n." John Lamb Papers, box 5, no. 1; New-York Historical Society.

16. Lee, *Letters* passim; Lee Family Papers, 1742–1795 (microfilm, University of Virginia Library).

17. Richard H. Lee, ed., *Memoir of the Life of Richard Henry Lee* (Philadelphia 1825) I, 240. Lee's most recent biographer calls the Letters of The Federal Farmer "Lee's greatest literary achievement," but he does not consider the grounds of attribution to Lee. Oliver Perry Chitwood, *Richard Henry Lee: Statesman of the Revolution* (Morgantown, W.Va. 1967) 173.

18. "It is not material whether the federal farmer belongs to Virginia or Kamtschatka—whether he owns five hundred negroes, or is a man of no property at all—if his arguments are cogent—his reasonings conclusive. . . . Nor is it of consequence to the publick, or to the general cause, whether mr. *Lee* is an enemy, or a devotee to the fame and to the merit, of general *Washington*. . . . We are not contending for the characters of men. . . . We wish to view every thing on the broad scale of independence to America—*the sovereignty of the United States*, and *the freedom* of the people. . . ." Helvidius Priscus, below, 4.12.9.

I

October 8th, 1787.

Dear Sir,

2.8.1   My letters to you last winter, on the subject of a well balanced national government for the United States, were the result of free enquiry;[1] when I passed from that subject to enquiries relative to our commerce, revenues, past administration, etc. I anticipated the anxieties I feel, on carefully examining the plan of government proposed by the convention. It appears to be a plan retaining some federal features; but to be the first important step, and to aim strongly to one consolidated government of the United States. It leaves the powers of government, and the representation of the people, so unnaturally divided between the general and state governments, that the operations of our system must be very uncertain. My uniform federal attachments, and the interest I have in the protection of property, and a steady execution of the laws, will convince you, that, if I am under any biass at all, it is in favor of any general system which shall promise those advantages. The instability of our laws increases my wishes for firm and steady government; but then, I can consent to no government, which, in my opinion, is not calculated equally to preserve the rights of all orders of men in the community. My object has been to join with those who have endeavoured to supply the defects in the forms of our governments by a steady and proper administration of them. Though I have long apprehended that fraudalent debtors, and embarrassed men, on the one hand, and men, on the other, unfriendly to republican equality, would produce an uneasiness among the people, and prepare the way, not for cool and deliberate reforms in the governments, but for changes calculated to promote the interests of particular orders of men.[2] Acquit me, sir, of any agency in the formation of the new system; I shall be satisfied with seeing, if it shall be adopted, a prudent administration. Indeed I am so much convinced of the truth of Pope's maxim, that "That which is best administered is best," that I am much inclined to subscribe to it from experience. I am not disposed to unreasonably contend about forms.[3] I know our situation is critical, and it behoves us to make the best of it.[4] A federal government of some sort is necessary. We have suffered the present to languish; and whether the confederation was capable or not originally of answering any valuable purposes, it is now but of little importance. I will pass by the men, and states, who have been particularly instrumental in preparing the way for a change, and, perhaps, for governments not very favourable to the people at large. A constitution is now presented which we may reject, or which we may accept, with or without amendments; and to which point we ought to direct our exertions, is the question. To determine this question, with propriety, we must attentively examine the system itself, and the probable consequences of either step. This I shall endeavour to do, so far as I am able, with candor and fairness; and leave you to decide upon the propriety of my opinions, the weight of my reasons, and how far my conclusions are well drawn. Whatever may be the conduct of others, on the present occasion, I do not mean, hastily and positively to decide on the merits of the constitution proposed. I shall be open to conviction, and always disposed to adopt that which, all things considered, shall appear to me to be most for the happiness of the community. It must be granted, that if men hastily and blindly adopt a system of government, they will as hastily and as blindly be led to alter or abolish it; and changes must ensue, one after another, till the peaceable and better part of the community will grow weary with changes, tumults and disorders, and be disposed to accept any government, however despotic, that shall promise stability and firmness.

2.8.2   The first principal question that occurs, is, Whether, considering our situation, we ought to precipitate the adoption of the proposed constitution? If we remain cool and temperate, we are in no immediate danger of any commotions; we are in a state of perfect peace, and in no danger of invasions; the state governments are in the full exercise of their powers; and our governments answer all present exigencies, except the regulation of trade, securing credit, in some cases, and providing for the interest, in some instances, of the public debts; and whether we adopt a change, three or nine months hence, can make but little odds with the private circumstances of individuals; their happiness and prosperity, after all, depend principally upon their own exertions. We are hardly recovered from a long and distressing war: The farmers, fishmen, &c. have not yet fully repaired the waste made by it. Industry and frugality are again assuming their proper station. Private debts are lessened, and public debts incurred by the war have been, by various ways, diminished; and the public lands have now become a productive source for diminishing them much more. I know uneasy men, who wish very much to precipitate, do not admit all these facts; but they are facts well known to all men who are thoroughly informed in the affairs of this country. It must, however, be admitted, that our federal system is defective, and that some of the state governments are not well administered; but, then, we impute to the defects in our governments many evils and embarrassments which are most clearly the result of the late war. We must allow men to conduct on the present occasion, as on all similar ones. They will urge a thousand pretences to answer their purposes on both sides. When we want a man to change his condition, we describe it as miserable, wretched, and despised; and draw a pleasing picture of that which we would have him assume. And when we wish the contrary, we reverse our descriptions. Whenever a clamor is raised, and idle men get to work, it is highly necessary to examine facts carefully, and without unreasonably suspecting men of falshood, to examine, and enquire attentively, under what impressions they act. It is too often the case in political concerns, that men state facts not as they are, but as they wish them to be; and almost every man, by calling to mind past scenes, will find this to be true.

2.8.3   Nothing but the passions of ambitious, impatient, or disorderly men, I conceive, will plunge us into commotions, if time should be taken fully to examine and consider the system proposed. Men who feel easy in their circumstances, and such as are not sanguine in their expectations relative to the consequences of the proposed change, will remain quiet under the existing governments. Many commercial and monied men, who are uneasy, not without just cause, ought to be respected; and, by no means, unreasonably disappointed in their expectations and hopes; but as to those who expect employments under the new constitution; as to those weak and ardent men who always expect to be gainers by revolutions, and whose lot it generally is to get out of one difficulty into another, they are very little to be regarded: and as to those who designedly avail themselves of this weakness and ardor, they are to be despised. It is natural for men, who wish to hasten the adoption of a measure, to tell us, now is the crisis—now is the critical moment which must be seized, or all will be lost: and to shut the door against free enquiry, whenever conscious the thing presented has defects in it, which time and investigation will probably discover. This has been the custom of tyrants and their dependants in all ages. If it is true, what has been so often said, that the people of this country cannot change their condition for the worse, I presume it still behoves them to endeavour deliberately to change it for the better. The fickle and ardent, in any community, are the proper tools for establishing despotic government. But it is deliberate and thinking men, who must establish and secure governments on free principles. Before they decide on the plan proposed, they will enquire whether it will probably be a blessing or a curse to this people.

The present moment discovers a new face in our affairs. Our object has been all along, to reform our federal system, and to strengthen our governments—to establish peace, order and justice in the community—but a new object now presents. The plan of government now proposed is evidently calculated totally to change, in time, our condition as a people. Instead of being thirteen republics, under a federal head, it is clearly designed to make us one consolidated government. Of this, I think, I shall fully convince you, in my following letters on this subject. This consolidation of the states has been the object of several men in this country for some time past. Whether such a change can ever be effected in any manner; whether it can be effected without convulsions and civil wars; whether such a change will not totally destroy the liberties of this country—time only can determine. 2.8.4

To have a just idea of the government before us, and to shew that a consolidated one is the object in view, it is necessary not only to examine the plan, but also its history, and the politics of its particular friends. 2.8.5

The confederation was formed when great confidence was placed in the voluntary exertions of individuals, and of the respective states; and the framers of it, to guard against usurpation, so limited and checked the powers, that, in many respects, they are inadequate to the exigencies of the union. We find, therefore, members of congress urging alterations in the federal system almost as soon as it was adopted. It was early proposed to vest congress with powers to levy an impost, to regulate trade, etc. but such was known to be the caution of the states in parting with power, that the vestment, even of these, was proposed to be under several checks and limitations. During the war, the general confusion, and the introduction of paper money, infused in the minds of people vague ideas respecting government and credit. We expected too much from the return of peace, and of course we have been disappointed. Our governments have been new and unsettled; and several legislatures, by making tender, suspension, and paper 2.8.6

money laws, have given just cause of uneasiness to creditors. By these and other causes, several orders of men in the community have been prepared, by degrees, for a change of government; and this very abuse of power in the legislatures, which, in some cases, has been charged upon the democratic part of the community, has furnished aristocratical men with those very weapons, and those very means, with which, in great measure, they are rapidly effecting their favourite object. And should an oppressive government be the consequence of the proposed change, posterity may reproach not only a few overbearing unprincipled men, but those parties in the states which have misused their powers.

2.8.7   The conduct of several legislatures, touching paper money, and tender laws, has prepared many honest men for changes in government, which otherwise they would not have thought of—when by the evils, on the one hand, and by the secret instigations of artful men, on the other, the minds of men were become sufficiently uneasy, a bold step was taken, which is usually followed by a revolution, or a civil war. A general convention for mere commercial purposes was moved for—the authors of this measure saw that the people's attention was turned solely to the amendment of the federal system; and that, had the idea of a total change been started, probably no state would have appointed members to the convention. The idea of destroying, ultimately, the state government, and forming one consolidated system, could not have been admitted—a convention, therefore, merely for vesting in congress power to regulate trade was proposed. This was pleasing to the commercial towns; and the landed people had little or no concern about it. September, 1786, a few men from the middle states met at Annapolis, and hastily proposed a convention to be held in May, 1787, for the purpose, generally, of amending the confederation—this was done before the delegates of Massachusetts, and of the other states arrived—still not a word was said about destroying the old constitution, and making a new one—The states still unsuspecting, and not aware that they were passing the Rubicon, appointed members to the new convention, for the sole and express purpose of revising and amending the confederation—and, probably, not one man in ten thousand in the United States, till within these ten or twelve days, had an idea that the old ship was to be destroyed, and he put to the alternative of embarking in the new ship presented, or of being left in danger of sinking—The States, I believe, universally supposed the convention would report alterations in the confederation, which would pass an examination in congress, and after being agreed to there, would be confirmed by all the legislatures, or be rejected. Virginia made a very respectable appointment, and placed at the head of it the first man in America: In this appointment there was a mixture of political characters; but Pennsylvania appointed principally those men who are esteemed aristocratical. Here the favourite moment for changing the government was evidently discerned by a few men, who seized it with address. Ten other states appointed, and tho' they chose men principally connected with commerce and the judicial department yet they appointed many good republican characters—had they all attended we should now see, I am persuaded a better system presented. The non-attendance of eight or nine men, who were appointed members of the convention, I shall ever consider as a very unfortunate event to the United States.[5]—Had they attended, I am pretty clear, that the result of the convention would not have had that strong tendency to aristocracy now discernable in every part of the plan.[6] There would not have been so great an accumulation of powers, especially as to the internal police of the country, in a few hands, as the constitution reported proposes to vest in them—the young visionary men, and the consolidating aristocracy, would have been more restrained than they have been. Eleven states met in the convention, and after four months close attention presented the new constitution, to be adopted or rejected by the people. The uneasy and fickle part of the community may be prepared to receive any form of government; but, I presume, the enlightened and substantial part will give any constitution presented for their adoption, a candid and thorough examination; and silence those designing or empty men, who weakly and rashly attempt to precipitate the adoption of a system of so much importance—We shall view the convention with proper respect—and, at the same time, that we reflect there were men of abilities and integrity in it, we must recollect how disproportionably the democratic and aristocratic parts of the community were represented—Perhaps the judicious friends and opposers of the new constitution will agree, that it is best to let it rest solely on its own merits, or be condemned for its own defects.

In the first place, I shall premise, that the plan proposed is a plan of accommodation—and that it is in this way only, and by giving up a part of our opinions, that we can ever expect to obtain a government founded in freedom and compact. This circumstance candid men will always keep in view, in the discussion of this subject. 2.8.8

The plan proposed appears to be partly federal, but principally however, calculated ultimately to make the states one consolidated government. 2.8.9

The first interesting question, therefore suggested, is, how far the states can be consolidated into one entire government on free principles. In considering this question extensive objects are to be taken into view, and important changes in the forms of government to be carefully attended to in all their consequences. The happiness of the people at large must be the great object with every honest statesman, and he will direct every movement to this point. If we are so situated as a people, as not to be able to enjoy equal happiness and advantages under one government, the consolidation of the states cannot be admitted.

There are three different forms of free government under which the United States may exist as one nation; and now is, perhaps, the time to determine to which we will direct our views.[7] 1. Distinct republics con- 2.8.10

nected under a federal head. In this case the respective state governments must be the principal guardians of the peoples rights, and exclusively regulate their internal police; in them must rest the balance of government. The congress of the states, or federal head, must consist of delegates amenable to, and removeable by the respective states: This congress must have general directing powers; powers to require men and monies of the states; to make treaties, peace and war; to direct the operations of armies, etc. Under this federal modification of government, the powers of congress would be rather advisory or recommendatory than coercive. 2. We may do away the several state governments, and form or consolidate all the states into one entire government, with one executive, one judiciary, and one legislature, consisting of senators and representatives collected from all parts of the union: In this case there would be a compleat consolidation of the states. 3. We may consolidate the states as to certain national objects, and leave them severally distinct independent republics, as to internal police generally. Let the general government consist of an executive, a judiciary, and balanced legislature, and its powers extend exclusively to all foreign concerns, causes arising on the seas to commerce, imports, armies, navies, Indian affairs, peace and war, and to a few internal concerns of the community; to the coin, post-offices, weights and measures, a general plan for the militia, to naturalization, *and, perhaps to bankruptcies,*[8] leaving the internal police of the community, in other respects, exclusively to the state governments; as the administration of justice in all causes arising internally, the laying and collecting of internal taxes, and the forming of the militia according to a general plan prescribed. In this case there would be a compleat consolidation, *quoad* certain objects only.[9]

2.8.11 Touching the first, or federal plan, I do not think much can be said in its favor: The sovereignty of the nation, without coercive and efficient powers to collect the strength of it, cannot always be depended on to answer the purposes of government; and in a congress of representatives of sovereign states, there must necessarily be an unreasonable mixture of powers in the same hands.

2.8.12 As to the second, or compleat consolidating plan, it deserves to be carefully considered at this time, by every American: If it be impracticable, it is a fatal error to model our governments, directing our views ultimately to it.

2.8.13 The third plan, or partial consolidation, is, in my opinion, the only one that can secure the freedom and happiness of this people. I once had some general ideas that the second plan was practicable,[10] but from long attention, and the proceedings of the convention, I am fully satisfied, that this third plan is the only one we can with safety and propriety proceed upon. Making this the standard to point out, with candor and fairness, the parts of the new constitution which appear to be improper, is my object. The convention appears to have proposed the partial consolidation evidently with a view to collect all powers ultimately, in the United States into one entire government; and from its views in this respect, and from the tenacity of the small states to have an equal vote in the senate, probably originated the greatest defects in the proposed plan.

Independant of the opinions of many great authors, that a free elective government cannot be extended over large territories, a few reflections must evince, that one government and general legislation alone, never can extend equal benefits to all parts of the United States: Different laws, customs, and opinions exist in the different states, which by a uniform system of laws would be unreasonably invaded. The United States contain about a million of square miles, and in half a century will, probably, contain ten millions of people; and from the center to the extremes is about 800 miles.

2.8.14

Before we do away the state governments, or adopt measures that will tend to abolish them, and to consolidate the states into one entire government, several principles should be considered and facts ascertained:— These, and my examination into the essential parts of the proposed plan, I shall pursue in my next.

Your's &c.
The Federal Farmer.

II

October 9, 1787.

Dear Sir,

The essential parts of a free and good government are a full and equal representation of the people in the legislature, and the jury trial of the vicinage in the administration of justice—a full and equal representation, is that which possesses the same interests, feelings, opinions, and views the people themselves would were they all assembled—a fair representation, therefore, should be so regulated, that every order of men in the community, according to the common course of elections, can have a share in it—in order to allow professional men, merchants, traders, farmers, mechanics, etc. to bring a just proportion of their best informed men respectively into the legislature, the representation must be considerably numerous[11]—We have about 200 state senators in the United States, and a less number than that of federal representatives cannot, clearly, be a full representation of this people, in the affairs of internal taxation and police, were there but one legislature for the whole union. The representation cannot be equal, or the situation of the people proper for one government only—if the extreme parts of the society cannot be represented as fully as the central—It is apparently impracticable that this should be the case in this extensive country—it would be impossible to collect a representation of the parts of the country five, six, and seven hundred miles from the seat of government.

2.8.15

2.8.16   Under one general government alone, there could be but one judiciary, one supreme and a proper number of inferior courts. I think it would be totally impracticable in this case to preserve a due administration of justice, and the real benefits of the jury trial of the vicinage,[12]—there are now supreme courts in each state in the union; and a great number of county and other courts subordinate to each supreme court—most of these supreme and inferior courts are itinerant, and hold their sessions in different parts every year of their respective states, counties and districts—with all these moving courts, our citizens, from the vast extent of the country must travel very considerable distances from home to find the place where justice is administered. I am not for bringing justice so near to individuals as to afford them any temptation to engage in law suits; though I think it one of the greatest benefits in a good government, that each citizen should find a court of justice within a reasonable distance, perhaps, within a day's travel of his home; so that, without great inconveniences and enormous expences, he may have the advantages of his witnesses and jury—it would be impracticable to derive these advantages from one judiciary—the one supreme court at most could only set in the centre of the union, and move once a year into the centre of the eastern and southern extremes of it—and, in this case, each citizen, on an average, would travel 150 or 200 miles to find this court—that, however, inferior courts might be properly placed in the different counties, and districts of the union, the appellate jurisdiction would be intolerable and expensive.

2.8.17   If it were possible to consolidate the states, and preserve the features of a free government, still it is evident that the middle states, the parts of the union, about the seat of government, would enjoy great advantages, while the remote states would experience the many inconveniences of remote provinces. Wealth, offices, and the benefits of government would collect in the centre: and the extreme states[13] and their principal towns, become much less important.[14]

2.8.18   There are other considerations which tend to prove that the idea of one consolidated whole, on free principles, is ill-founded—the laws of a free government rest on the confidence of the people, and operate gently—and never can extend their influence very far—if they are executed on free principles, about the centre, where the benefits of the government induce the people to support it voluntarily; yet they must be executed on the principles of fear and force in the extremes—This has been the case with every extensive republic of which we have any accurate account.[15]

2.8.19   There are certain unalienable and fundamental rights, which in forming the social compact, ought to be explicitly ascertained and fixed—a free and enlightened people, in forming this compact, will not resign all their rights to those who govern, and they will fix limits to their legislators and rulers, which will soon be plainly seen by those who are governed, as well as by those who govern: and the latter will know they cannot be passed unperceived by the former, and without giving a general alarm—These rights should be made the basis of every constitution: and if a people be so situated, or have such different opinions that they cannot agree in ascertaining and fixing them, it is a very strong argument against their attempting to form one entire society, to live under one system of laws only.—I confess, I never thought the people of these states differed essentially in these respects; they having derived all these rights from one common source, the British systems; and having in the formation of their state constitutions, discovered that their ideas relative to these rights are very similar. However, it is now said that the states differ so essentially in these respects, and even in the important article of the trial by jury, that when assembled in convention, they can agree to no words by which to establish that trial, or by which to ascertain and establish many other of these rights, as fundamental articles in the social compact.[16] If so, we proceed to consolidate the states on no solid basis whatever.

But I do not pay much regard to the reasons given for not bottoming the new constitution on a better bill of rights. I still believe a complete federal bill of rights to be very practicable.[17] Nevertheless I acknowledge the proceedings of the convention furnish my mind with many new and strong reasons, against a complete consolidation of the states. They tend to convince me, that it cannot be carried with propriety very far—that the convention have gone much farther in one respect than they found it practicable to go in another; that is, they propose to lodge in the general government very extensive powers—*powers* nearly, if not altogether, complete and unlimited, over the purse and the sword. But, in its organization, they furnish the strongest proof that the proper limbs, or parts of a government, to support and execute those powers on proper principles (or in which they can be safely lodged) cannot be formed. These powers must be lodged somewhere in every society; but then they should be lodged where the strength and guardians of the people are collected. They can be wielded, or safely used, in a free country only by an able executive and judiciary, a respectable senate, and a secure, full, and equal representation of the people. I think the principles I have premised or brought into view, are well founded—I think they will not be denied by any fair reasoner. It is in connection with these, and other solid principles, we are to examine the constitution. It is not a few democratic phrases, or a few well formed features, that will prove its merits; or a few small omissions that will produce its rejection among men of sense; they will enquire what are the essential powers in a community, and what are nominal ones; where and how the essential powers shall be lodged to secure government, and to secure true liberty.

In examining the proposed constitution carefully, we must clearly perceive an unnatural separation of these powers from the substantial representation of the people. The state governments will exist, with all their governors, senators, representatives, officers and expences; in these will be

2.8.20

2.8.21

nineteen-twentieths of the representatives of the people; they will have a near connection, and their members an immediate intercourse with the people; and the probability is, that the state governments will possess the confidence of the people, and be considered generally as their immediate guardians.

2.8.22   The general government will consist of a new species of executive, a small senate, and a very small house of representatives. As many citizens will be more than three hundred miles from the seat of this government as will be nearer to it, its judges and officers cannot be very numerous, without making our governments very expensive. Thus will stand the state and the general governments, should the constitution be adopted without any alterations in their organization; but as to powers, the general government will possess all essential ones, at least on paper, and those of the states a mere shadow of power. And therefore, unless the people shall make some great exertions to restore to the state governments their powers in matters of internal police; as the powers to lay and collect, exclusively, internal taxes, to govern the militia, and to hold the decisions of their own judicial courts upon their own laws final, the balance cannot possibly continue long; but the state governments must be annihilated, or continue to exist for no purpose.

2.8.23   It is however to be observed, that many of the essential powers given the national government are not exclusively given; and the general government may have prudence enough to forbear the exercise of those which may still be exercised by the respective states. But this cannot justify the impropriety of giving powers, the exercise of which prudent men will not attempt, and imprudent men will, or probably can, exercise only in a manner destructive of free government. The general government, organized as it is, may be adequate to many valuable objects, and be able to carry its laws into execution on proper principles in several cases; but I think its warmest friends will not contend, that it can carry all the powers proposed to be lodged in it into effect, without calling to its aid a military force, which must very soon destroy all elective governments in the country, produce anarchy, or establish despotism. Though we cannot have now a complete idea of what will be the operations of the proposed system, we may, allowing things to have their common course, have a very tolerable one. The powers lodged in the general government, if exercised by it, must intimately effect the internal police of the states, as well as external concerns; and there is no reason to expect the numerous state governments, and their connections, will be very friendly to the execution of federal laws in those internal affairs, which hitherto have been under their own immediate management. There is more reason to believe, that the general government, far removed from the people, and none of its members elected oftener than once in two years, will be forgot or neglected, and its laws in many cases disregarded, unless a multitude of officers and military force be continually kept in view, and employed to enforce the execution of the laws, and to make the government feared and respected. No position can be truer than this, that in this country either neglected laws, or a military execution of them, must lead to a revolution, and to the destruction of freedom. Neglected laws must first lead to anarchy and confusion; and a military execution of laws is only a shorter way to the same point—despotic government.[18]

Your's, &c.

The Federal Farmer.

III

October 10th, 1787.

Dear Sir,

The great object of a free people must be so to form their government and laws, and so to administer them, as to create a confidence in, and respect for the laws; and thereby induce the sensible and virtuous part of the community to declare in favor of the laws, and to support them without an expensive military force.[19] I wish, though I confess I have not much hope, that this may be the case with the laws of congress under the new constitution. I am fully convinced that we must organize the national government on different principals, and make the parts of it more efficient, and secure in it more effectually the different interests in the community; or else leave in the state governments some powers propose[d] to be lodged in it—at least till such an organization shall be found to be practicable. Not sanguine in my expectations of a good federal administration, and satisfied, as I am, of the impracticability of consolidating the states, and at the same time of preserving the rights of the people at large, I believe we ought still to leave some of those powers in the state governments, in which the people, in fact, will still be represented—to define some other powers proposed to be vested in the general government, more carefully, and to establish a few principles to secure a proper exercise of the powers given it. It is not my object to multiply objections, or to contend about inconsiderable powers or amendments; I wish the system adopted with a few alterations; but those, in my mind, are essential ones; if adopted without, every good citizen will acquiesce though I shall consider the duration of our governments, and the liberties of this people, very much dependant on the administration of the general government.[20] A wise and honest administration, may make the people happy under any government; but necessity only can justify even our leaving open avenues to the abuse of power, by wicked, unthinking, or ambitious men. I will examine, first, the organization of the proposed government, in order to judge; 2d, with propriety, what powers are improperly,

2.8.24

at least prematurely lodged in it. I shall examine, 3d, the undefined powers; and 4th, those powers, the exercise of which is not secured on safe and proper ground.

2.8.25   First. As to the organization—the house of representatives, the democrative branch, as it is called, is to consist of 65 members: that is, about one representative for fifty thousand inhabitants, to be chosen biennially—the federal legislature may increase this number to one for each thirty thousand inhabitants, abating fractional numbers in each state.— Thirty-three representatives will make a quorum for doing business, and a majority of those present determine the sense of the house.—I have no idea that the interests, feelings, and opinions of three or four millions of people, especially touching internal taxation, can be collected in such a house.—In the nature of things, nine times in ten, men of the elevated classes in the community only can be chosen—Connecticut, for instance, will have five representatives—not one man in a hundred of those who form the democrative branch in the state legislature, will, on a fair computation, be one of the five—The people of this country, in one sense, may all be democratic; but if we make the proper distinction between the few men of wealth and abilities, and consider them, as we ought, as the natural aristocracy of the country,[21] and the great body of the people, the middle and lower classes, as the democracy, this federal representative branch will have but very little democracy in it, even this small representation is not secured on proper principles.—The branches of the legislature are essential parts of the fundamental compact, and ought to be so fixed by the people, that the legislature cannot alter itself by modifying the elections of its own members. This, by a part of Art. 1. Sect. 4. the general legislature may do, it may evidently so regulate elections as to secure the choice of any particular description of men.—It may make the whole state one district—make the capital, or any places in the state, the place or places of election—it may declare that the five men (or whatever the number may be the state may chuse) who shall have the most votes shall be considered as chosen—In this case it is easy to perceive how the people who live scattered in the inland towns will bestow their votes on different men—and how a few men in a city, in any order or profession, may unite and place any five men they please highest among those that may be voted for—and all this may be done constitutionally, and by those silent operations, which are not immediately perceived by the people in general.—I know it is urged, that the general legislature will be disposed to regulate elections on fair and just principles:—This may be true—good men will generally govern well with almost any constitution: but why in laying the foundation of the social system, need we unnecessarily leave a door open to improper regulations?—This is a very general and unguarded clause, and many evils may flow from that part which authorises the congress to regulate elections—Were it omitted, the regulations of elections would be solely in the respective states, where the people are substantially represented; and where the elections ought to be regulated, otherwise to secure a representation from all parts of the community, in making the constitution, we ought to provide for dividing each state into a proper number of districts, and for confining the electors in each district to the choice of some men, who shall have a permanent interest and residence in it; and also for this essential object, that the representative elected shall have a majority of the votes of those electors who shall attend and give their votes.

In considering the practicability of having a full and equal representation of the people from all parts of the union, not only distances and different opinions, customs, and views, common in extensive tracts of country, are to be taken into view, but many differences peculiar to Eastern, Middle, and Southern states. These differences are not so perceivable among the members of congress, and men of general information in the states, as among the men who would properly form the democratic branch. The Eastern states are very democratic, and composed chiefly of moderate freeholders; they have but few rich men and no slaves; the Southern states are composed chiefly of rich planters and slaves; they have but few moderate freeholders, and the prevailing influence, in them, is generally a dissipated aristocracy: The Middle states partake partly of the Eastern, and partly of the Southern character. 2.8.26

Perhaps, nothing could be more disjointed, unweildly and incompetent to doing business with harmony and dispatch, than a federal house of representatives properly numerous for the great objects of taxation, et cetera collected from the several states; whether such men would ever act in concert; whether they would not worry along a few years, and then be the means of separating the parts of the union, is very problematical?—View this system in whatever form we can, propriety brings us still to this point, a federal government possessed of general and complete powers, as to those national objects which cannot well come under the cognizance of the internal laws of the respective states, and this federal government, accordingly, consisting of branches not very numerous. 2.8.27

The house of representatives is on the plan of consolidation, but the senate is intirely on the federal plan;[22] and Delaware will have as much constitutional influence in the senate, as the largest state in the union: and in this senate are lodged legislative, executive and judicial powers: Ten states in this union urge that they are small states, nine of which were present in the convention.—They were interested in collecting large powers into the hands of the senate, in which each state still will have its equal share of power. I suppose it was impracticable for the three large states, as they were called, to get the senate formed on any other principles: But this only proves, that we cannot form one general government on equal and just principles—and proves, that we ought not to lodge in it such extensive powers before we are convinced of the practicability of organizing it on just 2.8.28

and equal principles. The senate will consist of two members from each state, chosen by the state legislatures, every sixth year. The clause referred to, respecting the elections of representatives, empowers the general legislature to regulate the elections of senators also, ''except as to the places of chusing senators.''—There is, therefore, but little more security in the elections than in those of representatives: Fourteen senators make a quorum for business, and a majority of the senators present give the vote of the senate, except in giving judgment upon an impeachment, or in making treaties, or in expelling a member, when two-thirds of the senators present must agree— The members of the legislature are not excluded from being elected to any military offices, or any civil offices, except those created, or the emoluments of which shall be increased by themselves: two-thirds of the members present, of either house, may expel a member at pleasure. The senate is an independant branch of the legislature, a court for trying impeachments, and also a part of the executive, having a negative in the making of all treaties, and in appointing almost all officers.

2.8.29   The vice president is not a very important, if not an unncessary part of the system—he may be a part of the senate at one period, and act as the supreme executive magistrate at another—The election of this officer, as well as of the president of the United States seems to be properly secured;[23] but when we examine the powers of the president, and the forms of the executive, we shall perceive that the general government, in this part, will have a strong tendency to aristocracy, or the government of the few. The executive is, in fact, the president and senate in all transactions of any importance; the president is connected with, or tied to the senate; he may always act with the senate, but never can effectually counteract its views: The president can appoint no officer, civil or military, who shall not be agreeable to the senate; and the presumption is, that the will of so important a body will not be very easily controuled, and that it will exercise its powers with great address.

2.8.30   In the judicial department, powers ever kept distinct in well balanced governments, are no less improperly blended in the hands of the same men—in the judges of the supreme court is lodged, the law, the equity and the fact. It is not necessary to pursue the minute organical parts of the general government proposed.—There were various interests in the convention, to be reconciled, especially of large and small states; of carrying and non-carrying states; and of states more and states less democratic—vast labour and attention were by the convention bestowed on the organization of the parts of the constitution offered; still it is acknowledged there are many things radically wrong in the essential parts of this constitution—but it is said that these are the result of our situation: On a full examination of the subject, I believe it; but what do the laborious inquiries and determinations of the convention prove? If they prove any thing, they prove that we cannot consolidate the states on proper principles: The organization of the government presented proves, that we cannot form a general government in which all power can be safely lodged; and a little attention to the parts of the one proposed will make it appear very evident, that all the powers proposed to be lodged in it, will not be then well deposited, either for the purposes of government, or the preservation of liberty. I will suppose no abuse of powers in those cases, in which the abuse of it is not well guarded against—I will suppose the words authorising the general government to regulate the elections of its own members struck out of the plan, or free district elections, in each state, amply secured.—That the small representation provided for shall be as fair and equal as it is capable of being made—I will suppose the judicial department regulated on pure principles, by future laws, as far as it can be by the constitution, and consist[ent] with the situation of the country—still there will be an unreasonable accumulation of powers in the general government, if all be granted, enumerated in the plan proposed. The plan does not present a well balanced government. The senatorial branch of the legislative and the executive are substantially united, and the president, or the first executive magistrate, may aid the senatorial interest when weakest, but never can effectually support the democratic[,] however it may be oppressed;—the excellency, in my mind, of a well balanced government is that it consists of distinct branches, each sufficiently strong and independant to keep its own station, and to aid either of the other branches which may occasionally want aid.

The convention found that any but a small house of representatives would be expensive, and that it would be impracticable to assemble a large number of representatives. Not only the determination of the convention in this case, but the situation of the states, proves the impracticability of collecting, in any one point, a proper representation. 2.8.31

The formation of the senate, and the smallness of the house, being, therefore, the result of our situation, and the actual state of things, the evils which may attend the exercise of many powers in this national government may be considered as without a remedy. 2.8.32

All officers are impeachable before the senate only—before the men by whom they are appointed, or who are consenting to the appointment of these officers. No judgment of conviction, on an impeachment, can be given unless two thirds of the senators agree. Under these circumstances the right of impeachment, in the house, can be of but little importance; the house cannot expect often to convict the offender; and, therefore, probably, will but seldom or never exercise the right. In addition to the insecurity and inconveniences attending this organization beforementioned, it may be observed, that it is extremely difficult to secure the people against the fatal effects of corruption and influence. The power of making any law will be in the president, eight senators, and seventeen representatives, relative to the important objects enumerated in the constitution. Where there is a small representation a sufficient number to carry any measure, may, with ease, be influenced by bribes, offices and civilities; they may easily form private 2.8.33

juntoes, and out door meetings, agree on measures, and carry them by silent votes.

2.8.34   Impressed, as I am, with a sense of the difficulties there are in the way of forming the parts of a federal government on proper principles, and seeing a government so unsubstantially organized, after so arduous an attempt has been made, I am led to believe, that powers ought to be given to it with great care and caution.[24]

2.8.35   In the second place it is necessary, therefore, to examine the extent, and the probable operations of some of those extensive powers proposed to be vested in this government. These powers, legislative, executive, and judicial, respect internal as well as external objects. Those respecting external objects, as all foreign concerns, commerce, imposts, all causes arising on the seas, peace and war, and Indian affairs, can be lodged no where else, with any propriety, but in this government. Many powers that respect internal objects ought clearly to be lodged in it; as those to regulate trade between the states, weights and measures, the coin or current monies, post-offices, naturalization, etc. These powers may be exercised without essentially effecting the internal police of the respective states: But powers to lay and collect internal taxes, to form the militia, to make bankrupt laws, and to decide on appeals, questions arising on the internal laws of the respective states, are of a very serious nature, and carry with them almost all other powers. These taken in connection with the others, and powers to raise armies and build navies, proposed to be lodged in this government, appear to me to comprehend all the essential powers in the community, and those which will be left to the states will be of no great importance.

2.8.36   A power to lay and collect taxes at discretion, is, in itself, of very great importance. By means of taxes, the government may command the whole or any part of the subject's property. Taxes may be of various kinds; but there is a strong distinction between external and internal taxes. External taxes are impost duties, which are laid on imported goods; they may usually be collected in a few seaport towns, and of a few individuals, though ultimately paid by the consumer; a few officers can collect them, and they can be carried no higher than trade will bear, or smuggling permit—that in the very nature of commerce, bounds are set to them.[25] But internal taxes, as poll and land taxes, excises, duties on all written instruments, etc. may fix themselves on every person and species of property in the community; they may be carried to any lengths, and in proportion as they are extended, numerous officers must be employed to assess them, and to enforce the collection of them. In the United Netherlands the general government has compleat powers, as to external taxation; but as to internal taxes, it makes requisitions on the provinces. Internal taxation in this country is more important, as the country is so very extensive. As many assessors and collectors of federal taxes will be above three hundred miles from the seat of the federal government as will be less. Besides, to lay and collect internal taxes, in this extensive country, must require a great number of congressional ordinances, immediately operating upon the body of the people; these must continually interfere with the state laws, and thereby produce disorder and general dissatisfaction, till the one system of laws or the other, operating upon the same subjects, shall be abolished. These ordinances alone, to say nothing of those respecting the militia, coin, commerce, federal judiciary, etc. etc. will probably soon defeat the operations of the state laws and governments.

Should the general government think it politic, as some administrations (if not all) probably will, to look for a support in a system of influence, the government will take every occasion to multiply laws, and officers to execute them, considering these as so many necessary props for its own support.[26] Should this system of policy be adopted, taxes more productive than the impost duties will, probably, be wanted to support the government, and to discharge foreign demands, without leaving any thing for the domestic creditors. The internal sources of taxation then must be called into operation, and internal tax laws and federal assessors and collectors spread over this immense country. All these circumstances considered, is it wise, prudent, or safe, to vest the powers of laying and collecting internal taxes in the general government, while imperfectly organized and inadequate; and to trust to amending it hereafter, and making it adequate to this purpose? It is not only unsafe but absurd to lodge power in a government before it is fitted to receive it? [Sic.] It is confessed that this power and representation ought to go together. Why give the power first? Why give the power to the few, who, when possessed of it, may have address enough to prevent the increase of representation? Why not keep the power, and, when necessary, amend the constitution, and add to its other parts this power, and a proper increase of representation at the same time? Then men who may want the power will be under strong inducements to let in the people, by their representatives, into the government, to hold their due proportion of this power. If a proper representation be impracticable, then we shall see this power resting in the states, where it at present ought to be, and not inconsiderately given up.

When I recollect how lately congress, conventions, legislatures, and people contended in the cause of liberty, and carefully weighed the importance of taxation, I can scarcely believe we are serious in proposing to vest the powers of laying and collecting internal taxes in a government so imperfectly organized for such purposes. Should the United States be taxed by a house of representatives of two hundred members, which would be about fifteen members for Connecticut, twenty-five for Massachusetts, etc. still the middle and lower classes of people could have no great share, in fact, in taxation. I am aware it is said, that the representation proposed by the new constitution is sufficiently numerous; it may be for many purposes; but to suppose that this branch is sufficiently numerous to guard the rights of

2.8.37

2.8.38

the people in the administration of the government, in which the purse and sword is placed, seems to argue that we have forgot what the true meaning of representation is. I am sensible also, that it is said that congress will not attempt to lay and collect internal taxes; that it is necessary for them to have the power, though it cannot probably be exercised.[27]—I admit that it is not probable that any prudent congress will attempt to lay and collect internal taxes, especially direct taxes: but this only proves, that the power would be improperly lodged in congress, and that it might be abused by imprudent and designing men.

2.8.39   I have heard several gentlemen, to get rid of objections to this part of the constitution, attempt to construe the powers relative to direct taxes, as those who object to it would have them; as to these, it is said, that congress will only have power to make requisitions, leaving it to the states to lay and collect them.[28] I see but very little colour for this construction, and the attempt only proves that this part of the plan cannot be defended. By this plan there can be no doubt, but that the powers of congress will be complete as to all kinds of taxes whatever—Further, as to internal taxes, the state governments will have concurrent powers with the general government, and both may tax the same objects in the same year; and the objection that the general government may suspend a state tax, as a necessary measure for the promoting the collection of a federal tax, is not without foundation.[29]—As the states owe large debts, and have large demands upon them individually, there clearly would be a propriety in leaving in their possession exclusively, some of the internal sources of taxation, at least until the federal representation shall be properly encreased: The power in the general government to lay and collect internal taxes, will render its powers respecting armies, navies and the militia, the more exceptionable. By the constitution it is proposed that congress shall have power "to raise and support armies, but no appropriation of money to that use shall be for a longer term than two years; to provide and maintain a navy; to provide for calling forth the militia to execute the laws of the union, suppress insurrections, and repel invasions: to provide for organizing, arming, and disciplining the militia: reserving to the states the right to appoint the officers, and to train the militia according to the discipline prescribed by congress; congress will have unlimited power to raise armies, and to engage officers and men for any number of years; but a legislative act applying money for their support can have operation for no longer term than two years, and if a subsequent congress do not within the two years renew the appropriation, or further appropriate monies for the use of the army, the army will be left to take care of itself. When an army shall once be raised for a number of years, it is not probable that it will find much difficulty in getting congress to pass laws for applying monies to its support. I see so many men in America fond of a standing army, and especially among those who probably will have a large share in administering the federal system; it is very evident to me, that we shall have a large standing army as soon as the monies to support them can be possibly found. An army is a very agreeable place of employment for the young gentlemen of many families. A power to raise armies must be lodged some where; still this will not justify the lodging this power in a bare majority of so few men without any checks; or in the government in which the great body of the people, in the nature of things, will be only nominally represented. In the state governments the great body of the people, the yeomanry, etc. of the country, are represented: It is true they will chuse the members of congress, and may now and then chuse a man of their own way of thinking; but it is impossible for forty, or thirty thousand people in this country, one time in ten to find a man who can possess similar feelings, views, and interests with themselves: Powers to lay and collect taxes and to raise armies are of the greatest moment; for carrying them into effect, laws need not be frequently made, and the yeomanry, etc of the country ought substantially to have a check upon the passing of these laws; this check ought to be placed in the legislatures, or at least, in the few men the common people of the country, will, probably, have in congress, in the true sense of the word, "from among themselves."[30] It is true, the yeomanry of the country possess the lands, the weight of property, possess arms, and are too strong a body of men to be openly offended—and, therefore, it is urged, they will take care of themselves, that men who shall govern will not dare pay any disrespect to their opinions. It is easily perceived, that if they have not their proper negative upon passing laws in congress, or on the passage of laws relative to taxes and armies, they may in twenty or thirty years be by means imperceptible to them, totally deprived of that boasted weight and strength: This may be done in a great measure by congress, if disposed to do it, by modelling the militia. Should one fifth, or one eighth part of the men capable of bearing arms, be made a select militia, as has been proposed, and those the young and ardent part of the community, possessed of but little or no property, and all the others put upon a plan that will render them of no importance, the former will answer all the purposes of an army, while the latter will be defenceless. The state must train the militia in such form and according to such systems and rules as congress shall prescribe: and the only actual influence the respective states will have respecting the militia will be in appointing the officers. I see no provision made for calling out the *posse commitatus* for executing the laws of the union, but provision is made for congress to call forth the militia for the execution of them—and the militia in general, or any select part of it, may be called out under military officers, instead of the sheriff to enforce an execution of federal laws, in the first instance and thereby introduce an entire military execution of the laws.[31] I know that powers to raise taxes, to regulate the military strength of the community on some uniform plan, to provide for its defence and internal order, and for duly executing the laws, must be lodged somewhere; but still we ought not so to lodge them, as evidently to give one order of men in the community, undue advantages over others; or commit the many to the mercy, prudence, and moderation of the few. And so far as it may be necessary to lodge any of the peculiar powers in the general government, a more safe exercise of them ought to be secured, by requiring the consent of two-thirds or three-fourths of congress thereto—until the federal representation can be increased, so that the democratic members in congress may stand some tolerable chance of a reasonable negative, in behalf of the numerous, important, and democratic part of the community.

2.8.40   I am not sufficiently acquainted with the laws and internal police of all the states to discern fully, how general bankrupt laws, made by the union, would effect them, or promote the public good. I believe the property of debtors, in the several states, is held responsible for their debts in modes and forms very different. If uniform bankrupt laws can be made without producing real and substantial inconveniences, I wish them to be made by congress.[32]

2.8.41   There are some powers proposed to be lodged in the general government in the judicial department, I think very unnecessarily,[33] I mean powers respecting questions arising upon the internal laws of the respective states. It is proper the federal judiciary should have powers co-extensive with the federal legislature—that is, the power of deciding finally on the laws of the union. By Art. 3. Sect. 2. the powers of the federal judiciary are extended (among other things) to all cases between a state and citizens of another state—between citizens of different states—between a state or the citizens thereof, and foreign states, citizens or subjects. Actions in all these cases, except against a state government, are now brought and finally determined in the law courts of the states respectively; and as there are no words to exclude these courts of their jurisdiction in these cases, they will have concurrent jurisdiction with the inferior federal courts in them; and, therefore, if the new constitution be adopted without any amendment in this respect, all those numerous actions, now brought in the state courts between our citizens and foreigners, between citizens of different states, by state governments against foreigners, and by state governments against citizens of other states, may also be brought in the federal courts; and an appeal will lay in them from the state courts, or federal inferior courts, to the supreme judicial court of the union. In almost all these cases, either party may have the trial by jury in the state courts; excepting paper money and tender laws, which are wisely guarded against in the proposed constitution, justice may be obtained in these courts on reasonable terms; they must be more competent to proper decisions on the laws of their respective states, than the federal courts can possibly be. I do not, in any point of view, see the need of opening a new jurisdiction to these causes—of opening a new scene of expensive law suits—of suffering foreigners, and citizens of different states, to drag each other many hundred miles into the federal courts. It is true, those courts may be so organized by a wise and prudent legislature, as to make the obtaining of justice in them tolerably easy; they may in general be organized on the common law principles of the country: But this benefit is by no means secured by the constitution. The trial by jury is secured only in those few criminal cases, to which the federal laws will extend—as crimes committed on the seas, against the laws of nations, treason, and counterfeiting the federal securities and coin: But even in these cases, the jury trial of the vicinage is not secured—particularly in the large states, a citizen may be tried for a crime committed in the state, and yet tried in some states 500 miles from the place where it was committed; but the jury trial is not secured at all in civil causes. Though the convention have not established this trial, it is to be hoped that congress, in putting the new system into execution, will do it by a legislative act, in all cases in which it can be done with propriety. Whether the jury trial is not excluded [from] the supreme judicial court, is an important question. By Art. 3. Sect. 2. all cases affecting ambassadors, other public ministers, and consuls, and in those cases in which a state shall be party, the supreme court shall have jurisdiction. In all the other cases beforementioned, the supreme court shall have appellate jurisdiction, both as to *law and fact*, with such exception, and under such regulations, as the congress shall make. By court is understood a court consisting of judges; and the idea of a jury is excluded. This court, or the judges, are to have jurisdiction on appeals, in all the cases enumerated, as to law and fact; the judges are to decide the law and try the fact, and the trial of the fact being assigned to the judges by the constitution, a jury for trying the fact is excluded; however, under the exceptions and powers to make regulations, congress may, perhaps introduce the jury, to try the fact in most necessary cases.[34]

There can be but one supreme court in which the final jurisdiction will centre in all federal causes—except in cases where appeals by law shall not be allowed: The judicial powers of the federal courts extends in law and equity to certain cases: and, therefore, the powers to determine on the law, in equity, and as to the fact, all will concentre in the supreme court:—These powers, which by this constitution are blended in the same hands, the same judges, are in Great-Britain deposited in different hands—to wit, the decision of the law in the law judges, the decision in equity in the chancellor, and the trial of the fact in the jury. It is a very dangerous thing to vest in the same judge power to decide on the law, and also general powers in equity; for if the law restrain him, he is only to step into his shoes of equity, and give what judgment his reason or opinion may dictate; we have no precedents in this country, as yet, to regulate the divisions in equity as in Great Britain; equity, therefore, in the supreme court for many years will be mere discretion. I confess in the constitution of this supreme court, as left by the constitution, I do not see a spark of freedom or a shadow of our own or the British common law.

2.8.42

This court is to have appellate jurisdiction in all the other cases before

2.8.43

mentioned: Many sensible men suppose that cases before mentioned respect, as well the criminal cases as the civil ones, mentioned antecedently in the constitution, if so an appeal is allowed in criminal cases—contrary to the usual sense of law. How far it may be proper to admit a foreigner or the citizen of another state to bring actions against state governments, which have failed in performing so many promises made during the war, is doubtful: How far it may be proper so to humble a state, as to oblige it to answer to an individual in a court of law, is worthy of consideration; the states are now subject to no such actions; and this new jurisdiction will subject the states, and many defendants to actions, and processes, which were not in the contemplation of the parties, when the contract was made; all engagements existing between citizens of different states, citizens and foreigners, states and foreigners; and states and citizens of other states were made the parties contemplating the remedies then existing on the laws of the states— and the new remedy proposed to be given in the federal courts, can be founded on no principle whatever.

Your's &c.
The Federal Farmer.

IV

October 12th, 1787.

2.8.44   Dear Sir,

It will not be possible to establish in the federal courts the jury trial of the vicinage so well as in the state courts.

Third. There appears to me to be not only a premature deposit of some important powers in the general government—but many of those deposited there are undefined, and may be used to good or bad purposes as honest or designing men shall prevail. By Art. 1, Sect. 2, representatives and direct taxes shall be apportioned among the several states, etc.—same art. sect. 8, the congress shall have powers to lay and collect taxes, duties, etc. for the common defence and general welfare, but all duties, imposts and excises, shall be uniform throughout the United States: By the first recited clause, direct taxes shall be apportioned on the states. This seems to favour the idea suggested by some sensible men and writers, that congress, as to direct taxes, will only have power to make requisitions,[35] but the latter clause, power to lay and collect taxes, etc. seems clearly to favour the contrary opinion and, in my mind, the true one, that congress shall have power to tax immediately individuals, without the intervention of the state legislatures[;] in fact the first clause appears to me only to provide that each state shall pay a certain portion of the tax, and the latter to provide that congress shall have power to lay and collect taxes, that is to assess upon, and to collect of the individuals in the state, the state[']s quota; but these still I consider as undefined powers, because judicious men understand them differently.

It is doubtful whether the vice president is to have any qualifications; none are mentioned; but he may serve as president, and it may be inferred, he ought to be qualified therefore as the president; but the qualifications of the president are required only of the person to be elected president. By art. the 2, sect. 2. "But the congress may by law vest the appointment of such inferior officers as they think proper in the president alone, in the courts of law, or in the heads of the departments:" Who are inferior officers? May not a congress disposed to vest the appointment of all officers in the president, under this clause, vest the appointment of almost every officer in the president alone, and destroy the check mentioned in the first part of the clause, and lodged in the senate. It is true, this check is badly lodged, but then some check upon the first magistrate in appointing officers, ought it appears by the opinion of the convention, and by the general opinion, to be established in the constitution. By art. 3, sect. 2, the supreme court shall have appellate jurisdiction as to law and facts with such exceptions, etc. to what extent is it intended the exceptions shall be carried—Congress may carry them so far as to annihilate substantially the appellate jurisdiction, and the clause be rendered of very little importance.

2.8.45

4th. There are certain rights which we have always held sacred in the United States, and recognized in all our constitutions, and which, by the adoption of the new constitution in its present form, will be left unsecured.[36] By article 6, the proposed constitution, and the laws of the United States, which shall be made in pursuance thereof; and all treaties made, or which shall be made under the authority of the United States, shall be the supreme law of the land; and the judges in every state shall be bound thereby; any thing in the constitution or laws of any state to the contrary notwithstanding.

2.8.46

It is to be observed that when the people shall adopt the proposed constitution it will be their last and supreme act; it will be adopted not by the people of New-Hampshire, Massachusetts, etc. but by the people of the United States;[37] and wherever this constitution, or any part of it, shall be incompatible with the ancient customs, rights, the laws or the constitutions heretofore established in the United States, it will entirely abolish them and do them away: And not only this, but the laws of the United States which shall be made in pursuance of the federal constitution will be also supreme laws, and wherever they shall be incompatible with those customs, rights, laws or constitutions heretofore established, they will also entirely abolish them and do them away.

2.8.47

By the article before recited, treaties also made under the authority of the United States, shall be the supreme law: It is not said that these treaties shall be made in pursuance of the constitution—nor are there any con-

2.8.48

stitutional bounds set to those who shall make them: The president and two thirds of the senate will be empowered to make treaties indefinitely, and when these treaties shall be made, they will also abolish all laws and state constitutions incompatible with them. This power in the president and senate is absolute, and the judges will be bound to allow full force to whatever rule, article or thing the president and senate shall establish by treaty, whether it be practicable to set any bounds to those who make treaties, I am not able to say: if not, it proves that this power ought to be more safely lodged.

2.8.49   The federal constitution, the laws of congress made in pursuance of the constitution, and all treaties must have full force and effect in all parts of the United States; and all other laws, rights and constitutions which stand in their way must yield: It is proper the national laws should be supreme, and superior to state or district laws: but then the national laws ought to yield to unalienable or fundamental rights—and national laws, made by a few men, should extend only to a few national objects. This will not be the case with the laws of congress: To have any proper idea of their extent, we must carefully examine the legislative, executive and judicial powers proposed to be lodged in the general government, and consider them in connection with a general clause in art. 1. sect. 8, in these words (after inumerating a number of powers) "To make all laws which shall be necessary and proper for carrying into execution the foregoing powers, and all other powers vested by this constitution in the government of the United States, or in any department or officer thereof."—The powers of this government as has been observed, extend to internal as well as external objects, and to those objects to which all others are subordinate; it is almost impossible to have a just conception of these powers, or of the extent and number of the laws which may be deemed necessary and proper to carry them into effect, till we shall come to exercise those powers and make the laws. In making laws to carry those powers into effect, it is to be expected, that a wise and prudent congress will pay respect to the opinions of a free people, and bottom their laws on those principles which have been considered as essential and fundamental in the British, and in our government. But a congress of a different character will not be bound by the constitution to pay respect to those principles.

2.8.50   It is said, that when the people make a constitution, and delegate powers that all powers not delegated by them to those who govern is [sic] reserved in the people;[38] and that the people, in the present case, have reserved in themselves, and in their state governments, every right and power not expressly given by the federal constitution to those who shall administer the national government.[39] It is said on the other hand, that the people, when they make a constitution, yield all power not expressly reserved to themselves.[40] The truth is, in either case, it is mere matter of opinion and men usually take either side of the argument, as will best answer their purposes:

But the general presumption being, that men who govern, will, in doubtful cases, construe laws and constitutions most favourably for encreasing their own powers; all wise and prudent people, in forming constitutions, have drawn the line, and carefully described the powers parted with and the powers reserved. By the state constitutions, certain rights have been reserved in the people; or rather, they have been recognized and established in such a manner, that state legislatures are bound to respect them, and to make no laws infringing upon them. The state legislatures are obliged to take notice of the bills of rights of their respective states. The bills of rights, and the state constitutions, are fundamental compacts only between those who govern, and the people of the same state.

In the year 1788 the people of the United States make a federal constitution, which is a fundamental compact between them and their federal rulers; these rulers, in the nature of things, cannot be bound to take notice of any other compact. It would be absurd for them, in making laws, to look over thirteen, fifteen, or twenty state constitutions, to see what rights are established as fundamental, and must not be infringed upon, in making laws in the society. It is true, they would be bound to do it if the people, in their federal compact, should refer to the state constitutions, recognize all parts not inconsistent with the federal constitution, and direct their federal rulers to take notice of them accordingly; but this is not the case, as the plan stands proposed at present; and it is absurd, to suppose so unnatural an idea is intended or implied. I think my opinion is not only founded in reason, but I think it is supported by the report of the convention itself. If there are a number of rights established by the state constitutions, and which will remain sacred, and the general government is bound to take notice of them—it must take notice of one as well as another; and if unnecessary to recognize or establish one by the federal constitution, it would be unnecessary to recognize or establish another by it.[41] If the federal constitution is to be construed so far in connection with the state constitutions, as to leave the trial by jury in civil causes, for instance, secured; on the same principles it would have left the trial by jury in criminal causes, the benefits of the writ of habeas corpus, etc. secured; they all stand on the same footing; they are the common rights of Americans, and have been recognized by the state constitutions: But the convention found it necessary to recognize or re-establish the benefits of that writ, and the jury trial in criminal cases. As to *expost facto* laws, the convention has done the same in one case, and gone further in another. It is part of the compact between the people of each state and their rulers, that no *expost facto* laws shall be made. But the convention, by Art. I Sect. 10 have put a sanction upon this part even of the state compacts. In fact, the 9th and 10th Sections in Art. I. in the proposed constitution, are no more nor less, than a partial bill of rights; they establish certain principles as part of the compact upon which the federal legislators and officers can never infringe. It is here wisely stipulated, that the federal legislature shall

2.8.51

never pass a bill of attainder, or *expost facto* law; that no tax shall be laid on articles exported, etc. The establishing of one right implies the necessity of establishing another and similar one.

2.8.52   On the whole, the position appears to me to be undeniable, that this bill of rights ought to be carried farther, and some other principles established, as a part of this fundamental compact between the people of the United States and their federal rulers.

2.8.53   It is true, we are not disposed to differ much, at present, about religion; but when we are making a constitution, it is to be hoped, for ages and millions yet unborn, why not establish the free exercise of religion, as a part of the national compact. There are other essential rights, which we have justly understood to be the rights of freemen; as freedom from hasty and unreasonable search warrants, warrants not founded on oath, and not issued with due caution, for searching and seizing men's papers, property, and persons. The trials by jury in civil causes, it is said, varies so much in the several states, that no words could be found for the uniform establishment of it.[42] If so, the federal legislation will not be able to establish it by any general laws. I confess I am of opinion it may be established, but not in that beneficial manner in which we may enjoy it, for the reasons beforementioned. When I speak of the jury trial of the vicinage, or the trial of the fact in the neighbourhood,—I do not lay so much stress upon the circumstance of our being tried by our neighbours: in this enlightened country men may be probably impartially tried by those who do not live very near them: but the trial of facts in the neighbourhood is of great importance in other respects. Nothing can be more essential than the cross examining witnesses, and generally before the triers of the facts in question. The common people can establish facts with much more ease with oral than written evidence; when trials of facts are removed to a distance from the homes of the parties and witnesses, oral evidence becomes intolerably expensive, and the parties must depend on written evidence, which to the common people is expensive and almost useless; it must be frequently taken ex parte, and but very seldom leads to the proper discovery of truth.

2.8.54   The trial by jury is very important in another point of view. It is essential in every free country, that common people should have a part and share of influence, in the judicial as well as in the legislative department. To hold open to them the offices of senators, judges, and offices to fill which an expensive education is required, cannot answer any valuable purposes for them; they are not in a situation to be brought forward and to fill those offices; these, and most other offices of any considerable importance, will be occupied by the few. The few, the well born, etc. as Mr. Adams calls them,[43] in judicial decisions as well as in legislation, are generally disposed, and very naturally too, to favour those of their own description.

2.8.55   The trial by jury in the judicial department, and the collection of the people by their representatives in the legislature, are those fortunate inventions which have procured for them, in this country, their true proportion of influence, and the wisest and most fit means of protecting themselves in the community. Their situation, as jurors and representatives, enables them to acquire information and knowledge in the affairs and government of the society; and to come forward, in turn, as the centinels and guardians of each other. I am very sorry that even a few of our countrymen should consider jurors and representatives in a different point of view, as ignorant troublesome bodies, which ought not to have any share in the concerns of government.

I confess I do not see in what cases the congress can, with any pretence of right, make a law to suppress the freedom of the press; though I am not clear, that congress is restrained from laying any duties whatever on printing, and from laying duties particularly heavy on certain pieces printed, and perhaps congress may require large bonds for the payment of these duties. Should the printer say, the freedom of the press was secured by the constitution of the state in which he lived, congress might, and perhaps, with great propriety, answer, that the federal constitution is the only compact existing between them and the people; in this compact the people have named no others, and therefore congress, in exercising the powers assigned them, and in making laws to carry them into execution, are restrained by nothing beside the federal constitution, any more than a state legislature is restrained by a compact between the magistrates and people of a county, city, or town of which the people, in forming the state constitution, have taken no notice. 2.8.56

It is not my object to enumerate rights of inconsiderable importance; but there are others, no doubt, which ought to be established as a fundamental part of the national system.

It is worthy observation, that all treaties are made by foreign nations with a confederacy of thirteen states—that the western country is attached to thirteen states—thirteen states have jointly and severally engaged to pay the public debts.—Should a new government be formed of nine, ten, eleven, or twelve states, those treaties could not be considered as binding on the foreign nations who made them. However, I believe the probability to be, that if nine states adopt the constitution, the others will. 2.8.57

It may also be worthy our examination, how far the provision for amending this plan, when it shall be adopted, is of any importance. No measures can be taken towards amendments, unless two-thirds of the congress, or two-thirds of the legislatures of the several states shall agree.—While power is in the hands of the people, or democratic part of the community, more especially as at present, it is easy, according to the general course of human affairs, for the few influential men in the community, to obtain conventions, alterations in government, and to persuade the common people they may change for the better, and to get from them a part of the power: But when power is once transferred from the many to the few, all changes become 2.8.58

extremely difficult; the government, in this case, being beneficial to the few, they will be exceedingly artful and adroit in preventing any measures which may lead to a change; and nothing will produce it, but great exertions and severe struggles on the part of the common people. Every man of reflection must see, that the change now proposed, is a transfer of power from the many to the few, and the probability is, the artful and ever active aristocracy, will prevent all peaceable measures for changes, unless when they shall discover some favourable moment to increase their own influence.[44] I am sensible, thousands of men in the United States, are disposed to adopt the proposed constitution, though they perceive it to be essentially defective, under an idea that amendments of it, may be obtained when necessary. This is a pernicious idea, it argues a servility of character totally unfit for the support of free government; it is very repugnant to that perpetual jealousy respecting liberty, so absolutely necessary in all free states, spoken of by Mr. Dickinson.[45]—However, if our countrymen are so soon changed, and the language of 1774, is become odious to them, it will be in vain to use the language of freedom, or to attempt to rouse them to free enquiries: But I shall never believe this is the case with them, whatever present appearances may be, till I shall have very strong evidence indeed of it.

Your's, &c.
The Federal Farmer.

V

October 13th, 1787

Dear Sir,

2.8.59   Thus I have examined the federal constitution as far as a few days leisure would permit. It opens to my mind a new scene; instead of seeing powers cautiously lodged in the hands of numerous legislators, and many magistrates, we see all important powers collecting in one centre, where a few men will possess them almost at discretion. And instead of checks in the formation of the government, to secure the rights of the people against the usurpations of those they appoint to govern, we are to understand the equal division of lands among our people, and the strong arm furnished them by nature and situation, are to secure them against those usurpations. If there are advantages in the equal division of our lands, and the strong and manly habits of our people, we ought to establish governments calculated to give duration to them, and not governments which never can work naturally, till that equality of property, and those free and manly habits shall be destroyed; these evidently are not the natural basis of the proposed constitution. No man of reflection, and skilled in the science of government, can suppose these will move on harmoniously together for ages, or even for fifty years.[46] As to the little circumstances commented upon, by some writers, with applause—as the age of a representative, of the president, etc.—they have, in my mind, no weight in the general tendency of the system.

There are, however, in my opinion, many good things in the proposed system. It is founded on elective principles, and the deposits of powers in different hands, is essentially right. The guards against those evils we have experienced in some states in legislation are valuable indeed; but the value of every feature in this system is vastly lessened for the want of that one important feature in a free government, a representation of the people.[47] Because we have sometimes abused democracy, I am not among those men who think a democratic branch a nuisance; which branch shall be sufficiently numerous, to admit some of the best informed men of each order in the community into the administration of government.

2.8.60

While the radical defects in the proposed system are not so soon discovered, some temptations to each state, and to many classes of men to adopt it, are very visible. It uses the democratic language of several of the state constitutions, particularly that of Massachusetts; the eastern states will receive advantages so far as the regulation of trade, by a bare majority, is committed to it: Connecticut and New-Jersey will receive their share of a general impost: The middle states will receive the advantages surrounding the seat of government: The southern states will receive protection, and have their negroes represented in the legislature, and large back countries will soon have a majority in it. This system promises a large field of employment to military gentlemen, and gentlemen of the law; and in case the government shall be executed without convulsions, it will afford security to creditors, to the clergy, salary-men and others depending on money payments. So far as the system promises justice and reasonable advantages, in these respects, it ought to be supported by all honest men: but whenever it promises unequal and improper advantages to any particular states, or orders of men, it ought to be opposed.

2.8.61

I have, in the course of these letters observed, that there are many good things in the proposed constitution, and I have endeavoured to point out many important defects in it. I have admitted that we want a federal system—that we have a system presented, which, with several alterations may be made a tolerable good one—I have admitted there is a well founded uneasiness among creditors and mercantile men. In this situation of things, you ask me what I think ought to be done? My opinion in this case is only the opinion of an individual, and so far only as it corresponds with the opinions of the honest and substantial part of the community, is it entitled to consideration. Though I am fully satisfied that the state conventions ought most seriously to direct their exertions to altering and amending the system proposed before they shall adopt it—yet I have not sufficiently examined the subject, or formed an opinion, how far it will be practicable for those con-

2.8.62

ventions to carry their amendments. As to the idea, that it will be in vain for those conventions to attempt amendments, it cannot be admitted; it is impossible to say whether they can or not until the attempt shall be made; and when it shall be determined, by experience, that the conventions cannot agree in amendments, it will then be an important question before the people of the United States, whether they will adopt or not the system proposed in its present form. This subject of consolidating the states is new; and because forty or fifty men have agreed in a system, to suppose the good sense of this country, an enlightened nation, must adopt it without examination, and though in a state of profound peace, without endeavouring to amend those parts they perceive are defective, dangerous to freedom, and destructive of the valuable principles of republican government—is truly humiliating. It is true there may be danger in delay; but there is danger in adopting the system in its present form; and I see the danger in either case will arise principally from the conduct and views of two very unprincipled parties in the United States—two fires, between which the honest and substantial people have long found themselves situated. One party is composed of little insurgents, men in debt, who want no law, and who want a share of the property of others; these are called levellers, Shayites, etc. The other party is composed of a few, but more dangerous men, with their servile dependents; these avariciously grasp at all power and property; you may discover in all the actions of these men, an evident dislike to free and equal government, and they will go systematically to work to change, essentially, the forms of government in this country; these are called aristocrats, M[onarch]ites [?], etc. etc. Between these two parties is the weight of the community; the men of middling property, men not in debt on the one hand, and men, on the other, content with republican governments, and not aiming at immense fortunes, offices, and power. In 1786, the little insurgents, the levellers, came forth, invaded the rights of others, and attempted to establish governments according to their wills. Their movements evidently gave encouragement to the other party, which, in 1787, has taken the political field, and with its fashionable dependants, and the tongue and the pen, is endeavouring to establish in great haste, a politer kind of government. These two parties, which will probably be opposed or united as it may suit their interests and views, are really insignificant, compared with the solid, free, and independent part of the community. It is not my intention to suggest, that either of these parties, and the real friends of the proposed constitution, are the same men. The fact is, these aristocrats support and hasten the adoption of the proposed constitution, merely because they think it is a stepping stone to their favorite object. I think I am well founded in this idea; I think the general politics of these men support it, as well as the common observation among them, That the proffered plan is the best that can be got at present, it will do for a few years, and lead to something better. The sensible and judicious part of the community will carefully weigh all these circumstances; they will view the late convention as a respectable assembly of men—America probably never will see an assembly of men of a like number, more respectable. But the members of the convention met without knowing the sentiments of one man in ten thousand in these states, respecting the new ground taken. Their doings are but the first attempts in the most important scene ever opened. Though each individual in the state conventions will not, probably, be so respectable as each individual in the federal convention, yet as the state conventions will probably consist of fifteen hundred or two thousand men of abilities, and versed in the science of government, collected from all parts of the community and from all orders of men, it must be acknowledged that the weight of respectability will be in them—In them will be collected the solid sense and the real political character of the country. Being revisers of the subject, they will possess peculiar advantages. To say that these conventions ought not to attempt, coolly and deliberately, the revision of the system, or that they cannot amend it, is very foolish or very assuming. If these conventions, after examining the system, adopt it, I shall be perfectly satisfied, and wish to see men make the administration of the government an equal blessing to all orders of men. I believe the great body of our people to be virtuous and friendly to good government, to the protection of liberty and property; and it is the duty of all good men, especially of those who are placed as centinels to guard their rights—it is their duty to examine into the prevailing politics of parties, and to disclose them—while they avoid exciting undue suspicions, to lay facts before the people, which will enable them to form a proper judgment. Men who wish the people of this country to determine for themselves, and deliberately to fit the government to their situation, must feel some degree of indignation at those attempts to hurry the adoption of a system, and to shut the door against examination. The very attempts create suspicions, that those who make them have secret views, or see some defects in the system, which, in the hurry of affairs, they expect will escape thee ye of a free people.

What can be the views of those gentlemen in Pennsylvania, who precipitated decisions on this subject?[48] What can be the views of those gentlemen in Boston, who countenanced the Printers in shutting up the press against a fair and free investigation of this important system in the usual way.[49] The members of the convention have done their duty—why should some of them fly to their states—almost forget a propriety of behaviour, and precipitate measures for the adoption of a system of their own making? I confess candidly, when I consider these circumstances in connection with the unguarded parts of the system I have mentioned, I feel disposed to proceed with very great caution, and to pay more attention than usual to the conduct of particular characters. If the constitution presented be a good one, it will stand the test with a well informed people: all are agreed there shall be state conventions to examine it; and we must believe it will be

2.8.63

adopted, unless we suppose it is a bad one, or that those conventions will make false divisions respecting it. I admit improper measures are taken against the adoption of the system as well [as] for it—all who object to the plan proposed ought to point out the defects objected to, and to propose those amendments with which they can accept it, or to propose some other system of government, that the public mind may be known, and that we may be brought to agree in some system of government, to strengthen and execute the present, or to provide a substitute. I consider the field of enquiry just opened, and that we are to look to the state conventions for ultimate decisions on the subject before us; it is not to be presumed, that they will differ about small amendments, and lose a system when they shall have made it substantially good; but touching the essential amendments, it is to be presumed the several conventions will pursue the most rational measures to agree in and obtain them; and such defects as they shall discover and not remove, they will probably notice, keep them in view as the ground work of future amendments, and in the firm and manly language which every free people ought to use, will suggest to those who may hereafter administer the government, that it is their expectation, that the system will be so organized by legislative acts, and the government so administered, as to render those defects as little injurious as possible. Our countrymen are entitled to an honest and faithful government; to a government of laws and not of men; and also to one of their chusing—as a citizen of the country, I wish to see these objects secured, and licentious, assuming, and overbearing men restrained; if the constitution or social compact be vague and unguarded, then we depend wholly upon the prudence, wisdom and moderation of those who manage the affairs of government; or on what, probably, is equally uncertain and precarious, the success of the people oppressed by the abuse of government, in receiving it from the hands of those who abuse it, and placing it in the hands of those who will use it well.

2.8.64   In every point of view, therefore, in which I have been able, as yet, to contemplate this subject, I can discern but one rational mode of proceeding relative to it: and that is to examine it with freedom and candour, to have state conventions some months hence, which shall examine cooly every article, clause, and word in the system proposed, and to adopt it with such amendments as they shall think fit. How far the state conventions ought to pursue the mode prescribed by the federal convention of adopting or rejecting the plan in toto, I leave it to them to determine. Our examination of the subject hitherto has been rather of a general nature. The republican characters in the several states, who wish to make this plan more adequate to security of liberty and property, and to the duration of the principles of a free government, will, no doubt, collect their opinions to certain points, and accurately define those alterations and amendments they wish; if it shall be found they essentially disagree in them, the conventions will then be able to

determine whether to adopt the plan as it is, or what will be proper to be
done. 2.8.65

Under these impressions, and keeping in view the improper and unadvis-
able lodgment of powers in the general government, organized as it at present is, touching internal taxes, armies and militia, the elections of its own
members, causes between citizens of different states, etc. and the want of a
more perfect bill of rights, etc. I drop the subject for the present, and when I
shall have leisure to revise and correct my ideas respecting it, and to collect
into points the opinions of those who wish to make the system more secure
and safe, perhaps I may proceed to point out particularly for your consideration, the amendments which ought to be ingrafted into this system, not
only in conformity to my own, but the deliberate opinions of others—you
will with me perceive, that the objections to the plan proposed may, by a
more leisure examination be set in a stronger point of view, especially the
important one, that there is no substantial representation of the people
provided for in a government in which the most essential powers, even as to
the internal police of the country, is proposed to be lodged. 2.8.66

I think the honest and substantial part of the community will wish to see
this system altered, permanency and consistency given to the constitution
we shall adopt; and therefore they will be anxious to apportion the powers
to the features and organization of the government, and to see abuse in the
exercise of power more effectually guarded against. It is suggested, that
state officers, from interested motives will oppose the constitution
presented—I see no reason for this, their places in general will not be
effected, but new openings to offices and places of profit must evidently be
made by the adoption of the constitution in its present form.

Your's &c.
The Federal Farmer.

[The Additional Letters]

VI

December 25, 1787.

Dear Sir,

My former letters to you, respecting the constitution proposed, were 2.8.67
calculated merely to lead to a fuller investigation of the subject; having more
extensively considered it, and the opinions of others relative to it, I shall, in
a few letters, more particularly endeavour to point out the defects, and

propose amendments. I shall in this make only a few general and introductory observations, which, in the present state of the momentous question, may not be improper; and I leave you, in all cases, to decide by a careful examination of my works, upon the weight of my arguments, the propriety of my remarks, the uprightness of my intentions, and the extent of my candor—I presume I am writing to a man of candor and reflection, and not to an ardent, peevish, or impatient man.

2.8.68 When the constitution was first published, there appeared to prevail a misguided zeal to prevent a fair unbiassed examination of a subject of infinite importance to this people and their posterity—to the cause of liberty and the rights of mankind—and it was the duty of those who saw a restless ardor, or design, attempting to mislead the people by a parade of names and misrepresentations, to endeavour to prevent their having their intended effects. The only way to stop the passions of men in their career is, coolly to state facts, and deliberately to avow the truth—and to do this we are frequently forced into a painful view of men and measures.

2.8.69 Since I wrote to you in October, I have heard much said, and seen many pieces written, upon the subject in question; and on carefully examining them on both sides, I find much less reason for changing my sentiments, respecting the good and defective parts of the system proposed than I expected—The opposers, as well as the advocates of it, confirm me in my opinion, that this system affords, all circumstances considered, a better basis to build upon than the confederation. And as to the principal defects, as the smallness of the representation, the insecurity of elections, the undue mixture of powers in the senate, the insecurity of some essential rights, &c. the opposition appears, generally, to agree respecting them, and many of the ablest advocates virtually to admit them—Clear it is, the latter do not attempt manfully to defend these defective parts, but to cover them with a mysterious veil; they concede, they retract; they say we could do no better; and some of them, when a little out of temper, and hard pushed, use arguments that do more honor to their ingenuity, than to their candor and firmness.

2.8.70 Three states have now adopted the constitution without amendments;[50] these, and other circumstances, ought to have their weight in deciding the question, whether we will put the system into operation, adopt it, enumerate and recommend the necessary amendments, which afterwards, by three-fourths of the states, may be ingrafted into the system, or whether we will make the amendments prior to the adoption—I only undertake to shew amendments are essential and necessary—how far it is practicable to ingraft them into the plan, prior to the adoption, the state conventions must determine. Our situation is critical, and we have but our choice of evils—We may hazard much by adopting the constitution in its present form—we may hazard more by rejecting it wholly—we may hazard much by long contending about amendments prior to the adoption. The greatest political evils that can befal us, are discords and civil wars—the greatest blessings we can wish for, are peace, union, and industry, under a mild, free, and steady government. Amendments recommended will tend to guard and direct the administration—but there will be danger that the people, after the system shall be adopted, will become inattentive to amendments—Their attention is now awake—the discussion of the subject, which has already taken place, has had a happy effect—it has called forth the able advocates of liberty, and tends to renew, in the minds of the people, their true republican jealousy and vigilance, the strongest guard against the abuses of power; but the vigilance of the people is not sufficiently constant to be depended on— Fortunate it is for the body of a people, if they can continue attentive to their liberties, long enough to erect for them a temple, and constitutional barriers for their permanent security: when they are well fixed between the powers of the rulers and the rights of the people, they become visible boundaries, constantly seen by all, and any transgression of them is immediately discovered: they serve as centinels for the people at all times, and especially in those unavoidable intervals of inattention.

Some of the advocates, I believe, will agree to recommend *good* amendments; but some of them will only consent to recommend indefinite, specious, but unimportant ones; and this only with a view to keep the door open for obtaining, in some favourable moment, their main object, a complete consolidation of the states, and a government much higher toned, less republican and free than the one proposed. If necessity, therefore, should ever oblige us to adopt the system, and recommend amendments, the true friends of a federal republic must see they are well defined, and well calculated, not only to prevent our system of government moving further from republican principles and equality, but to bring it back nearer to them—they must be constantly on their guard against the address, flattery, and manœuvres of their adversaries. 2.8.71

The gentlemen who oppose the constitution, or contend for amendments in it, are frequently, and with much bitterness, charged with wantonly attacking the men who framed it. The unjustness of this charge leads me to make one observation upon the conduct of parties, &c.[51] Some of the advocates are only pretended federalists; in fact they wish for an abolition of the state governments. Some of them I believe to be honest federalists, who wish to preserve *substantially* the state governments united under an efficient federal head; and many of them are blind tools without any object. Some of the opposers also are only pretended federalists, who want no federal government, or one merely advisory. Some of them are the true federalists, their object, perhaps, more clearly seen, is the same with that of the honest federalists; and some of them, probably, have no distinct object. We might as well call the advocates and opposers tories and whigs, or any thing else, as federalists and anti-federalists. To be for or against the constitution, as it stands, is not much evidence of a federal disposition; if any 2.8.72

names are applicable to the parties, on account of their general politics, they are those of republicans and anti-republicans. The opposers are generally men who support the rights of the body of the people, and are properly republicans. The advocates are generally men not very friendly to those rights, and properly anti republicans.

2.8.73   Had the advocates left the constitution, as they ought to have done, to be adopted or rejected on account of its own merits or imperfections, I do not believe the gentlemen who framed it would ever have been even alluded to in the contest by the opposers. Instead of this, the ardent advocates begun by quoting names as incontestible authorities for the implicit adoption of the system, without any examination—treated all who opposed it as friends of anarchy; and with an indecent virulence addressed M[aso]n G[err]y, L[e]e, and almost every man of weight they could find in the opposition by name.[52] If they had been candid men they would have applauded the moderation of the opposers for not retaliating in this pointed manner, when so fair an opportunity was given them; but the opposers generally saw that it was no time to heat the passions; but, at the same time, they saw there was something more than mere zeal in many of their adversaries; they saw them attempting to mislead the people, and to precipitate their divisions, by the sound of names, and forced to do it, the opposers, in general terms, alledged those names were not of sufficient authority to justify the hasty adoption of the system contended for. The convention, as a body, was undoubtedly respectable; it was, generally, composed of members of the then and preceding Congresses: as a body of respectable men we ought to view it. To select individual names, is an invitation to personal attacks, and the advocates, for their own sake, ought to have known the abilities, politics, and situation of some of their favourite characters better, before they held them up to view in the manner they did, as men entitled to our implicit political belief: they ought to have known, whether all the men they so held up to view could, for their past conduct in public offices, be approved or not by the public records, and the honest part of the community. These ardent advocates seem now to be peevish and angry, because, by their own folly, they have led to an investigation of facts and of political characters, unfavourable to them, which they had not the discernment to foresee. They may well apprehend they have opened a door to some Junius,[53] or to some man, after his manner, with his polite addresses to men by name, to state serious facts, and unfold the truth; but these advocates may rest assured, that cool men in the opposition, best acquainted with the affairs of the country, will not, in the critical passage of a people from one constitution to another, pursue inquiries, which, in other circumstances, will be deserving of the highest praise. I will say nothing further about political characters, but examine the constitution; and as a necessary and previous measure to a particular examination, I shall state a few general positions and principles, which receive a general assent, and briefly notice the leading features of the confederation, and several state conventions, to which, through the whole investigation, we must frequently have recourse, to aid the mind in its determinations.

We can put but little dependance on the partial and vague information transmitted to us respecting antient governments; our situation as a people is peculiar: our people in general have a high sense of freedom; they are high spirited, though capable of deliberate measures; they are intelligent, discerning, and well informed; and it is to their condition we must mould the constitution and laws. We have no royal or noble families, and all things concur in favour of a government entirely elective. We have tried our abilities as free men in a most arduous contest, and have succeeded; but we now find the main spring of our movements were the love of liberty, and a temporary ardor, and not any energetic principle in the federal system.[54]   2.8.74

Our territories are far too extensive for a limited monarchy, in which the representatives must frequently assemble, and the laws operate mildly and systematically. The most elligible system is a federal republic, that is, a system in which national concerns may be transacted in the centre, and local affairs in state or district governments.   2.8.75

The powers of the union ought to be extended to commerce, the coin, and national objects; and a division of powers, and a deposit of them in different hands, is safest.

Good government is generally the result of experience and gradual improvements, and a punctual execution of the laws is essential to the preservation of life, liberty, and property. Taxes are always necessary, and the power to raise them can never be safely lodged without checks and limitation, but in a full and substantial representation of the body of the people; the quantity of power delegated ought to be compensated by the brevity of the time of holding it, in order to prevent the possessors increasing it. The supreme power is in the people, and rulers possess only that portion which is expressly given them; yet the wisest people have often declared this is the case on proper occasions, and have carefully formed stipulation to fix the extent, and limit the exercise of the power given.   2.8.76

The people by Magna Charta, &c. did not acquire powers, or receive privileges from the king, they only ascertained and fixed those they were entitled to as Englishmen; the title used by the king "we grant," was mere form. Representation, and the jury trial, are the best features of a free government ever as yet discovered, and the only means by which the body of the people can have their proper influence in the affairs of government.   2.8.77

In a federal system we must not only balance the parts of the same government, as that of the state, or that of the union; but we must find a balancing influence between the general and local governments—the latter is what men or writers have but very little or imperfectly considered   2.8.78

A free and mild government is that in which no laws can be made without the formal and free consent of the people, or of their constitutional repre-   2.8.79

sentatives; that is, of a substantial representative branch. Liberty, in its genuine sense, is security to enjoy the effects of our honest industry and labours, in a free and mild government, and personal security from all illegal restraints.

2.8.80 Of rights, some are natural and unalienable, of which even the people cannot deprive individuals: Some are constitutional or fundamental; these cannot be altered or abolished by the ordinary laws; but the people, by express acts, may alter or abolish them—These, such as the trial by jury, the benefits of the writ of habeas corpus, &c. individuals claim under the solemn compacts of the people, as constitutions, or at least under laws so strengthened by long usuage as not to be repealable by the ordinary legislature—and some are common or mere legal rights, that is, such as individuals claim under laws which the ordinary legislature may alter or abolish at pleasure.[55]

2.8.81 The confederation is a league of friendship among the states or sovereignties for the common defence and mutual welfare—Each state expressly retains its sovereignty, and all powers not expressly given to congress—All federal powers are lodged in a congress of delegates annually elected by the state legislatures, except in Connecticut and Rhode-Island, where they are chosen by the people—Each state has a vote in congress, pays its delegates, and may instruct or recall them; no delegate can hold any office of profit, or serve more than three years in any six years—Each state may be represented by not less than two, or more than seven delegates.

2.8.82 Congress (nine states agreeing) may make peace and war, treaties and alliances, grant letters of marque and reprisal, coin money, regulate the alloy and value of the coin, require men and monies of the states by fixed proportions, and appropriate monies, form armies and navies, emit bills of credit, and borrow monies.

2.8.83 Congress (seven states agreeing) may send and receive ambassadors, regulate captures, make rules for governing the army and navy, institute courts for the trial of piracies and felonies committed on the high seas, and for settling territorial disputes between the individual states, regulate weight and measures, post-offices, and Indian affairs.

2.8.84 No state, without the consent of congress, can send or receive embassies, make any agreement with any other state, or a foreign state, keep up any vessels of war or bodies of forces in time of peace, or engage in war, or lay any duties which may interfere with the treaties of congress—Each state must appoint regimental officers, and keep up a well regulated militia—Each state may prohibit the importation or exportation of any species of goods.

2.8.85 The free inhabitants of one state are intitled to the privileges and immunities of the free citizens of the other states—Credit in each state shall be given to the records and judicial proceedings in the others.

Canada, acceding, may be admitted, and any other colony may be admitted by the consent of nine states.

Alterations may be made by the agreement of congress, and confirmation of all the state legislatures.

The following, I think, will be allowed to be unalienable or fundamental rights in the United States:— 2.8.86

No man, demeaning himself peaceably, shall be molested on account of his religion or mode of worship—The people have a right to hold and enjoy their property according to known standing laws, and which cannot be taken from them without their consent, or the consent of their representatives; and whenever taken in the pressing urgencies of government, they are to receive a reasonable compensation for it—Individual security consists in having free recourse to the laws—The people are subject to no laws or taxes not assented to by their representatives constitutionally assembled—They are at all times intitled to the benefits of the writ of habeas corpus, the trial by jury in criminal and civil causes—They have a right, when charged, to a speedy trial in the vicinage; to be heard by themselves or counsel, not to be compelled to furnish evidence against themselves, to have witnesses face to face, and to confront their adversaries before the judge—No man is held to answer a crime charged upon him till it be substantially described to him; and he is subject to no unreasonable searches or seizures of his person, papers or effects—The people have a right to assemble in an orderly manner, and petition the government for a redress of wrongs—The freedom of the press ought not to be restrained—No emoluments, except for actual service—No hereditary honors, or orders of nobility, ought to be allowed—The military ought to be subordinate to the civil authority, and no soldier be quartered on the citizens without their consent—The militia ought always to be armed and disciplined, and the usual defence of the country—The supreme power is in the people, and power delegated ought to return to them at stated periods, and frequently—The legislative, executive, and judicial powers, ought always to be kept distinct—others perhaps might be added.

The organization of the state governments—Each state has a legislature, an executive, and a judicial branch—In general legislators are excluded from the important executive and judicial offices—Except in the Carolinas there is no constitutional distinction among Christian sects—The constitutions of New York, Delaware, and Virginia, exclude the clergy from offices civil and military—the other states do nearly the same in practice. 2.8.87

Each state has a democratic branch elected twice a-year in Rhode-Island and Connecticut, biennially in South Carolina, and annually in the other states—There are about 1500 representatives in all the states, or one to each 1700 inhabitants, reckoning five blacks for three whites—The states do not differ as to the age or moral characters of the electors or elected, nor materially as to their property. 2.8.88

Pennsylvania has lodged all her legislative powers in a single branch, and Georgia has done the same; the other eleven states have each in their legis- 2.8.89

latures a second or senatorial branch. In forming this they have combined various principles, and aimed at several checks and balances. It is amazing to see how ingenuity has worked in the several states to fix a barrier against popular instability. In Massachusetts the senators are apportioned on districts according to the taxes they pay, nearly according to property. In Connecticut the freemen, in September, vote for twenty counsellers, and return the names of those voted for in the several towns; the legislature takes the twenty who have the most votes, and give them to the people, who, in April, chuse twelve of them, who, with the governor and deputy governor, form the senatorial branch. In Maryland the senators are chosen by two electors from each county; these electors are chosen by the freemen, and qualified as the members in the democratic branch are: In these two cases checks are aimed at in the mode of election. Several states have taken into view the periods of service, age, property, &c. In South-Carolina a senator is elected for two years, in Delaware three, and in New-York and Virginia four, in Maryland five, and in the other states for one. In New-York and Virginia one-fourth part go out yearly. In Virginia a senator must be twenty-five years old, in South Carolina thirty. In New-York the electors must each have a freehold worth 250 dollars, in North-Carolina a freehold of fifty acres of land; in the other states the electors of senators are qualified as electors of representatives are. In Massachusetts a senator must have a freehold in his own right worth 1000 dollars, or any estate worth 2000, in New-Jersey any estate worth 2666, in South Carolina worth 1300 dollars, in North-Carolina 300 acres of land in fee, &c. The numbers of senators in each state are from ten to thirty-one, about 160 in the eleven states, about one of 14000 inhabitants.

2.8.90   Two states, Massachusetts and New-York, have each introduced into their legislatures a third, but incomplete branch. In the former, the governor may negative any law not supported by two-thirds of the senators, and two-thirds of the representatives: in the latter, the governor, chancellor, and judges of the supreme court may do the same.

2.8.91   Each state has a single executive branch. In the five eastern states the people at large elect their governors; in the other states the legislatures elect them. In South Carolina the governor is elected once in two years; in New-York and Delaware once in three, and in the other states annually. The governor of New-York has no executive council, the other governors have. In several states the governor has a vote in the senatorial branch—the governors have similar powers in some instances, and quite dissimilar ones in others. The number of executive counsellers in the states are from five to twelve. In the four eastern states, New-Jersey, Pennsylvania, and Georgia, they are of the men returned legislators by the people. In Pennsylvania the counsellers are chosen triennially, in Delaware every fourth year, in Virginia every three years, in South-Carolina biennially, and in the other states yearly.

Each state has a judicial branch; each common law courts, superior and inferior; some chancery and admiralty courts: The courts in general sit in different places, in order to accommodate the citizens. The trial by jury is had in all the common law courts, and in some of the admiralty courts. The democratic freemen principally form the juries; men destitute of property, of character, or under age, are excluded as in elections. Some of the judges are during good behaviour, and some appointed for a year, and some for years; and all are dependant on the legislatures for their salaries—Particulars respecting this department are too many to be noticed here.

The Federal Farmer.

VII

December 31, 1787.

Dear Sir,

In viewing the various governments instituted by mankind, we see their whole force reducible to two principles—the important springs which alone move the machines, and give them their intended influence and controul, are force and persuasion: by the former men are compelled, by the latter they are drawn. We denominate a government despotic or free, as the one or other principle prevails in it. Perhaps it is not possible for a government to be so despotic, as not to operate persuasively on some of its subjects; nor is it, in the nature of things, I conceive, for a government to be so free, or so supported by voluntary consent, as never to want force to compel obedience to the laws. In despotic governments one man, or a few men, independant of the people, generally make the laws, command obedience, and inforce it by the sword: one-fourth part of the people are armed, and obliged to endure the fatigues of soldiers, to oppress the others and keep them subject to the laws. In free governments the people, or their representatives, make the laws; their execution is principally the effect of voluntary consent and aid; the people respect the magistrate, follow their private pursuits, and enjoy the fruits of their labour with very small deductions for the public use.[56] The body of the people must evidently prefer the latter species of government; and it can be only those few who may be well paid for the part they take in enforcing despotism, that can, for a moment, prefer the former. Our true object is to give full efficacy to one principle, to arm persuasion on every side, and to render force as little necessary as possible. Persuasion is never dangerous not even in despotic governments; but military force, if often applied internally, can never fail to destroy the love and confidence, and break the spirits, of the people: and to render it totally impracticable

2.9.92

2.8.93

and unnatural for him or them who govern, and yield to this force against the people, to hold their places by the peoples' elections.

I repeat my observation, that the plan proposed will have a doubtful operation between the two principles; and whether it will preponderate towards persuasion or force is uncertain.

2.8.94 Government must exist—If the persuasive principle be feeble, force is infallibly the next resort. The moment the laws of congress shall be disregarded they must languish, and the whole system be convulsed—that moment we must have recourse to this next resort, and all freedom vanish.

2.8.95 It being impracticable for the people to assemble to make laws, they must elect legislators, and assign men to the different departments of the government.[57] In the representative branch we must expect chiefly to collect the confidence of the people, and in it to find almost entirely the force of persuasion. In forming this branch, therefore, several important considerations must be attended to. It must possess abilities to discern the situation of the people and of public affairs, a disposition to sympathize with the people, and a capacity and inclination to make laws congenial to their circumstances and condition: it must afford security against interested combinations, corruption and influence; it must possess the confidence, and have the voluntary support of the people.

2.8.96 I think these positions will not be controverted, nor the one I formerly advanced, that a fair and equal representation is that in which the interests, feelings, opinions and views of the people are collected, in such manner as they would be were the people all assembled. Having made these general observations, I shall proceed to consider further my principal position, viz. that there is no substantial representation of the people provided for in a government, in which the most essential powers, even as to the internal police of the country, are proposed to be lodged; and to propose certain amendments as to the representative branch: 1st, That there ought to be *an increase of the numbers of representatives:* And, 2dly, That the elections of them ought to be better secured.

2.8.97 1.[58] The representation is unsubstantial and ought to be increased. In matters where there is much room for opinion, you will not expect me to establish my positions with mathematical certainty; you must only expect my observations to be candid, and such as are well founded in the mind of the writer. I am in a field where doctors disagree; and as to genuine representation, though no feature in government can be more important, perhaps, no one has been less understood, and no one that has received so imperfect a consideration by political writers. The ephori in Sparta, and the tribunes in Rome, were but the shadow; the representation in Great-Britain is unequal and insecure. In America we have done more in establishing this important branch on its true principles, than, perhaps, all the world besides: yet even here, I conceive, that very great improvements in representation may be made. In fixing this branch, the situation of the people must be surveyed, and the number of representatives and forms of election apportioned to that situation. When we find a numerous people settled in a fertile and extensive country, possessing equality, and few or none of them oppressed with riches or wants, it ought to be the anxious care of the constitution and laws, to arrest them from national depravity, and to preserve them in their happy condition.[59] A virtuous people make just laws, and good laws tend to preserve unchanged a virtuous people. A virtuous and happy people by laws uncongenial to their characters, may easily be gradually changed into servile and depraved creatures. Where the people, or their representatives, make the laws, it is probable they will generally be fitted to the national character and circumstances, unless the representation be partial, and the imperfect substitute of the people. However, the people may be electors, if the representation be so formed as to give one or more of the natural classes of men in the society an undue ascendency over the others, it is imperfect; the former will gradually become masters, and the latter slaves. It is the first of all among the political balances, to preserve in its proper station each of these classes. We talk of balances in the legislature, and among the departments of government; we ought to carry them to the body of the people. Since I advanced the idea of balancing the several orders of men in a community, in forming a genuine representation, and seen that idea considered as chemerical,[60] I have been sensibly struck with a sentence in the marquis Beccaria's treatise: this sentence was quoted by congress in 1774, and is as follows:—"In every society there is an effort continually tending to confer on one part the height of power and happiness, and to reduce the others to the extreme of weakness and misery; the intent of good laws is to oppose this effort, and to diffuse their influence universally and equally."[61] Add to this Montesquieu's opinion, that "in a free state every man, who is supposed to be a free agent, ought to be concerned in his own government: therefore, the legislative should reside in the whole body of the people, or their representatives."[62] It is extremely clear that these writers had in view the several orders of men in society, which we call aristocratical, democratical, merchantile, mechanic, &c. and perceived the efforts they are constantly, from interested and ambitious views, disposed to make [efforts?] to elevate themselves and oppress others. Each order must have a share in the business of legislation actually and efficiently. It is deceiving a people to tell them they are electors, and can chuse their legislators, if they cannot, in the nature of things, chuse men from among themselves, and genuinely like themselves. I wish you to take another idea along with you; we are not only to balance these natural efforts, but we are also to guard against accidental combinations; combinations founded in the connections of offices and private interests, both evils which are increased in proportion as the number of men, among which the elected must be, are decreased. To set this matter in a proper point of view, we must form some general ideas and descriptions of the different classes of men, as they may be divided by occupations and politically: the first class is the aristocratical. There are three kinds of aristocracy spoken of in this country—the first is a constitutional one, which does not exist in the United States in our common acceptation of the word. Montesquieu, it is true, observes, that where a part of the persons in a society, for want of property, age, or moral character, are excluded any share in the government, the others, who alone are the constitutional electors and elected, form this aristocracy;[63] this, according to him, exists in each of the United States, where a considerable number of persons, as all convicted of crimes, under age, or not possessed of certain property, are excluded any share in the government;—the second is an aristocratic faction; a junto of unprincipled men, often distinguished for their wealth or abilities, who combine together and make their object their private interests and aggrandizement; the existence of this description is merely accidental, but particularly to be guarded against. The third is the natural aristocracy; this term we use to designate a respectable order of men, the line between whom and the natural democracy is in some degree arbitrary; we may place men on one side of this line, which others may place on the other, and in all disputes between the few and the many, a considerable number are wavering and uncertain themselves on which side they are, or ought to be. In my idea of our natural aristocracy in the United States, I include about four or five thousand men; and among these I reckon those who have been placed in the offices of governors, of members of Congress, and state senators generally, in the principal officers of Congress, of the army and militia, the superior judges, the most eminent professional men, &c. and men of large property[64]—the other persons and orders in the community form the natural democracy; this includes in general the yeomanry, the subordinate officers, civil and military, the fishermen, mechanics and traders, many of the merchants and professional men. It is easy to perceive that men of these two classes, the aristocratical, and democratical, with views equally honest, have sentiments widely different, especially respecting public and private expences, salaries, taxes, &c. Men of the first class associate more extensively, have a high sense of honor, possess abilities, ambition, and general knowledge; men of the second class are not so much used to combining great objects; they possess less ambition, and a larger share of honesty: their dependence is principally on middling and small estates, industrious pursuits, and hard labour, while that of the former is principally on the emoluments of large estates, and of the chief offices of government. Not only the efforts of these two great parties are to be balanced, but other interests and parties also, which do not always oppress each other merely for want of power, and for fear of the consequences; though they, in fact, mutually depend on each other; yet such are their general views, that the merchants alone would never fail to make laws favourable to themselves and oppressive to the farmers, &c. the farmers alone would act on like principles; the former would tax the land, the latter the trade. The manufacturers are often disposed to contend for monopolies, buyers make every exertion to lower prices, and sellers to raise them; men who live by fees and salaries endeavour to raise them, and the part of the people who pay them, endeavour to lower them; the public creditors to augment the taxes, and the people at large to lessen them. Thus, in every period of society, and in all the transactions of men, we see parties verifying the observation made by the Marquis; and those classes which have not their centinels in the government, in proportion to what they have to gain or lose, most infallibly be ruined.

Efforts among parties are not merely confined to property; they contend for rank and distinctions; all their passions in turn are enlisted in political controversies—Men, elevated in society, are often disgusted with the changeableness of the democracy, and the latter are often agitated with the passions of jealousy and envy: the yeomanry possess a large share of property and strength, are nervous and firm in their opinions and habits—the mechanics of towns are ardent and changeable, honest and credulous, they are inconsiderable for numbers, weight and strength, not always sufficiently stable for the supporting free governments: the fishing interest partakes partly of the strength and stability of the landed, and partly of the changeableness of the mechanic interest. As to merchants and traders, they are our agents in almost all money transactions; give activity to government, and possess a considerable share of influence in it. It has been observed by an able writer, that frugal industrious merchants are generally advocates for liberty. It is an observation, I believe, well founded, that the schools produce but few advocates for republican forms of government; [65] gentlemen of the law, divinity, physic, &c. probably form about a fourth part of the people; yet their political influence, perhaps, is equal to that of all the other descriptions of men; if we may judge from the appointments to Congress, the legal characters will often, in a small representation, be the majority; but the more the representatives are encreased, the more of the farmers, merchants, &c. will be found to be brought into the government.

These general observations will enable you to discern what I intend by different classes, and the general scope of my ideas, when I contend for uniting and balancing their interests, feelings, opinions, and views in the legislature; we may not only so unite and balance these as to prevent a change in the government by the gradual exaltation of one part to the depression of others, but we may derive many other advantages from the combination and full representation; a small representation can never be well informed as to the circumstances of the people, the members of it must be too far removed from the people, in general, to sympathize with them, and too few to communicate with them: a representation must be extremely imperfect where the representatives are not circumstanced to make the proper communications to their constituents, and where the constituents in turn cannot, with tolerable convenience, make known their wants, circum-

2.8.98

2.8.99

stances, and opinions, to their representatives; where there is but one representative to 30,000 or 40,000 inhabitants, it appears to me, he can only mix,
and be acquainted with a few respectable characters among his constituents,
even double the federal representation, and then there must be a very great
distance between the representatives and the people in general represented.
On the proposed plan, the state of Delaware, the city of Philadelphia, the
state of Rhode Island, the province of Main, the county of Suffolk in Massachusetts will have one representative each; there can be but little personal
knowledge, or but few communications, between him and the people at
large of either of those districts. It has been observed, that mixing only with
the respectable men, he will get the best information and ideas from them;
he will also receive impressions favourable to their purposes particularly.
Many plausible shifts have been made to divert the mind from dwelling on
this defective representation, these I shall consider in another place.[66]

2.8.100   Could we get over all our difficulties respecting a balance of interests and
party efforts, to raise some and oppress others, the want of sympathy,
information and intercourse between the representatives and the people, an
insuperable difficulty will still remain, I mean the constant liability of a small
number of representatives to private combinations; the tyranny of the one,
or the licentiousness of the multitude, are, in my mind, but small evils,
compared with the factions of the few. It is a consideration well worth
pursuing, how far this house of representatives will be liable to be formed
into private juntos, how far influenced by expectations of appointments and
offices, how far liable to be managed by the president and senate, and how
far the people will have confidence in them. To obviate difficulties on this
head, as well as objections to the representative branch, generally, several
observations have been made—these I will now examine, and if they shall
appear to be unfounded, the objections must stand unanswered.

2.8.101   That the people are the electors, must elect good men, and attend to the
administration.

It is said that the members of Congress, at stated periods, must return
home, and that they must be subject to the laws they may make, and to a
share of the burdens they may impose.

That the people possess the strong arm to overawe their rulers, and the
best checks in their national character against the abuses of power, that the
supreme power will remain in them.

That the state governments will form a part of, and a balance in the
system.

That Congress will have only a few national objects to attend to, and the
state governments many and local ones.

That the new Congress will be more numerous than the present, and that
any numerous body is unwieldy and mobbish.

That the states only are represented in the present Congress, and that the people will require a representation in the new one that in fifty or an hundred years the representation will be numerous.

That congress will have no temptation to do wrong; and that no system to enslave the people is practicable

That as long as the people are free they will preserve free governments; and that when they shall become tired of freedom, arbitrary government must take place.

These observations I shall examine in the course of my letters; and, I think, not only shew that they are not well founded, but point out the fallacy of some of them; and shew that others do not very well comport with the dignified and manly sentiments of a free and enlightened people.

The Federal Farmer.

XVI

January 20, 1788.

Dear Sir,

Having gone through with the organization of the government, I shall now proceed to examine more particularly those clauses which respect its powers. I shall begin with those articles and stipulations which are necessary for accurately ascertaining the extent of powers, and what is given, and for guarding, limiting, and restraining them in their exercise.[115] We often find, these articles and stipulations placed in bills of rights; but they may as well be incorporated in the body of the constitution, as selected and placed by themselves. The constitution, or whole social compact, is but one instrument, no more or less, than a certain number of articles or stipulations agreed to by the people, whether it consists of articles, sections, chapters, bills of rights, or parts of any other denomination, cannot be material. Many needless observations, and idle distinctions, in my opinion, have been made respecting a bill of rights. On the one hand, it seems to be considered as a necessary distinct limb of the constitution, and as containing a certain number of very valuable articles, which are applicable to all societies: and, on the other, as useless, especially in a federal government, possessing only enumerated power—nay, dangerous, as individual rights are numerous, and not easy to be enumerated in a bill of rights, and from articles, or stipulations, securing some of them, it may be inferred, that others not mentioned are surrendered.[116] There appears to me to be general indefinite propositions without much meaning—and the man who first advanced those of the

2.8.196

latter description, in the present case, signed the federal constitution, which directly contradicts him.[117] The supreme power is undoubtedly in the people, and it is a principle well established in my mind, that they reserve all powers not expressly delegated by them to those who govern; this is as true in forming a state as in forming a federal government. There is no possible distinction but this founded merely in the different modes of proceeding which take place in some cases. In forming a state constitution, under which to manage not only the great but the little concerns of a community: the powers to be possessed by the government are often too numerous to be enumerated; the people to adopt the shortest way often give general powers, indeed all powers, to the government, in some general words, and then, by a particular enumeration, take back, or rather say they however reserve certain rights as sacred, and which no laws shall be made to violate: hence the idea that all powers are given which are not reserved: but in forming a federal constitution, which *ex vi termine*, supposes state governments existing, and which is only to manage a few great national concerns, we often find it easier to enumerate particularly the powers to be delegated to the federal head, than to enumerate particularly the individual rights to be reserved; and the principle will operate in its full force, when we carefully adhere to it. When we particularly enumerate the powers given, we ought either carefully to enumerate the rights reserved, or be totally silent about them; we must either particularly enumerate both, or else suppose the particular enumeration of the powers given adequately draws the line between them and the rights reserved, particularly to enumerate the former and not the latter, I think most advisable: however, as men appear generally to have their doubts about these silent reservations, we might advantageously enumerate the powers given, and then in general words, according to the mode adopted in the 2d art. of the confederation, declare all powers, rights and privileges, are reserved, which are not explicitly and expressly given up. People, and very wisely too, like to be express and explicit about their essential rights, and not to be forced to claim them on the precarious and unascertained tenure of inferences and general principles, knowing that in any controversy between them and their rulers, concerning those rights, disputes may be endless, and nothing certain:—But admitting, on the general principle, that all rights are reserved of course, which are not expressly surrendered, the people could with sufficient certainty assert their rights on all occasions, and establish them with ease, still there are infinite advantages in particularly enumerating many of the most essential rights reserved in all cases; and as to the less important ones, we may declare in general terms, that all not expressly surrendered are reserved. We do not by declarations change the nature of things, or create new truths, but we give existence, or at least establish in the minds of the people truths and principles which they might never otherwise have thought of, or soon forgot. If a nation means its systems, religious or political, shall have duration, it ought to recognize the leading principles of them in the front page of every family book. What is the usefulness of a truth in theory, unless it exists constantly in the minds of the people, and has their assent:—we discern certain rights, as the freedom of the press, and the trial by jury, &c. which the people of England and of America of course believe to be sacred, and essential to their political happiness, and this belief in them is the result of ideas at first suggested to them by a few able men, and of subsequent experience; while the people of some other countries hear these rights mentioned with the utmost indifference; they think the privilege of existing at the will of a despot much preferable to them. Why this difference amongst beings every way formed alike. The reason of the difference is obvious—it is the effect of education, a series of notions impressed upon the minds of the people by examples, precepts and declarations. When the people of England got together, at the time they formed Magna Charta, they did not consider it sufficient, that they were indisputably entitled to certain natural and unalienable rights, not depending on silent titles, they, by a declaratory act, expressly recognized them, and explicitly declared to all the world, that they were entitled to enjoy those rights; they made an instrument in writing, and enumerated those they then thought essential, or in danger, and this wise men saw was not sufficient; and therefore, that the people might not forget these rights, and gradually become prepared for arbitrary government, their discerning and honest leaders caused this instrument to be confirmed near forty times, and to be read twice a year in public places, not that it would lose its validity without such confirmations, but to fix the contents of it in the minds of the people, as they successively come upon the stage.—Men, in some countries do not remain free, merely because they are entitled to natural and unalienable rights; men in all countries are entitled to them, not because their ancestors once got together and enumerated them on paper, but because, by repeated negociations and declarations, all parties are brought to realize them, and of course to believe them to be sacred. Were it necessary, I might shew the wisdom of our past conduct, as a people in not merely comforting ourselves that we were entitled to freedom, but in constantly keeping in view, in addresses, bills of rights, in news-papers, &c. the particular principles on which our freedom must always depend.[118]

It is not merely in this point of view, that I urge the engrafting in the constitution additional declaratory articles. The distinction, in itself just, that all powers not given are reserved, is in effect destroyed by this very constitution, as I shall particularly demonstrate—and even independent of this, the people, by adopting the constitution, give many general undefined powers to congress, in the constitutional exercise of which, the rights in question may be effected. Gentlemen who oppose a federal bill of rights, or further declaratory articles, seem to view the subject in a very narrow imperfect manner. These have for their objects, not only the enumeration of the rights reserved, but principally to explain the general powers delegated in certain material points, and to restrain those who exercise them by fixed known boundaries. Many explanations and restrictions necessary and use-

2.8.197

ful, would be much less so, were the people at large all well and fully acquainted with the principles and affairs of government. There appears to be in the constitution, a studied brevity, and it may also be probable, that several explanatory articles were omitted from a circumstance very common. What we have long and early understood ourselves in the common concerns of the community, we are apt to suppose is understood by others, and need not be expressed; and it is not unnatural or uncommon for the ablest men most frequently to make this mistake. To make declaratory articles unnecessary in an instrument of government, two circumstances must exist; the rights reserved must be indisputably so, and in their nature defined; the powers delegated to the government, must be precisely defined by the words that convey them, and clearly be of such extent and nature as that, by no reasonable construction, they can be made to invade the rights and prerogatives intended to be left in the people.

2.8.198   The first point urged, is, that all power is reserved not expressly given, that particular enumerated powers only are given, that all others are not given, but reserved, and that it is needless to attempt to restrian congress in the exercise of powers they possess not. This reasoning is logical, but of very little importance in the common affairs of men; but the constitution does not appear to respect it even in any view. To prove this, I might cite several clauses in it. I shall only remark on two or three. By article 1, section 9, "No title of nobility shall be granted by congress" Was this clause omitted, what power would congress have to make titles of nobility? in what part of the constitution would they find it? The answer must be, that congress would have no such power—that the people, by adopting the constitution, will not part with it. Why then by a negative clause, restrain congress from doing what it would have no power to do? This clause, then, must have no meaning, or imply, that were it omitted, congress would have the power in question, either upon the principle that some general words in the constitution may be so construed as to give it, or on the principle that congress possess the powers not expressly reserved. But this clause was in the confederation, and is said to be introduced into the constitution from very great caution. Even a cautionary provision implies a doubt, at least, that it is necessary; and if so in this case, clearly it is also alike necessary in all similar ones. The fact appears to be, that the people in forming the confederation, and the convention, in this instance, acted, naturally, they did not leave the point to be settled by general principles and logical inferences; but they settle the point in a few words, and all who read them at once understand them.

2.8.199   The trial by jury in criminal as well as in civil causes, has long been considered as one of our fundamental rights, and has been repeatedly recognized and confirmed by most of the state conventions.[119] But the constitution expressly establishes this trial in criminal, and wholly omits it in civil causes. The jury trial in criminal causes, and the benefit of the writ of habeas corpus, are already as effectually established as any of the fundamental or essential rights of the people in the United States. This being the case, why in adopting a federal constitution do we now establish these, and omit all others, or all others, at least with a few exceptions, such as again agreeing there shall be no ex post facto laws, no titles of nobility, &c. We must consider this constitution, when adopted, as the supreme act of the people, and in construing it hereafter, we and our posterity must strictly adhere to the letter and spirit of it, and in no instance depart from them: in construing the federal constitution, it will be not only impracticable, but improper to refer to the state constitutions. They are entirely distinct instruments and inferior acts: besides, by the people's now establishing certain fundamental rights, it is strongly implied, that they are of opinion, that they would not otherwise be secured as a part of the federal system, or be regarded in the federal administration as fundamental. Further, these same rights, being established by the state constitutions, and secured to the people, our recognizing them now, implies, that the people thought them insecure by the state establishments, and extinguished or put afloat by the new arrangement of the social system, unless re-established.—Further, the people, thus establishing some few rights, and remaining totally silent about others similarly circumstanced, the implication indubitably is, that they mean to relinquish the latter, or at least feel indifferent about them. Rights, therefore, inferred from general principles of reason, being precarious and hardly ascertainable in the common affairs of society, and the people, in forming a federal constitution, explicitly shewing they conceive these rights to be thus circumstanced, and accordingly proceed to enumerate and establish some of them, the conclusion will be, that they have established all which they esteem valuable and sacred. On every principle, then, the people especially having began, ought to go through enumerating, and establish particularly all the rights of individuals, which can by any possibility come in question in making and executing federal laws. I have already observed upon the excellency and importance of the jury trial in civil as well as in criminal causes, instead of establishing it in criminal causes only; we ought to establish it generally;—instead of the clause of forty or fifty words relative to this subject, why not use the language that has always been used in this country, and say, "the people of the United States shall always be entitled to the trial by jury." This would shew the people still hold the right sacred, and enjoin it upon congress substantially to preserve the jury trial in all cases, according to the usage and custom of the country. I have observed before, that it is *the jury trial* we want; the little different appendages and modifications tacked to it in the different states, are no more than a drop in the ocean: the jury trial is a solid uniform feature in a free government; it is the substance we would save, not the little articles of form.

Security against expost facto laws, the trial by jury, and the benefits of the writ of habeas corpus, are but a part of those inestimable rights the people of

2.8.200

the United States are entitled to, even in judicial proceedings, by the course of the common law. These may be secured in general words, as in New-York, the Western Territory, &c. by declaring the people of the United States shall always be entitled to judicial proceedings according to the course of the common law, as used and established in the said states. Perhaps it would be better to enumerate the particular essential rights the people are entitled to in these proceedings, as has been done in many of the states, and as has been done in England. In this case, the people may proceed to declare that no man shall be held to answer to any offence, till the same be fully described to him; nor to furnish evidence against himself: that, except in the government of the army and navy, no person shall be tried for any offence, whereby he may incur loss of life, or an infamous punishment, until he be first indicted by a grand jury: that every person shall have a right to produce all proofs that may be favourable to him, and to meet the witnesses against him face to face: that every person shall be entitled to obtain right and justice freely and without delay; that all persons shall have a right to be secure from all unreasonable searches and seizures of their persons, houses, papers, or possessions; and that all warrants shall be deemed contrary to this right, if the foundation of them be not previously supported by oath, and there be not in them a special designation of persons or objects of search, arrest, or seizure: and that no person shall be exiled or molested in his person or effects, otherwise than by the judgment of his peers, or according to the law of the land. A celebrated writer observes upon this last article, that in itself it may be said to comprehend the whole end of political society.[120] These rights are not necessarily reserved, they are established, or enjoyed but in few countries: they are stipulated rights, almost peculiar to British and American laws. In the execution of those laws, individuals, by long custom, by magna charta, bills of rights &c. have become entitled to them. A man, at first, by act of parliament, became entitled to the benefits of the writ of habeas corpus—men are entitled to these rights and benefits in the judicial proceedings of our state courts generally: but it will by no means follow, that they will be entitled to them in the federal courts, and have a right to assert them, unless secured and established by the constitution or federal laws. We certainly, in federal processes, might as well claim the benefits of the writ of habeas corpus, as to claim trial by a jury—the right to have council—to have witnesses face to face—to be secure against unreasonable search warrants, &c. was the constitution silent as to the whole of them:—but the establishment of the former, will evince that we could not claim them without it; and the omission of the latter, implies they are relinquished, or deemed of no importance. These are rights and benefits individuals acquire by compact; they must claim them under compacts, or immemorial usage—it is doubtful, at least, whether they can be claimed under immemorial usage in this country; and it is, therefore, we generally claim them under compacts, as charters and constitutions.

The people by adopting the federal constitution, give congress general powers to institute a distinct and new judiciary, new courts, and to regulate all proceedings in them, under the eight limitations mentioned in a former letter; and the further one, that the benefits of the habeas corpus act shall be enjoyed by individuals. Thus general powers being given to institute courts, and regulate their proceedings, with no provision for securing the rights principally in question, may not congress so exercise those powers, and constitutionally too, as to destroy those rights? clearly, in my opinion, they are not in any degree secured. But, admitting the case is only doubtful, would it not be prudent and wise to secure them and remove all doubts, since all agree the people ought to enjoy these valuable rights, a very few men excepted, who seem to be rather of opinion that there is little or nothing in them? Were it necessary I might add many observations to shew their value and political importance.

2.8.201

The constitution will give congress general powers to raise and support armies. General powers carry with them incidental ones, and the means necessary to the end. In the exercise of these powers, is there any provision in the constitution to prevent the quartering of soldiers on the inhabitants? you will answer, there is not. This may sometimes be deemed a necessary measure in the support of armies; on what principle can the people claim the right to be exempt from this burden? they will urge, perhaps, the practice of the country, and the provisions made in some of the state constitutions— they will be answered, that their claim thus to be exempt is not founded in nature, but only in custom and opinion, or at best, in stipulations in some of the state constitutions, which are local, and inferior in their operation, and can have no controul over the general government—that they had adopted a federal constitution—had noticed several rights, but had been totally silent about this exemption—that they had given general powers relative to the subject, which, in their operation, regularly destroyed the claim. Though it is not to be presumed, that we are in any immediate danger from this quarter, yet it is fit and proper to establish, beyond dispute, those rights which are particularly valuable to individuals, and essential to the permanency and duration of free government. An excellent writer observes, that the English, always in possession of their freedom, are frequently unmindful of the value of it:[121] we, at this period, do not seem to be so well off, having, in some instances abused ours; many of us are quite disposed to barter it away for what we call energy, coercion, and some other terms we use as vaguely as that of liberty—There is often as great a rage for change and novelty in politics, as in amusements and fashions.

2.8.202

All parties apparently agree, that the freedom of the press is a fundamental right, and ought not to be restrained by any taxes, duties, or in any manner whatever. Why should not the people, in adopting a federal constitution, declare this, even if there are only doubts about it. But, say the advocates, all powers not given are reserved:—true; but the great question is, are not powers given, in the excercise of which this right may be de-

2.8.203

stroyed? The people's or the printers claim to a free press, is founded on the fundamental laws, that is, compacts, and state constitutions, made by the people. The people, who can annihilate or alter those constitutions, can annihilate or limit this right. This may be done by giving general powers, as well as by using particular words. No right claimed under a state constitution, will avail against a law of the union, made in pursuance of the federal constitution: therefore the question is, what laws will congress have a right to make by the constitution of the union, and particularly touching the press? By art. 1. sect. 8. congress will have power to lay and collect taxes, duties, imposts and excise. By this congress will clearly have power to lay and collect all kind of taxes whatever—taxes on houses, lands, polls, industry, merchandize, &c.—taxes on deeds, bonds, and all written instruments—on writs, pleas, and all judicial proceedings, on licences, naval officers papers, &c. on newspapers, advertisements, &c. and to require bonds of the naval officers, clerks, printers, &c. to account for the taxes that may become due on papers that go through their hands. Printing, like all other business, must cease when taxed beyond its profits; and it appears to me, that a power to tax the press at discretion, is a power to destroy or restrain the freedom of it. There may be other powers given, in the exercise of which this freedom may be effected; and certainly it is of too much importance to be left thus liable to be taxed, and constantly to constructions and inferences. A free press is the channel of communication as to mercantile and public affairs; by means of it the people in large countries ascertain each others sentiments; are enabled to unite, and become formidable to those rulers who adopt improper measures. Newspapers may sometimes be the vehicles of abuse, and of many things not true; but these are but small inconveniencies, in my mind, among many advantages. A celebrated writer, I have several times quoted, speaking in high terms of the English liberties, says, "lastly the key stone was put to the arch, by the final establishment of the freedom of the press."[122] I shall not dwell longer upon the fundamental rights, to some of which I have attended in this letter, for the same reasons that these I have mentioned, ought to be expressly secured, lest in the exercise of general powers given they may be invaded: it is pretty clear, that some other of less importance, or less in danger, might with propriety also be secured.

I shall now proceed to examine briefly the powers proposed to be vested in the several branches of the government, and especially the mode of laying and collecting internal taxes.

The Federal Farmer.

XVII

January 23, 1788.

Dear Sir,

I believe the people of the United States are full in the opinion, that a free   2.8.204
and mild government can be preserved in their extensive territories, only
under the substantial forms of a federal republic. As several of the ablest
advocates for the system proposed, have acknowledged this (and I hope the
confessions they have published will be preserved and remembered) I shall
not take up time to establish this point.[123] A question then arises, how far
that system partakes of a federal republic.—I observed in a former letter,
that it appears to be the first important step to a consolidation of the states;
that its strong tendency is to that point.[124]

But what do we mean by a federal republic? and what by a consolidated   2.8.205
government? To erect a federal republic, we must first make a number of
states on republican principles; each state with a government organized for
the internal management of its affairs: The states, as such, must unite under
a federal head, and delegate to it powers to make and execute laws in certain
enumerated cases, under certain restrictions; this head may be a single
assembly, like the present congress, or the Amphictionic council; or it may
consist of a legislature, with one or more branches; of an executive, and of a
judiciary. To form a consolidated, or one entire government, there must be
no state, or local governments, but all things, persons and property, must be
subject to the laws of one legislature alone; to one executive, and one
judiciary. Each state government, as the government of New Jersey, &c. is
a consolidated, or one entire government, as it respects the counties, towns,
citizens and property within the limits of the state.—The state governments
are the basis, the pillar on which the federal head is placed, and the whole
together, when formed on elective principles, constitute a federal republic.
A federal republic in itself supposes state or local governments to exist, as
the body or props, on which the federal head rests, and that it cannot remain
a moment after they cease. In erecting the federal government, and always
in its councils, each state must be known as a sovereign body; but in erecting this government, I conceive, the legislature of the state, by the expressed or implied assent of the people, or the people of the state, under the
direction of the government of it, may accede to the federal compact: Nor
do I conceive it to be necessarily a part of a confederacy of states, that each
have an equal voice in the general councils. A confederated republic being
organized, each state must retain powers for managing its internal police,
and all delegate to the union power to manage general concerns: The quantity of power the union must possess is one thing, the mode of exercising the
powers given, is quite a different consideration; and it is the mode of exercising them, that makes one of the essential distinctions between one entire
or consolidated government, and a federal republic; that is, however the
government may be organized, if the laws of the union, in most important

concerns, as in levying and collecting taxes, raising troops, &c. operate immediately upon the persons and property of individuals, and not on states, extend to organizing the militia, &c. the government, as to its administration, as to making and executing laws, is not federal, but consolidated. To illustrate my idea—the union makes a requisition, and assigns to each state its quota of men or monies wanted; each state, by its own laws and officers, in its own way, furnishes its quota: here the state governments stand between the union and individuals; the laws of the union operate only on states, as such, and federally: Here nothing can be done without the meetings of the state legislatures—but in the other case the union, though the state legislatures should not meet for years together, proceeds immediately, by its own laws and officers, to levy and collect monies of individuals, to inlist men, form armies, &c. [H]ere the laws of the union operate immediately on the body of the people, on persons and property; in the same manner the laws of one entire consolidated government operate.— These two modes are very distinct, and in their operation and consequences have directly opposite tendencies: The first makes the existence of the state governments indispensable, and throws all the detail business of levying and collecting the taxes, &c. into the hands of those governments, and into the hands, of course, of many thousand officers solely created by, and dependent on the state. The last entirely excludes the agency of the respective states, and throws the whole business of levying and collecting taxes, &c. into the hands of many thousand officers solely created by, and dependent upon the union, and makes the existence of the state government of no consequence in the case. It is true, congress in raising any given sum in direct taxes, must by the constitution, raise so much of it in one state, and so much in another, by a fixed rule, which most of the states some time since agreed to: But this does not effect the principle in question, it only secures each state against any arbitrary proportions. The federal mode is perfectly safe and eligible, founded in the true spirit of a confederated republic; there could be no possible exception to it, did we not find by experience, that the states will sometimes neglect to comply with the reasonable requisitions of the union. It being according to the fundamental principles of federal republics, to raise men and monies by requisitions, and for the states individually to organize and train the militia, I conceive, there can be no reason whatever for departing from them, except this, that the states sometimes neglect to comply with reasonable requisitions, and that it is dangerous to attempt to compel a delinquent state by force, as it may often produce a war. We ought, therefore, to enquire attentively, how extensive the evils to be guarded against are, and cautiously limit the remedies to the extent of the evils. I am not about to defend the confederation, or to charge the proposed constitution with imperfections not in it; but we ought to examine facts, and strip them of the false colourings often given them by incautious observations, by unthinking or designing men. We ought to premise, that laws for raising men and monies, even in consolidated governments, are not often punctually complied with. Historians, except in extraordinary cases, but very seldom take notice of the detail collection of taxes; but these facts we have fully proved, and well attested; that the most energetic governments have relinquished taxes frequently, which were of many years standing. These facts amply prove, that taxes assessed, have remained many years uncollected. I agree there have been instances in the republics of Greece, Holland &c. in the course of several centuries, of states neglecting to pay their quotas of requisitions; but it is a circumstance certainly deserving of attention, whether these nations which have depended on requisitions principally for their defence, have not raised men and monies nearly as punctually as entire governments, which have taxed directly; whether we have not found the latter as often distressed for the want of troops and monies as the former. It has been said that the Amphictionic council, and the Germanic head, have not possessed sufficient powers to controul the members of the republic in a proper manner. Is this, if true, to be imputed to requisitions? Is it not principally to be imputed to the unequal powers of those members, connected with this important circumstance, that each member possessed power to league itself with foreign powers, and powerful neighbours, without the consent of the head. After all, has not the Germanic body a government as good as its neighbours in general? and did not the Grecian republic remain united several centuries, and form the theatre of human greatness? No government in Europe has commanded monies more plentifully than the government of Holland. As to the United States, the separate states lay taxes directly, and the union calls for taxes by way of requisitions; and is it a fact, that more monies are due in proportion on requisitions in the United States, than on the state taxes directly laid?—It is but about ten years since congress begun to make requisitions, and in that time, the monies, &c. required, and the bounties given for men required of the states, have amounted, specie value, to about 36 millions dollars, about 24 millions of dollars of which have been actually paid; and a very considerable part of the 12 millions not paid, remains so not so much from the neglect of the states, as from the sudden changes in paper money, &c. which in a great measure rendered payments of no service, and which often induced the union indirectly to relinquish one demand, by making another in a different form. Before we totally condemn requisitions, we ought to consider what immense bounties the states gave, and what prodigious exertions they made in the war, in order to comply with the requisitions of congress; and if since the peace they have been delinquent, ought we not carefully to enquire, whether that delinquency is to be imputed solely to the nature of requisitions? ought it not in part to be imputed to two other causes? I mean first, an opinion, that has extensively prevailed, that the requisitions for domestic interest have not been founded on just principles; and secondly, the circumstance, that the government itself, by proposing imposts, &c. has departed virtually from the constitutional system; which proposed changes, like all changes proposed in government, produce an inattention and negligence in the execution of the government in being.

2.8.206   I am not for depending wholly on requisitions; but I mention these few facts to shew they are not so totally futile as many pretend. For the truth of many of these facts I appeal to the public records; and for the truth of the others, I appeal to many republican characters, who are best informed in the affairs of the United States. Since the peace, and till the convention reported, the wisest men in the United States generally supposed, that certain limited funds would answer the purposes of the union: and though the states are by no means in so good a condition as I wish they were, yet, I think, I may very safely affirm, they are in a better condition than they would be had congress always possessed the powers of taxation now contended for. The fact is admitted, that our federal government does not possess sufficient powers to give life and vigor to the political system; and that we experience disappointments, and several inconveniencies; but we ought carefully to distinguish those which are merely the consequences of a severe and tedious war, from those which arise from defects in the federal system. There has been an entire revolution in the United States within thirteen years, and the least we can compute the waste of labour and property at, during that period, by the war, is three hundred million of dollars. Our people are like a man just recovering from a severe fit of sickness. It was the war that disturbed the course of commerce, introduced floods of paper money, the stagnation of credit, and threw many valuable men out of steady business. From these sources our greatest evils arise; men of knowledge and reflection must perceive it;—but then, have we not done more in three or four years past, in repairing the injuries of the war, by repairing houses and estates, restoring industry, frugality, the fisheries, manufactures, &c. and thereby laying the foundation of good government, and of indiviudal and political happiness, than any people ever did in a like time; we must judge from a view of the country and facts, and not from foreign newspapers, or our own, which are printed chiefly in the commercial towns, where imprudent living, imprudent importations, and many unexpected disappointments, have produced a despondency, and a disposition to view every thing on the dark side. Some of the evils we feel, all will agree, ought to be imputed to the defective administration of the governments. From these and various considerations, I am very clearly of opinion, that the evils we sustain, merely on account of the defects of the confederation, are but as a feather in the balance against a mountain, compared with those which would, infallibly, be the result of the loss of general liberty, and that happiness men enjoy under a frugal, free, and mild government.

2.8.207   Heretofore we do not seem to have seen danger any where, but in giving power to congress, and now no where but in congress wanting powers; and, without examining the extent of the evils to be remedied, by one step, we are for giving up to congress almost all powers of any importance without limitation. The defects of the confederation are extravagantly magnified, and every species of pain we feel imputed to them: and hence it is inferred, there must be a total change of the principles, as well as forms of government: and in the main point, touching the federal powers, we rest all on a logical inference, totally inconsistent with experience and sound political reasoning.[125]

It is said, that as the federal head must make peace and war, and provide for the common defence, it ought to possess all powers necessary to that end: that powers unlimited, as to the purse and sword, to raise men and monies, and form the militia, are necessary to that end; and, therefore, the federal head ought to possess them. This reasoning is far more specious than solid: it is necessary that these powers so exist in the body politic, as to be called into exercise whenever necessary for the public safety; but it is by no means true, that the man, or congress of men, whose duty it more immediately is to provide for the common defence, ought to possess them without limitation. But clear it is, that if such men, or congress, be not in a situation to hold them without danger to liberty, he or they ought not to possess them. It has long been thought to be a well founded position, that the purse and sword ought not to be placed in the same hands in a free government. Our wise ancestors have carefully separated them—placed the sword in the hands of their king, even under considerable limitations, and the purse in the hands of the commons alone: yet the king makes peace and war, and it is his duty to provide for the common defence of the nation. This authority at least goes thus far—that a nation, well versed in the science of government, does not conceive it to be necessary or expedient for the man entrusted with the common defence and general tranquility, to possess unlimitedly the powers in question, or even in any considerable degree. Could he, whose duty it is to defend the public, possess in himself independently, all the means of doing it consistent with the public good, it might be convenient: but the people of England know that their liberties and happiness would be in infinitely greater danger from the king's unlimited possession of these powers, than from all external enemies and internal commotions to which they might be exposed: therefore, though they have made it his duty to guard the empire, yet they have wisely placed in other hands, the hands of their representatives, the power to deal out and controul the means. In Holland their high mightinesses must provide for the common defence, but for the means they depend, in a considerable degree, upon requisitions made on the state or local assemblies. Reason and facts evince, that however convenient it might be for an executive magistrate, or federal head, more immediately charged with the national defence and safety, solely, directly, and independently to possess all the means; yet such magistrate, or head, never ought to possess them, if thereby the public liberties shall be endangered. The powers in question never have been, by nations wise and free, deposited, nor can they ever be, with safety, any where, but in the principal members of the national system;—where these form one entire

2.8.208

government, as in Great-Britain, they are separated and lodged in the principal members of it. But in a federal republic, there is quite a different organization; the people form this kind of government, generally, because their territories are too extensive to admit of their assembling in one legislature, or of executing the laws on free principles under one entire government. They convene in their local assemblies, for local purposes, and for managing their internal concerns, and unite their states under a federal head for general purposes. It is the essential characteristic of a confederated republic, that this head be dependant on, and kept within limited bounds by, the local governments; and it is because, in these alone, in fact, the people can be substantially assembled or represented. It is, therefore, we very universally see, in this kind of government, the congressional powers placed in a few hands, and accordingly limited, and specifically enumerated: and the local assemblies strong and well guarded, and composed of numerous members. Wise men will always place the controuling power where the people are substantially collected by their representatives. By the proposed system, the federal head will possess, without limitation, almost every species of power that can, in its exercise, tend to change the government, or to endanger liberty; while in it, I think it has been fully shewn, the people will have but the shadow of representation, and but the shadow of security for their rights and liberties. In a confederated republic, the division of representation, &c. in its nature, requires a correspondent division and deposit of powers relative to taxes and military concerns: and I think the plan offered stands quite alone, in confounding the principles of governments in themselves totally distinct. I wish not to exculpate the states for their improper neglects in not paying their quotas of requisitions; but, in applying the remedy, we must be governed by reason and facts. It will not be denied, that the people have a right to change the government when the majority chuse it, if not restrained by some existing compact—that they have a right to displace their rulers, and consequently to determine when their measures are reasonable or not—and that they have a right, at any time, to put a stop to those measures they may deem prejudicial to them, by such forms and negatives as they may see fit to provide. From all these, and many other well founded considerations, I need not mention, a question arises, what powers shall there be delegated to the federal head, to insure safety, as well as energy, in the government? I think there is a safe and proper medium pointed out by experience, by reason, and facts. When we have organized the government, we ought to give power to the union, so far only as experience and present circumstances shall direct, with a reasonable regard to time to come. Should future circumstances, contrary to our expectations, require that further powers be transferred to the union, we can do it far more easily, than get back those we may now imprudently give. The system proposed is untried: candid advocates and opposers admit, that it is, in a degree, a mere experiment, and that its organization is weak and imperfect; surely then, the safe ground is cautiously to vest power in it, and when we are sure we have given enough for ordinary exigencies, to be extremely careful how we delegate powers, which, in common cases, must necessarily be useless or abused, and of very uncertain effect in uncommon ones.

By giving the union power to regulate commerce, and to levy and collect taxes by imposts, we give it an extensive authority, and permanent productive funds, I believe quite as adequate to the present demands of the union, as exises and direct taxes can be made to the present demands of the separate states. The state governments are now about four times as expensive as that of the union; and their several state debts added together, are nearly as large as that of the union—Our impost duties since the peace have been almost as productive as the other sources of taxation, and when under one general system of regulations, the probability is, that those duties will be very considerably increased: Indeed the representation proposed will hardly justify giving to congress unlimited powers to raise taxes by imposts, in addition to the other powers the union must necessarily have. It is said, that if congress possess only authority to raise taxes by imposts, trade probably will be overburdened with taxes, and the taxes of the union be found inadequate to any uncommon exigencies: To this we may observe, that trade generally finds its own level, and will naturally and necessarily leave off any undue burdens laid upon it: further, if congress alone possess the impost, and also unlimited power to raise monies by excises and direct taxes, there must be much more danger that two taxing powers, the union and states, will carry excises and direct taxes to an unreasonable extent, especially as these have not the natural boundaries taxes on trade have. However, it is not my object to propose to exclude congress from raising monies by internal taxes, as by duties, excises, and direct taxes, but my opinion is, that congress, especially in its proposed organization, ought not to raise monies by internal taxes, except in strict conformity to the federal plan; that is, by the agency of the state governments in all cases, except where a state shall neglect, for an unreasonable time, to pay its quota of a requisition; and never where so many of the state legislatures as represent a majority of the people, shall formally determine an excise law or requisition is improper, in their next session after the same be laid before them. We ought always to recollect that the evil to be guarded against is found by our own experience, and the experience of others, to be mere neglect in the states to pay their quotas; and power in the union to levy and collect the neglecting states' quotas with interest, is fully adequate to the evil. By this federal plan, with this exception mentioned, we secure the means of collecting the taxes by the usual process of law, and avoid the evil of attempting to compel or coerce a state; and we avoid also a circumstance, which never yet could be, and I am fully confident never can be, admitted in a free federal republic; I mean a permanent and continued system of tax laws of the union, executed in the bowels of the states by many thousand officers, dependent as to the assessing and collecting federal taxes, solely upon the

2.8.209

union. On every principle then, we ought to provide, that the union render an exact account of all monies raised by imposts and other taxes; and that whenever monies shall be wanted for the purposes of the union, beyond the proceeds of the impost duties, requisitions shall be made on the states for the monies so wanted; and that the power of laying and collecting shall never be exercised, except in cases where a state shall neglect, a given time, to pay its quota. This mode seems to be strongly pointed out by the reason of the case, and spirit of the government; and I believe, there is no instance to be found in a federal republic, where the congressional powers ever extended generally to collecting monies by direct taxes or excises. Creating all these restrictions, still the powers of the union in matters of taxation, will be too unlimited; further checks, in my mind, are indispensably necessary. Nor do I conceive, that as full a representation as is practicable in the federal government, will afford sufficient security: the strength of the government, and the confidence of the people, must be collected principally in the local assemblies; every part or branch of the federal head must be feeble, and unsafely trusted with large powers. A government possessed of more power than its constituent parts will justify, will not only probably abuse it, but be unequal to bear its own burden; it may as soon be destroyed by the pressure of power, as languish and perish for want of it.

2.8.210 There are two ways further of raising checks, and guarding against undue combinations and influence in a federal system. The first is, in levying taxes, raising and keeping up armies, in building navies, in forming plans for the militia, and in appropriating monies for the support of the military, to require the attendance of a large proportion of the federal representatives, as two-thirds or three-fourths of them; and in passing laws, in these important cases, to require the consent of two-thirds or three-fourths of the members present. The second is, by requiring that certain important laws of the federal head, as a requisition or a law for raising monies by excise shall be laid before the state legislatures, and if disapproved of by a given number of them, say by as many of them as represent a majority of the people, the law shall have no effect. Whether it would be adviseable to adopt both, or either of these checks, I will not undertake to determine. We have seen them both exist in confederated republics. The first exists substantially in the confederation, and will exist in some measure in the plan proposed, as in chusing a president by the house, in expelling members; in the senate, in making treaties, and in deciding on impeachments, and in the whole in altering the constitution. The last exists in the United Netherlands, but in a much greater extent. The first is founded on this principle, that these important measures may, sometimes, be adopted by a bare quorum of members, perhaps, from a few states, and that a bare majority of the federal representatives may frequently be of the aristocracy, or some particular interests, connections, or parties in the community, and governed by motives, views, and inclinations not compatible with the general interest.—The last is founded on this principle, that the people will be substantially represented, only in their state or local assemblies; that their principal security must be found in them; and that, therefore, they ought to have ultimately a constitutional controul over such interesting measures.

I have often heard it observed, that our people are well informed, and will not submit to oppressive governments; that the state governments will be their ready advocates, and possess their confidence, mix with them, and enter into all their wants and feelings.[126] This is all true; but of what avail will these circumstances be, if the state governments, thus allowed to be the guardians of the people, possess no kind of power by the forms of the social compact, to stop in their passage, the laws of congress injurious to the people. State governments must stand and see the law take place; they may complain and petition—so may individuals; the members of them, in extreme cases, may resist, on the principles of self-defence—so may the people and individuals. 2.8.211

It has been observed, that the people, in extensive territories, have more power, compared with that of their rulers, than in small states.[127] Is not directly the opposite true? The people in a small state can unite and act in concert, and with vigour; but in large territories, the men who govern find it more easy to unite, while people cannot; while they cannot collect the opinions of each part, while they move to different points, and one part is often played off against the other. 2.8.212

It has been asserted, that the confederate head of a republic at best, is in general weak and dependent;—that the people will attach themselves to, and support their local governments, in all disputes with the union.[128] Admit the fact: is it any way to remove the inconvenience by accumulating powers upon a weak organization? The fact is, that the detail administration of affairs, in this mixed republics, depends principally on the local governments; and the people would be wretched without them: and a great proportion of social happiness depends on the internal administration of justice, and on internal police. The splendor of the monarch, and the power of the government are one thing. The happiness of the subject depends on very different causes: but it is to the latter, that the best men, the greatest ornaments of human nature, have most carefully attended: it is to the former tyrants and oppressors have always aimed, 2.8.213

The Federal Farmer.

1. It is intriguing to speculate why the letters begin in this way, especially since the "letters" of "last winter" could throw definitive light on the authorship; but my own speculations and search have been fruitless. There seems to be no record of any such letters or of the possible identity of the addressee, the Republican.

2. For an elaboration of the extreme parties, see I, 2.8.6–7; V, 2.8.62; VI, 2.8.68–73; VII, 2.8.97–98.

3. Alexander Pope, *Essay on Man*, epistle 3, lines 303–4. Pope's couplet was frequently discussed in the ratification literature, the classic case being the treatment in *The Federalist* no. 68, 461. See also Penn 3.12.4; [Maryland] Farmer II, 5.1.36. Generally the Anti-Federalist writers were more critical of the maxim than The Federal Farmer is here (but see III, 2.8.24–25; IX, 2.8.111; and he is specifically criticized on this point by a fellow Anti-Federalist writer, A Countryman (6.6.39). For Federalist discussions of the importance of good administration, see Poplicola 4.11.1 n.1.

4. The "critical" character of this period was not simply an invention of the Federalists or of Federalist historians. See VI, 2.8.70; Brutus I, 2.9.2; Old Whig IV, 3.3.18; Philadelphiensis I, 3.9.2.; Centinel IV, 2.7.91 n. 45.

5. The author is thinking of such men as Abraham Clark of New Jersey; Richard Caswell and Willie Jones of North Carolina; Patrick Henry, Thomas Nelson, and Richard Henry Lee of Virginia; all of whom were critics of the Constitution who had been elected to the Constitutional Convention but had declined to serve or failed to attend. See Farrand III, 557–59. Cf. Federal Farmer V, 2.8.62, and Lee's letter to Randolph, on 26 March 1787, expressing his confidence in the gentlemen appointed to the Convention (Lee, *Letters* II, 415). The discussion of the parties favoring and opposing the Constitution is continued in V, 2.8.62; VI, 2.8.68–73.

6. Pickering replied, "In the proposed Constitution there is no foundation for an aristocracy; for its officers (including in this term as well the legislative as the executive branches) do not hold their places by *hereditary* right, nor *for life*, nor by electing *one another;* neither is any portion of wealth or property a necessary qualification." Pickering and Upham, *The Life of Timothy Pickering* II, 353. However, it is not a conventional but the natural aristocracy that The Federal Farmer is concerned with. See III, 2.8.25; VII, 2.8.97.

7. Note that all of these, including the first, are described as forms under which the United States may exist *as one nation.* As Merrill Jensen says, the issue was not whether there was a "nation" before 1787. "There was a new nation, as the men of the time agreed: they disagreed as to whether the new nation should have a federal or a national government." Jensen, *New Nation* xiv. They also disagreed, however, about whether a nation *could* exist as a nation without a national government. Cf. James Wilson's similar statement of alternatives in his 24 November speech before the Pennsylvania ratifying convention. McMaster and Stone 225 ff; Elliot II, 427 ff.

8. See III, 2.8.35, where The Federal Farmer adds to the legitimate powers of the general government the regulation of trade between the states, but omits to mention the militia and bankruptcies. On bankruptcy laws, see XVIII, 2.8.221, where he concludes that the power to pass bankruptcy laws should not be given to the federal government.

9. The Federal Farmer displays a significant shift in terminology in this connection. Here he makes the then standard distinction between a federal plan, on the one side, a plan of consolidation, on the other side, and what he calls a "partial consolidation" in the middle, consisting of a combination of federal and consolidated or national principles. The distinctions are fundamentally identical to those drawn by Publius in *The Federalist* no. 39, 253–57. In his sixth essay, however, the advocates of the earlier and merely advisory "federal plan" become one kind of "pretended federalists" (the others being the advocates of the earlier "consolidation"), while the proponents of the earlier "partial consolidation" become the "true" or "honest federalists." See VI, 2.8.72. See Martin Diamond's essays, "What the Framers Meant by Federalism," *A Nation of States,* ed. Robert Goldwin, 2d ed. (Chicago 1974) 25–42; and "*The Federalists'* View of Federalism," *Essays on Federalism* (Claremont, Cal., 1961). On the characteristics of the "federal republic," see XVII, 2.8.204–5. For other important Anti-Federal discussions of the meaning of a federal system or fed-

eral republic, see Brutus I, 2.9.4–21; [Pennsylvania] Farmer 3.14.6–10; Henry 5.16.1–2; Clinton 6.13.2, 27.

10. Cf. Monroe's discussion of the desirability of consolidation if it were practicable, 5.21.12 n. 3.

11. On the question of a free and equal representation, see *The Federalist* nos. 35–36. Representation is one of The Federal Farmer's major themes. See III, 2.8.25–26, 39; V, 2.8.59–60; VI, 2.8.76–77; VII–XII, 2.8.93–165; XV, 2.8.190. The other major Anti-Federal discussions of representation will be found in Brutus I, 2.9.14–16; DeWitt 4.3.14; Cornelius 4.10.9; [Maryland] Farmer II, 5.1.22–32; V, 5.1.71–73; Chase 5.3.20; Republicus 5.13.3; Impartial Examiner 5.14.28–32.

12. On jury trials see IV, 2.8.44, 53–55; VI, 2.8.80; XV, 2.8.190–94.

13. A semicolon has been omitted here.

14. However, as Publius shrewdly argues, if the remote states share least in the circulation of the ordinary benefits of union, their exposed position gives them an unusually great dependence on the aid of the Union. The remote states get less out of the Union, but they need what they do get more, and thus the "proper equilibrium" is maintained. *The Federalist* no. 14, 87.

15. See below, n. 19.

16. See McMaster and Stone 144–45 (Wilson); Ford, *Pamphlets* 148–49 (An American Citizen), 361 (Iredell); Ford, *Essays* 165 (A Landholder), 397–98 (Hugh Williamson); Ford, *Pamphlets* 241 (Aristides). This point is made frequently by Federalists during the state ratification debates.

17. On the need for and functions of a Bill of Rights, see IV, 2.8.46–56; XVI, 2.8.196–203. On kinds of rights, see VI, 2.8.80–86.

18. Publius answers this argument (and its continuation in the next paper) in *The Federalist* no. 27. In no. 8, Publius describes in some detail an effect similar to that alluded to here by The Federal Farmer, but he derives it from a different cause, namely dissension among the states under an inadequate general government.

19. On the connection between free laws and the character of the people, see II, 2.8.18; V, 2.8.59; VII, 2.8.93–96; X, 2.8.127, 139; XVIII, 2.8.227. See also Cato III, 2.6.15–20; Centinel I, 2.7.9; Brutus I, 2.9.16; Federal Republican 3.6.21; Philadelphiensis II, 3.9.9; Turner 4.18; Columbian Patriot 4.28.2. This question is, of course, immediately connected with the question of representation; see above, n. 11.

20. An Anti-Federalist essayist, A Countryman from Dutchess County (6.6.42–64), points out that there is a substantial difficulty in the contention that good citizens should acquiesce even if essential alterations are not made.

21. On the natural aristocracy, see VI, 2.8.97.

22. A Countryman from Dutchess County makes the point, nearly always passed over even by the Anti-Federalists, that the Senate is not entirely on the federal plan, for each senator has one vote; whereas "by the present confederation, which is a union of the states, not a consolidation, *all the delegates,* from a state, have but one vote, and in the state senate, which is on the plan of consolidation, *each* senator has a vote" (6.6.45). Cf. [Pennsylvania] Farmer 3.14.14–15; Republicus 5.13.12. In the Additional Letters (XI, 2.8.143 ff) The Federal Farmer records a more favorable opinion of the "federal" basis of the senate. It should be noted that many Federalists defend the "federal" basis of the Senate as sound in principle and even assume that senators will be subject to instructions from their states. See especially Elliot II, 26 (Cabot), 47 (King); Ford, *Pamphlets* 40 (A Citizen of America), 206–7 (Fabius), 223 ff. (Aristides); Ford, *Essays* 29 (Cassius); *Pennsylvania Gazette* 30 January 1788 (A Freeman); *Virginia Independent Chronicle Extraordinary* 9 April 1788 (A Freeholder); *Maryland Journal* 1 August 1788 (Speech Intended to Have Been Delivered in Maryland Convention).

23. Publius presumably refers to The Federal Farmer when, in no. 68, 457–58, he writes that "the most plausible of [the opponents], who has appeared in print, has even deigned to admit that the election of the President is pretty well guarded." See Federal Farmer XIV, 2.8.177. James Wilson also noted that the scheme for selecting the President "is not objected to." McMaster and Stone 398. For criticism, however, see Republicus 5.13.13.

24. See Brutus IV, 2.9.48 n. 34.

25. Cf. *The Federalist* no. 35, 216–18.

26. Publius replies that if the government were interested in a system of influence, "the most certain road to the accomplishment of its aim would be to employ the State officers as much as possible, and to attach them to the Union by an accumulation of their emoluments." *The Federalist* no. 36, 228. The question of executive influence is discussed more fully and in broader terms in XIII, 2.8.166–72. Cf. Brutus III, 2.9.42 n. 29.

27. See Centinel II, 2.7.52 n. 30.

28. See Citizen of America, An Examination . . . , Ford, *Pamphlets* 49; and statement by Roger Sherman and Oliver Ellsworth, quoted by Old Whig VI, 3.3.37 and n. 35.

29. On the concurrent taxing powers of the national and state governments, see *The Federalist* nos. 32–34; no. 36, 227–29. Publius' basic argument is that a concurrent jurisdiction in this case was the only admissible substitute for an entire subordination of the states. For other Federal and Anti-Federal discussions of concurrent power to tax see McMaster and Stone 260 (Whitehill), 268–69 (Smilie); Ford, *Pamphlets* 50–51 (Webster); Ford, *Essays* 235–36 (Sherman); Elliot II, 333, 337, 372 (Smith); 339 (Williams), 346 (R. R. Livingston), 361–64 (Hamilton), 372 (Lansing); Elliot III, 306, 332 (Madison); Elliot IV, 75 (Spenser); Brutus I, 2.9.5; Old Whig VI, 3.3.33–39; Mason 5.17.1.

30. See above, n. 11.

31. The arguments here about the select militia and the *posse commitatus* versus military execution are answered directly, though not by name, in *The Federalist* no. 29, 182ff. Regarding the former, Publius professes himself perplexed how to treat the objections, but his raillery touches a sensitive point: "Where in the name of common sense are our fears to end if we may not trust our sons, our brothers, our neighbours, our fellow-citizens?" Ibid. 185.

32. On further reflection, The Federal Farmer concluded that the power to pass bankruptcy laws should not be given to the federal government. See XVIII, 2.8.221.

33. The judiciary is discussed fully in XV, 2.8.183–95. See Pickering's well-argued replies to The Federal Farmer's contentions on this head; Pickering and Upham, *The Life of Timothy Pickering* II, 359–60, 366–67.

34. See Democratic Federalist 3.5.6 n. 6.

35. See above, n. 28.

36. See above, n. 17.

37. Cf. Chief Justice Marshall's argument in *McCulloch* v. *Maryland*, 4 Wheat. 316, 403 (1819); and Publius in *The Federalist* no. 39, 253–54.

38. See Ford, *Essays* 163 (A Landholder); Ford, *Pamphlets* 77 (A Citizen of New York); *The Federalist* no. 84; Edmund Pendleton, letter to Lee, 14 June 1788, David John Mays, ed., *The Letters and Papers of Edmund Pendleton* (Charlottesville 1967) II, 532; *A Native of Virginia, Observations upon the Proposed Plan of Federal Government* (Petersburg 1787), reprinted in *The Writings of James Monroe* ed. S. M. Hamilton (1898–1903) I, 352 ff. (but not written by Monroe). For Anti-Federal rebuttals, see One of the Common People 4.8.1 n. 1; [New Hampshire] Farmer 4.17.2.

39. This argument is not entirely consistent with the preceding one, but Federalists, notably James Wilson, made them both. See [New Hampshire] Farmer 4.17.14 n. 9. See McMaster and Stone 143–44 (Wilson), 189 (Plain Truth), 377 (McKean); Ford, *Essays* 45–46 (Cassius); Ford, *Pamphlets* 242 (Aristides), 356 ff. (Iredell); Elliot IV, 259 (Pinckney). For Anti-Federal replies see Martin 2.4.38 n. 9; Brutus II, 2.9.26; Cincinnatus I, 6.1.4; DeWitt 4.3.7.

40. See Impartial Examiner 5.4.5; Henry 5.16.24. On this whole question, see Federal Farmer XVI, 2.8.196 ff.

41. See Brutus II, 2.9.30 n. 22.

42. See above, nn. 12, 16.

43. John Adams, *Defence* I, preface (*Works* IV, 290–91).

44. See VI, 2.8.71. For other Anti-Federal discussions of the ever-alert aristocracy, see [Maryland] Farmer IV, 5.1.26–32; Henry 5.16.7–8; Plebeian 6.11.2.

45. Dickinson, *Letters from a Farmer in Pennsylvania* XI.

46. See above, n. 19, and III, 2.8.39; see VI, 2.8.97; see below, n. 91. Cf. the arguments of A Citizen of America (Noah Webster) and A Landholder (Oliver Ellsworth), Ford, *Pamphlets* 57–61; Ford, *Essays* 166.

47. See above, n. 11.

48. See Pennsylvania Convention Minority 3.11.6–12; Centinel III, 2.7.70.

49. See below, Philadelphiensis I, 3.9.2–6.

50. Delaware, Pennsylvania, New Jersey.

51. On the parties, see above, n. 2; on the forms of "federalism" see above, nn. 7, 9. On Anti-Federal attacks on the framers, see Centinel III, 2.7.70.

52. The author probably refers here principally to the vigorous replies to and attacks on Mason, Gerry, and Lee made by A Landholder (Oliver Ellsworth) in a series of essays published in late 1787. See Ford, *Essays* 150–66, 173–77. A Landholder described Lee as possessing a "factious spirit" and an "implacable hatred to General Washington," and suggested that he was "the author of most of the scurrility poured out in the New York papers against the new constitution." Ford, *Essays* 161. Other Federalist writers referred to Lee, and especially to Mason and Gerry by name (all of them having published criticisms of the Constitution over their own names); but on the whole the Anti-Federalists at least equaled their opponents in personal attacks.

53. *The Letters of Junius* [Woodfall's Junius]; see VIII, 2.8.107 and n. 69.

54. "It is a pity that the expectations which actuated the authors of the existing confederation, neither have nor can be realized:—accustomed to see and admire the glorious spirit which moved all ranks of people in the most gloomy moments of the war, observing their steadfast attachment to Union, and the wisdom they so often manifested both in choosing and confiding in their rulers, those gentlemen were led to flatter themselves that the people of America only required to know what ought to be done, to do it. The amiable mistake induced them to institute a national government in such a manner, as though very fit to give advice, was yet destitute of power, and so constructed as to be very unfit to be trusted with it. They seem not to have been sensible that mere advice is a sad substitute for laws; nor to have recollected that the advice even of the allwise and best of Beings, has been always disregarded by a great majority of all the men that ever lived." A Citizen of New York [John Jay], "An Address to the People of the State of New-York," 1787, Ford, *Pamphlets* 71.

The Articles of Confederation, A Citizen of Philadelphia wrote, "was an honest and solemn covenant among our infant States, and virtue and common danger supplied its defects." McMaster and Stone 106.

55. Note that in the sequel the distinction made here is not maintained, and the list given is of "unalienable or fundamental rights in the United States" VI, 2.8.86. See II, 2.8.19, where The Federal Farmer also writes of "unalienable and fundamental rights."

56. See above, n. 19.

57. See above, n. 11.

58. The second point is not reached until letter XII, 2.8.148, at which time the numbering is abandoned.

59. See above, V, 2.8.59.

60. See above, II, 2.8.15. Publius contends that "the idea of an actual representation of all classes of the people by persons of each class is altogether visionary." *The Federalist* no. 35, 219. The Federal Farmer is not referring specifically to *The Federalist*, however, since the essay of Publius was first published on 5 January 1788, while this essay of The Federal Farmer is dated 31 December 1787.

61. Cesare Bonesana Beccaria, *An Essay on Crimes and Punishments* (London 1767), Introduction; quoted in "Address to Inhabitants of Quebec, October 26, 1774" (written by R. H. Lee), *Journals of the Continental Congress* I, 106. This edition of Beccaria's book, like the other early English translations, followed Beccaria's original (1764) organization of chapters. Beccaria himself later accepted an improved organization made in the 1766 translation into French by André Morellet. This is the preferable text, and it is the one used in the modern collection of Beccaria's works and in a recent Library of Liberal Arts paperback edition of *On Crimes and Punishments*. Unfortunately, the specific passage here, which was quoted by the Con-

tinental Congress and by several Anti-Federalists and which was the first sentence in the original introduction, was considerably altered in the revision, making the modern editions different in this crucial respect from those available to the American founding generation. See Cesare Beccaria, *Opere*, ed. Sergie Romagnoli (Florence 1958) I, 39; II, 862–63; Cesare Beccaria, *On Crimes and Punishments*, trans. Henry Paolucci (Indianapolis 1963).

62. *The Spirit of Laws* XI, ch. 6.

63. See Ibid. II, ch. 2.

64. John Adams gave good and influential expression to the stock of ideas on the natural aristocracy upon which the Anti-Federalists drew. See his *Defence*, letter 25 (*Works* IV, 396–98). For other Anti-Federalist discussions of the natural aristocracy, see above, III, 2.8.25; Cato VI, 2.6.43; Brutus III, 2.9.42; [Maryland] Farmer II, 5.1.26–32; Smith 6.12.22 n. 24. For Federalist replies, see McMaster and Stone 335–36 (Wilson); Elliot II, 256 (Hamilton); *Carlisle Gazette* 24 October 1787 (A Citizen).

65. While the thought is a common one, I have not been able to find the specific source of the observation about merchants. Regarding the schools, John Adams wrote: "Monarchies and aristocracies are in possession of the voice and influence of every university and academy in Europe. Democracy, simple democracy, never had a patron among men of letters. Democratical mixtures in government have lost almost all the advocates they ever had out of England and America." John Adams, *Defence*, preface (*Works* IV, 289).

66. This consideration takes place in letters VIII–X, 2.8.102–42.

• • • • •

115. On bills of rights see above, II, 2.8.19–20.

116. See above, nn. 38, 39, 40. For Federalist arguments that a bill of rights would be dangerous, see *The Federalist* no. 84, 579; McMaster and Stone 143–44, 253–54 (Wilson), 189 (Plain Truth), 296 (Yeates); Ford, *Pamphlets* 242 (Aristides), 360 (Marcus); Elliot III, 191 (Randolph), 620 (Madison); Elliot IV, 141 (Maclaine), 142 (Johnston), 149, 167 (Iredell), 316 (General Pinckney).

117. James Wilson, "Address to the Citizens of Philadelphia," McMaster and Stone, 143–44. See Brutus II, 2.9.30 n. 22.

118. For other expressions of this important theme, see Old Whig IV, 3.3.21–24; Impartial Examiner 5.14.5, 10; Henry 5.16.35–38; Delegate Who Has Catched Cold 5.19.13–17; Sentiments of Many, passim. A good statement of this view of a bill of rights is provided by Edmund Randolph in commenting on the Virginia Declaration of Rights. See Bernard Schwartz, *The Bill of Rights* (New York 1971) I, 249.

119. See II, 2.8.16 n. 12.

120. Blackstone, *Commentaries on the Laws of England* III, 379.

121. [While the precise reference has not been located, the context suggests De-Lolme, *The Constitution of England*, perhaps II, ch. 21. See text at n. 122 below (XVI, 2.8.203), which was located in DeLolme; see also text at n. 67 (VIII, 2.8.102), where The Federal Farmer identifies DeLolme and praises him.—M.D.]

122. DeLolme, *The Constitution of England* I, ch. 3.

123. See McMaster and Stone 264, 390 (Wilson); Ford, *Pamphlets* 39 (A Citizen of America), 121 (A Citizen of Philadelphia), 207 (Fabius), 247–48 (Aristides); Ford, *Essays* 238 (A Citizen of New Haven); Elliot II, 46 (Ames); Elliot IV, 58 (Davies). Publius, it should be noted, does not acknowledge this proposition. See *The Federalist* nos. 9, 15, 39. See Centinel V, 2.7.94.

124. I, 2.8.1.

125. Cf. *The Federalist*, esp. no. 23, 147–51; no. 31, 193–96.

126. See above, n. 80.

127. See *The Federalist* no. 28, 179; cf. the argument here with *The Federalist* no. 10.

128. See *The Federalist* no. 17, 107; no. 27, 172–73; McMaster and Stone 302, 325 (Wilson), Elliot II, 46 (Ames); 239, 267, 304, 354 (Hamilton); Elliot III, 18 (Nicholas), 257–59 (Madison). Cf. below, Brutus XI, 2.9.130 n. 87.

129. See Brutus V, 2.9.58–59; VI, 2.9.77–78.
130. See above, I, 2.8.10.
131. See Brutus XII, 2.9.155–57.
132. James Wilson, Philadelphia ratifying convention, McMaster and Stone 324.

Essays of Brutus

NEW YORK JOURNAL
October 1787–April 1788

The essays of Brutus are among the most important Anti-Federalist writings. In clear and forceful argument Brutus takes up in a highly competent way the major Anti-Federalist themes, such as consolidation,[1] the small republic, a bill of rights, and representation.[2] He provides the best Anti-Federalist rebuttal of the powerful Federalist argument, well known in the form given it by Publius, that the federal government must be given unlimited powers to meet the unlimited contingencies implicit in its vast responsibility. He provides an extended and excellent discussion—the best in the Anti-Federalist literature—of the judiciary to be established under the Constitution and its far-reaching implications.[3] In these latter respects and in general, the *Brutus* essays are the most direct Anti-Federal confrontation of the arguments of *The Federalist*.

The essays appeared in the *New York Journal* between October 1787 and April 1788, during which time the first seventy-seven papers of *The Federalist* also appeared. They were widely reprinted and referred to; but despite their importance and high quality, they had never been reprinted in their entirety until 1971.[4]

The essays have generally been attributed to Robert Yates on the authority of Paul Leicester Ford. The attribution is somewhat questionable, Ford himself having first attributed the essays to Thomas Treadwell (as did Samuel B. Harding), then changing his mind.[5] Ford does not give the evidence for concluding that Yates was the author. As Morton Borden correctly observes, the Brutus essays are clearly superior to the essays of Sydney, which have also been attributed to Yates;[6] if, however, the latter were written by Abraham Yates, as DePauw contends,[7] that would leave the field clear for Robert as Brutus. Ford does not give the evidence on which he formed his judgment, and no evidence one way or the other has been unearthed by the present editor.[8] (This Brutus is in any case not to be confused with Brutus [Virginia] 5.15.)

There follows an extended outline of the argument of Brutus.

Introduction—Importance of decision, need for care (I, 2.9.1–3).

I. Basic question: Is confederated government best for U.S.? (I, 2.9.1–21).

A. Government proposed is, though not perfect consolidation, so close as to terminate in it (I, 2.9.4–9).

  1. It is supreme within its sphere (necessary and proper clause); so far as its powers reach, it is a complete government, not a confederation (2.9.5).

  2. Powers are ostensibly limited but extend to everything of importance (2.9.5–9).

    a. Taxing power is complete and implies or draws with it all other powers (2.9.5).

    b. Judicial power is extensive and will eclipse state courts (2.9.7).

    c. Necessary and proper clause might be interpreted to give Congress complete control over states (2.9.8–9).

(Back then to question, 2.9.10).

B. Can free government be exercised over the whole U.S. reduced to one state? No.

  1. Authority denies it (2.9.11).

  2. History denies it (2.9.12).

  3. Reason denies it (2.9.13–20).

    a. Distinction between despotic government, pure democracy, free (representative) republic, the last being at issue here (2.9.13).

    b. Impossibility of a representation, in a country so large and populous as the U.S., that will speak the sentiments of the people without becoming too numerous for business (2.9.14–15).

    c. Free republic requires a similarity of manners, sentiments, interests in contrast to U.S. variety (2.9.16).

    d. Execution of laws in free republic depends on confidence of people, which must be lacking in so extensive a country (2.9.17–18).

    e. Legislature cannot have necessary knowledge of and time to deal with concerns and wants of different parts (2.9.19).

    f. In such an extensive republic officers of government would soon rise above control of people and abuse their power (2.9.20).

Above argument at least shows necessity, in forming government for this country, of (1) limiting and defining powers, (discussed in V–XV); (2) adjusting parts, (discussed in III, IV, XVI); (3) guarding against abuse of authority (discussed in II, 2.9.22–23).

II. Bill of Rights (II, 2.9.22–33).

A. The origins of civil government—kinds of individual rights. Foundation should be laid in express reservations by people of such of their essential national rights as are not necessary to be parted with (2.9.24; see IX, 2.9.102).

B. Bill of Rights as necessary for federal government as for states (2.9.26–33).

1. It is necessary, for example, in protection of individual in criminal prosecution (2.9.27–28).
2. It is necessary, for example, as certain provisions in proposed constitution themselves show (2.9.29–30; see IX, 2.9.103–4).
3. This is an original compact, doing away with all provisions of state constitutions that are inconsistent (2.9.31–32).
4. A Bill of Rights is all the more necessary in view of unrestrained power to make treaties, which become part of supreme law of land (2.9.33).

III. Organization of government—representation (III, IV, 2.9.34–54). (III and IV deal with the question of representation, particularly in the House of Representatives; the discussion is important but [especially IV] somewhat disorderly. The discussion may be grouped among the major headings, as follows.)

A. Representation of slaves unreasonable and unjust (III, 2.9.38–39).
B. Equal representation of states in Senate unreasonable and unjust (III, 2.9.40).
C. The representation is merely nominal—not sufficiently numerous to enable it to resemble the people, to contain representatives of several orders of people, to resist tendency of natural aristocracy to rule, to enable people to have knowledge of representatives (III, 2.9.41–42; IV, 2.9.45, 48–49).
D. There will be no security in so small a body as House of Representatives against influence and corruption (III, 2.9.42–44; IV, 2.9.47).
E. Feeble representation will not command confidence of people, which is necessary to the execution of the law in free government; thus execution by military force will be necessary (IV, 2.9.48–50).
F. Danger of "time/place/manner" provision (IV, 2.9.51–53).
G. Not sufficient to say good men will rule—constitutions are to regulate conduct of bad men (IV, 2.9.54).

IV. Legislative powers are broad and indefinite (V–X, 2.9.55–129). (Instead of proceeding with enquiry into the organization of the system, Brutus turns next to powers granted to legislature, V, 2.9.55. The discussion of organization is resumed in XVI, 2.9.197 ff.)

A. Preamble and necessary and proper clause, taken together, confer what amounts to a power to make laws at discretion. Rule of broad construction stated (V, 2.9.57).
B. Taxing power (V, VI, VIII, 2.9.55–92).
1. General welfare clause broadly construed. (V, 2.9.58; VI, 2.9.77–78).
2. The power to tax is unlimited (V, 2.9.59–60; VI, 2.9.71–78).
3. The power to tax will annihilate power of individual states (V, 2.9.61–63; VI, 2.9.64–70, 75–76).

    4. The argument that the power given to the general government must be unlimited because the exigencies of the federal government are unlimited is insufficient:

        a. National safety is not the only end; the states are responsible for managing internal concerns, which are in fact first objects of government and which also require revenue (V, 2.9.63; VI, 2.9.79–81).

        b. A distinction could have been drawn between external and internal taxes (V, 2.9.63; VII, 2.9.92).

        c. The aim of American governments is, or ought to be, not glory but domestic peace and justice (VII, 2.9.86–87).

        d. Granting the need for additional federal powers and granting that remote contingencies cannot be foreseen, yet the powers need not be unlimited, for rational judgments of need can be made (VII, 2.9.88–90).

C. Authority to borrow money is general and unlimited (VIII, 2.9.93–95).

D. Power to raise armies (VIII, IX, X, 2.9.93–129).

    1. This power is indefinite and unlimited (VIII, 2.9.96–97).

    2. Standing armies are dangerous to liberty (VIII, 2.9.99–101; IX, 2.9.105, 110; X, 2.9.115–20).

    3. Explicit prohibition of standing army is needed; a general reliance on sentiments of people and resistance of states not sufficient (IX, 2.9.106–9; X, 2.9.129).

    4. Answers to Federalist arguments of necessity of standing army and impracticality of restriction (IX, 2.9.111–14; X, 2.9.121–27).

V. Nature and extent of judicial power (XI–XV, 2.9.130–196). (This subject is little discussed in other writings, yet the real effects of the new system of government will be brought home to the people through the judiciary, which occupies a position totally independent. X, 2.9.130).

A. Judicial power of constitutional interpretation (X–XII, 2.9.115–158). (Without trying to give perfect explanation, will show that federal judiciary will subvert state judiciary, if not legislatures. XI, 2.9.133).

    1. Federal courts are vested with power to resolve, according to spirit as well as letter, all questions of construction of Constitution (XI, 2.9.134–38).

    2. Judicial power will subvert state governments and favor general government (XI, 2.9.139–44).

        a. Wide and general terms of the Constitution countenance such a construction. If necessary and proper clause does not grant additional powers, it does sanction broad construction (XI, 2.9.139–41).

        b. Court will be interested in broad interpretation (XI, 2.9.142).

        c. British precedent will favor it (XI, 2.9.143–44).

3. How judicial power will operate to extend legislative and judicial authority of federal government and finally destroy such authority of states (XII, 2.9.145–58; see XV, 2.9.194–96).

B. Other matters of which federal judiciary has cognizance (XIII–XIV, 2.9.159–85).

1. Authority in all cases arising under laws of U.S., which is proper (XIII, 2.9.159).
2. Power to decide all cases in law and equity under treaties is unintelligible—what is equity under treaty (XIII, 2.9.160)?
3. Jurisdiction over cases affecting ambassadors, where U.S. is a party, and between states is proper; but doubt if Supreme Court should have original jurisdiction (XIII, 2.9.160; XIV, 2.9.168).
4. Jurisdiction over controversies between state and citizen of another state not proper (extended discussion) (XIII, 2.9.161–67).
5. Appellate jurisdiction of Supreme Court is one of most objectionable parts of Constitution (XIV, 2.9.169).
   a. Appeals in criminal matters is new and harmful (XIV, 2.9.170–72).
   b. Appellate jurisdiction, as granted, in civil cases eliminates final jury trial of facts, despite confused denials of advocates, and will lead to great expense and delay (XIV, 173–78, 184–85).
   c. These extraordinary powers all the more objectionable because not needed; state courts provide protection of individual rights (XIV, 2.9.179–83).

C. Supreme Court under Constitution will be exalted above all other power in government and subject to no control (XV, 2.9.186–97).

1. Judges in England hold offices during good behavior but are more carefully circumscribed (2.9.187–88).
2. Proposed judiciary is independent in fullest sense; yet British reason for independence of crown does not apply here (2.9.189–90).
   a. No superior to correct errors or control decisions (2.9.191).
   b. No removal or diminution of salary for error (2.9.192).
   c. Power of Court often superior to legislature—can declare acts of legislature void (2.9.193–96).

D. Judiciary should be subject to control of some supreme body that is responsible to the people (XVI, 2.9.197).

VI. Senate (XVI, 2.9.197–204). (A very sketchy discussion).

A. Organization (2.9.198–202).

1. Election by state is proper for confederal system (2.9.198–99).
2. Term too long, and rotation and recall should be provided (2.9.200–201).

B. Powers (2.9.202–4). The Senate will possess a strange mixture of legislative, executive, and judicial powers, which will clash with each other.

1. Centinel, in his third letter (III, 2.7.77), thought that his proposed discussion of the dangers of consolidation had been rendered superfluous by the appearance of the first number of Brutus.

2. Cato contents himself with a very brief discussion of representation (V, 2.6.38), referring his reader to the able and full discussion of Brutus, which had appeared by the time Cato reached this subject.

3. Edward S. Corwin, recognizing the importance of the essays dealing with the judiciary, reprinted essays XI, XII, XV in his *Court over Constitution* (Princeton, N.J., 1938) 231–62.

4. William Jeffrey, Jr., "The Letters of Brutus—A Neglected Element in the Ratification Campaign of 1787–88," *University of Cincinnati Law Review* 40, no. 4 (1971): 643–777.

5. Ford, *Pamphlets* 117, 424; Harding, *The Contest over Ratification of the Federal Constitution in Massachusetts* 17 n. 3; Ford, *Essays* 295.

6. See below Sydney 6.9. Morton Borden, *The Antifederalist Papers* (East Lansing, Mich., 1965) 42.

7. DePauw, *The Eleventh Pillar* 131.

8. At one point Brutus disclaims the legal knowledge necessary to discuss fully the judiciary (below, XI, 2.9.132), which might seem to argue against the authorship of Yates, who was a lawyer and judge. But the legal knowledge actually displayed is considerable and argues rather in favor of Yates' authorship. William Jeffrey, Jr., makes the appealing suggestion of Melancton Smith, but the circumstantial case is not a very persuasive one. See *University of Cincinnati Law Review* 40, no. 4 (1971): 644–46.

I[1]

18 October 1787

To the Citizens of the State of New-York.

2.9.1   When the public is called to investigate and decide upon a question in which not only the present members of the community are deeply interested, but upon which the happiness and misery of generations yet unborn is in great measure suspended, the benevolent mind cannot help feeling itself peculiarly interested in the result.

In this situation, I trust the feeble efforts of an individual, to lead the minds of the people to a wise and prudent determination, cannot fail of being acceptable to the candid and dispassionate part of the community. Encouraged by this consideration, I have been induced to offer my thoughts upon the present important crisis of our public affairs.

2.9.2   Perhaps this country never saw so critical a period in their political concerns. We have felt the feebleness of the ties by which these United-States are held together, and the want of sufficient energy in our present confederation, to manage, in some instances, our general concerns. Various expedients have been proposed to remedy these evils, but none have succeeded. At length a Convention of the states has been assembled, they have formed a constitution which will now, probably, be submitted to the people to ratify or reject, who are the fountain of all power, to whom alone it of right belongs to make or unmake constitutions, or forms of government, at their pleasure. The most important question that was ever proposed to your decision, or to the decision of any people under heaven, is before you, and you are to decide upon it by men of your own election, chosen specially for this purpose. If the constitution, offered to your acceptance, be a wise one, calculated to preserve the invaluable blessings of liberty, to secure the inestimable rights of mankind, and promote human happiness, then, if you accept it, you will lay a lasting foundation of happiness for millions yet unborn; generations to come will rise up and call you blessed. You may rejoice in the prospects of this vast extended continent becoming filled with freemen, who will assert the dignity of human nature. You may solace yourselves with the idea, that society, in this favoured land, will fast advance to the highest point of perfection; the human mind will expand in knowledge and virtue, and the golden age be, in some measure, realised. But if, on the other hand, this form of government contains principles that will lead to the subversion of liberty—if it tends to establish a despotism, or, what is worse, a tyrannic aristocracy; then, if you adopt it, this only remaining assylum for liberty will be shut up, and posterity will execrate your memory.

Momentous then is the question you have to determine, and you are called upon by every motive which should influence a noble and virtuous mind, to examine it well, and to make up a wise judgment. It is insisted, indeed, that this constitution must be received, be it ever so imperfect. If it has its defects, it is said, they can be best amended when they are experienced. But remember, when the people once part with power, they can seldom or never resume it again but by force. Many instances can be produced in which the people have voluntarily increased the powers of their rulers; but few, if any, in which rulers have willingly abridged their authority. This is a sufficient reason to induce you to be careful, in the first instance, how you deposit the powers of government.   2.9.3

With these few introductory remarks, I shall proceed to a consideration of this constitution: 2.9.4

The first question that presents itself on the subject is, whether a confederated government be the best for the United States or not?[2] Or in other words, whether the thirteen United States should be reduced to one great republic, governed by one legislature, and under the direction of one executive and judicial; or whether they should continue thirteen confederated republics, under the direction and controul of a supreme federal head for certain defined national purposes only?

This enquiry is important, because, although the government reported by the convention does not go to a perfect and entire consolidation, yet it approaches so near to it, that it must, if executed, certainly and infallibly terminate in it.

2.9.5 This government is to possess absolute and uncontroulable power, legislative, executive and judicial, with respect to every object to which it extends, for by the last clause of section 8th, article 1st, it is declared "that the Congress shall have power to make all laws which shall be necessary and proper for carrying into execution the foregoing powers, and all other powers vested by this constitution, in the government of the United States; or in any department or office thereof." And by the 6th article, it is declared "that this constitution, and the laws of the United States, which shall be made in pursuance thereof, and the treaties made, or which shall be made, under the authority of the United States, shall be the supreme law of the land; and the judges in every state shall be bound thereby, any thing in the constitution, or law of any state to the contrary notwithstanding." It appears from these articles that there is no need of any intervention of the state governments, between the Congress and the people, to execute any one power vested in the general government, and that the constitution and laws of every state are nullified and declared void, so far as they are or shall be inconsistent with this constitution, or the laws made in pursuance of it, or with treaties made under the authority of the United States.—The government then, so far as it extends, is a complete one, and not a confederation. It is as much one complete government as that of New-York or Massachusetts, has as absolute and perfect powers to make and execute all laws, to appoint officers, institute courts, declare offences, and annex penalties, with respect to every object to which it extends, as any other in the world. So far therefore as its powers reach, all ideas of confederation are given up and lost. It is true this government is limited to certain objects, or to speak more properly, some small degree of power is still left to the states, but a little attention to the powers vested in the general government, will convince every candid man, that if it is capable of being executed, all that is reserved for the individual states must very soon be annihilated, except so far as they are barely necessary to the organization of the general government. The powers of the general legislature extend to every case that is of the least importance—there is nothing valuable to human nature, nothing dear to freemen, but what is within its power. It has authority to make laws which will affect the lives, the liberty, and property of every man in the United States; nor can the constitution or laws of any state, in any way prevent or impede the full and complete execution of every power given. The legislative power is competent to lay taxes, duties, imposts, and excises;[3]—there is no limitation to this power, unless it be said that the clause which directs the use to which those taxes, and duties shall be applied, may be said to be a limitation: but this is no restriction of the power at all, for by this clause they are to be applied to pay the debts and provide for the common defence and general welfare of the United States; but the legislature have authority to contract debts at their discretion; they are the sole judges of what is necessary to provide for the common defence, and they only are to determine what is for the general welfare; this power therefore is neither more nor less, than a power to lay and collect taxes, imposts, and excises, at their pleasure; not only [is] the power to lay taxes unlimited, as to the amount they may require, but it is perfect and absolute to raise them in any mode they please. No state legislature, or any power in the state governments, have any more to do in carrying this into effect, than the authority of one state has to do with that of another. In the business therefore of laying and collecting taxes, the idea of confederation is totally lost, and that of one entire republic is embraced. It is proper here to remark, that the authority to lay and collect taxes is the most important of any power that can be granted; it connects with it almost all other powers, or at least will in process of time draw all other after it; it is the great mean of protection, security, and defence, in a good government, and the great engine of oppression and tyranny in a bad one.[4] This cannot fail of being the case, if we consider the contracted limits which are set by this constitution, to the late [state?] governments, on this article of raising money. No state can emit paper money—lay any duties, or imposts, on imports, or exports, but by consent of the Congress; and then the net produce shall be for the benefit of the United States: the only mean therefore left, for any state to support its government and discharge its debts, is by direct taxation; and the United States have also power to lay and collect taxes, in any way they please. Every one who has thought on the subject, must be convinced that but small sums of money can be collected in any country, by direct taxe[s], when the foederal government begins to exercise the right of taxation in all its parts, the legislatures of the several states will find it impossible to raise monies to support their governments. Without money they cannot be supported, and they must dwindle away, and, as before observed, their powers absorbed in that of the general government.

It might be here shewn, that the power in the federal legislative, to raise and support armies at pleasure, as well in peace as in war, and their controul over the militia, tend, not only to a consolidation of the government, but the destruction of liberty.[5]—I shall not, however, dwell upon these, as a few observations upon the judicial power of this government, in addition to the preceding, will fully evince the truth of the position. 2.9.6

The judicial power of the United States is to be vested in a supreme court, and in such inferior courts as Congress may from time to time ordain and establish.[6] The powers of these courts are very extensive; their jurisdiction comprehends all civil causes, except such as arise between citizens of the same state; and it extends to all cases in law and equity arising under the constitution. One inferior court must be established, I presume, in each 2.9.7

state, at least, with the necessary executive officers appendant thereto. It is easy to see, that in the common course of things, these courts will eclipse the dignity, and take away from the respectability, of the state courts. These courts will be, in themselves, totally independent of the states, deriving their authority from the United States, and receiving from them fixed salaries; and in the course of human events it is to be expected, that they will swallow up all the powers of the courts in the respective states.

2.9.8 How far the clause in the 8th section of the 1st article may operate to do away all idea of confederated states, and to effect an entire consolidation of the whole into one general government, it is impossible to say. The powers given by this article are very general and comprehensive, and it may receive a construction to justify the passing almost any law. A power to make all laws, which shall be *necessary and proper*, for carrying into execution, all powers vested by the constitution in the government of the United States, or any department or officer thereof, is a power very comprehensive and definite [indefinite?], and may, for ought I know, be exercised in a such manner as entirely to abolish the state legislatures.[7] Suppose the legislature of a state should pass a law to raise money to support their government and pay the state debt, may the Congress repeal this law, because it may prevent the collection of a tax which they may think proper and necessary to lay, to provide for the general welfare of the United States? For all laws made, in pursuance of this constitution, are the supreme lay of the land, and the judges in every state shall be bound thereby, any thing in the constitution or laws of the different states to the contrary notwithstanding.—By such a law, the government of a particular state might be overturned at one stroke, and thereby be deprived of every means of its support.

2.9.9 It is not meant, by stating this case, to insinuate that the constitution would warrant a law of this kind; or unnecessarily to alarm the fears of the people, by suggesting, that the federal legislature would be more likely to pass the limits assigned them by the constitution, than that of an individual state, further than they are less responsible to the people. But what is meant is, that the legislature of the United States are vested with the great and uncontroulable powers, of laying and collecting taxes, duties, imposts, and excises; of regulating trade, raising and supporting armies, organizing, arming, and disciplining the militia, instituting courts, and other general powers. And are by this clause invested with the power of making all laws, *proper and necessary*, for carrying all these into execution; and they may so exercise this power as entirely to annihilate all the state governments, and reduce this country to one single government. And if they may do it, it is pretty certain they will; for it will be found that the power retained by individual states, small as it is, will be a clog upon the wheels of the government of the United States; the latter therefore will be naturally inclined to remove it out of the way. Besides, it is a truth confirmed by the unerring experience of ages, that every man, and every body of men, invested with power, are ever disposed to increase it, and to acquire a superiority over every thing that stands in their way. This disposition, which is implanted in human nature, will operate in the federal legislature to lessen and ultimately to subvert the state authority, and having such advantages, will most certainly succeed, if the federal government succeeds at all. It must be very evident then, that what this constitution wants of being a complete consolidation of the several parts of the union into one complete government, possessed of perfect legislative, judicial, and executive powers, to all intents and purposes, it will necessarily acquire in its exercise and operation.

Let us now proceed to enquire, as I at first proposed, whether it be best the thirteen United States should be reduced to one great republic, or not? It is here taken for granted, that all agree in this, that whatever government we adopt, it ought to be a free one; that it should be so framed as to secure the liberty of the citizens of America, and such an one as to admit of a full, fair, and equal representation of the people. The question then will be, whether a government thus constituted, and founded on such principles, is practicable, and can be exercised over the whole United States, reduced into one state? 2.9.10

If respect is to be paid to the opinion of the greatest and wisest men who have ever thought or wrote on the science of government, we shall be constrained to conclude, that a free republic cannot succeed over a country of such immense extent, containing such a number of inhabitants, and these encreasing in such rapid progression as that of the whole United States. Among the many illustrious authorities which might be produced to this point, I shall content myself with quoting only two. The one is the baron de Montesquieu, spirit of laws, chap. xvi. vol. I [book VIII]. "It is natural to a republic to have only a small territory, otherwise it cannot long subsist. In a large republic there are men of large fortunes, and consequently of less moderation; there are trusts too great to be placed in any single subject; he has interest of his own; he soon begins to think that he may be happy, great and glorious, by oppressing his fellow citizens; and that he may raise himself to grandeur on the ruins of his country. In a large republic, the public good is sacrificed to a thousand views; it is subordinate to exceptions, and depends on accidents. In a small one, the interest of the public is easier perceived, better understood, and more within the reach of every citizen; abuses are of less extent, and of course are less protected."[8] Of the same opinion is the marquis Beccarari. 2.9.11

History furnishes no example of a free republic, any thing like the extent of the United States. The Grecian republics were of small extent; so also was that of the Romans. Both of these, it is true, in process of time, extended their conquests over large territories of country; and the consequence was, that their governments were changed from that of free governments to those of the most tyrannical that ever existed in the world. 2.9.12

Not only the opinion of the greatest men, and the experience of mankind, 2.9.13

are against the idea of an extensive republic, but a variety of reasons may be drawn from the reason and nature of things, against it. In every government, the will of the sovereign is the law. In despotic governments, the supreme authority being lodged in one, his will is law, and can be as easily expressed to a large extensive territory as to a small one. In a pure democracy the people are the sovereign, and their will is declared by themselves; for this purpose they must all come together to deliberate, and decide. This kind of government cannot be exercised, therefore, over a country of any considerable extent; it must be confined to a single city, or at least limited to such bounds as that the people can conveniently assemble, be able to debate, understand the subject submitted to them, and declare their opinion concerning it.

2.9.14   In a free republic, although all laws are derived from the consent of the people, yet the people do not declare their consent by themselves in person, but by representatives, chosen by them, who are supposed to know the minds of their constituents, and to be possessed of integrity to declare this mind.[9]

In every free government, the people must give their assent to the laws by which they are governed. This is the true criterion between a free government and an arbitrary one. The former are ruled by the will of the whole, expressed in any manner they may agree upon; the latter by the will of one, or a few. If the people are to give their assent to the laws, by persons chosen and appointed by them, the manner of the choice and the number chosen, must be such, as to possess, be disposed, and consequently qualified to declare the sentiments of the people; for if they do not know, or are not disposed to speak the sentiments of the people, the people do not govern, but the sovereignty is in a few. Now, in a large extended country, it is impossible to have a representation, possessing the sentiments, and of integrity, to declare the minds of the people, without having it so numerous and unwieldly, as to be subject in great measure to the inconveniency of a democratic government.

2.9.15   The territory of the United States is of vast extent; it now contains near three millions of souls, and is capable of containing much more than ten times that number. Is it practicable for a country, so large and so numerous as they will soon become, to elect a representation, that will speak their sentiments, without their becoming so numerous as to be incapable of transacting public business? It certainly is not.

2.9.16   In a republic, the manners, sentiments, and interests of the people should be similar. If this be not the case, there will be a constant clashing of opinions; and the representatives of one part will be continually striving against those of the other.[10] This will retard the operations of government, and prevent such conclusions as will promote the public good. If we apply this remark to the condition of the United States, we shall be convinced that it forbids that we should be one government. The United States includes a variety of climates. The productions of the different parts of the union are very variant, and their interests, of consequence, diverse. Their manners and habits differ as much as their climates and productions; and their sentiments are by no means coincident. The laws and customs of the several states are, in many respects, very diverse, and in some opposite; each would be in favor of its own interests and customs, and, of consequence, a legislature, formed of representatives from the respective parts, would not only be too numerous to act with any care or decision, but would be composed of such heterogenous and discordant principles, as would constantly be contending with each other.

The laws cannot be executed in a republic, of an extent equal to that of the United States, with promptitude.   2.9.17

The magistrates in every government must be supported in the execution of the laws, either by an armed force, maintained at the public expence for that purpose; or by the people turning out to aid the magistrate upon his command, in case of resistance.

In despotic governments, as well as in all the monarchies of Europe, standing armies are kept up to execute the commands of the prince or the magistrate, and are employed for this purpose when occasion requires: But they have always proved the destruction of liberty, and [are] abhorrent to the spirit of a free republic. In England, where they depend upon the parliament for their annual support, they have always been complained of as oppressive and unconstitutional, and are seldom employed in executing of the laws; never except on extraordinary occasions, and then under the direction of a civil magistrate.

A free republic will never keep a standing army to execute its laws. It   2.9.18
must depend upon the support of its citizens. But when a government is to receive its support from the aid of the citizens, it must be so constructed as to have the confidence, respect, and affection of the people.[11] Men who, upon the call of the magistrate, offer themselves to execute the laws, are influenced to do it either by affection to the government, or from fear; where a standing army is at hand to punish offenders, every man is actuated by the latter principle, and therefore, when the magistrate calls, will obey: but, where this is not the case, the government must rest for its support upon the confidence and respect which the people have for their government and laws. The body of the people being attached, the government will always be sufficient to support and execute its laws, and to operate upon the fears of any faction which may be opposed to it, not only to prevent an opposition to the execution of the laws themselves, but also to compel the most of them to aid the magistrate; but the people will not be likely to have such confidence in their rulers, in a republic so extensive as the United States, as necessary for these purposes. The confidence which the people have in their rulers, in a free republic, arises from their knowing them, from their being responsible to them for their conduct, and from the power they have of displacing them

when they misbehave: but in a republic of the extent of this continent, the people in general would be acquainted with very few of their rulers: the people at large would know little of their proceedings, and it would be extremely difficult to change them. The people in Georgia and New-Hampshire would not know one another's mind, and therefore could not act in concert to enable them to effect a general change of representatives. The different parts of so extensive a country could not possibly be made acquainted with the conduct of their representatives, nor be informed of the reasons upon which measures were founded. The consequence will be, they will have no confidence in their legislature, suspect them of ambitious views, be jealous of every measure they adopt, and will not support the laws they pass.[12] Hence the government will be nerveless and inefficient, and no way will be left to render it otherwise, but by establishing an armed force to execute the laws at the point of the bayonet—a government of all others the most to be dreaded.

2.9.19   In a republic of such vast extent as the United-States, the legislature cannot attend to the various concerns and wants of its different parts. It cannot be sufficiently numerous to be acquainted with the local condition and wants of the different districts, and if it could, it is impossible it should have sufficient time to attend to and provide for all the variety of cases of this nature, that would be continually arising.

2.9.20   In so extensive a republic, the great officers of government would soon become above the controul of the people, and abuse their power to the purpose of aggrandizing themselves, and oppressing them. The trust committed to the executive offices, in a country of the extent of the United-States, must be various and of magnitude. The command of all the troops and navy of the republic, the appointment of officers, the power of pardoning offences, the collecting of all the public revenues, and the power of expending them, with a number of other powers, must be lodged and exercised in every state, in the hands of a few. When these are attended with great honor and emolument, as they always will be in large states, so as greatly to interest men to pursue them, and to be proper objects for ambitious and designing men, such men will be ever restless in their pursuit after them. They will use the power, when they have acquired it, to the purposes of gratifying their own interest and ambition, and it is scarcely possible, in a very large republic, to call them to account for their misconduct, or to prevent their abuse of power.[13]

2.9.21   These are some of the reasons by which it appears, that a free republic cannot long subsist over a country of the great extent of these states. If then this new constitution is calculated to consolidate the thirteen states into one, as it evidently is, it ought not to be adopted.

Though I am of opinion, that it is a sufficient objection to this government, to reject it, that it creates the whole union into one government, under the form of a republic, yet if this objection was obviated, there are exceptions to it, which are so material and fundamental, that they ought to determine every man, who is a friend to the liberty and happiness of mankind, not to adopt it. I beg the candid and dispassionate attention of my countrymen while I state these objections—they are such as have obtruded themselves upon my mind upon a careful attention to the matter, and such as I sincerely believe are well founded. There are many objections, of small moment, of which I shall take no notice—perfection is not to be expected in any thing that is the production of man—and if I did not in my conscience believe that this scheme was defective in the fundamental principles—in the foundation upon which a free and equal government must rest—I would hold my peace.

Brutus.

II
1 November 1787

To the Citizens of the State of New-York.

I flatter myself that my last address established this position, that to reduce the Thirteen States into one government, would prove the destruction of your liberties.

2.9.22

But lest this truth should be doubted by some, I will now proceed to consider its merits.

Though it should be admitted, that the argument[s] against reducing all the states into one consolidated government, are not sufficient fully to establish this point; yet they will, at least, justify this conclusion, that in forming a constitution for such a country, great care should be taken to limit and definite its powers, adjust its parts, and guard against an abuse of authority. How far attention has been paid to these objects, shall be the subject of future enquiry. When a building is to be erected which is intended to stand for ages, the foundation should be firmly laid. The constitution proposed to your acceptance, is designed not for yourselves alone, but for generations yet unborn. The principles, therefore, upon which the social compact is founded, ought to have been clearly and precisely stated, and the most express and full declaration of rights to have been made—But on this subject there is almost an entire silence.

2.9.23

If we may collect the sentiments of the people of America, from their own most solemn declarations, they hold this truth as self evident, that all men are by nature free. No one man, therefore, or any class of men, have a right, by the law of nature, or of God, to assume or exercise authority over their fellows. The origin of society then is to be sought, not in any natural right which one man has to exercise authority over another, but in the united

2.9.24

consent of those who associate. The mutual wants of men, at first dictated the propriety of forming societies; and when they were established, protection and defence pointed out the necessity of instituting government. In a state of nature every individual pursues his own interest; in this pursuit it frequently happened, that the possessions or enjoyments of one were sacrificed to the views and designs of another; thus the weak were a prey to the strong, the simple and unwary were subject to impositions from those who were more crafty and designing. In this state of things, every individual was insecure; common interest therefore directed, that government should be established, in which the force of the whole community should be collected, and under such directions, as to protect and defend every one who composed it. The common good, therefore, is the end of civil government, and common consent, the foundation on which it is established. To effect this end, it was necessary that a certain portion of natural liberty should be surrendered, in order, that what remained should be preserved: how great a proportion of natural freedom is necessary to be yielded by individuals, when they submit to government, I shall not now enquire. So much, however, must be given up, as will be sufficient to enable those, to whom the administration of the government is committed, to establish laws for the promoting the happiness of the community, and to carry those laws into effect. But it is not necessary, for this purpose, that individuals should relinquish all their natural rights. Some are of such a nature that they cannot be surrendered. Of this kind are the rights of conscience, the right of enjoying and defending life, etc. Others are not necessary to be resigned, in order to attain the end for which government is instituted, these therefore ought not to be given up. To surrender them, would counteract the very end of government, to wit, the common good.[14] From these observations it appears, that in forming a government on its true principles, the foundation should be laid in the manner I before stated, by expressly reserving to the people such of their essential natural rights, as are not necessary to be parted with.[15] The same reasons which at first induced mankind to associate and institute government, will operate to influence them to observe this precaution. If they had been disposed to conform themselves to the rule of immutable righteousness, government would not have been requisite. It was because one part exercised fraud, oppression, and violence on the other, that men came together, and agreed that certain rules should be formed, to regulate the conduct of all, and the power of the whole community lodged in the hands of rulers to enforce an obedience to them. But rulers have the same propensities as other men; they are as likely to use the power with which they are vested for private purposes, and to the injury and oppression of those over whom they are placed, as individuals in a state of nature are to injure and oppress one another. It is therefore as proper that bounds should be set to their authority, as that government should have at first been instituted to restrain private injuries.[16]

This principle, which seems so evidently founded in the reason and nature of things, is confirmed by universal experience. Those who have governed, have been found in all ages ever active to enlarge their powers and abridge the public liberty. This has induced the people in all countries, where any sense of freedom remained, to fix barriers against the encroachments of their rulers. The country from which we have derived our origin, is an eminent example of this. Their magna charta and bill of rights have long been the boast, as well as the security, of that nation. I need say no more, I presume, to an American, than, that this principle is a fundamental one, in all the constitutions of our own states; there is not one of them but what is either founded on a declaration or bill of rights, or has certain express reservation of rights interwoven in the body of them. From this it appears, that at a time when the pulse of liberty beat high and when an appeal was made to the people to form constitutions for the government of themselves, it was their universal sense, that such declarations should make a part of their frames of government. It is therefore the more astonishing, that this grand security, to the rights of the people, is not to be found in this constitution.

2.9.25

It has been said, in answer to this objection, that such declaration[s] of rights, however requisite they might be in the constitutions of the states, are not necessary in the general constitution, because, "in the former case, every thing which is not reserved is given, but in the latter the reverse of the proposition prevails, and every thing which is not given is reserved."[17] It requires but little attention to discover, that this mode of reasoning is rather specious than solid. The powers, rights, and authority, granted to the general government by this constitution, are as complete, with respect to every object to which they extend, as that of any state government—It reaches to every thing which concerns human happiness—Life, liberty, and property, are under its controul. There is the same reason, therefore, that the exercise of power, in this case, should be restrained within proper limits, as in that of the state governments. To set this matter in a clear light, permit me to instance some of the articles of the bills of rights of the individual states, and apply them to the case in question.[18]

2.9.26

For the security of life, in criminal prosecutions, the bills of rights of most of the states have declared, that no man shall be held to answer for a crime until he is made fully acquainted with the charge brought against him; he shall not be compelled to accuse, or furnish evidence against himself—The witnesses against him shall be brought face to face, and he shall be fully heard by himself or counsel. That it is essential to the security of life and liberty, that trial of facts be in the vicinity where they happen. Are not provisions of this kind as necessary in the general government, as in that of a particular state? The powers vested in the new Congress extend in many cases to life; they are authorised to provide for the punishment of a variety of capital crimes, and no restraint is laid upon them in its exercise, save

2.9.27

only, that "the trial of all crimes, except in cases of impeachment, shall be by jury; and such trial shall be in the state where the said crimes shall have been committed." No man is secure of a trial in the county where he is charged to have committed a crime; he may be brought from Niagara to New-York, or carried from Kentucky to Richmond for trial for an offence, supposed to be committed. What security is there, that a man shall be furnished with a full and plain description of the charges against him? That he shall be allowed to produce all proof he can in his favor? That he shall see the witnesses against him face to face, or that he shall be fully heard in his own defence by himself or counsel?

2.9.28   For the security of liberty it has been declared, "that excessive bail should not be required, nor excessive fines imposed, nor cruel or unusual punishments inflicted—That all warrants, without oath or affirmation, to search suspected places, or seize any person, his papers or property, are grievous and oppressive."[19]

These provisions are as necessary under the general government as under that of the individual states; for the power of the former is as complete to the purpose of requiring bail, imposing fines, inflicting punishments, granting search warrants, and seizing persons, papers, or property, in certain cases, as the other.

2.9.29   For the purpose of securing the property of the citizens, it is declared by all the states, "that in all controversies at law, respecting property, the ancient mode of trial by jury is one of the best securities of the rights of the people, and ought to remain sacred and inviolable."[20]

Does not the same necessity exist of reserving this right, under this national compact, as in that of these states? Yet nothing is said respecting it. In the bills of rights of the states it is declared, that a well regulated militia is the proper and natural defence of a free government—That as standing armies in time of peace are dangerous, they are not to be kept up, and that the military should be kept under strict subordination to, and controuled by the civil power.[21]

The same security is as necessary in this constitution, and much more so; for the general government will have the sole power to raise and to pay armies, and are under no controul in the exercise of it; yet nothing of this is to be found in this new system.

2.9.30   I might proceed to instance a number of other rights, which were as necessary to be reserved, such as, that elections should be free, that the liberty of the press should be held sacred; but the instances adduced, are sufficient to prove, that this argument is without foundation.—Besides, it is evident, that the reason here assigned was not the true one, why the framers of this constitution omitted a bill of rights; if it had been, they would not have made certain reservations, while they totally omitted others of more importance. We find they have, in the 9th section of the 1st article, declared, that the writ of habeas corpus shall not be suspended, unless in cases of rebellion—that no bill of attainder, or expost facto law, shall be passed— that no title of nobility shall be granted by the United States, &c. If every thing which is not given is reserved, what propriety is there in these excep- tions?[22] Does this constitution any where grant the power of suspending the habeas corpus, to make expost facto laws, pass bills of attainder, or grant titles of nobility? It certainly does not in express terms. The only answer that can be given is, that these are implied in the general powers granted. With equal truth it may be said, that all the powers, which the bills of right, guard against the abuse of, are contained or implied in the general ones granted by this constitution.

So far it is from being true, that a bill of rights is less necessary in the general constitution than in those of the states, the contrary is evidently the fact.—This system, if it is possible for the people of America to accede to it, will be an original compact; and being the last, will, in the nature of things, vacate every former agreement inconsistent with it. For it being a plan of government received and ratified by the whole people, all other forms, which are in existence at the time of its adoption, must yield to it. This is expressed in positive and unequivocal terms, in the 6th article, "That this constitution and the laws of the United States, which shall be made in pursuance thereof, and all treaties made, or which shall be made, under the authority of the United States, shall be the supreme law of the land; and the judges in every state shall be bound thereby, any thing in the *constitution*, or laws of any state, *to the contrary* notwithstanding.

"The senators and representatives before-mentioned, and the members of the several state legislatures, and all executive and judicial officers, both of the United States, and of the several states, shall be bound, by oath or affirmation, to support this constitution."

It is therefore not only necessarily implied thereby, but positively ex- pressed, that the different state constitutions are repealed and entirely done away, so far as they are inconsistent with this, with the laws which shall be made in pursuance thereof, or with treaties made, or which shall be made, under the authority of the United States; of what avail will the constitutions of the respective states be to preserve the rights of its citizens? should they be plead, the answer would be, the constitution of the United States, and the laws made in pursuance thereof, is the supreme law, and all legislatures and judicial officers, whether of the general or state governments, are bound by oath to support it. No priviledge, reserved by the bills of rights, or secured by the state government, can limit the power granted by this, or restrain any laws made in pursuance of it. It stands therefore on its own bottom, and must receive a construction by itself without any reference to any other[23]—And hence it was of the highest importance, that the most precise and express declarations and reservations of rights should have been made.

This will appear the more necessary, when it is considered, that not only the constitution and laws made in pursuance thereof, but all treaties made,

2.9.31

2.9.32

2.9.33

or which shall be made, under the authority of the United States, are the supreme law of the land, and supersede the constitutions of all the states. The power to make treaties, is vested in the president, by and with the advice and consent of two thirds of the senate. I do not find any limitation, or restriction, to the exercise of this power. The most important article in any constitution may therefore be repealed, even without a legislative act. Ought not a government, vested with such extensive and indefinite authority, to have been restricted by a declaration of rights? It certainly ought.

So clear a point is this, that I cannot help suspecting, that persons who attempt to persuade people, that such reservations were less necessary under this constitution than under those of the states, are wilfully endeavouring to deceive, and to lead you into an absolute state of vassalage.

Brutus.

III

15 November 1787

To the Citizens of the State of New-York.

2.9.34 In the investigation of the constitution, under your consideration, great care should be taken, that you do not form your opinions respecting it, from unimportant provisions, or fallacious appearances.

On a careful examination, you will find, that many of its parts, of little moment, are well formed; in these it has a specious resemblance of a free government—but this is not sufficient to justify the adoption of it—the gilded pill, is often found to contain the most deadly poison.

2.9.35 You are not however to expect, a perfect form of government, any more than to meet with perfection in man; your views therefore, ought to be directed to the main pillars upon which a free government is to rest; if these are well placed, on a foundation that will support the superstructure, you should be satisfied, although the building may want a number of ornaments, which, if your particular tastes were gratified, you would have added to it: on the other hand, if the foundation is insecurely laid, and the main supports are wanting, or not properly fixed, however the fabric may be decorated and adorned, you ought to reject it.

2.9.36 Under these impressions, it has been my object to turn your attention to the principal defects in this system.

I have attempted to shew, that a consolidation of this extensive continent, under one government, for internal, as well as external purposes, which is evidently the tendency of this constitution, cannot succeed, without a sacrifice of your liberties; and therefore that the attempt is not only preposterous, but extremely dangerous; and I have shewn, independent of this, that the plan is radically defective in a fundamental principle, which ought to be found in every free government; to wit, a declaration of rights.

I shall now proceed to take a nearer view of this system, to examine its parts more minutely, and shew that the powers are not properly deposited, for the security of public liberty.   2.9.37

The first important object that presents itself in the organization of this government, is the legislature. This is to be composed of two branches; the first to be called the general assembly, and is to be chosen by the people of the respective states, in proportion to the number of their inhabitants, and is to consist of sixty five members, with powers in the legislature to encrease the number, not to exceed one for every thirty thousand inhabitants. The second branch is to be called the senate, and is to consist of twenty-six members, two of which are to be chosen by the legislatures of each of the states.

In the former of these there is an appearance of justice, in the appoint-   2.9.38
ment of its members—but if the clause, which provides for this branch, be stripped of its ambiguity, it will be found that there is really no equality of representation, even in this house.

The words are "representatives and direct taxes, shall be apportioned among the several states, which may be included in this union, according to their respective numbers, which shall be determined by adding to the whole number of free persons, including those bound to service for a term of years, and excluding Indians not taxed, three fifths of all other persons."—What a strange and unnecessary accumulation of words are here used to conceal from the public eye, what might have been expressed in the following concise manner. Representatives are to be proportioned among the states respectively, according to the number of freemen and slaves inhabiting them, counting five slaves for three free men.

"In a free state," says the celebrated Montesquieu, "every man, who is   2.9.39
supposed to be a free agent, ought to be concerned in his own government, therefore the legislature should reside in the whole body of the people, or their representatives."[24] But it has never been alledged that those who are not free agents, can, upon any rational principle, have any thing to do in government, either by themselves or others. If they have no share in government, why is the number of members in the assembly, to be increased on their account? Is it because in some of the states, a considerable part of the property of the inhabitants consists in a number of their fellow men, who are held in bondage, in defiance of every idea of benevolence, justice, and religion, and contrary to all the principles of liberty, which have been publickly avowed in the late glorious revolution? If this be a just ground for representation, the horses in some of the states, and the oxen in others, ought to be represented—for a great share of property in some of them, consists in these animals; and they have as much controul over their own

actions, as these poor unhappy creatures, who are intended to be described in the above recited clause, by the words, "all other persons." By this mode of apportionment, the representatives of the different parts of the union, will be extremely unequal; in some of the southern states, the slaves are nearly equal in number to the free men; and for all these slaves, they will be entitled to a proportionate share in the legislature—this will give them an unreasonable weight in the government, which can derive no additional strength, protection, nor defence from the slaves, but the contrary. Why then should they be represented? What adds to the evil is, that these states are to be permitted to continue the inhuman traffic of importing slaves, until the year 1808—and for every cargo of these unhappy people, which unfeeling, unprincipled, barbarous, and avaricious wretches, may tear from their country, friends and tender connections, and bring into those states, they are to be rewarded by having an increase of members in the general assembly.

2.9.40   There[25] appears at the first view a manifest inconsistency, in the apportionment of representatives in the senate, upon the plan of a consolidated government.[26] On every principle of equity, and propriety, representation in a government should be in exact proportion to the numbers, or the aids afforded by the persons represented. How unreasonable, and unjust then is it, that Delaware should have a representation in the senate, equal to Massachusetts, or Virginia? The latter of which contains ten times her numbers, and is to contribute to the aid of the general government in that proportion? This article of the constitution will appear the more objectionable, if it is considered, that the powers vested in this branch of the legislature are very extensive, and greatly surpass those lodged in the assembly, not only for general purposes, but, in many instances, for the internal police of the states. The other branch of the legislature, in which, if in either, a f[a]int spark of democracy is to be found, should have been properly organized and established—but upon examination you will find, that this branch does not possess the qualities of a just representation, and that there is no kind of security, imperfect as it is, for its remaining in the hands of the people.

2.9.41   It has been observed, that the happiness of society is the end of government—that every free government is founded in compact; and that, because it is impracticable for the whole community to assemble, or when assembled, to deliberate with wisdom, and decide with dispatch, the mode of legislating by representation was devised.[27]

2.9.42   The very term, representative, implies, that the person or body chosen for this purpose, should resemble those who appoint them—a representation of the people of America, if it be a true one, must be like the people. It ought to be so constituted, that a person, who is a stranger to the country, might be able to form a just idea of their character, by knowing that of their representatives. They are the sign—the people are the thing signified. It is absurd to speak of one thing being the representative of another, upon any other principle. The ground and reason of representation, in a free government, implies the same thing. Society instituted government to promote the happiness of the whole, and this is the great end always in view in the delegation of powers. It must then have been intended, that those who are placed instead of the people, should possess their sentiments and feelings, and be governed by their interests, or, in other words, should bear the strongest resemblance of those in whose room they are substituted. It is obvious, that for an assembly to be a true likeness of the people of any country, they must be considerably numerous.—One man, or a few men, cannot possibly represent the feelings, opinions, and characters of a great multitude. In this respect, the new constitution is radically defective.—The house of assembly, which is intended as a representation of the people of America, will not, nor cannot, in the nature of things, be a proper one—sixty-five men cannot be found in the United States, who hold the sentiments, possess the feelings, or are acqainted with the wants and interests of this vast country. This extensive continent is made up of a number of different classes of people; and to have a proper representation of them, each class ought to have an opportunity of choosing their best informed men for the purpose; but this cannot possibly be the case in so small a number. The state of New-York, on the present apportionment, will send six members to the assembly: I will venture to affirm, that number cannot be found in the state, who will bear a just resemblance to the several classes of people who compose it. In this assembly, the farmer, merchant, mecanick, and other various orders of people, ought to be represented according to their respective weight and numbers; and the representatives ought to be intimately acquainted with the wants, understand the interests of the several orders in the society, and feel a proper sense and becoming zeal to promote their prosperity. I cannot conceive that any six men in this state can be found properly qualified in these respects to discharge such important duties: but supposing it possible to find them, is there the least degree of probability that the choice of the people will fall upon such men? According to the common course of human affairs, the natural aristocracy of the country will be elected.[28] Wealth always creates influence, and this is generally much increased by large family connections: this class in society will for ever have a great number of dependents; besides, they will always favour each other—it is their interest to combine—they will therefore constantly unite their efforts to procure men of their own rank to be elected—they will concenter all their force in every part of the state into one point, and by acting together, will most generally carry their election. It is probable, that but few of the merchants, and those the most opulent and ambitious, will have a representation from their body—few of them are characters sufficiently conspicuous to attract the notice of the electors of the state in so limited a representation. The great body of the yeomen of the country cannot expect any of their order in this assembly—the station will be too elevated for them to aspire to—the distance between the people and their representatives, will be so very great, that there is no probability that a farmer, however respectable, will be chosen—the mechanicks of every branch, must expect to be excluded from a seat in this Body—It will and must be esteemed a station too high and exalted to be filled by any but the first men in the state, in point of fortune; so that in reality there will be no part of the people represented, but the rich, even in that branch of the legislature, which is called the democratic.—The well born, and highest orders in life, as they term themselves, will be ignorant of the sentiments of the midling class of citizens, strangers to their ability, wants, and difficulties, and void of sympathy, and fellow feeling. This branch of the legislature will not only be an imperfect representation, but there will be no security in so small a body, against bribery, and corruption—It will consist at first, of sixty-five, and can never exceed one for every thirty thousand inhabitants; a majority of these, that is, thirty-three, are a quorum, and a majority of which, or seventeen, may pass any law—so that twenty-five men, will have the power to give away all the property of the citizens of these states—what security therefore can there be for the people, where their liberties and property are at the disposal of so few men? It will literally be a government in the hands of the few to oppress and plunder the many. You may conclude with a great degree of certainty, that it, like all others of a similar nature, will be managed by influence and corruption, and that the period is not far distant, when this will be the case, if it should be adopted; for even now there are some among us, whose characters stand high in the public estimation, and who have had a principal agency in framing this constitution, who do not scruple to say, that this is the only practicable mode of governing a people, who think with that degree of freedom which the Americans do[29]—this government will have in their gift a vast number of offices of great honor and emolument. The members of the legislature are not excluded from appointments; and twenty-five of them, as the case may be, being secured, any measure may be carried.

2.9.43   The rulers of this country must be composed of very different materials from those of any other, of which history gives us any account, if the majority of the legislature are not, before many years, entirely at the devotion of the executive—and these states will soon be under the absolute domination of one, or a few, with the fallacious appearance of being governed by men of their own election.

2.9.44   The more I reflect on this subject, the more firmly am I persuaded, that the representation is merely nominal—a mere burlesque; and that no security is provided against corruption and undue influence. No free people on earth, who have elected persons to legislate for them, ever reposed that confidence in so small a number. The British house of commons consists of five hundred and fifty-eight members; the number of inhabitants in Great-Britain, is computed at eight millions—this gives one member for a little more than fourteen thousand, which exceeds double the proportion this country can ever have: and yet we require a larger representation in proportion to our numbers, than Great-Britain, because this country is much more extensive, and differs more in its productions, interests, manners, and habits. The democratic branch of the legislatures of the several states in the union consists, I believe at present, of near two thousand; and this number was not thought too large for the security of liberty by the framers of our state constitutions: some of the states may have erred in this respect, but the difference between two thousand, and sixty-five, is so very great, that it will bear no comparison.

Other objections offer themselves against this part of the constitution—I shall reserve them for a future paper,[30] when I shall shew, defective as this representation is, no security is provided, that even this shadow of the right, will remain with the people.

Brutus.

IV

29 November 1787

To the People of the State of New-York.

There can be no free government where the people are not possessed of the power of making the laws by which they are governed, either in their own persons, or by others substituted in their stead.

2.9.45

Experience has taught mankind, that legislation by representatives is the most eligible, and the only practicable mode in which the people of any country can exercise this right, either prudently or beneficially. But then, it is a matter of the highest importance, in forming this representation, that it be so constituted as to be capable of understanding the true interests of the society for which it acts, and so disposed as to pursue the good and happiness of the people as its ultimate end. The object of every free government is the public good, and all lesser interests yield to it. That of every tyrannical government, is the happiness and aggrandisement of one, or a few, and to this the public felicity, and every other interest must submit.[31]—The reason of this difference in these governments is obvious. The first is so constituted as to collect the views and wishes of the whole people in that of their rulers, while the latter is so framed as to separate the interests of the governors from that of the governed. The principle of self love, therefore, that will influence the one to promote the good of the whole, will prompt the other to follow its own private advantage. The great art, therefore, in forming a good constitution, appears to be this, so to frame it, as that those to whom the

127

power is committed shall be subject to the same feelings, and aim at the same objects as the people do, who transfer to them their authority. There is no possible way to effect this but by an equal, full and fair representation; this, therefore, is the great desideratum in politics. However fair an appearance any government may make, though it may possess a thousand plausible articles and be decorated with ever so many ornaments, yet if it is deficient in this essential principle of a full and just representation of the people, it will be only like a painted sepulcher—For, without this it cannot be a free government; let the administration of it be good or ill, it still will be a government, not according to the will of the people, but according to the will of a few.

2.9.46   To test this new constitution then, by this principle, is of the last importance—It is to bring it to the touch-stone of national liberty, and I hope I shall be excused, if, in this paper, I pursue the subject commenced in my last number, to wit, the necessity of an equal and full representation in the legislature.—In that, I showed that it was not equal, because the smallest states are to send the same number of members to the senate as the largest, and, because the slaves, who afford neither aid or defence to the government, are to encrease the proportion of members. To prove that it was not a just or adequate representation, it was urged, that so small a number could not resemble the people, or possess their sentiments and dispositions. That the choice of members would commonly fall upon the rich and great, while the middling class of the community would be excluded. That in so small a representation there was no security against bribery and corruption.

2.9.47   The small number which is to compose this legislature, will not only expose it to the danger of that kind of corruption, and undue influence, which will arise from the gift of places of honor and emolument, or the more direct one of bribery, but it will also subject it to another kind of influence no less fatal to the liberties of the people, though it be not so flagrantly repugnant to the principles of rectitude. It is not to be expected that a legislature will be found in any country that will not have some of its members, who will pursue their private ends, and for which they will sacrifice the public good. Men of this character are, generally, artful and designing, and frequently possess brilliant talents and abilities; they commonly act in concert, and agree to share the spoils of their country among them; they will keep their object ever in view, and follow it with constancy. To effect their purpose, they will assume any shape, and, Proteus like, mould themselves into any form—where they find members proof against direct bribery or gifts of offices, they will endeavor to mislead their minds by specious and false reasoning, to impose upon their unsuspecting honesty by an affectation of zeal for the public good; they will form juntos, and hold out-door meetings; they will operate upon the good nature of their opponents, by a thousand little attentions, and teize them into compliance by the earnestness of so-

licitation. Those who are acquainted with the manner of conducting business in public assemblies, know how prevalent art and address are in carrying a measure, even over men of the best intentions, and of good understanding. The firmest security against this kind of improper and dangerous
influence, as well as all other, is a strong and numerous representation: in
such a house of assembly, so great a number must be gained over, before the
private views of individuals could be gratified that there could be scarce a
hope of success. But in the foederai assembly, seventeen men are all that is
necessary to pass a law. It is probable, it will seldom happen that more than
twenty-five will be requisite to form a majority, when it is considered what a
number of places of honor and emolument will be in the gift of the executive, the powerful influence that great and designing men have over the
honest and unsuspecting, by their art and address, their soothing manners
and civilities, and their cringing flattery, joined with their affected patriotism; when these different species of influence are combined, it is
scarcely to be hoped that a legislature, composed of so small a number, as
the one proposed by the new constitution, will long resist their force.

A[32] farther objection against the feebleness of the representation is, that it
will not possess the confidence of the people. The execution of the laws in a
free government must rest on this confidence, and this must be founded on
the good opinion they entertain of the framers of the laws. Every government must be supported, either by the people having such an attachment to
it, as to be ready, when called upon, to support it, or by a force at the
command of the government, to compel obedience. The latter mode destroys every idea of a free government; for the same force that may be
employed to compel obedience to good laws, might, and probably would be
used to wrest from the people their constitutional liberties.—Whether it is
practicable to have a representation for the whole union sufficiently numerous to obtain that confidence which is necessary for the purpose of internal
taxation, and other powers to which this proposed government extends, is
an important question. I am clearly of opinion, it is not, and therefore I have
stated this in my first number, as one of the reasons against going into an
entire consolidation[33] of the states—one of the most capital errors in the
system, is that of extending the powers of the foederal government to objects to which it is not adequate, which it cannot exercise without endangering public liberty, and which it is not necessary they should possess, in
order to preserve the union and manage our national concerns; of this,
however, I shall treat more fully in some future paper[34]—But, however this
may be, certain it is, that the representation in the legislature is not so
formed as to give reasonable ground for public trust.

2.9.48

In order for the people safely to repose themselves on their rulers, they
should not only be of their own choice. But it is requisite they should be
acquainted with their abilities to manage the public concerns with wisdom.
They should be satisfied that those who represent them are men of integrity,

2.9.49

who will pursue the good of the community with fidelity; and will not be turned aside from their duty by private interest, or corrupted by undue influence; and that they will have such a zeal for the good of those whom they represent, as to excite them to be diligent in their service; but it is impossible the people of the United States should have sufficient knowledge of their representatives, when the numbers are so few, to acquire any rational satisfaction on either of these points. The people of this state will have very little acquaintance with those who may be chosen to represent them; a great part of them will, probably, not know the characters of their own members, much less that of a majority of those who will compose the foederal assembly; they will consist of men, whose names they have never heard, and whose talents and regard for the public good, they are total strangers to;[35] and they will have no persons so immediately of their choice so near them, of their neighbours and of their own rank in life, that they can feel themselves secure in trusting their interests in their hands. The representatives of the people cannot, as they now do, after they have passed laws, mix with the people, and explain to them the motives which induced the adoption of any measure, point out its utility, and remove objections or silence unreasonable clamours against it.—The number will be so small that but a very few of the most sensible and respectable yeomanry of the country can ever have any knowledge of them: being so far removed from the people, their station will be elevated and important, and they will be considered as ambitious and designing. They will not be viewed by the people as part of themselves, but as a body distinct from them, and having separate interests to pursue; the consequence will be, that a perpetual jealousy will exist in the minds of the people against them; their conduct will be narrowly watched; their measures scrutinized; and their laws opposed, evaded, or reluctantly obeyed. This is natural, and exactly corresponds with the conduct of individuals towards those in whose hands they intrust important concerns. If the person confided in, be a neighbour with whom his employer is intimately acquainted, whose talents, he knows, are sufficient to manage the business with which he is charged, his honesty and fidelity unsuspected, and his friendship and zeal for the service of this principal unquestionable, he will commit his affairs into his hands with unreserved confidence, and feel himself secure; all the transactions of the agent will meet with the most favorable construction, and the measures he takes will give satisfaction. But, if the person employed be a stranger, whom he has never seen, and whose character for ability or fidelity he cannot fully learn—If he is constrained to choose him, because it was not in his power to procure one more agreeable to his wishes, he will trust him with caution, and be suspicious of all his conduct.

2.9.50   If then this government should not derive support from the good will of the people, it must be executed by force, or not executed at all; either case would lead to the total destruction of liberty.—The convention seemed aware of this, and have therefore provided for calling out the militia to execute the laws of the union. If this system was so framed as to command that respect from the people, which every good free government will obtain, this provision was unnecessary—the people would support the civil magistrate.[36] This power is a novel one, in free governments—these have depended for the execution of the laws on the Posse Comitatus, and never raised an idea, that the people would refuse to aid the civil magistrate in executing those laws they themselves had made. I shall now dismiss the subject of the incompetency of the representation, and proceed, as I promised, to shew, that, impotent as it is, the people have no security that they will enjoy the exercise of the right of electing this assembly, which, at best, can be considered but as the shadow of representation.

By section 4, article 1, the Congress are authorized, at any time, by law, to make, or alter, regulations respecting the time, place, and manner of holding elections for senators and representatives, except as to the places of choosing senators. By this clause the right of election itself, is, in a great measure, transferred from the people to their rulers.—One would think, that if any thing was necessary to be made a fundamental article of the original compact, it would be, that of fixing the branches of the legislature, so as to put it out of its power to alter itself by modifying the election of its own members at will and pleasure. When a people once resign the privilege of a fair election, they clearly have none left worth contending for. 2.9.51

It is clear that, under this article, the foederal legislature may institute such rules respecting elections as to lead to the choice of one description of men. The weakness of the representation, tends but too certainly to confer on the rich and *well-born*, all honours; but the power granted in this article, may be so exercised, as to secure it almost beyond a possibility of controul. The proposed Congress may make the whole state one district, and direct, that the capital (the city of New-York, for instance) shall be the place for holding the election; the consequence would be, that none but men of the most elevated rank in society would attend, and they would as certainly choose men of their own class; as it is true what the *Apostle Paul* saith, that "no man ever yet hated his own flesh, but nourisheth and cherisheth it."[37]—They may declare that those members who have the greatest number of votes, shall be considered as duly elected; the consequence would be that the people, who are dispersed in the interior parts of the state, would give their votes for a variety of candidates, while any order, or profession, residing in populous places, by uniting their interests, might procure whom they pleased to be chosen—and by this means the representatives of the state may be elected by one tenth part of the people who actually vote. This may be effected constitutionally, and by one of those silent operations which frequently takes place without being noticed, but which often produces such changes as entirely to alter a government, subvert a free constitution, and rivet the chains on a free people before they 2.9.52

perceive they are forged. Had the power of regulating elections been left under the direction of the state legislatures, where the people are not only nominally but substantially represented, it would have been secure; but if it was taken out of their hands, it surely ought to have been fixed on such a basis as to have put it out of the power of the foederal legislature to deprive the people of it by law. Provision should have been made for marking out the states into districts, and for choosing, by a majority of votes, a person out of each of them of permanent property and residence in the district which he was to represent.

2.9.53   If the people of America will submit to a constitution that will vest in the hands of any body of men a right to deprive them by law of the privilege of a fair election, they will submit to almost any thing. Reasoning with them will be in vain, they must be left until they are brought to reflection by feeling oppression—they will then have to wrest from their oppressors, by a strong hand, that which they now possess, and which they may retain if they will exercise but a moderate share of prudence and firmness.

2.9.54   I know it is said that the dangers apprehended from this clause are merely imaginary, that the proposed general legislature will be disposed to regulate elections upon proper principles, and to use their power with discretion, and to promote the public good. On this, I would observe, that constitutions are not so necessary to regulate the conduct of good rulers as to restrain that of bad ones.—Wise and good men will exercise power so as to promote the public happiness under any form of government. If we are to take it for granted, that those who administer the government under this system, will always pay proper attention to the rights and interests of the people, nothing more was necessary than to say who should be invested with the powers of government, and leave them to exercise it at will and pleasure. Men are apt to be deceived both with respect to their own dispositions and those of others. Though this truth is proved by almost every page of the history of nations, to wit, that power, lodged in the hands of rulers to be used at discretion, is almost always exercised to the oppression of the people, and the aggrandizement of themselves; yet most men think if it was lodged in their hands they would not employ it in this manner.—Thus when the prophet *Elisha* told *Hazael,* "I know the evil that thou wilt do unto the children of Israel; their strong holds wilt thou set on fire, and their young men, wilt thou slay with the sword, and wilt dash their children, and rip up their women with child." Hazael had no idea that he ever should be guilty of such horrid cruelty, and said to the prophet, "Is thy servant a dog that he should do this great thing." Elisha answered, "The Lord hath shewed me that thou shalt be king of Syria."[38] The event proved, that Hazael only wanted an opportunity to perpetrate these enormities without restraint, and he had a disposition to do them, though he himself knew it not.

Brutus.

V

13 December 1787

To the People of the State of New-York.

It was intended in this Number to have prosecuted the enquiry into the organization of this new system; particularly to have considered the dangerous and premature union of the President and Senate, and the mixture of legislative, executive, and judicial powers in the Senate.

2.9.55

But there is such an intimate connection between the several branches in whom the different species of authority is lodged, and the powers with which they are invested, that on reflection it seems necessary first to proceed to examine the nature and extent of the powers granted to the legislature.

This enquiry will assist us the better to determine, whether the legislature is so constituted, as to provide proper checks and restrictions for the security of our rights, and to guard against the abuse of power—For the means should be suited to the end; a government should be framed with a view to the objects to which it extends: if these be few in number, and of such a nature as to give but small occasion or opportunity to work oppression in the exercise of authority, there will be less need of a numerous representation, and special guards against abuse, than if the powers of the government are very extensive, and include a great variety of cases.[39] It will also be found necessary to examine the extent of these powers, in order to form a just opinion how far this system can be considered as a confederation, or a consolidation of the states. Many of the advocates for, and most of the opponents to this system, agree that the form of government most suitable for the United States, is that of a confederation.[40] The idea of a confederated government is that of a number of independent states entering into a compact, for the conducting certain general concerns, in which they have a common interest, leaving the management of their internal and local affairs to their separate governments. But whether the system proposed is of this nature cannot be determined without a strict enquiry into the powers proposed to be granted.

2.9.56

This constitution considers the people of the several states as one body corporate, and is intended as an original compact, it will therefore dissolve all contracts which may be inconsistent with it. This not only results from its nature, but is expressly declared in the *6th article* of it. The design of the constitution is expressed in the preamble, to be, "in order to form a more perfect union, to establish justice, insure domestic tranquility, provide for the common defence, promote the general welfare, and secure the blessings of liberty to ourselves and posterity." These are the ends this government is to accomplish, and for which it is invested with certain powers, among these

2.9.57

is the power "to make all laws which are *necessary and proper* for carrying into execution the foregoing powers, and *all other* powers vested by this constitution in the government of the United States, or in any department or officer thereof." It is a rule in construing a law to consider the objects the legislature had in view in passing it, and to give it such an explanation as to promote their intention. The same rule will apply in explaining a constitution. The great objects then are declared in this preamble in general and indefinite terms to be to provide for the common defence, promote the general welfare, and an express power being vested in the legislature to make all laws which shall be necessary and proper for carrying into execution all the powers vested in the general government. The inference is natural that the legislature will have an authority to make all laws which they shall judge necessary for the common safety, and to promote the general welfare. This amounts to a power to make laws at discretion: No terms can be found more indefinite than these, and it is obvious, that the legislature alone must judge what laws are proper and necessary for the purpose. It may be said, that this way of explaining the constitution, is torturing and making it speak what it never intended. This is far from my intention, and I shall not even insist upon this implied power, but join issue with those who say we are to collect the idea of the powers given from the express words of the clauses granting them; and it will not be difficult to shew that the same authority is expressly given which is supposed to be implied in the forgoing paragraphs.

2.9.58   In the 1st article, 8th section, it is declared, "that Congress shall have power to lay and collect taxes, duties, imposts and excises, to pay the debts, and provide for the common defence, and general welfare of the United States." In the preamble, the intent of the constitution, among other things, is declared to be to provide for the common defence, and promote the general welfare, and in this clause the power is in express words given to Congress "to provide for the common defence, and general welfare."—And in the last paragraph of the same section there is an express authority to make all laws which shall be necessary and proper for carrying into execution this power. It is therefore evident, that the legislature under this constitution may pass any law which they may think proper. It is true the 9th section restrains their power with respect to certain objects. But these restrictions are very limited, some of them improper, some unimportant, and others not easily understood, as I shall hereafter shew. It has been urged that the meaning I give to this part of the constitution is not the true one, that the intent of it is to confer on the legislature the power to lay and collect taxes, etc. in order to provide for the common defence and general welfare.[41] To this I would reply, that the meaning and intent of the constitution is to be collected from the words of it, and I submit to the public, whether the construction I have given it is not the most natural and easy. But admitting the contrary opinion to prevail, I shall nevertheless, be able to shew, that the same powers are substantially vested in the general government, by several other articles in the constitution. It invests the legislature with authority to lay and collect taxes, duties, imposts and excises, in order to provide for the common defence, and promote the general welfare, and to pass all laws which shall be necessary and proper for carrying this power into effect. To comprehend the extent of this authority, it will be requisite to examine 1st. what is included in this power to lay and collect taxes, duties, imposts and excises.

2d. What is implied in the authority, to pass all laws which shall be necessary and proper for carrying this power into execution.

3d. What limitation, if any, is set to the exercise of this power by the constitution.

1st. To detail the particulars comprehended in the general terms, taxes, duties, imposts and excises, would require a volume, instead of a single piece in a news-paper. Indeed it would be a task far beyond my ability, and to which no one can be competent, unless possessed of a mind capable of comprehending every possible source of revenue; for they extend to every possible way of raising money, whether by direct or indirect taxation. Under this clause may be imposed a poll-tax, a land-tax, a tax on houses and buildings, on windows and fire places, on cattle and on all kinds of personal property:—It extends to duties on all kinds of goods to any amount, to tonnage and poundage on vessels, to duties on written instruments, newspapers, almanacks, and books:—It comprehends an excise on all kinds of liquors, spirits, wines, cyder, beer, etc. and indeed takes in duty or excise on every necessary or conveniency of life; whether of foreign or home growth or manufactory. In short, we can have no conception of any way in which a government can raise money from the people, but what is included in one or other of three general terms. We may say then that this clause commits to the hands of the general legislature every conceivable source of revenue within the United States. Not only are these terms very comprehensive, and extend to a vast number of objects, but the power to lay and collect has great latitude; it will lead to the passing a vast number of laws, which may affect the personal rights of the citizens of the states, expose their property to fines and confiscation, and put their lives in jeopardy: it opens a door to the appointment of a swarm of revenue and excise officers to pray [sic] upon the honest and industrious part of the community, eat up their substance, and riot on the spoils of the country. 2.9.59

2d. We will next enquire into what is implied in the authority to pass all laws which shall be necessary and proper to carry this power into execution. 2.9.60

It is, perhaps, utterly impossible fully to define this power. The authority granted in the first clause can only be understood in its full extent, by descending to all the particular cases in which a revenue can be raised; the number and variety of these cases are so endless, and as it were infinite, that no man living has, as yet, been able to reckon them up. The greatest geniuses in the world have been for ages employed in the research, and when mankind had supposed that the subject was exhausted they have been astonished with the refined improvements that have been made in modern times, and especially in the English nation on the subject—If then the objects of this power cannot be comprehended, how is it possible to understand the extent of that power which can pass all laws which shall be necessary and proper for carrying it into execution? It is truly incomprehensible. A case cannot be conceived of, which is not included in this power. It is well known that the subject of revenue is the most difficult and extensive in the science of government. It requires the greatest talents of a statesman, and the most numerous and exact provisions of the legislature. The command of the revenues of a state gives the command of every thing in it.—He that has the purse will have the sword, and they that have both, have every thing; so that the legislature having every source from which money can be drawn under their direction, with a right to make all laws necessary and proper for drawing forth all the resource of the country, would have, in fact, all power.[42]

2.9.61 Were I to enter into the detail, it would be easy to shew how this power in its operation, would totally destroy all the powers of the individual states.[43] But this is not necessary for those who will think for themselves, and it will be useless to such as take things upon trust, nothing will awaken them to reflection, until the iron hand of oppression compel them to it.

2.9.62 I shall only remark, that this power, given to the federal legislature, directly annihilates all the powers of the state legislatures.[44] There cannot be a greater solecism in politics than to talk of power in a government, without the command of any revenue. It is as absurd as to talk of an animal without blood, or the subsistence of one without food.[45] Now the general government having in their controul every possible source of revenue, and authority to pass any law they may deem necessary to draw them forth, or to facilitate their collection; no source of revenue is therefore left in the hands of any state. Should any state attempt to raise money by law, the general government may repeal or arrest it in the execution, for all their laws will be the supreme law of the land: If then any one can be weak enough to believe that a government can exist without having the authority to raise money to pay a door-keeper to their assembly, he may believe that the state government can exist, should this new constitution take place.[46]

2.9.63 It is agreed by most of the advocates of this new system, that the government which is proper for the United States should be a confederated one; that the respective states ought to retain a portion of their sovereignty, and that they should preserve not only the forms of their legislatures, but also the power to conduct certain internal concerns. How far the powers to be retained by the states shall extend, is the question; we need not spend much time on this subject, as it respects this constitution, for a government without the power to raise money is one only in name. It is clear that the legislatures of the respective states must be altogether dependent on the will of the general legislature, for the means of supporting their government. The legislature of the United States will have a right to exhaust every source of revenue in every state, and to annul all laws of the states which may stand in the way of effecting it; unless therefore we can suppose the state governments can exist without money to support the officers who execute them, we must conclude they will exist no longer than the general legislature choose they should. Indeed the idea of any government existing, in any respect, as an independent one, without any means of support in their own hands, is an absurdity. If therefore, this constitution has in view, what many of its framers and advocates say it has, to secure and guarantee to the separate states the exercise of certain powers of government[,] it certainly ought to have left in their hands some sources of revenue. It should have marked the line in which the general government should have raised money, and set bounds over which they should not pass, leaving to the separate states other means to raise supplies for the support of their governments, and to discharge their respective debts. To this it is objected, that the general government ought to have power competent to the purposes of the union; they are to provide for the common defence, to pay the debts of the United States, support foreign ministers, and the civil establishment of the union, and to do these they ought to have authority to raise money adequate to the purpose. On this I observe, that the state governments have also contracted debts, they require money to support their civil officers, and how this is to be done, if they give to the general government a power to raise money in every way in which it can possibly be raised, with such a controul over the state legislatures as to prohibit them, whenever the general legislature may think proper, from raising any money.[47] It is again objected that it is very difficult, if not impossible, to draw the line of distinction between the powers of the general and state governments on this subject. The first, it is said, must have the power of raising the money necessary for the purposes of the union, if they are limited to certain objects the revenue may fall short of a sufficiency for the public exigencies, they must therefore have discretionary power. The line may be easily and accurately drawn between the powers of the two governments on this head. The distinction between external and internal taxes, is not a novel one in this country, it is a plain one, and easily understood. The first includes impost duties on all imported goods; this species of taxes it is proper should be laid by the general government; many reasons might be urged to shew that no danger is to be apprehended from their exercise of it. They may be collected in few places, and from few hands with certainty and expedition. But few officers are necessary to be imployed in collecting them, and there is no danger of oppression in laying them, because, if they are laid higher than trade will bear, the merchants will cease importing, or smuggle their goods. We have therefore sufficient security, arising from the nature of the thing, against burdensome and intolerable impositions from this kind of tax.[48] But the case is far otherwise with regard to direct taxes; these include poll taxes, land taxes, excises, duties on written instruments, on every thing we eat, drink, or wear; they take hold of every species of property, and come home to every man's house and packet. These are often so oppressive, as to grind the face of the poor, and render the lives of the common people a burden to them. The great and only security the people can have against oppression from this kind of taxes, must rest in their representatives. If they are sufficiently numerous to be well informed of the circumstances, and ability of those who send them, and have a proper regard for the people, they will be secure. The general legislature, as I have shewn in a former paper, will not be thus qualified, and therefore, on this account, ought not to exercise the power of direct taxation. If the power of laying imposts will not be sufficient, some other specific mode of raising a revenue should have been assigned the general government; many may be suggested in which their power may be accurately defined and limited, and it would be much better to give them authority to lay and collect a duty on exports, not to exceed a certain rate per cent, than to have surrendered every kind of resource that the country has, to the complete abolition of the state governments, and which will introduce such an infinite number of laws and ordinances, fines and penalties, courts, and judges, collectors, and excisemen, that when a man can number them, he may enumerate the stars of Heaven.

I shall resume this subject in my next, and by an induction of particulars shew, that this power, in its exercise, will subvert all state authority, and will work to the oppression of the people, and that there are no restrictions in the constitution that will soften its rigour, but rather the contrary.

Brutus.

VI
27 December 1787

2.9.64   It is an important question, whether the general government of the United States should be so framed, as to absorb and swallow up the state governments? or whether, on the contrary, the former ought not to be confined to certain defined national objects, while the latter should retain all the powers which concern the internal police of the states?

2.9.65   I have, in my former papers, offered a variety of arguments to prove, that a simple free government could not be exercised over this whole continent, and that therefore we must either give up our liberties and submit to an arbitrary one, or frame a constitution on the plan of confederation. Further reasons might be urged to prove this point—but it seems unnecessary, because the principal advocates of the new constitution admit of the position. The question therefore between us, this being admitted, is, whether or not this system is so formed as either directly to annihilate the state governments, or that in its operation it will certainly effect it. If this is answered in the affirmative, then the system ought not to be adopted, without such amendments as will avoid this consequence. If on the contrary it can be shewn, that the state governments are secured in their rights to manage the internal police of the respective states, we must confine ourselves in our enquiries to the organization of the government and the guards and provisions it contains to prevent a misuse or abuse of power.[49] To determine this question, it is requisite, that we fully investigate the nature, and the extent of the powers intended to be granted by this constitution to the rulers.

In my last number I called your attention to this subject, and proved, as I think, uncontrovertibly, that the powers given the legislature under the 8th section of the 1st article, had no other limitation than the discretion of the Congress. It was shewn, that even if the most favorable construction was given to this paragraph, that the advocates for the new constitution could wish, it will convey a power to lay and collect taxes, imposts, duties, and excises, according to the discretion of the legislature, and to make all laws which they shall judge proper and necessary to carry this power into execution. This I shewed would totally destroy all the power of the state governments. To confirm this, it is worth while to trace the operation of the government in some particular instances.   2.9.66

The general government is to be vested with authority to levy and collect taxes, duties, and excises; the separate states have also power to impose taxes, duties, and excises, except that they cannot lay duties on exports and imports without the consent of Congress. Here then the two governments have concurrent jurisdiction; both may lay impositions of this kind. But then the general government have supperadded to this power, authority to make all laws which shall be necessary and proper for carrying the foregoing power into execution. Suppose then that both governments should lay taxes, duties, and excises, and it should fall so heavy on the people that they would be unable, or be so burdensome that they would refuse to pay them both—would it not be necessary that the general legislature should suspend the collection of the state tax? It certainly would. For, if the people could not, or would not pay both, they must be discharged from the tax to the state, or the tax to the general government could not be collected.—The conclusion therefore is inevitable, that the respective state governments will not have the power to raise one shilling in any way, but by the permission of the Congress. I presume no one will pretend, that the states can exercise legislative authority, or administer justice among their citizens for any length of time, without being able to raise a sufficiency to pay those who administer their governments.   2.9.67

2.9.68   If this be true, and if the states can raise money only by permission of the general government, it follows that the state governments will be dependent on the will of the general government for their existence.

What will render this power in Congress effectual and sure in its operation is, that the government will have complete judicial and executive authority to carry all their laws into effect, which will be paramount to the judicial and executive authority of the individual states: in vain therefore will be all interference of the legislatures, courts, or magistrates of any of the states on the subject; for they will be subordinate to the general government, and engaged by oath to support it, and will be constitutionally bound to submit to their decisions.[50]

2.9.69   The general legislature will be empowered to lay any tax they chuse, to annex any penalties they please to the breach of their revenue laws; and to appoint as many officers as they may think proper to collect the taxes. They will have authority to farm the revenues and to vest the farmer general, with his subalterns, with plenary powers to collect them, in any way which to them may appear eligible. And the courts of law, which they will be authorized to institute, will have cognizance of every case arising under the revenue laws, the conduct of all the officers employed in collecting them; and the officers of these courts will execute their judgments. There is no way, therefore, of avoiding the destruction of the state governments, whenever the Congress please to do it, unless the people rise up, and, with a strong hand, resist and prevent the execution of constitutional laws.[51] The fear of this, will, it is presumed, restrain the general government, for some time, within proper bounds; but it will not be many years before they will have a revenue, and force, at their command, which will place them above any apprehensions on that score.

2.9.70   How far the power to lay and collect duties and excises, may operate to dissolve the state governments, and oppress the people, it is impossible to say. It would assist us much in forming a just opinion on this head, to consider the various objects to which this kind of taxes extend, in European nations, and the infinity of laws they have passed respecting them. Perhaps, if leisure will permit, this may be essayed in some future paper.[52]

2.9.71   It was observed in my last number, that the power to lay and collect duties and excises, would invest the Congress with authority to impose a duty and excise on every necessary and convenience of life. As the principal object of the government, in laying a duty or excise, will be, to raise money, it is obvious, that they will fix on such articles as are of the most general use and consumption; because, unless great quantities of the article, on which the duty is laid, is used, the revenue cannot be considerable. We may therefore presume, that the articles which will be the object of this species of taxes will be either the real necessaries of life; or if not these, such as from custom and habit are esteemed so. I will single out a few of the productions of our own country, which may, and probably will, be of the number.

Cider is an article that most probably will be one of those on which an excise will be laid, because it is one, which this country produces in great abundance, which is in very general use, is consumed in great quantities, and which may be said too not to be a real necessary of life. An excise on this would raise a large sum of money in the United States. How would the power, to lay and collect an excise on cider, and to pass all laws proper and necessary to carry it into execution, operate in its exercise? It might be necessary, in order to collect the excise on cider, to grant to one man, in each county, an exclusive right of building and keeping cider-mills, and oblige him to give bonds and security for payment of the excise; or, if this was not done, it might be necessary to license the mills, which are to make this liquor, and to take from them security, to account for the excise; or, if otherwise, a great number of officers must be employed, to take account of the cider made, and to collect the duties on it. 2.9.72

Porter, ale, and all kinds of malt-liquors, are articles that would probably be subject also to an excise. It would be necessary, in order to collect such an excise, to regulate the manufactory of these, that the quantity made might be ascertained or otherwise security could not be had for the payment of the excise. Every brewery must then be licensed, and officers appointed, to take account of its product, and to secure the payment of the duty, or excise, before it is sold. Many other articles might be named, which would be objects of this species of taxation, but I refrain from enumerating them. It will probably be said, by those who advocate this system, that the observations already made on this head, are calculated only to inflame the minds of the people, with the apprehension of dangers merely imaginary. That there is not the least reason to apprehend, the general legislature will exercise their power in this manner. To this I would only say, that these kinds of taxes exist in Great Britain, and are severely felt. The excise on cider and perry, was imposed in that nation a few years ago, and it is in the memory of every one, who read the history of the transaction, what great tumults it occasioned. 2.9.73

This power, exercised without limitation, will introduce itself into every corner of the city, and country—It will wait upon the ladies at their toilett, and will not leave them in any of their domestic concerns; it will accompany them to the ball, the play, and the assembly; it will go with them when they visit, and will, on all occasions, sit beside them in their carriages, nor will it desert them even at church; it will enter the house of every gentleman, watch over his cellar, wait upon his cook in the kitchen, follow the servants into the parlour, preside over the table, and note down all he eats or drinks; it will attend him to his bed-chamber, and watch him while he sleeps; it will take cognizance of the professional man in his office, or his study; it will watch the merchant in the counting-house, or in his store; it will follow the mechanic to his shop, and in his work, and will haunt him in his family, and in his bed; it will be a constant companion of the industrious farmer in all his 2.9.74

labour, it will be with him in the house, and in the field, observe the toil of his hands, and the sweat of his brow; it will penetrate into the most obscure cottage; and finally, it will light upon the head of every person in the United States. To all these different classes of people, and in all these circumstances, in which it will attend them, the language in which it will address them, will be GIVE! GIVE!

2.9.75   A power that has such latitude, which reaches every person in the community in every conceivable circumstance, and lays hold of every species of property they possess, and which has no bounds set to it, but the discretion of those who exercise it[,] I say, such a power must necessarily, from its very nature, swallow up all the power of the state governments.

2.9.76   I shall add but one other observation on this head, which is this—It appears to me a solecism, for two men, or bodies of men, to have unlimited power respecting the same object. It contradicts the scripture maxim, which saith, "no man can serve two masters,"[53] the one power or the other must prevail, or else they will destroy each other, and neither of them effect their purpose. It may be compared to two mechanic powers, acting upon the same body in opposite directions, the consequence would be, if the powers were equal, the body would remain in a state of rest, or if the force of the one was superior to that of the other, the stronger would prevail, and overcome the resistance of the weaker.

2.9.77   But it is said, by some of the advocates of this system, "That the idea that Congress can levy taxes at pleasure, is false, and the suggestion wholly unsupported: that the preamble to the constitution is declaratory of the purposes of the union, and the assumption of any power not necessary to establish justice, &c. to provide for the common defence, &c. will be unconstitutional. Besides, in the very clause which gives the power of levying duties and taxes, the purposes to which the money shall be appropriated, are specified, viz. to pay the debts, and provide for the common defence and general welfare."* I would ask those, who reason thus, to define what ideas are included under the terms, to provide for the common defence and general welfare? Are these terms definite, and will they be understood in the same manner, and to apply to the same cases by every one? No one will pretend they will. It will then be matter of opinion, what tends to the general welfare; and the Congress will be the only judges in the matter. To provide for the general welfare, is an abstract proposition, which mankind differ in the explanation of, as much as they do on any political or moral proposition that can be proposed; the most opposite measures may be pursued by different parties, and both may profess, that they have in view the general welfare; and both sides may be honest in their professions, or both may have sinister views. Those who advocate this new constitution declare, they

*Vide an examination into the leading principles of the federal constitution, printed in Philadelphia, Page 34.[54]

are influenced by a regard to the general welfare; those who oppose it, declare they are moved by the same principle; and I have no doubt but a number on both sides are honest in their professions; and yet nothing is more certain than this, that to adopt this constitution, and not to adopt it, cannot both of them be promotive of the general welfare.

It is as absurd to say, that the power of Congress is limited by these general expressions, "to provide for the common safety, and general welfare," as it would be to say, that it would be limited, had the constitution said they should have power to lay taxes, &c. at will and pleasure. Were this authority given, it might be said, that under it the legislature could not do injustice, or pursue any measures, but such as were calculated to promote the public good, and happiness. For every man, rulers as well as others, are bound by the immutable laws of God and reason, always to will what is right. It is certainly right and fit, that the governors of every people should provide for the common defence and general welfare; every government, therefore, in the world, even the greatest despot, is limited in the exercise of his power. But however just this reasoning may be, it would be found, in practice, a most pitiful restriction. The government would always say, their measures were designed and calculated to promote the public good; and there being no judge between them and the people, the rulers themselves must, and would always, judge for themselves.   2.9.78

There are others of the favourers of this system, who admit, that the power of the Congress under it, with respect to revenue, will exist without limitation, and contend, that so it ought to be.   2.9.79

It is said, "The power to raise armies, to build and equip fleets, and to provide for their support, ought to exist without limitation, because it is impossible to foresee, or to define, the extent and variety of national exigencies, or the correspondent extent and variety of the means which may be necessary to satisfy them.["]

This, it is said, "is one of those truths which, to correct and unprejudiced minds, carries its own evidence along with it. It rests upon axioms as simple as they are universal: the means ought to be proportioned to the end; the person, from whose agency the attainment of any end is expected, ought to possess the means by which it is to be attained."*

This same writer insinuates, that the opponents to the plan promulgated by the convention, manifests a want of candor, in objecting to the extent of the powers proposed to be vested in this government; because he asserts, with an air of confidence, that the powers ought to be unlimited as to the object to which they extend; and that this position, if not self-evident, is at least clearly demonstrated by the foregoing mode of reasoning. But with submission to this author's better judgment, I humbly conceive his reasoning will appear, upon examination, more specious than solid. The means,   2.9.80

*Vide the Federalist, No. 23.[55]

says the gentleman, ought to be proportioned to the end: admit the proposition to be true it is then necessary to enquire, what is the end of the government of the United States, in order to draw any just conclusions from it. Is this end simply to preserve the general government, and to provide for the common defence and general welfare of the union only? certainly not: for beside this, the state governments are to be supported, and provision made for the managing such of their internal concerns as are allotted to them. It is admitted, "that the circumstances of our country are such, as to demand a compound, instead of a simple, a confederate, instead of a sole government," that the objects of each ought to be pointed out, and that each ought to possess ample authority to execute the powers committed to them.[56] The government then, being complex in its nature, the end it has in view is so also; and it is as necessary, that the state governments should possess the means to attain the ends expected from them, as for the general government. Neither the general government, nor the state governments, ought to be vested with all the powers proper to be exercised for promoting the ends of government. The powers are divided between them—certain ends are to be attained by the one, and other certain ends by the other; and these, taken together, include all the ends of good government. This being the case, the conclusion follows, that each should be furnished with the means, to attain the ends, to which they are designed.

2.9.81   To apply this reasoning to the case of revenue; the general government is charged with the care of providing for the payment of the debts of the United States; supporting the general government, and providing for the defence of the union. To obtain these ends, they should be furnished with means. But does it thence follow, that they should command all the revenues of the United States! Most certainly it does not. For if so, it will follow, that no means will be left to attain other ends, as necessary to the happiness of the country, as those committed to their care. The individual states have debts to discharge; their legislatures and executives are to be supported, and provision is to be made for the administration of justice in the respective states. For these objects the general government has no authority to provide; nor is it proper it should. It is clear then, that the states should have the command of such revenues, as to answer the ends they have to obtain. To say, "that the circumstances that endanger the safety of nations are infinite,"[57] and from hence to infer, that all the sources of revenue in the states should be yielded to the general government, is not conclusive reasoning: for the Congress are authorized only to controul in general concerns, and not regulate local and internal ones; and these are as essentially requisite to be provided for as those. The peace and happiness of a community is as intimately connected with the prudent direction of their domestic affairs, and the due administration of justice among themselves, as with a competent provision for their defence against foreign invaders, and indeed more so.

Upon the whole, I conceive, that there cannot be a clearer position than this, that the state governments ought to have an uncontroulable power to raise a revenue, adequate to the exigencies of their governments; and, I presume, no such power is left them by this constitution.

2.9.82

Brutus.

VII
3 January 1788

The result of our reasoning in the two preceeding numbers is this, that in a confederated government, where the powers are divided between the general and the state government, it is essential to its existence, that the revenues of the country, without which no government can exist, should be divided between them, and so apportioned to each, as to answer their respective exigencies, as far as human wisdom can effect such a division and apportionment.

2.9.83

It has been shewn, that no such allotment is made in this constitution, but that every source of revenue is under the controul of the Congress; it therefore follows, that if this system is intended to be a complex and not a simple, a confederate and not an entire consolidated government, it contains in it the sure seeds of its own dissolution.—One of two things must happen— Either the new constitution will become a mere *nudum pactum,* and all the authority of the rulers under it be cried down, as has happened to the present confederation—Or the authority of the individual states will be totally supplanted, and they will retain the mere form without any of the powers of government.—To one or the other of these issues, I think, this new government, if it is adopted, will advance with great celerity.

2.9.84

It is said, I know, that such a separation of the sources of revenue, cannot be made without endangering the public safety—"unless (says a writer) it can be shewn that the circumstances which may affect the public safety are reducible within certain determinate limits; unless the contrary of this position can be fairly and rationally disputed; it must be admitted as a necessary consequence, that there can be no limitation of that authority which is to provide for the defence and protection of the community, &c."*

2.9.85

The pretended demonstration of this writer will instantly vanish, when it is considered, that the *protection and defence* of the community is not intended to be entrusted *solely* into the hands of the general government, and by his own confession it ought not to be. It is true this system commits to the general government the protection and defence of the community against foreign force and invasion, against piracies and felonies on the high

2.9.86

Federalist, No. 23.

seas, and against insurrections among ourselves. They are also authorised
to provide for the administration of justice in certain matters of a general
concern, and in some that I think are not so. But it ought to be left to the
state governments to provide for the protection and defence of the citizen
against the hand of private violence, and the wrongs done or attempted by
individuals to each other—Protection and defence against the murderer, the
robber, the thief, the cheat, and the unjust person, is to be derived from the
respective state governments.—The just way of reasoning therefore on this
subject is this, the general government is to provide for the protection and
defence of the community against foreign attacks, &c., they therefore ought
to have authority sufficient to effect this, so far as is consistent with the
providing for our internal protection and defence. The state governments
are entrusted with the care of administring justice among its citizens, and
the management of other internal concerns, they ought therefore to retain
power adequate to the end. The preservation of internal peace and good
order, and the due administration of law and justice, ought to be the first
care of every government.—The happiness of a people depends infinitely
more on this than it does upon all that glory and respect which nations
acquire by the most brilliant martial achievements—and I believe history
will furnish but few examples of nations who have duly attended to these,
who have been subdued by foreign invaders. If a proper respect and submission to the laws prevailed over all orders of men in our country; and if a
spirit of public and private justice, oeconomy and industry influenced the
people, we need not be under any apprehensions but what they would be
ready to repel any invasion that might be made on the country.[58] And more
than this, I would not wish from them—A defensive war is the only one I
think justifiable[59]—I do not make these observations to prove, that a government ought not to be authorised to provide for the protection and defence of a country against external enemies, but to shew that this is not the
most important, much less the only object of their care.[60]

2.9.87   The European governments are almost all of them framed, and administered with a view to arms, and war, as that in which their chief glory
consists; they mistake the end of government—it was designed to save
men[']s lives, not to destroy them. We ought to furnish the world with an
example of a great people, who in their civil institutions hold chiefly in view,
the attainment of virtue, and happiness among ourselves. Let the monarchs
in Europe, share among them the glory of depopulating countries, and
butchering thousands of their innocent citizens, to revenge private quarrels,
or to punish an insult offered to a wife, a mistress, or a favorite: I envy them
not the honor, and I pray heaven this country may never be ambitious of
it.[61] The czar Peter the great, acquired great glory by his arms; but all this
was nothing, compared with the true glory which he obtained, by civilizing
his rude and barbarous subjects, diffusing among them knowledge, and
establishing, and cultivating the arts of life: by the former he desolated

countries, and drenched the earth with human blood: by the latter he soft-
ened the ferocious nature of his people, and pointed them to the means of
human happiness. The most important end of government then, is the
proper direction of its internal policy, and oeconomy; this is the province of
the state governments, and it is evident, and is indeed admitted, that these
ought to be under their controul. Is it not then preposterous, and in the
highest degree absurd, when the state governments are vested with powers
so essential to the peace and good order of society, to take from them the
means of their own preservation?

The idea, that the powers of congress in respect to revenue ought to be   2.9.88
unlimited, "because the circumstances which may affect the public safety
are not reducible to certain determinate limits," is novel, as it relates to the
government of the united states. The inconveniencies which resulted from
the feebleness of the present confederation was discerned, and felt soon
after its adoption. It was soon discovered, that a power to require money,
without either the authority or means to enforce a collection of it, could not
be relied upon either to provide for the common defence, the discharge of
the national debt, or for support of government. Congress therefore, so
early as February 1781, recommended to the states to invest them with a
power to levy an impost of five per cent ad valorem, on all imported goods,
as a fund to be appropriated to discharge the debts already contracted, or
which should hereafter be contracted for the support of the war, to be
continued until the debts should be fully and finally discharged. There is not
the most distant idea held out in this act, that an unlimited power to collect
taxes, duties and excises was necessary to be vested in the united states,
and yet this was a time of the most pressing danger and distress. The idea
then was, that if certain definite funds were assigned to the union, which
were certain in their natures, productive, and easy of collection, it would
enable them to answer their engagements, and provide for their defence,
and the impost of five per cent was fixed upon for the purpose.

This same subject was revived in the winter and spring of 1783, and after a   2.9.89
long consideration of the subject, and many schemes were proposed; the
result was, a recommendation of the revenue system of April 1783; this
system does not suggest an idea that it was necessary to grant the United
States unlimited authority in matters of revenue. A variety of amendments
were proposed to this system, some of which are upon the journals of
Congress, but it does not appear that any of them proposed to invest the
general government with discretionary power to raise money. On the contrary, all of them limit them to certain definite objects, and fix the bounds
over which they could not pass. This recommendation was passed at the
conclusion of the war, and was founded on an estimate of the whole national
debt. It was computed, that one million and an half of dollars, in addition to
the impost, was a sufficient sum to pay the annual interest of the debt, and
gradually to abolish the principal.—Events have proved that their estimate

was sufficiently liberal, as the domestic debt appears upon its being adjusted to be less than it was computed, and since this period a considerable portion of the principal of the domestic debt has been discharged by the sale of the western lands. It has been constantly urged by Congress, and by individuals, ever since, until lately, that had this revenue been appropriated by the states, as it was recommended, it would have been adequate to every exigency of the union. Now indeed it is insisted, that all the treasures of the country are to be under the controul of that body, whom we are to appoint to provide for our protection and defence against foreign enemies. The debts of the several states, and the support of the governments of them are to trust to fortune and accident. If the union should not have occasion for all the money they can raise, they will leave a portion for the state, but this must be a matter of mere grace and favor. Doctrines like these would not have been listened to by any state in the union, at a time when we were pressed on every side by a powerful enemy, and were called upon to make greater exertions than we have any reason to expect we shall ever be again. The ability and character of the convention, who framed the proferred constitution, is sounded forth and reiterated by every declaimer and writer in its favor, as a powerful argument to induce its adoption. But are not the patriots who guided our councils in the perilous times of the war, entitled to equal respect. How has it happened, that none of these perceived a truth, which it is pretended is capable of such clear demonstration, that the power to raise a revenue should be deposited in the general government without limitation? Were the men so dull of apprehension, so incapable of reasoning as not to be able to draw the inference?[62] The truth is, no such necessity exists. It is a thing practicable, and by no means so difficult as is pretended, to limit the powers of the general government in respect to revenue, while yet they may retain reasonable means to provide for the common defence.

2.9.90
It is admitted, that human wisdom cannot foresee all the variety of circumstances that may arise to endanger the safety of nations—and it may with equal truth be added, that the power of a nation, exerted with its utmost vigour, may not be equal to repel a force with which it may be assailed, much less may it be able, with its ordinary resources and power, to oppose an extraordinary and unexpected attack;—but yet every nation may form a rational judgment, what force will be competent to protect and defend it, against any enemy with which it is probable it may have to contend. In extraordinary attacks, every country must rely upon the spirit and special exertions of its inhabitants—and these extraordinary efforts will always very much depend upon the happiness and good order the people experience from a wise and prudent administration of their internal government.[63] The states are as capable of making a just estimate on this head, as perhaps any nation in the world.—We have no powerful nation in our neighbourhood; if we are to go to war, it must either be with the Aboriginal natives, or with European nations. The first are so unequal to a contest with this whole

continent, that they are rather to be dreaded for the depredations they may make on our frontiers, than for any impression they will ever be able to make on the body of the country. Some of the European nations, it is true, have provinces bordering upon us, but from these, unsupported by their European forces, we have nothing to apprehend; if any of them should attack us, they will have to transport their armies across the atlantic, at immense expence, while we should defend ourselves in our own country, which abounds with every necessary of life. For defence against any assault, which there is any probability will be made upon us, we may easily form an estimate.

I may be asked to point out the sources, from which the general government could derive a sufficient revenue, to answer the demands of the union. Many might be suggested, and for my part, I am not disposed to be tenacious of my own opinion on the subject. If the object be defined with precision, and will operate to make the burden fall any thing nearly equal on the different parts of the union, I shall be satisfied. 2.9.91

There is one source of revenue, which it is agreed, the general government ought to have the sole controul of. This is an impost upon all goods imported from foreign countries. This would, of itself, be very productive, and would be collected with ease and certainty.—It will be a fund too, constantly encreasing—for our commerce will grow, with the productions of the country; and these, together with our consumption of foreign goods, will encrease with our population.[64] It is said, that the impost will not produce a sufficient sum to satisfy the demands of the general government; perhaps it would not. Let some other then, equally well defined, be assigned them:— that this is practicable is certain, because such particular objects were proposed by some members of Congress when the revenue system of April 1783, was agitated in that body. It was then moved, that a tax at the rate of ninetieths[65] of a dollar on surveyed land, and a house tax of half a dollar on a house, should be granted to the United States. I do not mention this, because I approve of raising a revenue in this mode. I believe such a tax would be difficult in its collection, and inconvenient in its operation. But it shews, that it has heretofore been the sense of some of those, who now contend, that the general government should have unlimited authority in matters of revenue, that their authority should be definite and limitted on that head.—My own opinion is, that the objects from which the general government should have authority to raise a revenue, should be of such a nature, that the tax should be raised by simple laws, with few officers, with certainty and expedition, and with the least interference with the internal police of the states.—Of this nature is the impost on imported goods—and it appears to me that a duty on exports, would also be of this nature—and therefore, for ought I can discover, this would be the best source of revenue to grant the general government. I know neither the Congress nor the state legislatures will have authority under the new constitution to raise a revenue 2.9.92

in this way. But I cannot perceive the reason of the restriction. It appears to me evident, that a tax on articles exported, would be as nearly equal as any that we can expect to lay, and it certainly would be collected with more ease and less expence than any direct tax. I do not however, contend for this mode, it may be liable to well founded objections that have not occurred to me. But this I do contend for, that some mode is practicable, and that limits must be marked between the general government, and the states on this head, or if they be not, either the Congress in the exercise of this power, will deprive the state legislatures of the means of their existence, or the states by resisting the constitutional authority of the general government, will render it nugatory.

Brutus.

VIII
10 January 1788

2.9.93   The next powers vested by this constitution in the general government, which we shall consider, are those, which authorise them to "borrow money on the credit of the United States, and to raise and support armies." I take these two together and connect them with the power to lay and collect taxes, duties, imposts and excises, because their extent, and the danger that will arise from the exercise of these powers, cannot be fully understood, unless they are viewed in relation to each other.

2.9.94   The power to borrow money is general and unlimited, and the clause so often before referred to, authorises the passing any laws proper and necessary to carry this into execution. Under this authority, the Congress may mortgage any or all the revenues of the union, as a fund to loan money upon, and it is probably, in this way, they may borrow of foreign nations, a principal sum, the interest of which will be equal to the annual revenues of the country.—By this means, they may create a national debt, so large, as to exceed the ability of the country ever to sink. I can scarcely contemplate a greater calamity that could befal this country, than to be loaded with a debt exceeding their ability ever to discharge. If this be a just remark, it is unwise and improvident to vest in the general government a power to borrow at discretion, without any limitation or restriction.

2.9.95   It may possibly happen that the safety and welfare of the country may require, that money be borrowed, and it is proper when such a necessity arises that the power should be exercised by the general government.—But it certainly ought never to be exercised, but on the most urgent occasions, and then we should not borrow of foreigners if we could possibly avoid it.

The constitution should therefore have so restricted, the exercise of this power as to have rendered it very difficult for the government to practise it. The present confederation requires the assent of nine states to exercise this, and a number of the other important powers of the confederacy—and it would certainly have been a wise provision in this constitution, to have made it necessary that two thirds of the members should assent to borrowing money—when the necessity was indispensible, this assent would always be given, and in no other cause ought it to be.

The power to raise armies, is indefinite and unlimited, and authorises the raising forces, as well in peace as in war. Whether the clause which impowers the Congress to pass all laws which are proper and necessary, to carry this into execution, will not authorise them to impress men for the army, is a question well worthy consideration? If the general legislature deem it for the general welfare to raise a body of troops, and they cannot be procured by voluntary enlistments, it seems evident, that it will be proper and necessary to effect it, that men be impressed from the militia to make up the deficiency.   2.9.96

These powers taken in connection, amount to this: that the general government have unlimitted authority and controul over all the wealth and all the force of the union. The advocates for this scheme, would favor the world with a new discovery, if they would shew, what kind of freedom or independency is left to the state governments, when they cannot command any part of the property or of the force of the country, but at the will of the Congress. It seems to me as absurd, as it would be to say, that I was free and independent, when I had conveyed all my property to another, and was tenant to will to him, and had beside, given an indenture of myself to serve him during life.—The power to keep up standing armies in time of peace, has been justly objected, to this system, as dangerous and improvident. The advocates who have wrote in its favor, have some of them ridiculed the objection, as though it originated in the distempered brain of its opponents,[66] and others have taken pains to shew, that it is a power that was proper to be granted to the rulers in this constitution.[67] That you may be enabled to form a just opinion on this subject, I shall first make some remarks, tending to prove, that this power ought to be restricted, and then animadvert on the arguments which have been adduced to justify it.   2.9.97

I take it for granted, as an axiom in politic, that the people should never authorise their rulers to do any thing, which if done, would operate to their injury.   2.9.98

It seems equally clear, that in a case where a power, if given and exercised, will generally produce evil to the community, and seldom good—and which, experience has proved, has most frequently been exercised to the great injury, and very often to the total destruction of the government; in such a case, I say, this power, if given at all, should if possible be so restricted, as to prevent the ill effect of its operation.

Let us then enquire, whether standing armies in time of peace, would be   2.9.99

ever beneficial to our country—or if in some extraordinary cases, they might be necessary; whether it is not true, that they have generally proved a scourge to a country, and destructive of their liberty.

I shall not take up much of your time in proving a point, in which the friends of liberty, in all countries, have so universally agreed. The following extract from Mr. Pultney's speech, delivered in the house of commons of Great-Britain, on a motion for reducing the army, is so full to the point, and so much better than any thing I can say, that I shall be excused for inserting it.[68] He says, "I have always been, and always shall be against a standing army of any kind; to me it is a terrible thing, whether under that of a parliamentary, or any other designation; a standing army is still a standing army by whatever name it is called; they are a body of men distinct from the body of the people; they are governed by different laws, and blind obedience, and an entire submission to the orders of their commanding officer, is their only principle; the nations around us, sir, are already enslaved, and have been enslaved by those very means; by means of their standing armies they have every one lost their liberties; it is indeed impossible that the liberties of the people in any country can be preserved where a numerous standing army is kept up. Shall we then take our measures from the example of our neighbours? No, sir, on the contrary, from their misfortunes we ought to learn to avoid those rocks upon which they have split.

2.9.100 "It signifies nothing to tell me that our army is commanded by such gentlemen as cannot be supposed to join in any measures for enslaving their country; it may be so; I have a very good opinion of many gentlemen now in the army; I believe they would not join in any such measures; but their lives are uncertain, nor can we be sure how long they will be kept in command, they may all be dismissed in a moment, and proper tools of power put in their room. Besides, sir, we know the passions of men, we know how dangerous it is to trust the best of men with too much power. Where was a braver army than that under Jul. Caesar? Where was there ever an army that had served their country more faithfully? That army was commanded generally by the best citizens of Rome, by men of great fortune and figure in their country, yet that army enslaved their country. The affections of the soldiers towards their country, the honor and integrity of the under officers, are not to be depended on. By the military law the administration of justice is so quick, and the punishment so severe, that neither the officer nor soldier dare dispute the orders of his supreme commander; he must not consult his own inclination. If an officer were commanded to pull his own father out of this house, he must do it; he dares not disobey; immediate death would be the sure consequence of the least grumbling: and if an officer were sent into the court of request, accompanied by a body of musketeers with screwed bayonets, and with orders to tell us what we ought to do, and how we were to vote: I know what would be the duty of this house; I know it would be our duty to order the officer to be hanged at the door of the lobby; but I doubt, sir, I doubt much, if such a spirit could be found in the house, or in any house of commons that will ever be in England.

"Sir, I talk not of imaginary things? I talk of what has happened to an English house of commons, from an English army; not only from an English army, but an army that was raised by that very house of commons, an army that was paid by them, and an army that was commanded by generals appointed by them; therefore do not let us vainly imagine, that an army, raised and maintained by authority of parliament, will always be so submissive to them. If an army be so numerous as to have it in their power to overawe the parliament, they will be submissive as long as the parliament does nothing to disoblige their favourite general; but when that case happens, I am afraid, that in place of the parliament's dismissing the army, the army will dismiss the parliament."—If this great man's reasoning be just, it follows, that keeping up a standing army, would be in the highest degree dangerous to the liberty and happiness of the community—and if so, the general government ought not to have authority to do it; for no government should be empowered to do that which if done, would tend to destroy public liberty.

2.9.101

Brutus.

IX
17 January 1788

The design of civil government is to protect the rights and promote the happiness of the people.

2.9.102

For this end, rulers are invested with powers. But we cannot from hence justly infer that these powers should be unlimited. There are certain rights which mankind possess, over which government ought not to have any controul, because it is not necessary they should, in order to attain the end of its institution. There are certain things which rulers should be absolutely prohibited from doing, because, if they should do them, they would work an injury, not a benefit to the people. Upon the same principles of reasoning, if the exercise of a power, is found generally or in most cases to operate to the injury of the community, the legislature should be restricted in the exercise of that power, so as to guard, as much as possible, against the danger. These principles seem to be the evident dictates of common sense, and what ought to give sanction to them in the minds of every American, they are the great principles of the late revolution, and those which governed the framers of all our state constitutions. Hence we find, that all the state constitutions, contain either formal bills of rights, which set bounds to the powers of the legislature, or have restrictions for the same purpose in the body of the constitutions. Some of our new political Doctors, indeed, reject the idea of the necessity, or propriety of such restrictions in any elective government, but especially in the general one.[69]

2.9.103 But it is evident, that the framers of this new system were of a contrary opinion, because they have prohibited the general government, the exercise of some powers, and restricted them in that of others.

I shall adduce two instances, which will serve to illustrate my meaning, as well as to confirm the truth of the preceeding remark.

In the 9th section, it is declared, "no bill of attainder shall be passed." This clause takes from the legislature all power to declare a particular person guilty of a crime by law. It is proper the legislature should be deprived of the exercise of this power, because it seldom is exercised to the benefit of the community, but generally to its injury.

2.9.104 In the same section it is provided, that "the privilege of the writ of habeas corpus shall not be suspended, unless when in cases of rebellion and invasion, the public safety may require it." This clause limits the power of the legislature to deprive a citizen of the right of habeas corpus, to particular cases viz. those of rebellion and invasion; the reason is plain, because in no other cases can this power be exercised for the general good.

Let us apply these remarks to the case of standing armies in times of peace. If they generally prove the destruction of the happiness and liberty of the people, the legislature ought not to have power to keep them up, or if they had, this power should be so restricted, as to secure the people against the danger arising from the exercise of it.

2.9.105 That standing armies are dangerous to the liberties of a people was proved in my last number—If it was necessary, the truth of the position might be confirmed by the history of almost every nation in the world. A cloud of the most illustrious patriots of every age and country, where freedom has been enjoyed, might be adduced as witnesses in support of the sentiment. But I presume it would be useless, to enter into a laboured argument, to prove to the people of America, a position, which has so long and so generally been received by them as a kind of axiom.

2.9.106 Some of the advocates for this new system controvert this sentiment, as they do almost every other that has been maintained by the best writers on free government.—Others, though they will not expressly deny, that standing armies in times of peace are dangerous, yet join with these in maintaining, that it is proper the general government should be vested with the power to do it.[70] I shall now proceed to examine the arguments they adduce in support of their opinions.

2.9.107 A writer, in favor of this system, treats this objection as a ridiculous one.[71] He supposes it would be as proper to provide against the introduction of Turkish janizaries, or against making the Alcoran a rule of faith.

From the positive, and dogmatic manner, in which this author delivers his opinions, and answers objections made to his sentiments—one would conclude, that he was some pedantic pedagogue who had been accustomed to deliver his dogmas to pupils, who always placed implicit faith in what he delivered.

But, why is this provision so ridiculous? because, says this author, it is unnecessary. But, why is it unnecessary? "because, the principles and habits, as well as the power of the Americans are directly opposed to standing armies; and there is as little necessity to guard against them by positive constitutions, as to prohibit the establishment of the Mahometan religion." It is admitted then, that a standing army in time of peace, is an evil. I ask then, why should this government be authorised to do evil? If the principles and habits of the people of this country are opposed to standing armies in time of peace, if they do not contribute to the public good, but would endanger the public liberty and happiness, why should the government be vested with the power? No reason can be given, why rulers should be authorised to do, what, if done, would oppose the principles and habits of the people, and endanger the public safety, but there is every reason in the world, that they should be prohibited from the exercise of such a power. But this author supposes, that no danger is to be apprehended from the exercise of this power, because, if armies are kept up, it will be by the people themselves, and therefore, to provide against it, would be as absurd as for a man to "pass a law in his family, that no troops should be quartered in his family by his consent." This reasoning supposes, that the general government is to be exercised by the people of America themselves—But such an idea is groundless and absurd. There is surely a distinction between the people and their rulers, even when the latter are representatives of the former.—They certainly are not identically the same, and it cannot be disputed, but it may and often does happen, that they do not possess the same sentiments or pursue the same interests. I think I have shewn, that as this government is constituted, there is little reason to expect, that the interest of the people and their rulers will be the same.

2.9.108

Besides, if the habits and sentiments of the people of America are to be relied upon, as the sole security against the encroachment of their rulers, all restrictions in constitutions are unnecessary; nothing more is requisite, than to declare who shall be authorized to exercise the powers of government, and about this we need not be very careful—for the habits and principles of the people will oppose every abuse of power. This I suppose to be the sentiments of this author, as it seems to be of many of the advocates of this new system. An opinion like this, is as directly opposed to the principles and habits of the people of America, as it is to the sentiments of every writer of reputation on the science of government, and repugnant to the principles of reason and common sense.[72]

2.9.109

The idea that there is no danger of the establishment of a standing army, under the new constitution, is without foundation.

2.9.110

It is a well known fact, that a number of those who had an agency in producing this system, and many of those who it is probable will have a principal share in the administration of the government under it, if it is adopted, are avowedly in favour of standing armies. It is a language common among them, "That no people can be kept in order, unless the government have an army to awe them into obedience; it is necessary to support the dignity of government, to have a military establishment."[73] And there will not be wanting a variety of plausible reason to justify the raising one, drawn from the danger we are in from the Indians on our frontiers, or from the European provinces in our neighbourhood. If to this we add, that an army will afford a decent support, and agreeable employment to the young men of many families, who are too indolent to follow occupations that will require care and industry, and too poor to live without doing any business[,] we can have little reason to doubt, but that we shall have a large standing army, as soon as this government can find money to pay them, and perhaps sooner.[74]

2.9.111   A writer, who is the boast of the advocates of this new constitution, has taken great pains to shew, that this power was proper and necessary to be vested in the general government.

He sets out with calling in question the candour and integrity of those who advance the objection, and with insinuating, that it is their intention to mislead the people, by alarming their passions, rather than to convince them by arguments addressed to their understandings.[75]

The man who reproves another for a fault, should be careful that he himself be not guilty of it. How far this writer has manifested a spirit of candour, and has pursued fair reasoning on this subject, the impartial public will judge, when his arguments pass before them in review.

2.9.112   He first attempts to shew, that this objection is futile and disingenuous, because the power to keep up standing armies, in time of peace, is vested, under the present government, in the legislature of every state in the union, except two. Now this is so far from being true, that it is expressly declared, by the present articles of confederation, that no body of forces "shall be kept up by any state, in time of peace, except such number only, as in the judgment of the United States in Congress assembled, shall be deemed requisite to garrison the forts necessary for the defence of such state."[76] Now, was it candid and ingenuous to endeavour to persuade the public, that the general government had no other power than your own legislature have on this head; when the truth is, your legislature have no authority to raise and keep up any forces?

He next tells us, that the power given by this constitution, on this head, is similar to that which Congress possess under the present confederation. As little ingenuity is manifested in this representation as in that of the former.

2.9.113   I shall not undertake to enquire whether or not Congress are vested with a power to keep up a standing army in time of peace; it has been a subject warmly debated in Congress, more than once, since the peace; and one of the most respectable states in the union, were so fully convinced that they had no such power, that they expressly instructed their delegates to enter a solemn protest against it on the journals of Congress, should they attempt to exercise it.

But should it be admitted that they have the power, there is such a striking dissimilarity between the restrictions under which the present Congress can exercise it, and that of the proposed government, that the comparison will serve rather to shew the impropriety of vesting the proposed government with the power, than of justifying it.

It is acknowledged by this writer, that the powers of Congress, under the present confederation, amount to little more than that of recommending. If they determine to raise troops, they are obliged to effect it through the authority of the state legislatures. This will, in the first instance, be a most powerful restraint upon them, against ordering troops to be raised. But if they should vote an army, contrary to the opinion and wishes of the people, the legislatures of the respective states would not raise them. Besides, the present Congress hold their places at the will and pleasure of the legislatures of the states who send them, and no troops can be raised, but by the assent of nine states out of the thirteen. Compare the power proposed to be lodged in the legislature on this head, under this constitution, with that vested in the present Congress, and every person of the least discernment, whose understanding is not totally blinded by prejudice, will perceive, that they bear no analogy to each other. Under the present confederation, the representatives of nine states, out of thirteen, must assent to the raising of troops, or they cannot be levied: under the proposed constitution, a less number than the representatives of two states, in the house of representatives, and the representatives of three states and an half in the senate, with the assent of the president, may raise any number of troops they please. The present Congress are restrained from an undue exercise of this power, from this consideration, they know [that] the state legislatures, through whose authority it must be carried into effect, would not comply with the requisition for the purpose, if it was evidently opposed to the public good: the proposed constitution authorizes the legislature to carry their determinations into execution, without the intervention of any other body between them and the people. The Congress under the present form are amenable to, and removable by, the legislatures of the respective states, and are chosen for one year only: the proposed constitution does not make the members of the legislature accountable to, or removeable by the state legislatures at all; and they are chosen, the one house for six, and the other for two years; and cannot be removed until their time of service is expired, let them conduct [themselves] ever so badly.—The public will judge, from the above comparison, how just a claim this writer has to that candour he affects to possess. In the mean time, to convince him, and the advocates for this system, that I possess some share of candor, I pledge myself to give up all opposition to it, on the

2.9.114

head of standing armies, if the power to raise them be restricted as it is in the present confederation; and I believe I may safely answer, not only for myself, but for all who make the objection, that they will be satisfied with less.

Brutus.

X
24 January 1788

To the People of the State of New-York.

2.9.115   The liberties of a people are in danger from a large standing army, not only because the rulers may employ them for the purposes of supporting themselves in any usurpations of power, which they may see proper to exercise, but there is great hazard, that an army will subvert the forms of the government, under whose authority, they are raised, and establish one, according to the pleasure of their leader.

2.9.116   We are informed, in the faithful pages of history, of such events frequently happening.—Two instances have been mentioned in a former paper.[77] They are so remarkable, that they are worthy of the most careful attention of every lover of freedom.—They are taken from the history of the two most powerful nations that have ever existed in the world; and who are the most renowned, for the freedom they enjoyed, and the excellency of their constitutions:—I mean Rome and Britain.

2.9.117   In the first, the liberties of the commonwealth was destroyed, and the constitution overturned, by an army, lead by Julius Cesar, who was appointed to the command, by the constitutional authority of that commonwealth. He changed it from a free republic, whose fame had sounded, and is still celebrated by all the world, into that of the most absolute despotism. A standing army effected this change, and a standing army supported it through a succession of ages, which are marked in the annals of history, with the most horrid cruelties, bloodshed, and carnage;—The most devilish, beastly, and unnatural vices, that ever punished or disgraced human nature.

The same army, that in Britain, vindicated the liberties of that people from the encroachments and despotism of a tyrant king, assisted Cromwell, their General, in wresting from the people, that liberty they had so dearly earned.

2.9.118   You may be told, these instances will not apply to our case:—But those who would persuade you to believe this, either mean to deceive you, or have not themselves considered the subject.

I firmly believe, no country in the world had ever a more patriotic army, than the one which so ably served this country, in the late war.

2.9.119   But had the General who commanded them, been possessed of the spirit of a Julius Cesar or a Cromwell, the liberties of this country, had in all probability, terminated with the war; or had they been maintained, might have cost more blood and treasure, than was expended in the conflict with Great-Britain. When an anonimous writer addressed the officers of the army at the close of the war, advising them not to part with their arms, until justice was done them—the effect it had is well known.[78] It affected them like an electric shock. He wrote like Cesar; and had the commander in chief, and a few more officers of rank, countenanced the measure, the desperate resolution had been taken, to refuse to disband. What the consequences of such a determination would have been, heaven only knows.—The army were in the full vigor of health and spirits, in the habit of discipline, and possessed of all our military stores and apparatus. They would have acquired great accessions of strength from the country.—Those who were disgusted at our republican forms of government (for such there then were, of high rank among us) would have lent them all their aid.—We should in all probability have seen a constitution and laws, dictated to us, at the head of an army, and at the point of a bayonet, and the liberties for which we had so severely struggled, snatched from us in a moment. It remains a secret, yet to be revealed, whether this measure was not suggested, or at least countenanced, by some, who have had great influence in producing the present system.—Fortunately indeed for this country, it had at the head of the army, a patriot as well as a general; and many of our principal officers, had not abandoned the characters of citizens, by assuming that of soldiers, and therefore, the scheme proved abortive. But are we to expect, that this will always be the case? Are we so much better than the people of other ages and of other countries, that the same allurements of power and greatness, which led them aside from their duty, will have no influence upon men in our country? Such an idea, is wild and extravagant.—Had we indulged such a delusion, enough has appeared in a little time past, to convince the most credulous, that the passion for pomp, power and greatness, works as powerfully in the hearts of many of our better sort, as it ever did in any country under heaven.—Were the same opportunity again to offer, we should very probably be grossly disappointed, if we made dependence, that all who then rejected the overture, would do it again.

From these remarks, it appears, that the evil[79] to be feared from a large standing army in time of peace, does not arise solely from the apprehension, that the rulers may employ them for the purpose of promoting their own ambitious views, but that equal, and perhaps greater danger, is to be apprehended from their overturning the constitutional powers of the government, and assuming the power to dictate any form they please.   2.9.120

The advocates for power, in support of this right in the proposed government, urge that a restraint upon the discretion of the legislatures, in respect to military establishments in time of peace, would be improper to be imposed, because they say, it will be necessary to maintain small garrisons on   2.9.121

the frontiers, to guard against the depredations of the Indians, and to be prepared to repel any encroachments or invasions that may be made by Spain or Britain.[80]

2.9.122 The amount of this argument striped of the abundant verbages with which the author has dressed it, is this:

It will probably be necessary to keep up a small body of troops to garrison a few posts, which it will be necessary to maintain, in order to guard against the sudden encroachments of the Indians, or of the Spaniards and British; and therefore, the general government ought to be invested with power to raise and keep up a standing army in time of peace, without restraint; at their discretion.

I confess, I cannot perceive that the conclusion follows from the premises. Logicians say, it is not good reasoning to infer a general conclusion from particular premises: though I am not much of a Logician, it seems to me, this argument is very like that species of reasoning.

2.9.123 When the patriots in the parliament in Great-Britain, contended with such force of argument, and all the powers of eloquence, against keeping up standing armies in time of peace, it is obvious, they never entertained an idea, that small garrisons on their frontiers, or in the neighbourhood of powers, from whom they were in danger of encroachments, or guards, to take care of public arsenals would thereby be prohibited.

2.9.124 The advocates for this power farther urge that it is necessary, because it may, and probably will happen, that circumstances will render it requisite to raise an army to be prepared to repel attacks of an enemy, before a formal declaration of war, which in modern times has fallen into disuse.[81] If the constitution prohibited the raising an army, until a war actually commenced, it would deprive the government of the power of providing for the defence of the country, until the enemy were within our territory. If the restriction is not to extend to the raising armies in cases of emergency, but only to the keeping them up, this would leave the matter to the discretion of the legislature; and they might, under the pretence that there was danger of an invasion, keep up the army as long as they judged proper—and hence it is inferred, that the legislature should have authority to raise and keep up an army without any restriction. But from these premises nothing more will follow than this, that the legislature should not be so restrained, as to put it out of their power to raise an army, when such exigencies as are instanced shall arise. But it does not thence follow, that the government should be empowered to raise and maintain standing armies at their discretion as well in peace as in war. If indeed, it is impossible to vest the general government with the power of raising troops to garrison the frontier posts, to guard arsenals, or to be prepared to repel an attack, when we saw a power preparing to make one, without giving them a general and indefinite authority, to raise and keep up armies, without any restriction or qualification, then this reasoning might have weight; but this has not been proved nor can it be.

2.9.125 It is admitted that to prohibit the general government, from keeping up standing armies, while yet they were authorised to raise them in case of exigency, would be an insufficient guard against the danger. A discretion of such latitude would give room to elude the force of the provision.

It is also admitted that an absolute prohibition against raising troops, except in cases of actual war, would be improper; because it will be requisite to raise and support a small number of troops to garrison the important frontier posts, and to guard arsenals; and it may happen, that the danger of an attack from a foreign power may be so imminent, as to render it highly proper we should raise an army, in order to be prepared to resist them. But to raise and keep up forces for such purposes and on such occasions, is not included in the idea, of keeping up standing armies in times of peace.

It is a thing very practicable to give the government sufficient authority to provide for these cases, and at the same time to provide a reasonable and competent security against the evil of a standing army—a clause to the following purpose would answer the end:

2.9.126

As standing armies in time of peace are dangerous to liberty, and have often been the means of overturning the best constitutions of government, no standing army, or troops of any description whatsoever, shall be raised or kept up by the legislature, except so many as shall be necessary for guards to the arsenals of the United States, or for garrisons to such posts on the frontiers, as it shall be deemed absolutely necessary to hold, to secure the inhabitants, and facilitate the trade with the Indians: unless when the United States are threatened with an attack or invasion from some foreign power, in which case the legislature shall be authorised to raise an army to be prepared to repel the attack; provided that no troops whatsoever shall be raised in time of peace, without the assent of two thirds of the members, composing both houses of the legislature.

A clause similar to this would afford sufficient latitude to the legislature to raise troops in all cases that were really necessary, and at the same time competent security against the establishment of that dangerous engine of despotism a standing army.

2.9.127

The same writer who advances the arguments I have noticed, makes a number of other observations with a view to prove that the power to raise and keep up armies, ought to be discretionary in the general legislature; some of them are curious; he instances the raising of troops in Massachusetts and Pennsylvania, to shew the necessity of keeping a standing army in time of peace;[82] the least reflection must convince every candid mind that both these cases are totally foreign to his purpose—Massachusetts raised a body of troops for six months, at the expiration of which they were to disband of course; this looks very little like a standing army. But beside, was that commonwealth in a state of peace at that time? So far from it that they were in the most violent commotions and contents, and their legislature had formally declared that an unnatural rebellion existed within the state. The situation of Pennsylvania was similar; a number of armed men had levied war against the authority of the state, and openly avowed their intention of withdrawing their allegiance from it. To what purpose examples are brought, of states raising troops for short periods in times of war or insurrections, on a question concerning the propriety of keeping up standing armies in times of peace, the public must judge.

2.9.128   It is farther said, that no danger can arise from this power being lodged in the hands of the general government, because the legislatures will be a check upon them, to prevent their abusing it.[83]

This is offered, as what force there is in it will hereafter receive a more particular examination. At present, I shall only remark, that it is difficult to conceive how the state legislatures can, in any case, hold a check over the general legislature, in a constitutional way. The latter has, in every instance to which their powers extend, complete controul over the former. The state legislatures can, in no case, by law, resolution, or otherwise, of right, prevent or impede the general government, from enacting any law, or executing it, which this constitution authorizes them to enact or execute. If then the state legislatures check the general legislatures [sic], it must be by exciting the people to resist constitutional laws. In this way every individual, or every body of men, may check any government, in proportion to the influence they may have over the body of the people. But such kinds of checks as these, though they sometimes correct the abuses of government, oftner destroy all government.[84]

2.9.129   It is further said, that no danger is to be apprehended from the exercise of this power, because it is lodged in the hands of representatives of the people; if they abuse it, it is in the power of the people to remove them, and chuse others who will pursue their interests.[85] Not to repeat what has been said before, That it is unwise in any people, to authorize their rulers to do, what, if done, would prove injurious—I have, in some former numbers, shewn, that the representation in the proposed government will be a mere shadow without the substance.[86] I am so confident that I am well founded in this opinion, that I am persuaded, if it was to be adopted or rejected, upon a fair discussion of its merits, without taking into contemplation circumstances extraneous to it, as reasons for its adoption, nineteen-twentieths of the sensible men in the union would reject it on this account alone; unless its powers were confined to much fewer objects than it embraces.

Brutus.

XI
31 January 1788

2.9.130   The nature and extent of the judicial power of the United States, proposed to be granted by this constitution, claims our particular attention.

Much has been said and written upon the subject of this new system on both sides, but I have not met with any writer, who has discussed the judicial powers with any degree of accuracy. And yet it is obvious, that we can form but very imperfect ideas of the manner in which this government will work, or the effect it will have in changing the internal police and mode of distributing justice at present subsisting in the respective states, without a thorough investigation of the powers of the judiciary and of the manner in which they will operate. This government is a complete system, not only for making, but for executing laws. And the courts of law, which will be constituted by it, are not only to decide upon the constitution and the laws made in pursuance of it, but by officers subordinate to them to execute all their decisions. The real effect of this system of government, will therefore be brought home to the feelings of the people, through the medium of the judicial power.[87] It is, moreover, of great importance, to examine with care the nature and extent of the judicial power, because those who are to be vested with it, are to be placed in a situation altogether unprecedented in a free country. They are to be rendered totally independent, both of the people and the legislature, both with respect to their offices and salaries. No errors they may commit can be corrected by any power above them, if any such power there be, nor can they be removed from office for making ever so many erroneous adjudications.

The only causes for which they can be displaced, is, conviction of treason, bribery, and high crimes and misdemeanors.   2.9.131

This part of the plan is so modelled, as to authorise the courts, not only to carry into execution the powers expressly given, but where these are wanting or ambiguously expressed, to supply what is wanting by their own decisions.

That we may be enabled to form a just opinion on this subject, I shall, in considering it,

1st. Examine the nature and extent of the judicial powers—and

2d. Enquire, whether the courts who are to exercise them, are so constituted as to afford reasonable ground of confidence, that they will exercise them for the general good.

With a regard to the nature and extent of the judicial powers, I have to   2.9.132
regret my want of capacity to give that full and minute explanation of them that the subject merits. To be able to do this, a man should be possessed of a degree of law knowledge far beyond what I pretend to. A number of hard words and technical phrases are used in this part of the system, about the meaning of which gentlemen learned in the law differ.

Its advocates know how to avail themselves of these phrases. In a number   2.9.133
of instances, where objections are made to the powers given to the judicial, they give such an explanation to the technical terms as to avoid them.

Though I am not competent to give a perfect explanation of the powers granted to this department of the government, I shall yet attempt to trace ˙ ˌ

some of the leading features of it, from which I presume it will appear, that they will operate to a total subversion of the state judiciaries, if not, to the legislative authority of the states.

2.9.134   In article 3d, sect. 2d, it is said, "The judicial power shall extend to all cases in law and equity arising under this constitution, the laws of the United States, and treaties made, or which shall be made, under their authority, &c."

The first article to which this power extends, is, all cases in law and equity arising under this constitution.

What latitude of construction this clause should receive, it is not easy to say. At first view, one would suppose, that it meant no more than this, that the courts under the general government should exercise, not only the powers of courts of law, but also that of courts of equity, in the manner in which those powers are usually exercised in the different states. But this cannot be the meaning, because the next clause authorises the courts to take cognizance of all cases in law and equity arising under the laws of the United States; this last article, I conceive, conveys as much power to the general judicial as any of the state courts possess.

2.9.135   The cases arising under the constitution must be different from those arising under the laws, or else the two clauses mean exactly the same thing.

The cases arising under the constitution must include such, as bring into question its meaning, and will require an explanation of the nature and extent of the powers of the different departments under it.

This article, therefore, vests the judicial with a power to resolve all questions that may arise on any case on the construction of the constitution, either in law or in equity.[88]

2.9.136   1st. They are authorised to determine all questions that may arise upon the meaning of the constitution in law. This article vests the courts with authority to give the constitution a legal construction, or to explain it according to the rules laid down for construing a law.—These rules give a certain degree of latitude of explanation. According to this mode of construction, the courts are to give such meaning to the constitution as comports best with the common, and generally received acceptation of the words in which it is expressed, regarding their ordinary and popular use, rather than their grammatical propriety. Where words are dubious, they will be explained by the context. The end of the clause will be attended to, and the words will be understood, as having a view to it; and the words will not be so understood as to bear no meaning or a very absurd one.

2.9.137   2d. The judicial are not only to decide questions arising upon the meaning of the constitution in law, but also in equity.

By this they are empowered, to explain the constitution according to the reasoning spirit of it, without being confined to the words or letter.[89]

"From this method of interpreting laws (says Blackstone) by the reason of them, arises what we call equity;" which is thus defined by Grotius, "the correction of that, wherein the law, by reason of its universality, is deficient["]; for since in laws all cases cannot be foreseen, or expressed, it is necessary, that when the decrees of the law cannot be applied to particular cases, there should some where be a power vested of defining those circumstances, which had they been foreseen the legislator would have expressed; and these are the cases, which according to Grotius, ["]lex non exacte definit, sed arbitrio boni viri permittet."

The same learned author observes, "That equity, thus depending   2.9.138 essentially upon each individual case, there can be no established rules and fixed principles of equity laid down, without destroying its very essence, and reducing it to a positive law."[90]

From these remarks, the authority and business of the courts of law, under this clause, may be understood.

They will give the sense of every article of the constitution, that may from time to time come before them. And in their decisions they will not confine themselves to any fixed or established rules, but will determine, according to what appears to them, the reason and spirit of the constitution. The opinions of the supreme court, whatever they may be, will have the force of law; because there is no power provided in the constitution, that can correct their errors, or controul their adjudications. From this court there is no appeal. And I conceive the legislature themselves, cannot set aside a judgment of this court, because they are authorised by the constitution to decide in the last resort. The legislature must be controuled by the constitution, and not the constitution by them. They have therefore no more right to set aside any judgment pronounced upon the construction of the constitution, than they have to take from the president, the chief command of the army and navy, and commit it to some other person. The reason is plain; the judicial and executive derive their authority from the same source, that the legislature do theirs; and therefore in all cases, where the constitution does not make the one responsible to, or controulable by the other, they are altogether independent of each other.

The judicial power will operate to effect, in the most certain, but yet silent   2.9.139 and imperceptible manner, what is evidently the tendency of the constitution:—I mean, an entire subversion of the legislative, executive and judicial powers of the individual states. Every adjudication of the supreme court, on any question that may arise upon the nature and extent of the general government, will affect the limits of the state jurisdiction. In proportion as the former enlarge the exercise of their powers, will that of the latter be restricted.

That the judicial power of the United States, will lean strongly in favour of   2.9.140 the general government, and will give such an explanation to the constitution, as will favour an extension of its jurisdiction, is very evident from a variety of considerations.

1st. The constitution itself strongly countenances such a mode of con-   2.9.141

struction. Most of the articles in this system, which convey powers of any considerable importance, are conceived in general and indefinite terms, which are either equivocal, ambiguous, or which require long definitions to unfold the extent of their meaning. The two most important powers committed to any government, those of raising money, and of raising and keeping up troops, have already been considered, and shewn to be unlimitted by any thing but the discretion of the legislature.[91] The clause which vests the power to pass all laws which are proper and necessary, to carry the powers given into execution, it has been shewn, leaves the legislature at liberty, to do every thing, which in their judgment is best.[92] It is said, I know, that this clause confers no power on the legislature, which they would not have had without it[93]—though I believe this is not the fact, yet, admitting it to be, it implies that the constitution is not to receive an explanation strictly, according to its letter; but more power is implied than is expressed. And this clause, if it is to be considered, as explanatory of the extent of the powers given, rather than giving a new power, is to be understood as declaring, that in construing any of the articles conveying power, the spirit, intent and design of the clause, should be attended to, as well as the words in their common acceptation.

This constitution gives sufficient colour for adopting an equitable construction, if we consider the great end and design it professedly has in view—these appear[94] from its preamble to be, "to form a more perfect union, establish justice, insure domestic tranquility, provide for the common defence, promote the general welfare, and secure the blessings of liberty to ourselves and posterity." The design of this system is here expressed, and it is proper to give such a meaning to the various parts, as will best promote the accomplishment of the end; this idea suggests itself naturally upon reading the preamble, and will countenance the court in giving the several articles such a sense, as will the most effectually promote the ends the constitution had in view—how this manner of explaining the constitution will operate in practice, shall be the subject of future enquiry.

2.9.142   2d. Not only will the constitution justify the courts in inclining to this mode of explaining it, but they will be interested in using this latitude of interpretation. Every body of men invested with office are tenacious of power; they feel interested, and hence it has become a kind of maxim, to hand down their offices, with all its rights and privileges, unimpared to their successors; the same principle will influence them to extend their power, and increase their rights; this of itself will operate strongly upon the courts to give such a meaning to the constitution in all cases where it can possibly be done, as will enlarge the sphere of their own authority. Every extension of the power of the general legislature, as well as of the judicial powers, will increase the powers of the courts; and the dignity and importance of the judges, will be in proportion to the extent and magnitude of the powers they exercise. I add, it is highly probable the emolument of the judges will be increased, with the increase of the business they will have to transact and its importance. From these considerations the judges will be interested to extend the powers of the courts, and to construe the constitution as much as possible, in such a way as to favour it; and that they will do it, appears probable.

3d. Because they will have precedent to plead, to justify them in it. It is well known, that the courts in England, have by their own authority, extended their jurisdiction far beyond the limits set them in their original institution, and by the laws of the land.

2.9.143

The court of exchequer is a remarkable instance of this. It was originally intended principally to recover the king's debts, and to order the revenues of the crown. It had a common law jurisdiction, which was established merely for the benefit of the king's accomptants. We learn from Blackstone, that the proceedings in this court are grounded on a writ called quo minus, in which the plaintiff suggests, that he is the king's farmer or debtor, and that the defendant hath done him the damage complained of, by which he is less able to pay the king.[95] These suits, by the statute of Rutland, are expressly directed to be confined to such matters as specially concern the king, or his ministers in the exchequer. And by the articuli super cartas, it is enacted, that no common pleas be thenceforth held in the exchequer contrary to the form of the great charter: but now any person may sue in the exchequer. The surmise of being debtor to the king being matter of form, and mere words of course; and the court is open to all the nation.

When the courts will have a precedent[96] before them of a court which extended its jurisdiction in opposition to an act of the legislature, is it not to be expected that they will extend theirs, especially when there is nothing in the constitution expressly against it? and they are authorised to construe its meaning, and are not under any controul?

2.9.144

This power in the judicial, will enable them to mould the government, into almost any shape they please.—The manner in which this may be effected we will hereafter examine.

Brutus.

XII
7 February 1788

In my last, I shewed, that the judicial power of the United States under the first clause of the second section of article eight, would be authorized to explain the constitution, not only according to its letter, but according to its spirit and intention; and having this power, they would strongly incline to

2.9.145

give it such a construction as to extend the powers of the general government, as much as possible, to the diminution, and finally to the destruction, of that of the respective states.

I shall now proceed to shew how this power will operate in its exercise to effect these purposes. In order to perceive the extent of its influence, I shall consider,

First. How it will tend to extend the legislative authority.

Second. In what manner it will increase the jurisdiction of the courts, and

Third. The way in which it will diminish, and destroy, both the legislative and judicial authority of the United States.

2.9.146   First. Let us enquire how the judicial power will effect an extension of the legislative authority.

Perhaps the judicial power will not be able, by direct and positive decrees, ever to direct the legislature, because it is not easy to conceive how a question can be brought before them in a course of legal discussion, in which they can give a decision, declaring, that the legislature have certain powers which they have not exercised, and which, in consequence of the determination of the judges, they will be bound to exercise. But it is easy to see, that in their adjudications they may establish certain principles, which being received by the legislature, will enlarge the sphere of their power beyond all bounds.

2.9.147   It is to be observed, that the supreme court has the power, in the last resort, to determine all questions that may arise in the course of legal discussion, on the meaning and construction of the constitution. This power they will hold under the constitution, and independent of the legislature. The latter can no more deprive the former of this right, than either of them, or both of them together, can take from the president, with the advice of the senate, the power of making treaties, or appointing ambassadors.

2.9.148   In determining these questions, the court must and will assume certain principles, from which they will reason, in forming their decisions. These principles, whatever they may be, when they become fixed, by a course of decisions, will be adopted by the legislature, and will be the rule by which they will explain their own powers. This appears evident from this consideration, that if the legislature pass laws, which, in the judgment of the court, they are not authorised to do by the constitution, the court will not take notice of them; for it will not be denied, that the constitution is the highest or supreme law.[97] And the courts are vested with the supreme and uncontroulable power, to determine, in all cases that come before them, what the constitution means; they cannot, therefore, execute a law, which, in their judgment, opposes the constitution, unless we can suppose they can make a superior law give way to an inferior. The legislature, therefore, will not go over the limits by which the courts may adjudge they are confined. And there is little room to doubt but that they will come up to those bounds, as often as occasion and opportunity may offer, and they may judge it proper to do it. For as on the one hand, they will not readily pass laws which they know the courts will not execute, so on the other, we may be sure they will not scruple to pass such as they know they will give effect, as often as they may judge it proper.

From these observations it appears, that the judgment of the judicial, on the constitution, will become the rule to guide the legislature in their construction of their powers.

2.9.149

What the principles are, which the courts will adopt, it is impossible for us to say; but taking up the powers as I have explained them in my last number, which they will possess under this clause, it is not difficult to see, that they may, and probably will, be very liberal ones.

We have seen, that they will be authorized to give the constitution a construction according to its spirit and reason, and not to confine themselves to its letter.

To discover the spirit of the constitution, it is of the first importance to attend to the principal ends and designs it has in view. These are expressed in the preamble, in the following words, viz. "We, the people of the United States, in order to form a more perfect union, establish justice, insure domestic tranquility, provide for the common defence, promote the general welfare, and secure the blessings of liberty to ourselves and our posterity, do ordain and establish this constitution," &c. If the end of the government is to be learned from these words, which are clearly designed to declare it, it is obvious it has in view every object which is embraced by any government. The preservation of internal peace—the due administration of justice—and to provide for the defence of the community, seems to include all the objects of government; but if they do not, they are certainly comprehended in the words, "to provide for the general welfare." If it be further considered, that this constitution, if it is ratified, will not be a compact entered into by states, in their corporate capacities, but an agreement of the people of the United States, as one great body politic, no doubt can remain, but that the great end of the constitution, if it is to be collected from the preamble, in which its end is declared, is to constitute a government which is to extend to every case for which any government is instituted, whether external or internal. The courts, therefore, will establish this as a principle in expounding the constitution, and will give every part of it such an explanation, as will give latitude to every department under it, to take cognizance of every matter, not only that affects the general and national concerns of the union, but also of such as relate to the administration of private justice, and to regulating the internal and local affairs of the different parts.

2.9.150

Such a rule of exposition is not only consistent with the general spirit of the preamble, but it will stand confirmed by considering more minutely the different clauses of it.

2.9.151

The first object declared to be in view is, "To form a perfect union." It is to be observed, it is not an union of states or bodies corporate; had this been the case the existence of the state governments, might have been secured. But it is a union of the people of the United States considered as one body, who are to ratify this constitution, if it is adopted. Now to make a union of this kind perfect, it is necessary to abolish all inferior governments, and to give the general one compleat legislative, executive and judicial powers to every purpose. The courts therefore will establish it as a rule in explaining the constitution to give it such a construction as will best tend to perfect the union or take from the state governments every power of either making or executing laws. The second object is "to establish justice." This must include not only the idea of instituting the rule of justice, or of making laws which shall be the measure or rule of right, but also of providing for the application of this rule or of administering justice under it. And under this the courts will in their decisions extend the power of the government to all cases they possibly can, or otherwise they will be restricted in doing what appears to be the intent of the constitution they should do, to wit, pass laws and provide for the execution of them, for the general distribution of justice between man and man. Another end declared is "to insure domestic tranquility." This comprehends a provision against all private breaches of the peace, as well as against all public commotions or general insurrections; and to attain the object of this clause fully, the government must exercise the power of passing laws on these subjects, as well as of appointing magistrates with authority to execute them. And the courts will adopt these ideas in their expositions. I might proceed to the other clause, in the preamble, and it would appear by a consideration of all of them separately, as it does by taking them together, that if the spirit of this system is to be known from its declared end and design in the preamble, its spirit is to subvert and abolish all the powers of the state government, and to embrace every object to which any government extends.

2.9.152   As it sets out in the preamble with this declared intention, so it proceeds in the different parts with the same idea. Any person, who will peruse the 8th section with attention, in which most of the powers are enumerated, will perceive that they either expressly or by implication extend to almost every thing about which any legislative power can be employed. But if this equitable mode of construction is applied to this part of the constitution; nothing can stand before it.

This will certainly give the first clause in that article a construction which I confess I think the most natural and grammatical one, to authorise the Congress to do any thing which in their judgment will tend to provide for the general welfare, and this amounts to the same thing as general and unlimited powers of legislation in all cases.

(To be continued.)

14 February 1788

(Continued from last Thursday's paper.)

This same manner of explaining the constitution, will fix a meaning, and a very important one too, to the 12th [18th?] clause of the same section, which authorises the Congress to make all laws which shall be proper and necessary for carrying into effect the foregoing powers, &c. A voluminous writer in favor of this system, has taken great pains to convince the public, that this clause means nothing: for that the same powers expressed in this, are implied in other parts of the constitution.[98] Perhaps it is so, but still this will undoubtedly be an excellent auxilliary to assist the courts to discover the spirit and reason of the constitution, and when applied to any and every of the other clauses granting power, will operate powerfully in extracting the spirit from them.

2.9.153

I might instance a number of clauses in the constitution, which, if explained in an *equitable* manner, would extend the powers of the government to every case, and reduce the state legislatures to nothing; but, I should draw out my remarks to an undue length, and I presume enough has been said to shew, that the courts have sufficient ground in the exercise of this power, to determine, that the legislature have no bounds set to them by this constitution, by any supposed right the legislatures of the respective states may have, to regulate any of their local concerns.

2.9.154

I proceed, 2d, To inquire, in what manner this power will increase the jurisdiction of the courts.

2.9.155

I would here observe, that the judicial power extends, expressly, to all civil cases that may arise save such as arise between citizens of the same state, with this exception to those of that description, that the judicial of the United States have cognizance of cases between citizens of the same state, claiming lands under grants of different states. Nothing more, therefore, is necessary to give the courts of law, under this constitution, complete jurisdiction of all civil causes, but to comprehend cases between citizens of the same state not included in the foregoing exception.

I presume there will be no difficulty in accomplishing this. Nothing more is necessary than to set forth, in the process, that the party who brings the suit is a citizen of a different state from the one against whom the suit is brought, and there can be little doubt but that the court will take cognizance of the matter, and if they do, who is to restrain them?[99] Indeed, I will freely confess, that it is my decided opinion, that the courts ought to take cognizance of such causes, under the powers of the constitution. For one of the great ends of the constitution is, "to establish justice." This supposes that this cannot be done under the existing governments of the states; and there is certainly as good reason why individuals, living in the same state, should

2.9.156

have justice, as those who live in different states. Moreover, the constitution expressly declares, that "the citizens of each state shall be entitled to all the privileges and immunities of citizens in the several states." It will therefore be no fiction, for a citizen of one state to set forth, in a suit, that he is a citizen of another; for he that is entitled to all the privileges and immunities of a country, is a citizen of that country. And in truth, the citizen of one state will, under this constitution, be a citizen of every state.

2.9.157   But supposing that the party, who alledges that he is a citizen of another state, has recourse to fiction in bringing in his suit, it is well known, that the courts have high authority to plead, to justify them in suffering actions to be brought before them by such fictions. In my last number I stated, that the court of exchequer tried all causes in virtue of such a fiction. The court of king's bench, in England, extended their jurisdiction in the same way. Originally, this court held pleas, in civil cases, only of trespasses and other injuries alledged to be committed *vi et armis*. They might likewise, says Blackstone,[100] upon the division of the *aula regia,* have originally held pleas of any other civil action whatsoever (except in real actions which are now very seldom in use) provided the defendant was an officer of the court, or in the custody of the marshall or prison-keeper of this court, for breach of the peace, &c. In process of time, by a fiction, this court began to hold pleas of any personal action whatsoever; it being surmised, that the defendant has been arrested for a supposed trespass that "he has never committed, and being thus in the custody of the marshall of the court, the plaintiff is at liberty to proceed against him, for any other personal injury: which surmise of being in the marshall's custody, the defendant is not at liberty to dispute." By a much less fiction, may the pleas of the courts of the United States extend to cases between citizens of the same state. I shall add no more on this head, but proceed briefly to remark, in what way this power will diminish and destroy both the legislative and judicial authority of the states.

2.9.158   It is obvious that these courts will have authority to decide upon the validity of the laws of any of the states, in all cases where they come in question before them. Where the constitution gives the general government exclusive jurisdiction, they will adjudge all laws made by the states, in such cases, void *ab initio.* Where the constitution gives them concurrent jurisdiction, the laws of the United States must prevail, because they are the supreme law. In such cases, therefore, the laws of the state legislatures must be repealed, restricted, or so construed, as to give full effect to the laws of the union on the same subject. From these remarks it is easy to see, that in proportion as the general government acquires power and jurisdiction, by the liberal construction which the judges may give the constitution, will those of the states lose its rights, until they become so trifling and unimportant, as not to be worth having. I am much mistaken, if this system will not operate to effect this with as much celerity, as those who have the administration of it will think prudent to suffer it. The remaining objections to the judicial power shall be considered in a future paper.

Brutus.

XIII
21 February 1788

Having in the two preceding numbers, examined the nature and tendency of the judicial power, as it respects the explanation of the constitution, I now proceed to the consideration of the other matters, of which it has cognizance.—The next paragraph extends its authority, to all cases, in law and equity, arising under the laws of the United States. This power, as I understand it, is a proper one. The proper province of the judicial power, in any government, is, as I conceive, to declare what is the law of the land.[101] To explain and enforce those laws, which the supreme power or legislature may pass; but not to declare what the powers of the legislature are. I suppose the cases in equity, under the laws, must be so construed, as to give the supreme court not only a legal, but equitable jurisdiction of cases which may be brought before them, or in other words, so, as to give them, not only the powers which are now exercised by our courts of law, but those also, which are now exercised by our court of chancery. If this be the meaning, I have no other objection to the power, than what arises from the undue extension of the legislative power. For, I conceive that the judicial power should be commensurate with the legislative. Or, in other words, the supreme court should have authority to determine questions arising under the laws of the union.

2.9.159

The next paragraph which gives a power to decide in law and equity, on all cases arising under treaties, is unintelligible to me. I can readily comprehend what is meant by deciding a case under a treaty. For as treaties will be the law of the land, every person who have rights or privileges secured by treaty, will have aid of the courts of law, in recovering them. But I do not understand, what is meant by equity arising under a treaty. I presume every right which can be claimed under a treaty, must be claimed by virtue of some article or clause contained in it, which gives the right in plain and obvious words; or at least, I conceive, that the rules for explaining treaties, are so well ascertained, that there is no need of having recourse to an equitable construction. If under this power, the courts are to explain treaties, according to what they conceive are their spirit, which is nothing less than a power to give them whatever extension they may judge proper, it is a dangerous and improper power. The cases affecting ambassadors, public ministers, and consuls—of admiralty and maritime jurisdiction; con-

2.9.160

troversies to which the United States are a party, and controversies between states, it is proper should be under the cognizance of the courts of the union, because none but the general government, can, or ought to pass laws on their subjects. But, I conceive the clause which extends the power of the judicial to controversies arising between a state and citizens of another state, improper in itself, and will, in its exercise, prove most pernicious and destructive.

2.9.161   It is improper, because it subjects a state to answer in a court of law, to the suit of an individual.[102] This is humiliating and degrading to a government, and, what I believe, the supreme authority of no state ever submitted to.

The states are now subject to no such actions. All contracts entered into by individuals with states, were made upon the faith and credit of the states; and the individuals never had in contemplation any compulsory mode of obliging the government to fulfil its engagements.

2.9.162   The evil consequences that will flow from the exercise of this power, will best appear by tracing it in its operation. The constitution does not direct the mode in which an individual shall commence a suit against a state or the manner in which the judgement of the court shall be carried into execution, but it gives the legislature full power to pass all laws which shall be proper and necessary for the purpose. And they certainly must make provision for these purposes, or otherwise the power of the judicial will be nugatory. For, to what purpose will the power of a judicial be, if they have no mode, in which they can call the parties before them? Or of what use will it be, to call the parties to answer, if after they have given judgement, there is no authority to execute the judgment? We must, therefore, conclude, that the legislature will pass laws which will be effectual in this head. An individual of one state will then have a legal remedy against a state for any demand he may have against a state to which he does not belong. Every state in the union is largely indebted to individuals. For the payment of these debts they have given notes payable to the bearer. At least this is the case in this state. Whenever a citizen of another state becomes possessed of one of these notes, he may commence an action in the supreme court of the general government; and I cannot see any way in which he can be prevented from recovering. It is easy to see, that when this once happens, the notes of the state will pass rapidly from the hands of citizens of the state to those of other states.

2.9.163   And when the citizens of other states possess them, they may bring suits against the state for them, and by this means, judgments and executions may be obtained against the state for the whole amount of the state debt. It is certain the state, with the utmost exertions it can make, will not be able to discharge the debt she owes, under a considerable number of years, perhaps with the best management, it will require twenty or thirty years to discharge it. This new system will protract the time in which the ability of the state will enable them to pay off their debt, because all the funds of the state will be transferred to the general government, except those which arise from internal taxes.

The situation of the states will be deplorable. By this system, they will surrender to the general government, all the means of raising money, and at the same time, will subject themselves to suits at law, for the recovery of the debts they have contracted in effecting the revolution. 2.9.164

The debts of the individual states will amount to a sum, exceeding the domestic debt of the United States; these will be left upon them, with power in the judicial of the general government, to enforce their payment, while the general government will possess an exclusive command of the most productive funds, from which the states can derive money, and a command of every other source of revenue paramount to the authority of any state.

It may be said that the apprehension that the judicial power will operate in this manner is merely visionary, for that the legislature will never pass laws that will work these effects. Or if they were disposed to do it, they cannot provide for levying an execution on a state, for where will the officer find property whereon to levy? 2.9.165

To this I would reply, if this is a power which will not or cannot be executed, it was useless and unwise to grant it to the judicial. For what purpose is a power given which it is imprudent or impossible to exercise? If it be improper for a government to exercise a power, it is improper they should be vested with it. And it is unwise to authorise a government to do what they cannot effect.

As to the idea that the legislature cannot provide for levying an execution on a state, I believe it is not well founded. I presume the last paragraph of the 8th section of article 1, gives the Congress express power to pass any laws they may judge proper and necessary for carrying into execution the power vested in the judicial department. And they must exercise this power, or otherwise the courts of justice will not be able to carry into effect the authorities with which they are invested. For the constitution does not direct the mode in which the courts are to proceed, to bring parties before them, to try causes, or to carry the judgment of the courts into execution. Unless they are pointed out by law, how are these to proceed, in any of the cases of which they have cognizance? They have the same authority to establish regulations in respect to these matters, where a state is a party, as where an individual is a party. The only difficulty is, on whom shall process be served, when a state is a party, and how shall execution be levied. With regard to the first, the way is easy, either the executive or legislative of the state may be notified, and upon proof being made of the service of the notice, the court may proceed to a hearing of the cause. Execution may be levied on any property of the state, either real or personal. The treasury may be seized by the officers of the general government, or any lands the property of the state, may be made subject to seizure and sale to satisfy any 2.9.166

judgment against it. Whether the estate of any individual citizen may not be made answerable for the discharge of judgments against the state, may be worth consideration. In some corporations this is the case.

2.9.167   If the power of the judicial under this clause will extend to the cases above stated, it will, if executed, produce the utmost confusion, and in its progress, will crush the states beneath its weight. And if it does not extend to these cases, I confess myself utterly at a loss to give it any meaning. For if the citizen of one state, possessed of a written obligation, given in pursuance of a solemn act of the legislature, acknowledging a debt due to the bearer, and promising to pay it, cannot recover in the supreme court, I can conceive of no case in which they can recover. And it appears to me ridiculous to provide for obtaining judgment against a state, without giving the means of levying execution.

Brutus.

XIV
28 February 1788

2.9.168   The second paragraph of sect. 2d. art. 3, is in these words: "In all cases affecting ambassadors, other public ministers and consuls, and those in which a state shall be a party, the supreme court shall have original jurisdiction. In all the other cases before mentioned, the supreme court shall have appellate jurisdiction, both as to law and fact, with such exceptions, and under such regulations as the Congress shall make.["]

Although it is proper that the courts of the general government should have cognizance of all matters affecting ambassadors, foreign ministers, and consuls; yet I question much the propriety of giving the supreme court original jurisdiction in all cases of this kind.

Ambassadors, and other public ministers, claim, and are entitled by the law of nations, to certain privileges, and exemptions, both for their persons and their servants.

2.9.169   The meanest servant of an ambassador is exempted by the law of nations from being sued for debt. Should a suit be brought against such an one by a citizen, through inadvertency or want of information, he will be subject to an action in the supreme court. All the officers concerned in issuing or executing the process will be liable to like actions. Thus may a citizen of a state be compelled, at great expence and inconveniency, to defend himself against a suit, brought against him in the supreme court, for inadvertently commencing an action against the most menial servant of an ambassador for a just debt.

The appellate jurisdiction granted to the supreme court, in this paragraph, has justly been considered as one of the most objectionable parts of the constitution: under this power, appeals may be had from the inferior courts to the supreme, in every case to which the judicial power extends, except in the few instances in which the supreme court will have original jurisdiction.

By this article, appeals will lie to the supreme court, in all criminal as well as civil causes. This I know, has been disputed by some; but I presume the point will appear clear to any one, who will attend to the connection of this paragraph with the one that precedes it. In the former, all the cases, to which the power of the judicial shall extend, whether civil or criminal, are enumerated. There is no criminal matter, to which the judicial power of the United States will extend; but such as are included under some one of the cases specified in this section. For this section is intended to define all the cases, of every description, to which the power of the judicial shall reach. But in all these cases it is declared, the supreme court shall have appellate jurisdiction, except in those which affect ambassadors, other public ministers and consuls, and those in which a state shall be a party. If then this section extends the power of the judicial, to criminal cases, it allows appeals in such cases. If the power of the judicial is not extended to criminal matters by this section, I ask, by what part of this system does it appear, that they have any cognizance of them?

2.9.170

I believe it is a new and unusual thing to allow appeals in criminal matters. It is contrary to the sense of our laws, and dangerous to the lives and liberties of the citizen. As our law now stands, a person charged with a crime has a right to a fair and impartial trial by a jury of his country [county?], and their verdict is final. If he is acquitted no other court can call upon him to answer for the same crime. But by this system, a man may have had ever so fair a trial, have been acquitted by ever so respectable a jury of his country; and still the officer of the government who prosecutes, may appeal to the supreme court. The whole matter may have a second hearing. By this means, persons who may have disobliged those who execute the general government, may be subjected to intolerable oppression. They may be kept in long and ruinous confinement, and exposed to heavy and insupportable charges, to procure the attendence of witnesses, and provide the means of their defence, at a great distance from their places of residence.

2.9.171

I can scarcely believe there can be a considerate citizen of the United States, that will approve of this appellate jurisdiction, as extending to criminal cases, if they will give themselves time for reflection.

2.9.172

Whether the appellate jurisdiction as it respects civil matters, will not prove injurious to the rights of the citizens, and destructive of those privileges which have ever been held sacred by Americans, and whether it will not render the administration of justice intolerably burthensome, intricate, and dilatory, will best appear, when we have considered the nature and operation of this power.

It has been the fate of this clause, as it has of most of those, against which unanswerable objections have been offered, to be explained different ways, by the advocates and opponents to the constitution. I confess I do not know

2.9.173

what the advocates of the system, would make it mean, for I have not been fortunate enough to see in any publication this clause taken up and considered. It is certain however, they do not admit the explanation which those who oppose the constitution give it, or otherwise they would not so frequently charge them with want of candor, for alledging that it takes away the trial by jury[;] appeals from an inferior to a superior court, as practised in the civil law courts, are well understood. In these courts, the judges determine both on the law and the fact; and appeals are allowed from the inferior to the superior courts, on the whole merits: the superior tribunal will re-examine all the facts as well as the law, and frequently new facts will be introduced, so as many times to render the cause in the court of appeals very different from what it was in the court below.

2.9.174   If the appellate jurisdiction of the supreme court, be understood in the above sense, the term is perfectly intelligible. The meaning then is, that in all the civil causes enumerated, the supreme court shall have authority to re-examine the whole merits of the case, both with respect to the facts and the law which may arise under it, without the intervention of a jury; that this is the sense of this part of the system appears to me clear, from the express words of it, "in all the other cases before mentioned, the supreme court shall have appellate jurisdiction, both as to law and fact, &c." Who are the supreme court? Does it not consist of the judges? and they are to have the same jurisdiction of the fact as they are to have of the law. They will therefore have the same authority to determine the fact as they will have to determine the law, and no room is left for a jury on appeals to the supreme court.

2.9.175   If we understand the appellate jurisdiction in any other way, we shall be left utterly at a loss to give it a meaning; the common law is a stranger to any such jurisdiction: no appeals can lie from any of our common law courts, upon the merits of the case; the only way in which they can go up from an inferior to a superior tribunal is by habeas corpus before a hearing, or by certiorari, or writ of error, after they are determined in the subordinate courts; but in no case, when they are carried up, are the facts re-examined, but they are always taken as established in the inferior courts.[103]

(To be continued.)

XIV
6 March 1788

(Continued.)

2.9.176   It may still be insisted that this clause does not take away the trial by jury on appeals, but that this may be provided for by the legislature, under that paragraph which authorises them to form regulations and restrictions for the court in the exercise of this power.

The natural meaning of this paragraph seems to be no more than this, that Congress may declare, that certain cases shall not be subject to the appellate jurisdiction, and they may point out the mode in which the court shall proceed in bringing up the causes before them, the manner of their taking evidence to establish the facts, and the method of the courts proceeding. But I presume they cannot take from the court the right of deciding on the fact, any more than they can deprive them of the right of determining on the law, when a cause is once before them; for they have the same jurisdiction as to fact, as they have as to the law. But supposing the Congress may under this clause establish the trial by jury on appeals, it[104] does not seem to me that it will render this article much less exceptionable. An appeal from one court and jury, to another court and jury, is a thing altogether unknown in the laws of our state, and in most of the states in the union. A practice of this kind prevails in the eastern states; actions are there commenced in the inferior courts, and an appeal lies from them on the whole merits to the superior courts: the consequence is well known, very few actions are determined in the lower courts; it is rare that a case of any importance is not carried by appeal to the supreme court, and the jurisdiction of the inferior courts is merely nominal; this has proved so burthensome to the people in Massachusetts, that it was one of the principal causes which excited the insurrection in that state, in the year past; very few sensible and moderate men in that state but what will admit, that the inferior courts are almost entirely useless, and answer very little purpose, save only to accumulate costs against the poor debtors who are already unable to pay their just debts.

But the operation of the appellate power in the supreme judicial of the United States, would work infinitely more mischief than any such power can do in a single state. 2.9.177

The trouble and expence to the parties would be endless and intolerable. No man can say where the supreme court are to hold their sessions, the presumption is, however, that it must be at the seat of the general government: in this case parties must travel many hundred miles, with their witnesses and lawyers, to prosecute or defend a suit; no man of midling fortune, can sustain the expence of such a law suit, and therefore the poorer and midling class of citizens will be under the necessity of submitting to the demands of the rich and the lordly, in cases that will come under the cognizance of this court. If it be said, that to prevent this oppression, the supreme court will set in different parts of the union, it may be replied, that this would only make the oppression somewhat more tolerable, but by no means so much as to give a chance of justice to the poor and midling class. It is utterly impossible that the supreme court can move into so many different parts of the Union, as to make it convenient or even tolerable to attend before them with witnesses to try causes from every part of the United states; if to avoid the expence and inconvenience of calling witnesses from a great distance, to give evidence before the supreme court, the expedient of taking the deposition of witnesses in writing should be adopted, it would not help the matter. It is of great importance in the distribution of justice that witnesses should be examined face to face, that the parties should have the fairest opportunity of cross examining them in order to bring out the whole truth; there is something in the manner in which a witness delivers his testimony which cannot be committed to paper, and which yet very frequently gives a complexion to his evidence, very different from what it would bear if committed to writing, besides the expence of taking written testimony would be enormous; those who are acquainted with the costs that arise in the courts, where all the evidence is taken in writing, well know that they exceed beyond all comparison those of the common law courts, where witnesses are examined viva voce.

2.9.178   The costs accruing in courts generally advance with the grade of the court; thus the charges attending a suit in our common pleas, is much less than those in the supreme court, and these are much lower than those in the court of chancery; indeed the costs in the last mentioned court, are in many cases so exorbitant and the proceedings so dilatory that the suitor had almost as well give up his demand as to prosecute his suit. We have just reason to suppose, that the costs in the supreme general court will exceed either of our courts; the officers of the general court will be more dignified than those of the states, the lawyers of the most ability will practice in them, and the trouble and expence of attending them will be greater. From all these considerations, it appears, that the expence attending suits in the supreme court will be so great, as to put it out of the power of the poor and midling class of citizens to contest a suit in it.

2.9.179   From these remarks it appears, that the administration of justice under the powers of the judicial will be dilatory; that it will be attended with such an heavy expence as to amount to little short of a denial of justice to the poor and middling class of people who in every government stand most in need of the protection of the law; and that the trial by jury, which has so justly been the boast of our fore fathers as well as ourselves is taken away under them.

These extraordinary powers in this court are the more objectionable, because there does not appear the least necessity for them, in order to secure a due and impartial distribution of justice.

2.9.180   The want of ability or integrity, or a disposition to render justice to every suitor, has not been objected against the courts of the respective states: so far as I have been informed, the courts of justice in all the states, have ever been found ready, to administer justice with promptitude and impartiality according to the laws of the land; It is true in some of the states, paper money has been made, and the debtor authorised to discharge his debts with it, at a depreciated value, in orders, tender laws have been passed, obliging the creditor to receive on execution other property than money in discharge of his demand, and in several of the states laws have been made unfavorable to the creditor and tending to render property insecure.

But these evils have not happened from any defect in the judicial departments of the states; the courts indeed are bound to take notice of these laws, and so will the courts of the general government be under obligation to observe the laws made by the general legislature not repugnant to the constitution; but so far have the judicial been from giving undue latitude of construction to laws of this kind, that they have invariably strongly inclined to the other side. All the acts of our legislature, which have been charged with being of this complexion, have uniformly received the strictest construction by the judges, and have been extended to no cases but to such as came within the strict letter of the law. In this way, have our courts, I will not say evaded the law, but so limited it in its operation as to work the least possible injustice: the same thing has taken place in Rhode-Island, which has justly rendered herself infamous, by her tenaciously adhering to her paper money system. The judges there gave a decision, in opposition to the words of the Statute, on this principle, that a construction according to the words of it, would contradict the fundamental maxims of their laws and constitution.[105]

2.9.181

No pretext therefore, can be formed, from the conduct of the judicial courts which will justify giving such powers to the supreme general court, for their decisions have been such as to give just ground of confidence in them, that they will firmly adhere to the principles of rectitude, and there is no necessity of lodging these powers in the courts, in order to guard against the evils justly complained of, on the subject of security of property under this constitution. For it has provided, "that no state shall emit bills of credit, or make any thing but gold and silver coin a tender in payment of debts." It has also declared, that "no state shall pass any law impairing the obligation of contracts."—These prohibitions give the most perfect security against those attacks upon property which I am sorry to say some of the states have but too wantonly made, by passing laws sanctioning fraud in the debtor against his creditor. For "this constitution will be the supreme law of the land, and the judges in every state will be bound thereby; any thing in the constitution and laws of any state to the contrary notwithstanding."

2.9.182

The courts of the respective states might therefore have been securely trusted, with deciding all cases between man and man, whether citizens of the same state or of different states, or between foreigners and citizens, and indeed for ought I see every case that can arise under the constitution or laws of the United States, ought in the first instance to be tried in the court of the state, except those which might arise between states, such as respect ambassadors, or other public ministers, and perhaps such as call in question the claim of lands under grants from different states. The state courts would

2.9.183

be under sufficient controul, if writs of error were allowed from the state courts to the supreme court of the union; according to the practice of the courts in England and of this state, on all cases in which the laws of the union are concerned, and perhaps to all cases in which a foreigner is a party.

2.9.184   This method would preserve the good old way of administering justice, would bring justice to every man's door, and preserve the inestimable right of trial by jury. It would be following, as near as our circumstances will admit, the practice of the courts in England, which is almost the only thing I would wish to copy in their government.

But as this system now stands, there is to be as many inferior courts as Congress may see fit to appoint, who are to be authorised to originate and in the first instance to try all the cases falling under the description of this article; there is no security that a trial by jury shall be had in these courts, but the trial here will soon become, as it is in Massachusetts' inferior courts, mere matter of form; for an appeal may be had to the supreme court on the whole merits. This court is to have power to determine in law and in equity, on the law and the fact, and this court is exalted above all other power in the government, subject to no controul, and so fixed as not to be removeable, but upon impeachment, which I shall hereafter shew, is much the same thing as not to be removeable at all.

2.9.185   To obviate the objections made to the judicial power it has been said, that the Congress, in forming the regulations and exceptions which they are authorised to make respecting the appellate jurisdiction, will make provision against all the evils which are apprehended from this article. On this I would remark, that this way of answering the objection made to the power, implies an admission that the power is in itself improper without restraint, and if so, why not restrict it in the first instance.

The just way of investigating any power given to a government, is to examine its operation supposing it to be put in exercise. If upon enquiry, it appears that the power, if exercised, would be prejudicial, it ought not to be given. For to answer objections made to a power given to a government, by saying it will never be exercised, is really admitting that the power ought not to be exercised, and therefore ought not to be granted.

Brutus.

XV
20 March 1788

(Continued.)[106]

2.9.186   I said in my last number, that the supreme court under this constitution would be exalted above all other power in the government, and subject to no controul. The business of this paper will be to illustrate this, and to shew the danger that will result from it. I question whether the world ever saw, in any period of it, a court of justice invested with such immense powers, and yet placed in a situation so little responsible. Certain it is, that in England, and in the several states, where we have been taught to believe, the courts of law are put upon the most prudent establishment, they are on a very different footing.

The judges in England, it is true, hold their offices during their good behaviour, but then their determinations are subject to correction by the house of lords; and their power is by no means so extensive as that of the proposed supreme court of the union.—I believe they in no instance assume the authority to set aside an act of parliament under the idea that it is inconsistent with their constitution. They consider themselves bound to decide according to the existing laws of the land, and never undertake to controul them by adjudging that they are inconsistent with the constitution—much less are they vested with the power of giving an *equitable* construction to the constitution.

2.9.187

The judges in England are under the controul of the leigislature, for they are bound to determine according to the laws passed by them. But the judges under this constitution will controul the legislature, for the supreme court are authorised in the last resort,[107] to determine what is the extent of the powers of the Congress; they are to give the constitution an explanation, and there is no power above them to set[108] aside their judgment. The framers of this constitution appear to have followed that of the British, in rendering the judges independent, by granting them their offices during good behaviour, without following the constitution of England, in instituting a tribunal in which their errors may be corrected; and without adverting to this, that the judicial under this system have a power which is above the legislative, and which indeed transcends any power before given to a judicial by any free government under heaven.

2.9.188

I do not object to the judges holding their commissions during good behaviour. I suppose it a proper provision provided they were made properly responsible. But I say, this system has followed the English government in this, while it has departed from almost every other principle of their jurisprudence, under the idea, of rendering the judges independent; which, in the British constitution, means no more than that they hold their places during good behaviour, and have fixed salaries, they have made the judges *independent,* in the fullest sense of the word. There is no power above them, to controul any of their decisions. There is no authority that can remove them, and they cannot be controuled by the laws of the legislature. In short, they are independent of the people, of the legislature, and of every power under heaven. Men placed in this situation will generally soon feel themselves independent of heaven itself. Before I proceed to illustrate the truth of these assertions, I beg liberty to make one remark—Though in my opin-

2.9.189

ion the judges ought to hold their offices during good behaviour, yet I think it is clear, that the reasons in favour of this establishment of the judges in England, do by no means apply to this country.

2.9.190   The great reason assigned, why the judges in Britain ought to be commissioned during good behaviour, is this, that they may be placed in a situation, not to be influenced by the crown, to give such decisions, as would tend to increase its powers and prerogatives. While the judges held their places at the will and pleasure of the king, on whom they depended not only for their offices, but also for their salaries, they were subject to every undue influence. If the crown wished to carry a favorite point, to accomplish which the aid of the courts of law was necessary, the pleasure of the king would be signified to the judges. And it required the spirit of a martyr, for the judges to determine contrary to the king's will.—They were absolutely dependent upon him both for their offices and livings. The king, holding his office during life, and transmitting it to his posterity as an inheritance, has much stronger inducements to increase the prerogatives of his office than those who hold their offices for stated periods, or even for life. Hence the English nation gained a great point, in favour of liberty. When they obtained the appointment of the judges, during good behaviour, they got from the crown a concession, which deprived it of one of the most powerful engines with which it might enlarge the boundaries of the royal prerogative and encroach on the liberties of the people. But these reasons do not apply to this country, we have no hereditary monarch; those who appoint the judges do not hold their offices for life, nor do they descend to their children. The same arguments, therefore, which will conclude in favor of the tenor of the judge's offices for good behaviour, lose a considerable part of their weight when applied to the state and condition of America. But much less can it be shewn, that the nature of our government requires that the courts should be placed beyond all account more independent, so much so as to be above controul.

2.9.191   I have said that the judges under this system will be *independent* in the strict sense of the word: To prove this I will shew—That there is no power above them that can controul their decisions, or correct their errors. There is no authority that can remove them from office for any errors or want of capacity, or lower their salaries, and in many cases their power is superior to that of the legislature.

1st. There is no power above them that can correct their errors or controul their decisions—The adjudications of this court are final and irreversible, for there is no court above them to which appeals can lie, either in error or on the merits.—In this respect it differs from the courts in England, for there the house of lords is the highest court, to whom appeals, in error, are carried from the highest of the courts of law.

2.9.192   2d. They cannot be removed from office or suffer a dimunition of their salaries, for any error in judgement or want of capacity.

It is expressly declared by the constitution,—"That they shall at stated times receive a compensation for their services which shall not be diminished during their continuance in office."

The only clause in the constitution which provides for the removal of the judges from office, is that which declares, that "the president, vice-president, and all civil officers of the United States, shall be removed from office, on impeachment for, and conviction of treason, bribery, or other high crimes and misdemeanors." By this paragraph, civil officers, in which the judges are included, are removable only for crimes. Treason and bribery are named, and the rest are included under the general terms of high crimes and misdemeanors.—Errors in judgement, or want of capacity to discharge the duties of the office, can never be supposed to be included in these words, *high crimes and misdemeanors*. A man may mistake a case in giving judgment, or manifest that he is incompetent to the discharge of the duties of a judge, and yet give no evidence of corruption or want of integrity. To support the charge, it will be necessary to give in evidence some facts that will shew, that the judges commited the error from wicked and corrupt motives.

3d. The power of this court is in many cases superior to that of the legislature. I have shewed, in a former paper, that this court will be authorised to decide upon the meaning of the constitution, and that, not only according to the natural and ob[vious] meaning of the words, but also according to the spirit and intention of it.[109] In the exercise of this power they will not be subordinate to, but above the legislature. For all the departments of this government will receive their powers, so far as they are expressed in the constitution, from the people immediately, who are the source of power. The legislature can only exercise such powers as are given them by the constitution, they cannot assume any of the rights annexed to the judicial, for this plain reason, that the same authority which vested the legislature with their powers, vested the judicial with theirs—both are derived from the same source, both therefore are equally valid, and the judicial hold their powers independently of the legislature, as the legislature do of the judicial.—The supreme court then have a right, independent of the legislature, to give a construction to the constitution and every part of it, and there is no power provided in this system to correct their construction or do it away. If, therefore, the legislature pass any laws, inconsistent with the sense the judges put upon the constitution, they will declare it void; and therefore in this respect their power is superior to that of the legislature.[110] In England the judges are not only subject to have their decisions set aside by the house of lords, for error, but in cases where they give an explanation to the laws or constitution of the country, contrary to the sense of the parliament, though the parliament will not set aside the judgement of the court, yet, they have authority, by a new law, to explain a former one, and

2.9.193

by this means to prevent a reception of such decisions. But no such power is in the legislature. The judges are supreme—and no law, explanatory of the constitution, will be binding on them.

From the preceding remarks, which have been made on the judicial powers proposed in this system, the policy of it may be fully developed.

2.9.194   I have, in the course of my observation on this constitution, affirmed and endeavored to shew, that it was calculated to abolish entirely the state governments, and to melt down the states into one entire government, for every purpose as well internal and local, as external and national. In this opinion the opposers of the system have generally agreed—and this has been uniformly denied by its advocates in public. Some individuals, indeed, among them, will confess, that it has this tendency, and scruple not to say, it is what they wish; and I will venture to predict, without the spirit of prophecy, that if it is adopted[111] without amendments, or some such precautions as will ensure amendments immediately after its adoption, that the same gentlemen who have employed their talents and abilities with such success to influence the public mind to adopt this plan, will employ the same to persuade the people, that it will be for their good to abolish the state governments as useless and burdensome.

2.9.195   Perhaps nothing could have been better conceived to facilitate the abolition of the state governments than the constitution of the judicial. They will be able to extend the limits of the general government gradually, and by insensible degrees, and to accomodate themselves to the temper of the people. Their decisions on the meaning of the constitution will commonly take place in cases which arise between individuals, with which the public will not be generally acquainted; one adjudication will form a precedent to the next, and this to a following one. These cases will immediately affect individuals only; so that a series of determinations will probably take place before even the people will be informed of them. In the mean time all the art and address of those who wish for the change will be employed to make converts to their opinion. The people will be told, that their state officers, and state legislatures are a burden and expence without affording any solid advantage, for that all the laws passed by them, might be equally well made by the general legislature. If to those who will be interested in the change, be added, those who will be under their influence, and such who will submit to almost any change of government, which they can be persuaded to believe will ease them of taxes, it is easy to see, the party who will favor the abolition of the state governments would be far from being inconsiderable.—In this situation, the general legislature, might pass one law after another, extending the general and abridging the state jurisdictions, and to sanction their proceedings would have a course of decisions of the judicial to whom the constitution has committed the power of explaining the constitution.—If the states remonstrated, the constitutional mode of deciding upon the validity of the law, is with the supreme court, and neither people, nor state legislatures, nor the general legislature can remove them or reverse their decrees.

Had the construction of the constitution been left with the legislature, they would have explained it at their peril; if they exceed their powers, or sought to find, in the spirit of the constitution, more than was expressed in the letter, the people from whom they derived their power could remove them, and do themselves right; and indeed I can see no other remedy that the people can have against their rulers for encroachments of this nature. A constitution is a compact of a people with their rulers; if the rulers break the compact, the people have a right and ought to remove them and do themselves justice; but in order to enable them to do this with the greater facility, those whom the people chuse at stated periods, should have the power in the last resort to determine the sense of the compact; if they determine contrary to the understanding of the people, an appeal will lie to the people at the period when the rulers are to be elected, and they will have it in their power to remedy the evil; but when this power is lodged in the hands of men independent of the people, and of their representatives, and who are not, constitutionally, accountable for their opinions, no way is left to controul them but *with a high hand and an outstretched arm.*

2.9.196

Brutus.

XVI
10 April 1788

When great and extraordinary powers are vested in any man, or body of men, which in their exercise, may operate to the oppression of the people, it is of high importance that powerful checks should be formed to prevent the abuse of it.

2.9.197

Perhaps no restraints are more forcible, than such as arise from responsibility to some superior power.—Hence it is that the true policy of a republican government is, to frame it in such manner, that all persons who are concerned in the government, are made accountable to some superior for their conduct in office.—This responsibility should ultimately rest with the People. To have a government well administered in all its parts, it is requisite the different departments of it should be separated and lodged as much as may be in different hands. The legislative power should be in one body, the executive in another, and the judicial in one different from either—But still each of these bodies should be accountable for their conduct.[112] Hence it is impracticable, perhaps, to maintain a perfect distinction between these several departments—For it is difficult, if not impossible, to call to account the several officers in government, without in some degree mixing the legislative and judicial. The legislature in a free republic are chosen[113] by the people at stated periods, and their responsibility consists, in their being amenable to the people. When the term, for which they are chosen, shall expire, who will then have opportunity to displace them if they disapprove of their conduct—but it would be improper that the judicial should be elective, because their business requires that they should possess a degree of law knowledge, which is acquired only by a regular education, and besides it is fit that they should be placed, in a certain degree in an independent situation, that they may maintain firmness and steadiness in their decisions.[114] As the people therefore ought not to elect the judges, they cannot be amenable to them immediately, some other mode of amenability must therefore be devised for these, as well as for all other officers which do not spring from the immediate choice of the people: this is to be effected by making one court subordinate to another, and by giving them cognizance of the behaviour of all officers; but on this plan we at last arrive at some supreme, over whom there is no power to controul but the people themselves. This supreme controling power should be in the choice of the people, or else you establish an authority independent, and not amenable at all, which is repugnant to the principles of a free government. Agreeable to these principles I suppose the supreme judicial ought to be liable to be called to account, for any misconduct, by some body of men, who depend upon the people for their places; and so also should all other great officers in the State, who are not made amenable to some superior officers. This policy seems in some measure to have been in view of the framers of the new system, and to have given rise to the institution of a court of impeachments—How far this Court will be properly qualified to execute the trust which will be reposed in them, will be the business of a future paper to investigate. To prepare the way to do this, it shall be the business of this, to make some remarks upon the constitution and powers of the Senate, with whom the power of trying impeachments is lodged.

2.9.198   The following things may be observed with respect to the constitution of the Senate.

1st. They are to be elected by the legislatures of the States and not by the people, and each State is to be represented by an equal number.

2d. They are to serve for six years, except that one third of those first chosen are to go out of office at the expiration of two years, one third at the expiration of four years, and one third at the expiration of six years, after which this rotation is to be preserved, but still every member will serve for the term of six years.

3d. If vacancies happen by resignation or otherwise, during the recess of the legislature of any State, the executive is authorised to make temporary appointments until the next meeting of the legislature.

4. No person can be a senator who has not arrived to the age of thirty

years, been nine years a citizen of the United States, and who is not at the time he is elected an inhabitant of the State for which he is elected.

The apportionment of members of Senate among the States is not according to numbers, or the importance of the States; but is equal. This, on the plan of a consolidated government, is unequal and improper; but is proper on the system of confederation—on this principle I approve of it.[115] It is indeed the only feature of any importance in the constitution of a confederated government. It was obtained after a vigorous struggle of that part of the Convention who were in favor of preserving the state governments. It is to be regretted, that they were not able to have infused other principles into the plan, to have secured the government of the respective states, and to have marked with sufficient precision the line between them and the general government.

2.9.199

The term for which the senate are to be chosen, is in my judgment too long, and no provision being made for a rotation will, I conceive, be of dangerous consequence.

2.9.200

It is difficult to fix the precise period for which the senate should be chosen. It is a matter of opinion, and our sentiments on the matter must be formed, by attending to certain principles. Some of the duties which are to be performed by the senate, seem evidently to point out the propriety of their term of service being extended beyond the period of that of the assembly. Besides as they are designed to represent the aristocracy of the country, it seems fit they should possess more stability, and so continue a longer period than that branch who represent the democracy. The business of making treaties and some other which it will be proper to commit to the senate, requires that they should have experience, and therefore that they should remain some time in office to acquire it.—But still it is of equal importance that they should not be so long in office as to be likely to forget the hand that formed them, or be insensible of their interests. Men long in office are very apt to feel themselves independent [and] to form and pursue interests separate from those who appointed them. And this is more likely to be the case with the senate, as they will for the most part of the time be absent from the state they represent, and associate with such company as will possess very little of the feelings of the middling class of people. For it is to be remembered that there is to be a *federal city,* and the inhabitants of it will be the great and the mighty of the earth. For these reasons I would shorten the term of their service to four years. Six years is a long period for a man to be absent from his home, it would have a tendency to wean him from his constituents.

A rotation in the senate, would also in my opinion be of great use. It is probable that senators once chosen for a state will, as the system now stands, continue in office for life. The office will be honorable if not lucrative. The persons who occupy it will probably wish to continue in it, and therefore use all their influence and that of their friends to continue in

2.9.201

office.—Their friends will be numerous and powerful, for they will have it in their power to confer great favors; besides it will before long be considered as disgraceful not to be re-elected. It will therefore be considered as a matter of delicacy to the character of the senator not to return him again.—Every body acquainted with public affairs knows how difficult it is to remove from office a person who is [has?] long been in it. It is seldom done except in cases of gross misconduct. It is rare that want of competent ability procures it. To prevent this inconvenience I conceive it would be wise to determine, that a senator should not be eligible after he had served for the period assigned by the constitution for a certain number of years; perhaps three would be sufficient. A farther benefit would be derived from such an arrangement; it would give opportunity to bring forward a greater number of men to serve their country, and would return those, who had served, to their state, and afford them the advantage of becoming better acquainted with the condition and politics of their constituents. It farther appears to me proper, that the legislatures should retain the right which they now hold under the confederation, of recalling their members. It seems an evident dictate of reason, that when a person authorises another to do a piece of business for him, he should retain the power to displace him, when he does not conduct according to his pleasure. This power in the state legislatures, under confederation, has not been exercised to the injury of the government, nor do I see any danger of its being so exercised under the new system. It may operate much to the public benefit.

2.9.202   These brief remarks are all I shall make on the organization of the senate. The powers with which they are invested will require a more minute investigation.

This body will possess a strange mixture of legislative, executive and judicial powers, which in my opinion will in some cases clash with each other.

1. They are one branch of the legislature, and in this respect will possess equal powers in all cases with the house of representatives; for I consider the clause which gives the house of representatives the right of originating bills for raising a revenue as merely nominal, seeing the senate be[116] authorised to propose or concur with amendments.

2. They are a branch of the executive in the appointment of ambassadors and public ministers, and in the appointment of all other officers, not otherwise provided for; whether the forming of treaties, in which they are joined with the president, appertains to the legislative or the executive part of the government, or to neither, is not material.

3. They are part of the judicial, for they form the court of impeachments.

2.9.203   It has been a long established maxim, that the legislative, executive and judicial departments in government should be kept distinct. It is said, I know, that this cannot be done. And therefore that this maxim is not just, or at least that it should only extend to certain leading features in a government. I admit that this distinction cannot be perfectly preserved. In a due ballanced government, it is perhaps absolutely necessary to give the executive qualified legislative powers, and the legislative or a branch of them judicial powers in the last resort. It may possibly also, in some special cases, be adviseable to associate the legislature, or a branch of it, with the executive, in the exercise of acts of great national importance. But still the maxim is a good one, and a separation of these powers should be sought as far as is practicable. I can scarcely imagine that any of the advocates of the system will pretend, that it was necessary to accumulate all these powers in the senate.

There is a propriety in the senate's possessing legislative powers; this is the principal end which should be held in view in their appointment. I need not here repeat what has so often and ably been advanced on the subject of a division of the legislative power into two branches—The arguments in favor of it I think conclusive. But I think it equally evident, that a branch of the legislature should not be invested with the power of appointing officers. This power in the senate is very improperly lodged for a number of reasons—These shall be detailed in a future number.[117]

2.9.204

Brutus.

1. This essay was replied to by Pelatiah Webster in a pamphlet, "The Weakness of Brutus Exposed," published in Philadelphia in 1787; Ford, *Pamphlets* 117-31.

2. Cf. Federal Farmer I, 2.8.9, whose argument Brutus follows in many respects. Jeffrey points to numerous specific similarities. *University of Cincinnati Law Review* 40, no. 4 (1971): 643 ff., passim, nn. 5, 10, 32, 35, 45, 60, 64.

3. The taxing power is discussed at length in essays V–VIII, 2.9.55–101.

4. See V, 2.9.60–61; cf. Federal Farmer IV, 2.8.51.

5. These powers are discussed in VIII–X, 2.9.93–129.

6. The judiciary is discussed in XI–XV, 2.4.130–96.

7. The classic exposition of the meaning of the necessary and proper clause is in *The Federalist* no. 33. See also Ford, *Pamphlets* 233–34 (Aristides), 356–57 (Iredell); McMaster and Stone 329–30 (Wilson). For other Anti-Federalist discussions of this clause see Centinel V, 2.7.97; Federal Farmer IV, 2.8.49; Old Whig II, 3.3.12; Countryman from Dutchess County 6.6.25 n. 12.

8. Beccaria, *An Essay on Crimes and Punishments* ch. 26, "Of the Spirit of Family in States." On editions of this work, see above, Federal Farmer VI, 2.8.97 n. 61.

9. The subject of representation is discussed at length in essays III and IV, 2.9.34–54.

10. The argument here should, of course, be compared with that of Publius in *The Federalist* no. 10. See also Federal Farmer VIII, 2.8.108, and Cato III, 2.6.13 n. 8.

11. Cf. Federal Farmer III, 2.8.24 n. 19; and Brutus IV, 2.9.47.

12. See IV, 2.9.48–50.

13. Cf. the discussion of the executive by Franklin in the Philadelphia Convention, Farrand I, 81–85 (2 June). Brutus does not treat the executive at any length. For the discussion by Federal Farmer, see above, XIV, 2.8.177–82. See also "The Weakness of Brutus Exposed," Ford, *Pamphlets* 130; and Federal Farmer XIV, 2.8.179 n. 107.

14. Cf. Federal Farmer's scheme of rights, VI, 2.8.80–86.

15. See IX, 2.9.102.

16. Brutus' argument calls to mind the more famous but fundamentally identical statement by Publius: "If men were angels, no government would be necessary. If

angels were to govern men, neither external nor internal controuls on government would be necessary. In framing a government which is to be administered by men over men, the great difficulty lies in this: you must first enable the government to controul the governed; and in the next place, oblige it to controul itself." *The Federalist* no. 51, 349. Publius differs from Brutus in his solution of this difficulty; and to understand the Anti-Federalists it is necessary to grasp both the difference and the profound agreement upon which it rests. See IV, 2.9.45–46; XVI, 2.9.197.

17. James Wilson, "Address to Citizens of Philadelphia," McMaster and Stone 143. Wilson's argument is not the "piece of foolishness" that William Jeffrey calls it (*University of Cincinnati Law Review* 40, no. 4 [1971]: 681n), as is suggested by the great efforts made by the Anti-Federalists in refuting it. The fuller view is that Wilson's argument has a solid basis but is insufficient to prove that a bill of rights is unnecessary.

18. These bills of rights can be found in Thorpe, *Federal and State Constitutions.*

19. The quotation is from the Maryland constitution of 1776, Declaration of Rights, arts. XXII–XXIII. Virginia, Massachusetts, New Hampshire, North Carolina, and Pennsylvania had similar provisions.

20. The quotation is from the North Carolina constitution, Declaration of Rights, art. XIV. Maryland, Massachusetts, New Hampshire, Virginia, and Pennsylvania had similar provisions.

21. The constitutions of Virginia, Pennsylvania, Maryland, North Carolina, New York, Massachusetts, New Hampshire had such provisions regarding the militia. The constitutions of Massachusetts, Maryland, New Hampshire prohibited the keeping up of standing armies "without the consent of the legislature." The constitutions of North Carolina, Pennsylvania, Virginia advised the avoidance of standing armies "in time of peace." See *The Federalist* no. 24, 153 and note; no. 26, 167–68. For Brutus' criticism of Publius on standing army, see IX, 2.9.111–14.

22. Edmund Randolph was one of the few Federalists who attempted to meet this objection (see Elliot III, 464–66), though McKean and Yeates made similar but weaker attempts in the Pennsylvania ratifying convention (McMaster and Stone 278–79, 296. For other Anti-Federal discussions of this point see, Federal Farmer IV, 2.8.51–52; XVI, 2.8.196–97; Agrippa XIV, 4.6.66; Henry 5.16.24, 36; Cincinnatus I, 6.1.4–5; Old Whig II, 3.3.7 ff.

23. Cf. Old Whig III, 3.3.15; Agrippa VI, 4.6.22 ff; One of the Common People 4.8.1 ff. For Federalist arguments, of varying penetration, that the new government will be limited by existing state bills of rights, see Ford, *Pamphlets* 48 (A Citizen of America), 148 (An American Citizen); Ford, *Essays* 398 (Williamson); McMaster and Stone 112–13 (A Citizen of Pennsylvania); New Hampshire *Freeman's Oracle* 18 January 1788 (Alfredus); *The Country Journal and the Poughkeepsie Advertiser* 15 April 1788 (A Friend to Good Government); *Massachusetts Centinel* 28 November 1787 (One of the Middle Interest). "The State Declarations of Rights are not repealed by this Constitution," Roger Sherman said in the Philadelphia convention, "and being in force are sufficient." Farrand II, 588 (12 September).

24. *The Spirit of Laws* XI, ch. 6. Brutus abridges the part of Montesquieu's comment relating to representation.

25. This is not a new paragraph in the original.

26. Cf. XVI, 2.9.199, where Brutus takes a different view. The question of the apportionment of Senate seats equally among the states was one on which the Anti-Federalists were equivocal. Like Brutus, The Federal Farmer seems to have changed his mind; see above, III, 2.8.28; XI, 2.8.143. See also Martin 2.4.35, 42; Centinel I, 2.7.23; Impartial Examiner 5.14.34; Symmes 4.5.2

27. Above, II, 2.9.23–24. For references to other Anti-Federalist discussions see Federal Farmer II, 2.8.15 n. 11.

28. Cf. *The Federalist* nos. 35–36; for other Anti-Federalist discussions of the natural aristocracy see Federal Farmer VII, 2.8.97 n. 64.

29. Brutus probably refers to Alexander Hamilton and Gouverneur Morris and perhaps also to Nathaniel Gorham and Rufus King. Farrand I, 282–311, 381–82, 375–76, 392–93, 513–14; II, 490–91. While no one in the Convention expressed exactly the opinion Brutus describes, John Francis Mercer—an Anti-Federalist and probably

the author of the essays of A [Maryland] Farmer—came close; see Farrand II, 284–85, and [Maryland] Farmer II, 5.1.29. Cf. Federal Farmer III, 2.8.37.

30. Essay IV, 2.9.45–54.

31. Note that Brutus does not seem to acknowledge here a possibility of a tyranny of the many; but see V, 2.9.56. Cf. Federal Farmer V, 2.8.60; Agrippa XVI, 4.6.73; [Maryland] Farmer I, 5.1.15 and n. 11; Henry 5.16.14. On the Federalist side see, in addition to *The Federalist* no. 10, Ford, *Pamphlets* 200–201 (Fabius), 354 (Marcus); *Virginia Independent Chronicle* 6 February 1788 (The State Soldier).

32. This is not a new paragraph in the original.

33. The original reads, "going into so an entire consolidation. . . ."

34. See below, V–X, 2.9.55–129. Many Anti-Federalists made this somewhat desperate argument. See Federal Farmer III, 2.8.34; Mason 5.17.1; Smith 6.12.9, 38–40.

35. The original reads, "and of whose talents . . . they are total strangers to. . . ."

36. Cf. *The Federalist* nos. 27–28.

37. Ephesians 5:29.

38. II Kings 8:13.

39. Compare Publius' different formulation of the issue, *The Federalist* nos. 23, 150–51; no. 31, 197. Cf. VI, 2.9.66.

40. See above, Federal Farmer XVII, 2.8.204 n. 123.

41. See Ford, *Pamphlets* 50–51 (A Citizen of America), and McMaster and Stone 274–75 (McKean, answering Smilie, ibid. 268–69). Cf. *The Federalist* no. 41. See Brutus VI, 2.9.77–78.

42. "As the duties of superintending the national defence and of securing the public peace against foreign or domestic violence, involve a provision for casualties and dangers, to which no possible limit can be assigned, the power of making that provision ought to know no other bounds than the exigencies of the nation and the resources of the community." *The Federalist* no. 31, 195–96, and generally nos. 30–36.

43. In addition to the discussion immediately following, Brutus treats this question in essay VI, 2.9.64–82.

44. Publius replies to this argument in *The Federalist* nos. 32 and 34.

45. "Money is, with propriety, considered as the vital principle of the body politic; as that which sustains its life and motion and enables it to perform its most essential functions." *The Federalist* no. 30, 188.

46. "This mode of reasoning," Publius argues, "appears sometimes to turn upon the suggestion of usurpation in the national government; at other times it seems to be designed only as a deduction from the constitutional operation of its intended powers. It is only in the latter light, that it can be admitted to have any pretensions to fairness. . . . [A]ll observations founded upon the danger of usurpation, ought to be referred to the composition and structure of the government, not to the nature or extent of its powers." *The Federalist* no. 31, 197.

47. Publius argues that there is no legal or constitutional power in either the national or the state governments to annul the taxes of the other. "And in practice there is little reason to apprehend any inconvenience; because in a short course of time the wants of the States will naturally reduce themselves within *a very narrow compass;* and in the interim, the United States will in all probability find it convenient to abstain wholly from those objects to which the particular States would be inclined to resort." *The Federalist* no. 34, 210. See above, Federal Farmer III, 2.8.39 n. 29.

48. Discussed in *The Federalist* no. 35, 216–18.

49. See above, n. 39.

50. No state interposition here!

51. See below, n. 84.

52. Brutus does not reach this question.

53. Matthew 6:24; Luke 16:13.

54. See Ford, *Pamphlets* 50 (Noah Webster). The quotation is slightly altered from the original. See above, V, 2.9.58.

55. P. 147. The statement is slightly revised from the original.

56. Publius does not quite admit this. He says: "*If* the circumstances of our coun-

try are such, as to demand a compound instead of a simple, a confederate instead of a sole government, the essential point which will remain to be adjusted, will be to discriminate the OBJECTS, *as far as it can be done,* which shall appertain to the different provinces or departments of power; allowing to each the most ample authority for fulfilling the objects committed to its charge." *The Federalist* no. 23 (italics added). Other Federalists were less equivocal. See for example McMaster and Stone 99 (P. Webster); Ford, *Pamphlets* 121–22, 128 (A Citizen of Philadelphia), 252 (Aristides); Ford, *Essays* 238 ff. (*A Citizen of New Haven*); Elliot III, 301 (Pendleton). On the critical importance of the line to be drawn between federal and state powers see Monroe 5.21.17 n. 8.

57. *The Federalist* no. 23, 147.

58. Cf. the forceful argument to this effect made by George Mason in the Constitutional Convention, Farrand I, 112–13 (4 June); see below, Old Whig VIII, 3.3.53–54; Philadelphiensis VI, 3.9.37–38; [Maryland] Farmer V, 5.1.82; Henry 5.16.2.

59. Publius calls the policy "of tying up the hands of government from offensive war founded upon reasons of state" a "novel and absurd experiment in politics." *The Federalist* no. 34, 211. See [New Hampshire] Farmer 4.17.4.

60. See the exchange between Roger Sherman and James Madison regarding the objects of the general government, Farrand I, 133–36 (6 June).

61. Cf. the intriguing discussion of the causes of hostilities among nations in *The Federalist* no. 6.

62. See above, Federal Farmer VI, 2.8.74 n. 54.

63. On the comparative merits of the administration of the state and federal governments, see *The Federalist* no. 27, 172–75. See below, n. 87.

64. See *The Federalist* no. 41, 276–77. Publius points out that the growth of imports for consumption will not grow in the same proportion as the growth of the population and economy in general. See Centinel II, 2.7.52 n. 30.

65. The space is left blank by Brutus.

66. See *The Federalist* no. 24; Ford, *Pamphlets* 51–52 (A Citizen of America), 234–35 (Aristides). Some of the more interesting of the Anti-Federal discussions of the dangers of a standing army, in addition to that of Brutus, are those of Federal Republican 3.6.21; DeWitt 4.3.9, 14, 28–29; [New Hampshire] Farmer 4.17.4; [Maryland] Farmer II, 5.1.33, 45–49; Impartial Examiner 5.14.8.

67. James Wilson, "Address to Citizens of Philadelphia," McMaster and Stone 145–46; *The Federalist* no. 24, 155–57. See also Ford, *Pamphlets* 234–36 (Aristides), 363–66 (Marcus); Ford, *Essays* 156–57 (A Landholder); McMaster and Stone 101, 107 (Pelatiah Webster), 170 (A Federalist), 373 (McKean). Other Federalists denied that a "standing army," properly speaking, is provided for. See An American Citizen [Tench Coxe], in Ford, *Pamphlets* 150–51.

68. *Cobbett's Parliamentary History of England* (London 1811), VIII (1722–33), 904–10.

69. See *The Federalist* no. 84; Mason 2.2.1 n. 1; Federal Farmer IV, 2.8.50 nn. 38–40.

70. See above, nn. 66, 67.

71. A Citizen of America [Noah Webster], "An Examination . . . ," Ford, *Pamphlets* 51–52. Compare in this connection the more subtle argument of An American Citizen [Tench Coxe] in Ford, *Pamphlets* 150–51.

72. See Federal Farmer X, 2.8.127 n. 80.

73. I know of no such Federalist language. James Wilson did argue in favor of the power to maintain a standing army as necessary to secure "the dignity and safety" of the country. McMaster and Stone 145–46. Publius, tough-minded as ever, admits that military force may have to turn inward: "seditions and insurrections are unhappily maladies as inseparable from the body politic, as tumours and eruptions from the natural body; that the idea of governing at all times by the simple force of law (which we have been told is the only admissible principle of republican government) has no place but in the reveries of those political doctors, whose sagacity disdains the admonitions of experimental instruction." *The Federalist* no. 28, 176. See above, n. 66.

The possibility of military enforcement of federal law was a major Anti-Federal concern. See for example Cato III, 2.6.17; Federal Farmer II, 2.8.23; Pennsylvania Convention Minority 3.11.50; Columbian Patriot 4.28.4.

74. Cf. Federal Farmer III, 2.8.39.

75. *The Federalist* no. 24, 154–55.

76. Article VI. Publius' statement is that "*two* only [of the State constitutions] contained an interdiction of standing armies in time of peace; that the other eleven had either observed a profound silence on the subject, or had in express terms admitted the right of the legislature to authorize their existence." *The Federalist* no. 24, 153–54. Publius refers in his next paper (no. 25, 159–60) to the provision in the Articles of Confederation prohibiting the states from maintaining military forces in peacetime without the consent of Congress.

77. VIII, 2.9.100–101.

78. See John Marshall, *The Life of George Washington* (Philadelphia 1804–7; 2d ed. 1839) IV, 74 ff.

79. The original reads, "evils."

80. *The Federalist* no. 24, 155–57.

81. *The Federalist* no. 25, 161; see Marcus [James Iredell], Ford, *Pamphlets* 364–65.

82. *The Federalist* no. 25, 162–63.

83. *The Federalist* no. 26, 168–69.

84. See VI, 2.9.69; Federal Farmer X, 2.8.128 n. 82; Henry, 5.16.2, 14; Smith 6.12.31. Publius agrees, indeed insists, that the states have no constitutional check on the general legislature. See *The Federalist* nos. 15, 16, especially p. 103. Cf. Tocqueville, *Democracy in America* I, ch. 8, subsection entitled "What Distinguishes the Federal Constitution of the United States of America from All Other Federal Constitutions." On the states as arms of revolution, see *The Federalist* no. 26, 168–69; no. 28, 178–79; no. 46, 321–22; no. 60, 404.

85. *The Federalist* no. 26, 169.

86. See above, essays I, III, IV, 2.9.1–21, 34–54.

87. The federal government, Publius argued two months earlier, "must carry its agency to the persons of the citizens. It must stand in need of no intermediate legislations, but must itself be empowered to employ the arm of the ordinary magistrate to execute its own resolutions. The majesty of the national authority must be manifested through the medium of the courts of justice. The government of the Union, like that of each State, must be able to address itself immediately to the hopes and fears of individuals; and to attract to its support those passions which have the strongest influence upon the human heart. It must, in short, possess all the means, and have a right to resort to all the methods, of executing the powers, with which it is intrusted, that are possessed and exercised by the governments of the particular States." *The Federalist* no. 16, 102–3. Jeffrey suggests that there is a contradiction between this argument and Publius' statement the next day (no. 17, 106) that the administration of private justice and other local matters can never be desirable cares of a general jurisdiction. Jeffrey thinks that the "entire performance must have been the cause of much innocent merriment among knowledgeable New Yorkers, as well as the source of considerable irritation to Federalists who had abundant reasons to feel ashamed at his sophistries and pettifogging." *University of Cincinnati Law Review* 40, no. 4 (1971): 739 n. 47. Careless readers may have had some such reactions, yet it is to be hoped that there were not many who came to such harsh conclusions on such slender evidence. Even on their face, the two statements of Publius are not contradictory, though it is true that their reconciliation points to further questions. These statements are, moreover, part of a larger and subtle argument by Publius looking to the eventual replacement of the state governments by the federal government in the hearts and minds of the people. The attentive reader can follow this argument in *The Federalist* no. 16, 102–3; no. 17, 106–7; and no. 27, 171–74. See above, Cato III, 2.6.20 n. 14; Federal Farmer XVIII, 2.8.13 n. 128. See John Smilie's keen analysis in the Pennsylvania ratifying convention, McMaster and Stone 270–71. See also Smith 6.12.31.

88. See below, n. 101.

89. Cf. Publius' narrow interpretation of the "equity" jurisdiction, *The Federalist* no. 80, 539-40.

90. Blackstone, *Commentaries on the Laws of England* I, 61-62.

91. Above, I, V-X, 2.9.1-21, 55-129.

92. See I, 2.9.1-21; V, 55-63; XII, 2.9.153 ff.

93. See *The Federalist* no. 33, and above, n. 7.

94. The original reads, "there appears."

95. *Commentaries on the Laws of England* III, 45.

96. The original reads, "president."

97. Cf. *The Federalist* no. 78, 524-26. The power of judicial review of acts of the legislature was explicitly assumed by a number of Anti-Federalist and Federalist writers, though seldom so thoughtfully argued as by Brutus and Publius. See for example, Martin 2.4.89; Centinel XVI, 2.7.168; Ford, *Pamphlets* 234 (Aristides); McMaster and Stone 304-5 (Wilson). Cf. the provocative comparison of Brutus and Publius in Ann Stuart Diamond, "The Anti-Federalist Brutus," *Political Science Reviewer*, Fall 1976.

98. Referring, no doubt, to *The Federalist*, especially no. 33, 204-6, and no. 44, 302-5, both of which had been published at this time.

99. See The Federal Farmer's suggestion that fictional residence or action in the federal city may be used as the means of establishing federal jurisdiction, XVIII, 2.8.224.

100. *Commentaries on the Laws of England* III, 42.

101. This premise is of course also the basis of Publius' different conclusion. No. 78, 525: "The interpretation of the laws is the proper and peculiar province of the courts. A constitution is, in fact, and must be regarded by the judges as, a fundamental law. It therefore belongs to them to ascertain its meaning as well as the meaning of any particular act proceeding from the legislative body. If there should happen to be an irreconcilable variance between the two, that which has the superior obligation and validity ought, of course, to be preferred; or, in other words, the Constitution ought to be preferred to the statute, the intention of the people to the intention of their agents." *The Federalist* no. 78.

102. See *Chisholm* v. *Georgia*, 2 Dall. 419 (1793), the outcry over which led to the Eleventh Amendment.

103. See the discussion of this matter by A Democratic Federalist, below, 3.5.6, and references collected there in n. 6.

104. The original reads, "on appeals. It does not. . ."

105. *Trevett* v. *Weeden* (1786); see Frank G. Bates, *Rhode Island and the Formation of the Union* (New York 1898) 131-38; William W. Crosskey, *Politics and the Constitution* II, 965-68.

106. The "continued" signifies merely that the series is being continued, apparently because there was a larger than usual gap between the last essay and this one. There is no essay by Brutus in the *Journal* between "XIV continued," on 6 March, and this one; and this is evidently the whole of XV and not a continuation.

107. The original reads, "last report."

108. The original reads, "sit aside."

109. See XI, 2.9.130-44.

110. Publius denies that the power to declare an act of the legislature void supposes "a superiority of the judicial to the legislative power. It only supposes that the power of the people is superior to both, and that where the will of the legislature, declared in its statutes, stands in opposition to that of the people, declared in the Constitution, the judges ought to be governed by the latter rather than the former. They ought to regulate their decisions by the fundamental laws rather than by those which are not fundamental." *The Federalist* no. 78, 525.

111. The original reads, "adoption."

112. Although a system of separation of functions is advocated, there is nothing in Brutus like Publius' discussion of separation of powers in *The Federalist* no. 51, and there is no articulation of the connection between the principle of *responsibility*, on

which so much emphasis is laid, and the principle of *balanced government*. See above, Centinel I, 2.7.7 n. 4; II, 2.7.50 n. 29.

113. The original reads, ''in a free and republic are chosen. . . .'' Jeffrey suggests ''in a free and [equal?] republic are chosen. . . .'' *University of Cincinnati Law Review* 40, no. 4 (1971): 773, n. 73.

114. Cf. *The Federalist* no. 78.

115. Cf. above, III, 2.9.40.

116. The original reads, ''the Senate we authorised. . .''

117. No further essays were published.

Pennsylvania: Introduction

The first state to take action on the Constitution was Pennsylvania, where sharp party divisions centered upon the state's 1776 constitution, which established what one historian called "the first triumph of democracy" and another "the most democratic form of government ever tried by an American state."[1] The government was one of legislative dominance—the traditional form in the Proprietary regime—a multiple and weak executive, and a judiciary dependent on the legislature. The defenders of this constitution, the "Constitutionalists," later Anti-Federalists, saw it as the means of protecting the ordinary people of Pennsylvania, particularly the farm people, from the wealthier, better educated, better connected commercial and propertied classes. The opponents, the "Republicans," saw it as defective in principle, because of its lack of provision for stability and balance, and as illiberal and undemocratic in practice.[2] Additional objects of contention were the severe test oaths required of citizens by the constitution and subsequent legislation, and the Bank of North America, whose Pennsylvania charter was abruptly repealed by the Constitutionalist-controlled legislature leading to a Republican legislative victory in 1786. Political power alternated between these groups—often by popular response to excessive partisanship and vindictiveness on one side or the other—with the Republicans increasingly looking to a more energetic federal government, while the Constitutionalists remained steadfastly local. Samuel Bannister Harding describes the situation in Pennsylvania on the eve of the ratification debate as follows:

In the State were two parties, embittered by a dozen years of violent struggle. On the one side, and for the moment in power, stood the greater proportion of the men of property, of education, of large ideas, and federal views; six of the eight delegates sent by the State to the Federal convention had come from their number, and the other two—Franklin and Ingersoll—if not neutral, were at most but moderate Constitutionalists. On the other side the leadership had been assumed by men of obscure birth, of little education or property, and of the narrowest views. Small wonder, then, that the cause espoused by the first met with the violent condemnation of the second, and that the contest which ensued was unprecedented in virulence and animosity.[3]

Moving very quickly, the Republican-controlled legislature called for a convention to meet on 20 November. While they did not achieve for Pennsylvania the honor of being the first state to ratify—Delaware having unanimously ratified on 7 December—the Pennsylvania convention acceded to the Constitution on 12 December by the substantial margin of 46 to 23. The Pennsylvania Anti-Federalists remained unreconciled, however, and continued to press their attack on the Constitution, providing much material for the debate in other states.

1. Douglass, *Rebels and Democrats* 214. Samuel Bannister Harding, "Party Struggles over the First Pennsylvania Constitution," *Annual Report of the American Historical Association for the Year 1894* (Washington, D.C., 1895) 376. See also Harry Marlin Tinkcom, *The Republicans and Federalists in Pennsylvania 1790–1801* (Harrisburg 1950) 1; and David Hawke, *In the Midst of a Revolution* (Philadelphia 1961). For a general background in Pennsylvania see, in addition to the above, Brunhouse, *The Counter Revolution in Pennsylvania, 1776–1790;* Paul Leicester Ford, "The Adoption of the Pennsylvania Constitution of 1776," *Political Science Quarterly* September 1895; Jensen, *New Nation;* Charles H. Lincoln, *The Revolutionary Movement in Pennsylvania, 1760–1776* (Philadelphia 1901); McDonald, *We the People;* McDonald, *E Pluribus Unum;* Allan Nevins, *The American States during and after the Revolution, 1775–1789* (New York 1924); J. Paul Selsam, *The Pennsylvania Constitution of 1776* (Philadelphia 1935).

2. McDonald may exaggerate when he says that in the Pennsylvania ratifying convention it was Wilson who argued on democratic grounds and Smilie and Findley who took the ground of republican principle; but there is enough truth in this view to seriously qualify and complicate the common terms of the arguments about the degree of "democracy" in both the Pennsylvania and the U.S. constitutions. See *We the People* 165.

3. Harding, *Annual Report of the American Historical Association 1894* 391.

The Address and Reasons of Dissent of the Minority of the Convention of Pennsylvania To Their Constituents

PENNSYLVANIA PACKET AND DAILY ADVERTISER
18 December 1787

Failing in its attempt to secure the pages of the official journal to spread its views (a not uncommon practice in faction-torn Pennsylvania) the minority of the state ratifying convention published its Address and Reasons of Dissent in the *Pennsylvania Packet and Daily Advertiser*. The Address was frequently reprinted and commented on by both Federalist and Anti-Federalist writers.[1] The author was probably Samuel Bryan, even though he was not a member of the convention.[2]

The Address consists of three parts: (1) a description of events leading up to and concluding the Pennsylvania ratifying convention (3.11.1–2); (2) a list of proposed amendments, many of which found their way into the Bill of Rights (3.11.12–15); and (3) the three general grounds of dissent—(a) that an extensive territory cannot be governed on the principles of freedom, except as a confederation of republics (3.11.16–17), (b) that the government under the Constitution will not be a confederation but a consolidation founded on a destruction of the states (3.11.18–30), (c) that the Constitution is defective (3.11.30–56) in its failure to provide (i) a bill of rights, (ii) adequate representation, (iii) the traditional safeguards of the common law, (iv) a due separation of powers, (v) protection against excessive and tyrannical taxation, and (vi) adequate representation for Pennsylvania. For all of these reasons the government will not possess the confidence of the people and will have to rely on a standing army and a strictly controlled militia, leading to the suppression of individual liberty as well as to great expense.

---

1. For Centinel's complaint that the distribution of the Address was hampered by unfriendly postal arrangements, see Centinel XVIII, 2.7.182 n. 96. See the essays of A Freeman, addressed to the Minority of the Pennsylvania Convention, published in the *Pennsylvania Gazette* 23 January, 30 January, and 6 February 1788. These were, in turn, replied to by [Pennsylvania] Farmer, whose essay is printed below, 3.14. Noah Webster replied in a forceful and interesting essay, published under the pseudonym "America" in the New York *Daily Advertiser* 31 December 1787, and

reprinted in his *Collection of Essays* (Boston 1790). McMaster and Stone print some of the responses, beginning at p. 483, including Francis Hopkinson's Federalist parable, "The New Roof" (pp. 510–16), which appeared in the *Pennsylvania Packet* 29 December 1787.

2. Samuel Bryan claimed authorship in letters to Jefferson, 27 February 1801 and 24 July 1807, and in a letter to Albert Gallatin, 18 December 1790. Files of Ratification of Constitution project, National Archives. See Centinel 2.7. intro. n. 4. The attribution is strengthened by several striking similarities between passages in the Address of the Pennsylvania Convention minority, and in the Centinel letters, although of course one author might, under the circumstances, very well have drawn on another. Cf. the following passages of Centinel and the Pennsylvania Convention Minority, respectively: V, 2.7.95; 3.11.22. III, 2.7.73; 3.11.26. I, 2.7.9; 3.11.48. IV, 2.7.93; 3.11.56. IX, 2.7.129; 3.11.4–5. III, 2.7.70; 3.11.8.

3.11.1   It was not until after the termination of the late glorious contest, which made the people of the United States, an independent nation, that any defect was discovered in the present confederation. It was formed by some of the ablest patriots in America. It carried us successfully through the war; and the virtue and patriotism of the people, with their disposition to promote the common cause, supplied the want of power in Congress.

3.11.2   The requisition of Congress for the five *per cent.* impost was made before the peace, so early as the first of February, 1781, but was prevented taking effect by the refusal of one state; yet it is probable every state in the union would have agreed to this measure at that period, had it not been for the extravagant terms in which it was demanded. The requisition was new moulded in the year 1783, and accompanied with an additional demand of certain supplementary funds for 25 years. Peace had now taken place, and the United States found themselves labouring under a considerable foreign and domestic debt, incurred during the war. The requisition of 1783 was commensurate with the interest of the debt, as it was then calculated; but it has been more accurately ascertained since that time. The domestic debt has been found to fall several millions of dollars short of the calculation, and it has lately been considerably diminished by large sales of the western lands. The states have been called on by Congress annually for supplies until the general system of finance proposed in 1783 should take place.

3.11.3   It was at this time that the want of an efficient federal government was first complained of, and that the powers vested in Congress were found to be inadequate to the procuring of the benefits that should result from the union. The impost was granted by most of the states, but many refused the supplementary funds; the annual requisitions were set at nought by some of the states, while others complied with them by legislative acts, but were tardy in their payments, and Congress found themselves incapable of complying with their engagements, and supporting the federal government. It was found that our national character was sinking in the opinion of foreign nations. The Congress could make treaties of commerce, but could not enforce the observance of them. We were suffering from the restrictions of foreign nations, who had shackled our commerce, while we were unable to retaliate: and all now agreed that it would be advantageous to the union to enlarge the powers of Congress; that they should be enabled in the amplest manner to regulate commerce, and to lay and collect duties on the imports throughout the United States. With this view a convention was first proposed by Virginia, and finally recommended by Congress for the different states to appoint deputies to meet in convention, "for the purposes of revising and amending the present articles of confederation, so as to make them adequate to the exigencies of the union." This recommendation the legislatures of twelve states complied with so hastily as not to consult their constituents on the subject; and though the different legislatures had no authority from their constituents for the purpose, they probably apprehended the necessity would justify the measure; and none of them extended their ideas at that time further than "revising and amending the present articles of confederation." Pennsylvania by the act appointing deputies expressly confined their powers to this object; and though it is probable that some of the members of the assembly of this state had at that time in contemplation to annihilate the present confederation, as well as the constitution of Pennsylvania, yet the plan was not sufficiently matured to communicate it to the public.

The majority of the legislature of this commonwealth, were at that time under the influence of the members from the city of Philadelphia. They agreed that the deputies sent by them to convention should have no compensation for their services, which determination was calculated to prevent the election of any member who resided at a distance from the city. It was in vain for the minority to attempt electing delegates to the convention, who understood the circumstances, and the feelings of the people, and had a common interest with them. They found a disposition in the leaders of the majority of the house to chuse themselves and some of their dependants. The minority attempted to prevent this by agreeing to vote for some of the leading members, who they knew had influence enough to be appointed at any rate, in hopes of carrying with them some respectable citizens of Philadelphia, in whose principles and integrity they could have more confidence; but even in this they were disappointed, except in one member: the eighth member was added at a subsequent session of the assembly.[1]   3.11.4

The Continental convention met in the city of Philadelphia at the time appointed. It was composed of some men of excellent characters; of others who were more remarkable for their ambition and cunning, than their patriotism; and of some who had been opponents to the independence of the United States. The delegates from Pennsylvania were, six of them, uniform and decided opponents to the constitution of this commonwealth. The con-   3.11.5

vention sat upwards of four months. The doors were kept shut, and the members brought under the most solemn engagements of secrecy.* Some of those who opposed their going so far beyond their powers, retired, hopeless, from the convention, others had the firmness to refuse signing the plan altogether; and many who did sign it, did it not as a system they wholly approved, but as the best that could be then obtained, and notwithstanding the time spent on this subject, it is agreed on all hands to be a work of haste and accommodation.

3.11.6 Whilst the gilded chains were forging in the secret conclave, the meaner instruments of despotism without, were busily employed in alarming the fears of the people with dangers which did not exist, and exciting their hopes of greater advantages from the expected plan than even the best government on earth could produce.

3.11.7 The proposed plan had not many hours issued forth from the womb of suspicious secrecy, until such as were prepared for the purpose, were carrying about petitions for people to sign, signifying their approbation of the system, and requesting the legislature to call a convention. While every measure was taken to intimidate the people against opposing it, the public papers teemed with the most violent threats against those who should dare to think for themselves, and *tar and feathers* were liberally promised to all those who would not immediately join in supporting the proposed government be it what it would. Under such circumstances petitions in favour of calling a convention were signed by great numbers in and about the city, before they had leisure to read and examine the system, many of whom, now they are better acquainted with it, and have had time to investigate its principles, are heartily opposed to it. The petitions were speedily handed into the legislature.

3.11.8 Affairs were in this situation when on the 28th of September last a resolution was proposed to the assembly by a member of the house who had been also a member of the federal convention, for calling a state convention, to be elected within *ten* days for the purpose of examining and adopting the proposed constitution of the United States, though at this time the house had not received it from Congress. This attempt was opposed by a minority, who after offering every argument in their power to prevent the precipitate measure, without effect, absented themselves from the house as the only alternative left them, to prevent the measure taking place previous to their constituents being acquainted with the business—That violence and outrage which had been so often threatened was now practised; some of the members were seized the next day by a mob collected for the purpose, and forcibly dragged to the house, and there detained by force whilst the quorum of the legislature, *so formed,* compleated their resolution. We shall dwell no longer on this subject, the people of Pennsylvania have been already ac-

*The Journals of the conclave are still concealed.

quainted therewith.[2] We would only further observe that every member of the legislature, previously to taking his seat, by solemn oath or affirmation, declares, "that he will not do or consent to any act or thing whatever that shall have a tendency to lessen or abridge their rights and privileges, as declared in the constitution of this state." And that constitution which they are so solemnly sworn to support cannot legally be altered but by a recommendation of a council of censors, who alone are authorised to propose alterations and amendments, and even these must be published at least *six months*, for the consideration of the people.[3]—The proposed system of government for the United States, if adopted, will alter and may annihilate the constitution of Pennsylvania; and therefore the legislature had no authority whatever to recommend the calling a convention for that purpose. This proceeding could not be considered as binding on the people of this commonwealth. The house was formed by violence, some of the members composing it were detained there by force, which alone would have vitiated any proceedings, to which they were otherwise competent; but had the legislature been legally formed, this business was absolutely without their power.[4]

In this situation of affairs were the subscribers elected members of the convention of Pennsylvania. A convention called by a legislature in direct violation of their duty, and composed in part of members, who were compelled to attend for that purpose, to consider of a constitution proposed by a convention of the United States, who were not appointed for the purpose of framing a new form of government, but whose powers were expressly confined to altering and amending the present articles of confederation.— Therefore the members of the continental convention in proposing the plan acted as individuals, and not as deputies from Pennsylvania.* The assembly who called the state convention acted as individuals, and not as the legislature of Pennsylvania; nor could they or the convention chosen on their recommendation have authority to do any act or thing, that can alter or annihilate the constitution of Pennsylvania (both of which will be done by the new constitution) nor are their proceedings in our opinion, at all binding on the people.

3.11.9

The election for members of the convention was held at so early a period and the want of information was so great, that some of us did not know of it until after it was over, and we have reason to believe that great numbers of the people of Pennsylvania have not yet had an opportunity of sufficiently

3.11.10

---

*The continental convention in direct violation of the 13th article of the confederation, have declared, "that the ratification of nine states shall be sufficient for the establishment of this constitution, between the states so ratifying the same."—Thus has the plighted faith of the states been sported with! They had solemnly engaged that the confederation now subsisting should be inviolably preserved by each of them, and the union thereby formed, should be perpetual, unless the same should be altered by mutual consent.

examining the proposed constitution.—We apprehend that no change can take place that will affect the internal government or constitution of this commonwealth, unless a majority of the people should evidence a wish for such a change; but on examining the number of votes given for members of the present state convention, we find that of upwards of *seventy thousand* freemen who are intitled to vote in Pennsylvania, the whole convention has been elected by about *thirteen thousand* voters, and though *two thirds* of the members of the convention have thought proper to ratify the proposed constitution, yet those *two thirds* were elected by the votes of only *six thousand and eight hundred* freemen.

3.11.11 In the city of Philadelphia and some of the eastern counties, the junto that took the lead in the business agreed to vote for none but such as would solemnly promise to adopt the system in *toto,* without exercising their judgment. In many of the counties the people did not attend the elections as they had not an opportunity of judging of the plan. Others did not consider themselves bound by the call of a set of men who assembled at the state-house in Philadelphia, and assumed the name of the legislature of Pennsylvania; and some were prevented from voting by the violence of the party who were determined at all events to force down the measure. To such lengths did the tools of despotism carry their outrage, that in the night of the election for members of convention, in the city of Philadelphia; several of the subscribers (being then in the city to transact your business) were grossly abused, ill-treated and insulted while they were quiet in their lodgings, though they did not interfere, nor had any thing to do with the said election, but as they apprehend, because they were supposed to be adverse to the proposed constitution, and would not tamely surrender those sacred rights, which you had committed to their charge.

3.11.12 The convention met, and the same disposition was soon manifested in considering the proposed constitution, that had been exhibited in every other stage of the business. We were prohibited by an express vote of the convention, from taking any question on the separate articles of the plan, and reduced to the necessity of adopting or rejecting *in toto.*—'Tis true the majority permitted us to debate on each article, but restrained us from proposing amendments.—They also determined not to permit us to enter on the minutes our reasons of dissent against any of the articles, nor even on the final question our reasons of dissent against the whole. Thus situated we entered on the examination of the proposed system of government, and found it to be such as we could not adopt, without, as we conceived, surrendering up your dearest rights. We offered our objections to the convention, and opposed those parts of the plan, which, in our opinion, would be injurious to you, in the best manner we were able; and closed our arguments by offering the following propositions to the convention.

3.11.13 1. The right of conscience shall be held inviolable; and neither the legis-

lative, executive nor judicial powers of the United States shall have authority to alter, abrogate, or infringe any part of the constitution of the several
states, which provide for the preservation of liberty in matters of religion.

2. That in controversies respecting property, and in suits between man
and man, trial by jury shall remain as heretofore, as well in the federal
courts, as in those of the several states.[5]

3. That in all capital and criminal prosecutions, a man has a right to
demand the cause and nature of his accusation, as well in the federal courts,
as in those of the several states; to be heard by himself and his counsel; to be
confronted with the accusers and witnesses; to call for evidence in his favor,
and a speedy trial by an impartial jury of his vicinage, without whose
unanimous consent, he cannot be found guilty, nor can he be compelled to
give evidence against himself; and that no man be deprived of his liberty,
except by the law of the land or the judgment of his peers.

4. That excessive bail ought not to be required, nor excessive fines imposed, nor cruel nor unusual punishments inflicted.

5. That warrants unsupported by evidence, whereby any officer or messenger may be commanded or required to search suspected places, or to
seize any person or persons, his or their property, not particularly described, are grievous and oppressive, and shall not be granted either by the
magistrates of the federal government or others.

6. That the people have a right to the freedom of speech, of writing and
publishing their sentiments, therefore, the freedom of the press shall not be
restrained by any law of the United States.[6]

7. That the people have a right to bear arms for the defence of themselves
and their own state, or the United States, or for the purpose of killing game;
and no law shall be passed for disarming the people or any of them, unless
for crimes committed, or real danger of public injury from individuals; and
as standing armies in the time of peace are dangerous to liberty, they ought
not to be kept up: and that the military shall be kept under strict subordination to and be governed by the civil powers.

8. The inhabitants of the several states shall have liberty to fowl and hunt
in seasonable times, on the lands they hold, and on all other lands in the
United States not inclosed, and in like manner to fish in all navigable waters,
and others not private property, without being restrained therein by any
laws to be passed by the legislature of the United States.[7]

9. That no law shall be passed to restrain the legislatures of the several
states from enacting laws for imposing taxes, except imposts and duties on
goods imported or exported, and that no taxes, except imposts and duties
upon goods imported and exported, and postage on letters shall be levied by
the authority of Congress.

10. That the house of representatives be properly increased in number;
that elections shall remain free; that the several states shall have power to

regulate the elections for senators and representatives, without being controuled either directly or indirectly by any interference on the part of the Congress; and that elections of representatives be annual.

11. That the power of organizing, arming and disciplining the militia (the manner of disciplining the militia to be prescribed by Congress) remain with the individual states, and that Congress shall not have authority to call or march any of the militia out of their own state, without the consent of such state, and for such length of time only as such state shall agree.

That the sovereignty, freedom and independency of the several states shall be retained, and every power, jurisdiction and right which is not by this constitution expressly delegated to the United States in Congress assembled.

12. That the legislative, executive, and judicial powers be kept separate; and to this end that a constitutional council be appointed, to advise and .assist the president, who shall be responsible for the advice they give, hereby the senators would be relieved from almost constant attendance; and also that the judges be made completely independent.

13. That no treaty which shall be directly opposed to the existing laws of the United States in Congress assembled, shall be valid until such laws shall be repealed, or made conformable to such treaty; neither shall any treaties be valid which are in contradiction to the constitution of the United States, or the constitutions of the several states.

14. That the judiciary power of the United States shall be confined to cases affecting ambassadors, other public ministers and consuls; to cases of admiralty and maritime jurisdiction; to controversies to which the United States shall be a party; to controversies between two or more states—between a state and citizens of different states—between citizens claiming lands under grants of different states; and between a state or the citizen thereof and foreign states, and in criminal cases, to such only as are expressly enumerated in the constitution, and that the United States in Congress assembled, shall not have power to enact laws, which shall alter the laws of descents and distribution of the effects of deceased persons, the titles of lands or goods, or the regulation of contracts in the individual states.

3.11.14   After reading these propositions, we declared our willingness to agree to the plan, provided it was so amended as to meet these propositions, or something similar to them: and finally moved the convention to adjourn, to give the people of Pennsylvania time to consider the subject, and determine for themselves; but these were all rejected, and the final vote was taken, when our duty to you induced us to vote against the proposed plan, and to decline signing the ratification of the same.

3.11.15   During the discussion we met with many insults, and some personal abuse; we were not even treated with decency, during the sitting of the convention, by the persons in the gallery of the house; however, we flatter ourselves that in contending for the preservation of those invaluable rights you have thought proper to commit to our charge, we acted with a spirit becoming freemen, and being desirous that you might know the principles which actuated our conduct, and being prohibited from inserting our reasons of dissent on the minutes of the convention, we have subjoined them for your consideration, as to you alone we are accountable. It remains with you whether you will think those inestimable privileges, which you have so ably contended for, should be sacrificed at the shrine of despotism, or whether you mean to contend for them with the same spirit that has so often baffled the attempts of an aristocratic faction, to rivet the shackles of slavery on you and your unborn posterity.

Our objections are comprised under three general heads of dissent, viz.

We dissent, first, because it is the opinion of the most celebrated writers on government, and confirmed by uniform experience, that a very extensive territory cannot be governed on the principles of freedom, otherwise than by a confederation of republics, possessing all the powers of internal government; but united in the management of their general, and foreign concerns. 3.11.16

If any doubt could have been entertained of the truth of the foregoing principle, it has been fully removed by the concession of *Mr. Wilson*, one of majority on this question; and who was one of the deputies in the late general convention. In justice to him, we will give his own words; they are as follows, viz.[8] "The extent of country for which the new constitution was required, produced another difficulty in the business of the federal convention. It is the opinion of some celebrated writers, that to a small territory, the democratical; to a middling territory (as Montesquieu has termed it) the monarchial; and to an extensive territory, the despotic form of government is best adapted. Regarding then the wide and almost unbounded jurisdiction of the United States, at first view, the hand of despotism seemed necessary to controul, connect, and protect it; and hence the chief embarrassment rose. For, we know that, altho' our constituents would chearfully submit to the legislative restraints of a free government, they would spurn at every attempt to shackle them with despotic power."—And again in another part of his speech he continues.—"Is it probable that the dissolution of the state governments, and the establishment of one *consolidated empire* would be eligible in its nature, and satisfactory to the people in its administration? I think not, as I have given reasons to shew that so extensive a territory could not be governed, connected, and preserved, but by the *supremacy of despotic power*. All the exertions of the most potent emperors of Rome were not capable of keeping that empire together, which in extent was far inferior to the dominion of America."[9] 3.11.17

We dissent, secondly, because the powers vested in Congress by this constitution, must necessarily annihilate and absorb the legislative, executive, and judicial powers of the several states, and produce from their ruins 3.11.18

one consolidated government, which from the nature of things will be *an iron handed despotism,* as nothing short of the supremacy of despotic sway could connect and govern these United States under one government.

3.11.19   As the truth of this position is of such decisive importance, it ought to be fully investigated, and if it is founded to be clearly ascertained; for, should it be demonstrated, that the powers vested by this constitution in Congress, will have such an effect as necessarily to produce one consolidated government, the question then will be reduced to this short issue, viz. whether satiated with the blessings of liberty; whether repenting of the folly of so recently asserting their unalienable rights, against foreign despots at the expence of so much blood and treasure, and such painful and arduous struggles, the people of America are now willing to resign every privilege of freemen, and submit to the dominion of an absolute government, that will embrace all America in one chain of despotism; or whether they will with virtuous indignation, spurn at the shackles prepared for them, and confirm their liberties by a conduct becoming freemen.

3.11.20   That the new government will not be a confederacy of states, as it ought, but one consolidated government, founded upon the destruction of the several governments of the states, we shall now shew.

    The powers of Congress under the new constitution, are complete and unlimited over the *purse* and the *sword,* and are perfectly independent of, and supreme over, the state governments; whose intervention in these great points is entirely destroyed. By virtue of their power of taxation, Congress may command the whole, or any part of the property of the people. They may impose what imposts upon commerce; they may impose what land taxes, poll taxes, excises, duties on all written instruments, and duties on every other article that they may judge proper; in short, every species of taxation, whether of an external or internal nature is comprised in section the 8th, of article the 1st, viz. "The Congress shall have power to lay and collect taxes, duties, imposts, and excises, to pay the debts, and provide for the common defence and general welfare of the United States."

3.11.21   As there is no one article of taxation reserved to the state governments, the Congress may monopolise every source of revenue, and thus indirectly demolish the state governments, for without funds they could not exist, the taxes, duties and excises imposed by Congress may be so high as to render it impracticable to levy further sums on the same articles; but whether this should be the case or not, if the state governments should presume to impose taxes, duties or excises, on the same articles with Congress, the latter may abrogate and repeal the laws whereby they are imposed, upon the allegation that they interfere with the due collection of their taxes, duties or excises, by virtue of the following clause, part of section 8th, article 1st. viz. "To make all laws which shall be necessary and proper for carrying into execution the foregoing powers, and all other powers vested by this constitution in the government of the United States, or in any department or officer thereof."[10]

The Congress might gloss over this conduct by construing every purpose for which the state legislatures now lay taxes, to be for the *"general welfare,"* and therefore as of their ju[ris]diction.

And the supremacy of the laws of the United States is established by article 6th, viz. "That this constitution and the laws of the United States, which shall be made in pursuance thereof, and *all treaties* made, or which shall be made, under the authority of the United States, shall be the *supreme law* of the *land;* and *the judges in every state shall be bound thereby; any thing in the constitution or laws of any state to the contrary notwithstanding."* It has been alledged that the words "pursuant to the constitution," are a restriction upon the authority of Congress;[11] but when it is considered that by other sections they are invested with every efficient power of government, and which may be exercised to the absolute destruction of the state governments, without any violation of even the forms of the constitution, this seeming restriction, as well as every other restriction in it, appears to us to be nugatory and delusive; and only introduced as a blind upon the real nature of the government. In our opinion, "pursuant to the constitution," will be co-extensive with the *will* and *pleasure* of Congress, which, indeed, will be the only limitation of their powers.

3.11.22

We apprehend that two co-ordinate sovereignties would be a solecism in politics.[12] That therefore as there is no line of distinction drawn between the general, and state governments; as the sphere of their jurisdiction is undefined, it would be contrary to the nature of things, that both should exist together, one or the other would necessarily triumph in the fullness of dominion. However the contest could not be of long continuance, as the state governments are divested of every means of defence, and will be obliged by "the supreme law of the land" *to yield at discretion.*

3.11.23

It has been objected to this total destruction of the state governments, that the existence of their legislatures is made essential to the organization of Congress; that they must assemble for the appointment of the senators and president general of the United States.[13] True, the state legislatures may be continued for some years, as boards of appointment, merely, after they are divested of every other function, but the framers of the constitution foreseeing that the people will soon be disgusted with this solemn mockery of a government without power and usefulness, have made a provision for relieving them from the imposition, in section 4th, of article 1st, viz. "The times, places, and manner of holding elections for senators and representatives, shall be prescribed in each state by the legislature thereof; *but the Congress may at any time, by law make or alter such regulations; except as to the place of chusing senators."*

3.11.24

As Congress have the controul over the time of the appointment of the

3.11.25

president general, of the senators and of the representatives of the United States, they may prolong their existence in office, for life, by postponing the time of their election and appointment, from period to period, under various pretences, such as an apprehension of invasion, the factious disposition of the people, or any other plausible pretence that the occasion may suggest; and having thus obtained life-estates in the government, they may fill up the vacancies themselves, by their controul over the mode of appointment; with this exception in regard to the senators, that as the place of appointment for them, must, by the constitution, be in the particular state, they may depute some body in the respective states, to fill up the vacancies in the senate, occasioned by death, until they can venture to assume it themselves. In this manner, may the only restriction in this clause be evaded. By virtue of the foregoing section, when the spirit of the people shall be gradually broken; when the general government shall be firmly established, and when a numerous standing army shall render opposition vain, the Congress may compleat the system of despotism, in renouncing all dependance on the people, by continuing themselves, and children in the government.

3.11.26   The celebrated *Montesquieu*, in his Spirit of Laws, vol. 1, page 12th, says, "That in a democracy there can be no exercise of sovereignty, but by the suffrages of the people, which are their will; now the sovereigns will is the sovereign himself; the laws therefore, which establish the right of suffrage, are fundamental to this government. In fact, it is as important to regulate in a republic in what manner, by whom, and concerning what suffrages are to be given, as it is in a monarchy to know who is the prince, and after what manner he ought to govern."[14] The *time, mode* and *place* of the election of representatives, senators and president general of the United States, ought not to be under the controul of Congress, but fundamentally ascertained and established.

3.11.27   The new constitution, consistently with the plan of consolidation, contains no reservation of the rights and privileges of the state governments, which was made in the confederation of the year 1778, by article the 2d, viz. "That each state retains its sovereignty, freedom and independence, and every power, jurisdiction and right, which is not by this confederation expressly delegated to the United States in Congress assembled."

The legislative power vested in Congress by the foregoing recited sections, is so unlimited in its nature; may be so comprehensive and boundless [in] its exercise, that this alone would be amply sufficient to annihilate the state governments, and swallow them up in the grand vortex of general empire.

3.11.28   The judicial powers vested in Congress are also so various and extensive, that by legal ingenuity they may be extended to every case, and thus absorb the state judiciaries, and when we consider the decisive influence that a general judiciary would have over the civil polity of the several states, we do not hesitate to pronounce that this power, unaided by the legislative, would effect a consolidation of the states under one government.

The powers of a court of equity, vested by this constitution, in the tribu- nals of Congress; powers which do not exist in Pennsylvania, unless so far as they can be incorporated with jury trial, would, in this state, greatly contribute to this event. The rich and wealthy suitors would eagerly lay hold of the infinite mazes, perplexities and delays, which a court of chancery, with the appellate powers of the supreme court in fact as well as law would furnish him with, and thus the poor man being plunged in the bottomless pit of legal discussion, would drop his demand in despair.   3.11.29

In short, consolidation pervades the whole constitution. It begins with an annunciation that such was the intention. The main pillars of the fabric correspond with it, and the concluding paragraph is a confirmation of it. The preamble begins with the words, "We the people of the United States," which is the style of a compact between individuals entering into a state of society, and not that of a confederation of states.[15] The other features of consolidation, we have before noticed.   3.11.30

Thus we have fully established the position, that the powers vested by this constitution in Congress, will effect a consolidation of the states under one government, which even the advocates of this constitution admit, could not be done without the sacrifice of all liberty.

3. We dissent, Thirdly, Because if it were practicable to govern so exten- sive a territory as these United States includes, on the plan of a consolidated government, consistent with the principles of liberty and the happiness of the people, yet the construction of this constitution is not calculated to attain the object, for independent of the nature of the case, it would of itself, necessarily, produce a despotism, and that not by the usual gradations, but with the celerity that has hitherto only attended revolutions effected by the sword.   3.11.31

To establish the truth of this position, a cursory investigation of the prin- ciples and form of this constitution will suffice.

The first consideration that this review suggests, is the omission of a BILL of RIGHTS, ascertaining and fundamentally establishing those unalienable and personal rights of men, without the full, free, and secure enjoyment of which there can be no liberty, and over which it is not necessary for a good government to have the controul. The principal of which are the rights of conscience, personal liberty by the clear and unequivocal establishment of the writ of *habeas corpus*, jury trial in criminal and civil cases, by an impartial jury of the vicinage or county, with the common-law proceedings, for the safety of the accused in criminal prosecutions; and the liberty of the press, that scourge of tyrants, and the grand bulwark of every other liberty and privilege; the stipulations heretofore made in favor of them in the state constitutions, are entirely superceded by this constitution.   3.11.32

3.11.33   The legislature of a free country should be so formed as to have a competent knowledge of its constituents, and enjoy their confidence. To produce these essential requisites, the representation ought to be fair, equal, and sufficiently numerous, to possess the same interests, feelings, opinions, and views, which the people themselves would possess, were they all assembled; and so numerous as to prevent bribery and undue influence, and so responsible to the people, by frequent and fair elections, as to prevent their neglecting or sacrificing the views and interests of their constituents, to their own pursuits.

3.11.34   We will now bring the legislature under this constitution to the test of the foregoing principles, which will demonstrate, that it is deficient in every essential quality of a just and safe representation.

    The house of representatives is to consist of 65 members; that is one for about every 50,000 inhabitants, to be chosen every two years. Thirty-three members will form a quorum for doing business; and 17 of these, being the majority, determine the sense of the house.

    The senate, the other constituent branch of the legislature, consists of 26 members being *two* from each state, appointed by their legislatures every six years—fourteen senators make a quorum; the majority of whom, eight, determines the sense of that body: except in judging on impeachments, or in making treaties, or in expelling a member, when two thirds of the senators present, must concur.

    The president is to have the controul over the enacting of laws, so far as to make the concurrence of *two* thirds of the representatives and senators present necessary, if he should object to the laws.

3.11.35   Thus it appears that the liberties, happiness, interests, and great concerns of the whole United States, may be dependent upon the integrity, virtue, wisdom, and knowledge of 25 or 26 men—How unadequate and unsafe a representation! Inadequate, because the sense and views of 3 or 4 millions of people diffused over so extensive a territory comprising such various climates, products, habits, interests, and opinions, cannot be collected in so small a body; and besides, it is not a fair and equal representation of the people even in proportion to its number, for the smallest state has as much weight in the senate as the largest, and from the smallness of the number to be chosen for both branches of the legislature; and from the mode of election and appointment, which is under the controul of Congress; and from the nature of the thing, men of the most elevated rank in life, will alone be chosen. The other orders in the society, such as farmers, traders, and mechanics, who all ought to have a competent number of their best informed men in the legislature, will be totally unrepresented.[16]

3.11.36   The representation is unsafe, because in the exercise of such great powers and trusts, it is so exposed to corruption and undue influence, by the gift of the numerous places of honor and emoluments at the disposal of the executive; by the arts and address of the great and designing; and by direct bribery.

The representation is moreover inadequate and unsafe, because of the long terms for which it is appointed, and the mode of its appointment, by which Congress may not only controul the choice of the people, but may so manage as to divest the people of this fundamental right, and become self-elected.

The number of members in the house of representatives *may* be encreased to one for every 30,000 inhabitants. But when we consider, that this cannot be done without the consent of the senate, who from their share in the legislative, in the executive, and judicial departments, and permanency of appointment, will be the great efficient body in this government, and whose weight and predominancy would be abridged by an increase of the representatives, we are persuaded that this is a circumstance that cannot be expected. On the contrary, the number of representatives will probably be continued at 65, although the population of the country may swell to treble what it now is; unless a revolution should effect a change.[17]

3.11.37

We have before noticed the judicial power as it would effect a consolidation of the states into one government; we will now examine it, as it would affect the liberties and welfare of the people, supposing such a government were practicable and proper.

3.11.38

The judicial power, under the proposed constitution, is founded on the well-known principles of the *civil law*, by which the judge determines both on law and fact, and appeals are allowed from the inferior tribunals to the superior, upon the whole question; so that *facts* as well as *law*, would be re-examined, and even new facts brought forward in the court of appeals; and to use the words of a very eminent Civilian—"The cause is many times another thing before the court of appeals, than what it was at the time of the first sentence."[18]

That this mode of proceeding is the one which must be adopted under this constitution, is evident from the following circumstances:—1st. That the trial by jury, which is the grand characteristic of the common law, is secured by the constitution, only in criminal cases.—2d. That the appeal from both *law* and *fact* is expressly established, which is utterly inconsistent with the principles of the common law, and trials by jury. The only mode in which an appeal from law and fact can be established, is, by adopting the principles and practice of the civil law; unless the United States should be drawn into the absurdity of calling and swearing juries, merely for the purpose of contradicting their verdicts, which would render juries contemptible and worse than useless.—3d. That the courts to be established would decide on all cases *of law and equity*, which is a well known characteristic of the civil law, and these courts would have conusance not only of the laws of the United States and of treaties, and of cases affecting ambassadors, but of all

3.11.39

cases of *admiralty and maritime jurisdiction,* which last are matters belonging exclusively to the civil law, in every nation in Christendom.

3.11.40   Not to enlarge upon the loss of the invaluable right of trial by an unbiassed jury, so dear to every friend of liberty, the monstrous expence and inconveniences of the mode of proceedings to be adopted, are such as will prove intolerable to the people of this country. The lengthy proceedings of the civil law courts in the chancery of England, and in the courts of Scotland and France, are such that few men of moderate fortune can endure the expence of; the poor man must therefore submit to the wealthy. Length of purse will too often prevail against right and justice. For instance, we are told by the learned judge *Blackstone,* that a question only on the property of an ox, of the value of *three* guineas, originating under the civil law proceedings in Scotland, after many interlocutory orders and sentences below, was carried at length from the court of sessions, the highest court in that part of Great Britain, by way of *appeal* to the house of lords, *where* the question of law and fact was finally determined. He adds, that no pique or spirit could in the court of king's bench or common pleas at Westminster, have given continuance to such a cause for a tenth part of the time, nor have cost a twentieth part of the expence. Yet the costs in the courts of king's bench and common pleas in England, are infinitely greater than those which the people of this country have ever experienced. We abhor the idea of losing the transcendant privilege of trial by jury, with the loss of which, it is remarked by the same learned author, that in Sweden, the liberties of the commons were extinguished by an aristocratic senate: and that *trial by jury* and the liberty of the people went out together.[19] At the same time we regret the intolerable delay, the enormous expences and infinite vexation to which the people of this country will be exposed from the voluminous proceedings of the courts of civil law, and especially from the appellate jurisdiction, by means of which a man may be drawn from the utmost boundaries of this extensive country to the seat of the supreme court of the nation to contend, perhaps with a wealthy and powerful adversary. The consequence of this establishment will be an absolute confirmation of the power of aristocratical influence in the courts of justice: for the common people will not be able to contend or struggle against it.

3.11.41   Trial by jury in criminal cases may also be excluded by declaring that the libeller for instance shall be liable to an action of debt for a specified sum; thus evading the common law prosecution by indictment and trial by jury. And the common course of proceeding against a ship for breach of revenue laws by information (which will be classed among civil causes) will at the civil law be within the resort of a court, where no jury intervenes. Besides, the benefit of jury trial, in cases of a criminal nature, which cannot be evaded, will be rendered of little value, by calling the accused to answer far from home; there being no provision that the trial be by a jury of the neighbourhood or country. Thus an inhabitant of Pittsburgh, on a charge of crime committed on the banks of the Ohio, may be obliged to defend himself at the side of the Delaware, and so *vice versa*. To conclude this head: we observe that the judges of the courts of Congress would not be independent, as they are not debarred from holding other offices, during the pleasure of the president and senate, and as they may derive their support in part from fees, alterable by the legislature.

The next consideration that the constitution presents, is the undue and dangerous mixture of the powers of government; the same body possessing legislative, executive, and judicial powers. The senate is a constituent branch of the legislature, it has judicial power in judging on impeachments, and in this case unites in some measure the characters of judge and party, as all the principal officers are appointed by the president-general, with the concurrence of the senate and therefore they derive their offices in part from the senate. This may biass the judgments of the senators and tend to screen great delinquents from punishment. And the senate has, moreover, various and great executive powers, viz. in concurrence with the president-general, they form treaties with foreign nations, that may controul and abrogate the constitutions and laws of the several states. Indeed, there is no power, privilege or liberty of the state governments, or of the people, but what may be affected by virtue of this power. For all treaties, made by them, are to be the "supreme law of the land, any thing in the constitution or laws of any state, to the contrary notwithstanding." | 3.11.42

And this great power may be exercised by the president and 10 senators (being two-thirds of 14, which is a quorum of that body). What an inducement would this offer to the ministers of foreign powers to compass by bribery *such concessions* as could not otherwise be obtained. It is the unvaried usage of all free states, whenever treaties interfere with the positive laws of the land, to make the intervention of the legislature necessary to give them operation. This became necessary, and was afforded by the parliament of Great-Britain. In consequence of the late commercial treaty between that kingdom and France—As the senate judges on impeachments, who is to try the members of the senate for the abuse of this power! And none of the great appointments to office can be made without the consent of the senate. | 3.11.43

Such various, extensive, and important powers combined in one body of men, are inconsistent with all freedom; the celebrated Montesquieu tells us, that "when the legislative and executive powers are united in the same person, or in the same body of magistrates, there can be no liberty, because apprehensions may arise, lest the same monarch or *senate* should enact tyrannical laws, to execute them in a tyrannical manner." | 3.11.44

"Again, there is no liberty, if the power of judging be not separated from the legislative and executive powers. Were it joined with the legislative, the life and liberty of the subject would be exposed to arbitrary controul: for the judge would then be legislator. Were it joined to the executive power, the judge might behave with all the violence of an oppressor. There would be an end of every thing, were the same man, or the same body of the nobles, or of the people, to exercise those three powers; that of enacting laws; that of executing the public resolutions; and that of judging the crimes or differences of individuals."[20]

3.11.45 The president general is dangerously connected with the senate; his coincidence with the views of the ruling junto in that body, is made essential to his weight and importance in the government, which will destroy all independency and purity in the executive department, and having the power of pardoning without the concurrence of a council, he may skreen from punishment the most treasonable attempts that may be made on the liberties of the people, when instigated by his coadjutors in the senate. Instead of this dangerous and improper mixture of the executive with the legislative and judicial, the supreme executive powers ought to have been placed in the president, with a small independent council, made personally responsible for every appointment to office or other act, by having their opinions recorded; and that without the concurrence of the majority of the quorum of this council, the president should not be capable of taking any step.

3.11.46 We have before considered internal taxation, as it would effect the destruction of the state governments, and produce one consolidated government. We will now consider that subject as it affects the personal concerns of the people.

The power of direct taxation applies to every individual, as congress, under this government, is expressly vested with the authority of laying a capitation or poll tax upon every person to any amount. This is a tax that, however oppressive in its nature, and unequal in its operation, is certain as to its produce and simple in its collection; it cannot be evaded like the objects of imposts or excise, and will be paid, because all that a man hath will he give for his head. This tax is so congenial to the nature of despotism, that it has ever been a favorite under such governments. Some of those who were in the late general convention from this state have long laboured to introduce a poll-tax among us.

3.11.47 The power of direct taxation will further apply to every individual, as congress may tax land, cattle, trades, occupations, etc. in any amount, and every object of internal taxation is of that nature, that however oppressive, the people will have but this alternative, except to pay the tax, or let their property be taken, for all resistance will be in vain. The standing army and select militia would enforce the collection.

3.11.48 For the moderate exercise of this power, there is no controul left in the state governments, whose intervention is destroyed. No relief, or redress of grievances can be extended, as heretofore by them. There is not even a declaration of RIGHTS to which the people may appeal for the vindication of their wrongs in the court of justice. They must therefore, implicitly obey the most arbitrary laws, as the worst of them will be pursuant to the principles and form of the constitution, and that strongest of all checks upon the conduct of administration, *responsibility to the people,* will not exist in this government. The permanency of the appointments of senators and representatives, and the controul the congress have over their election, will place them independent of the sentiments and resentment of the people, and the administration having a greater interest in the government than in the community, there will be no consideration to restrain them from oppression and tyranny. In the government of this state, under the old confederation, the members of the legislature are taken from among the people, and their interests and welfare are so inseparably connected with those of their constituents, that they can derive no advantage from oppressive laws and taxes, for they would suffer in common with their fellow citizens; would participate in the burthens they impose on the community, as they must return to the common level, after a short period; and notwithstanding every ex[er]-tion of influence, every means of corruption, a necessary rotation excludes them from permanency in the legislature.

This large state is to have but ten members in that Congress which is to have the liberty, property and dearest concerns of every individual in this vast country at absolute command and even these ten persons, who are to be our only guardians; who are to supercede the legislature of Pennsylvania, will not be of the choice of the people, nor amenable to them. From the mode of their election and appointment they will consist of the lordly and high-minded; of men who will have no congenial feelings with the people, but a perfect indifference for, and contempt of them; they will consist of those harpies of power, that prey upon the very vitals; that riot on the miseries of the community. But we will suppose, although in all probability it may never be realized in fact, that our deputies in Congress have the welfare of their constituents at heart, and will exert themselves in their behalf, what security could even this afford; what relief could they extend to their oppressed constituents? To attain this, the majority of the deputies of the twelve other states in Congress must be alike well disposed; must alike forego the sweets of power, and relinquish the pursuits of ambition, which from the nature of things is not to be expected. If the people part with a responsible representation in the legislature, founded upon fair, certain and frequent elections, they have nothing left they can call their own. Miserable is the lot of that people whose every concern depends on the WILL and PLEASURE of their rulers. Our soldiers will become Janissaries, and our officers of government Bashaws; in short, the system of despotism will soon be compleated.

From the foregoing investigation, it appears that the Congress under this constitution will not possess the confidence of the people, which is an essential requisite in a good government; for unless the laws command the confidence and respect of the great body of the people, so as to induce them to support them, when called on by the civil magistrate, they must be executed by the aid of a numerous standing army, which would be in-

3.11.49

3.11.50

consistent with every idea of liberty; for the same force that may be employed to compel obedience to good laws, might and probably would be used to wrest from the people their constitutional liberties. The framers of this constitution appear to have been aware of this great deficiency; to have been sensible that no dependence could be placed on the people for their support: but on the contrary, that the government must be executed by force. They have therefore made a provision for this purpose in a permanent STANDING ARMY, and a MILITIA that may be subjected to as strict discipline and government.

3.11.51   A standing army in the hands of a government placed so independent of the people, may be made a fatal instrument to overturn the public liberties; it may be employed to enforce the collection of the most oppressive taxes, and to carry into execution the most arbitrary measures. An ambitious man who may have the army at his devotion, may step up into the throne, and seize upon absolute power.

The absolute unqualified command that Congress have over the militia may be made instrumental to the destruction of all liberty, both public and private; whether of a personal, civil or religious nature.

3.11.52   First, the personal liberty of every man probably from sixteen to sixty years of age, may be destroyed by the power Congress have in organizing and governing of the militia. As militia they may be subjected to fines to any amount, levied in a military manner; they may be subjected to corporal punishments of the most disgraceful and humiliating kind, and to death itself, by the sentence of a court martial: To this our young men will be more immediately subjected, as a select militia, composed of them, will best answer the purposes of government.

3.11.53   Secondly, The rights of conscience may be violated, as there is no exemption of those persons who are conscientiously scrupulous of bearing arms.[21] These compose a respectable proportion of the community in the state. This is the more remarkable, because even when the distresses of the late war, and the evident disaffection of many citizens of that description, inflamed our passions, and when every person, who was obliged to risque his own life, must have been exasperated against such as on any account kept back from the common danger, yet even then, when outrage and violence might have been expected, the rights of conscience were held sacred.

At this momentous crisis, the framers of our state constitution made the most express and decided declaration and stipulations in favour of the rights of conscience: but now when no necessity exists, those dearest rights of men are left insecure.

3.11.54   Thirdly, The absolute command of Congress over the militia may be destructive of public liberty; for under the guidance of an arbitrary government, they may be made the unwilling instruments of tyranny. The militia of Pennsylvania may be marched to New England or Virginia to quell an insurrection occasioned by the most galling oppression, and aided by the standing army, they will no doubt be successful in subduing their liberty and independency; but in so doing, although the magnanimity of their minds will be extinguished, yet the meaner passions of resentment and revenge will be increased, and these in turn will be the ready and obedient instruments of despotism to enslave the others; and that with an irritated vengeance. Thus may the militia be made the instruments of crushing the last efforts of expiring liberty, of riveting the chains of despotism on their fellow citizens, and on one another. This power can be exercised not only without violating the constitution, but in strict conformity with it; it is calculated for this express purpose, and will doubtless be executed accordingly.

As this government will not enjoy the confidence of the people, but be executed by force, it will be a very expensive and burthensome government. The standing army must be numerous, and as a further support, it will be the policy of this government to multiply officers in every department: judges, collectors, tax-gatherers, excisemen and the whole host of revenue officers will swarm over the land, devouring the hard earnings of the industrious. Like the locusts of old, impoverishing and desolating all before them.   3.11.55

We have not noticed the smaller, nor many of the considerable blemishes, but have confined our objections to the great and essential defects; the main pillars of the constitution; which we have shewn to be inconsistent with the liberty and happiness of the people, as its establishment will annihilate the state governments, and produce one consolidated government that will eventually and speedily issue in the supremacy of despotism.   3.11.56

In this investigation, we have not confined our views to the interests or welfare of this state, in preference to the others. We have overlooked all local circumstances—we have considered this subject on the broad scale of the general good; we have asserted the cause of the present and future ages: the cause of liberty and mankind.

Nathaniel Breading,	John Ludwig,
John Smilie	Abraham Lincoln
Richard Baird	John Bishop
Adam Orth	Joseph Heister
John A. Hanna	Joseph Powel
John Whitehill	James Martin
John Harris	William Findley
Robert Whitehill	John Baird
John Reynolds	James Edgar
Jonathan Hoge	William Todd.
Nicholas Lutz	

The yeas and nays upon the final vote were as follows, viz.

YEAS.

George Latimer	James Wilson	John Hunn
Benjamin Rush	Thomas M'Kean	George Gray
Hilary Baker	William M'Pherson	Samuel Ashmead

Enoch Edwards	Sebastian Graff	William Wilson
Henry Wynkoop	John Hubley	John Boyd
John Barclay	Jasper Yates	Thomas Scott
Thomas Yardley	Henry Slagle	John Nevill
Abraham Stout	Thomas Campbell	John Allison
Thomas Bull	Thomas Hartley	Jonathan Roberts
Anthony Wayne	David Grier	John Richards
William Gibbons	John Black	F. A. Muhlenberg
Richard Downing	Benjamin Pedan	James Morris
Thomas Cheyney	John Arndt	Timothy Pickering
John Hannum	Stephen Balliott	Benjamin Elliot
Stephen Chambers	Joseph Horsefield	
Robert Coleman	David Deshler	

46

NAYS.

John Whitehill	John Bishop	James Edgar
John Harris	Joseph Heister	Nathaniel Breading
John Reynolds	James Martin	John Smilie
Robert Whitehill	Joseph Powell	Richard Baird
Jonathan Hoge	William Findley	William Brown
Nicholas Lutz	John Baird	Adam Orth
John Ludwig	William Todd	John Andre Hannah
Abraham Lincoln	James Marshall	

23

Philadelphia, Dec. 12, 1787.

1. The eighth member was Benjamin Franklin, who had not been chosen at the first election because of doubt about his willingness to serve. See the reply by some of the majority to the "Address of the Minority of the Assembly," McMaster and Stone 79–83.

2. McMaster and Stone 65–71; see Pennsylvania House Minority above 3.2.3.

3. Constitution of Pennsylvania, 1776, sec. 47; Thorpe, *Federal and State Constitutions* V, 3091–92. See "Minutes of the Council of Censors, 1783–1784," *Pennsylvania Archives* 3d series, X (1896), 785 ff.

4. This is presumably the argument referred to by Publius when he claims that the enemies of the proposed Constitution question "that fundamental principle of republican government, which admits the right of the people to alter or abolish the established constitution whenever they find it inconsistent with their happiness. . . ." *The Federalist* no. 78, 527. Note however that the Minority of the Pennsylvania Convention does not make the argument Publius attributes to it and that Publius himself is here cautioning against ill-considered change.

5. This proposal is criticized by Publius in *The Federalist* no. 83, 563–68.

6. See the penetrating discussion by America (Noah Webster) of the difficulties of defining and applying a guarantee of freedom of the press. The New York *Daily Advertiser* 31 December 1787, reprinted in Webster's *Collection of Essays* (1790).

7. America gleefully shows how irrelevant this proposal is in free America, where every man is lord of this own land, and how much it derives from the "feudal tyranny" of Europe. Ibid.

8. McMaster and Stone 220. This is Wilson's speech at the Pennsylvania ratifying convention, given on 24 November 1787.

9. McMaster and Stone 225. Exactly the same portions of the speech are quoted by Centinel V, 2.7.94.

10. Cf. *The Federalist* on taxation, especially nos. 32 and 33. The question of concurrent taxation was of course very widely discussed. See McMaster and Stone 260 (Whitehill), 268–69 (Smilie); for other citations see Federal Farmer III, 2.8.39 n. 29.

11. Wilson in Pennsylvania Convention, McMaster and Stone 308; see also Ford, *Essays* 45–46 (Cassius), and *The Federalist* no. 33, 207. On the Anti-Federal side see Centinel V, 2.7.97, and Federal Farmer IV, 2.8.49; the latter, in criticizing the absence of this language from the treaty-making power, seems to imply that it does restrict the authority of Congress.

12. Cf. the argument following and Centinel V, 2.7.99.

13. This argument was made frequently, but the reference here is doubtless to James Wilson in his influential speech of 6 October and in the Pennsylvania convention; see McMaster and Stone 147, 264; for other citations see Centinel II, 2.7.36 n. 16. For an argument similar to the one here see Republican Federalist 4.13.23, 26. The deeper Anti-Federal reply is not that Congress will usurp the state's elective roles but that participation of that kind is not sufficient to maintain the states as truly significant parts of the federal republic. See Federal Farmer X, 2.8.132 n. 84.

14. *The Spirit of Laws* II, ch. 2. The same compressed version of Montesquieu's statement is used by Centinel (III, 2.7.73).

15. A Freeman replied that "tho' the convention propose that it should be the act of the people, yet it is in their capacities as citizens of *the several members of our confederacy*—for they are expressly declared to be the people of *the United States*—to which idea the expression is *strictly* confined, and the *general* term of *America*, which is constantly used in speaking of us *as a nation*, is carefully omitted; a pointed view was evidently had to our *existing union.*" *Pennsylvania Gazette* 23 January 1788. Cf. Henry's denunciation of the language of the preamble, 5.16.1, and the discussion in the North Carolina ratifying convention Elliot IV, 15–16, and McMaster and Stone 256–57 (Whitehill).

16. Cf. *The Federalist* nos. 35–36; see Federal Farmer II, 2.8.15 n. 11.

17. See Publius' ingenious, and in its implications profound, contention that the balance of interest will be such that representation will be increased, *The Federalist* no. 58, 392–95. For other Federalist discussions of this question see Federal Farmer X, 2.8.137 n. 88.

18. The source of this quotation has not been found. See above, Democratic Federalist 3.5.6 n. 6.

19. *Commentaries* III, 380–81. I do not find the discussion of Scottish proceedings.

20. Montesquieu, *The Spirit of Laws* XI, ch. 6.

21. See Centinel III, 2.7.76 n. 39.

Massachusetts: Introduction

As winter wore on, the focus of debate moved northward. By January 1788 five states had ratified the Constitution—Delaware, Pennsylvania, New Jersey, Georgia, and Connecticut—all with comparative ease and in four cases unanimously or nearly so.[1] But among these only Pennsylvania was a major state, and there the opposition was unreconciled to defeat. The Massachusetts convention was to meet on 14 January; and an unfavorable decision there would strengthen the opponents of the Constitution in the remaining states, while giving encouragement to the adamant Pennsylvania Anti-Federalists.

The contest over ratification in Massachusetts was preceded by a decade of factional contention, leading to civil disturbances and culminating in the famous Shays Rebellion.[2] The rebellion centered in western Massachusetts, where the economic depression following the dislocation of the war was most severe, where hard currency was scarce, and where the courts and lawyers were a target of popular resentment. Opposition to the Constitution was centered in this western part of the state, but there was a distinct lack of leadership. Few of the eastern Anti-Federalists, who provided essays and pamphlets read all over the country, were elected to the ratifying convention, where the Anti-Federalists, while strong in numbers, had no spokesmen able to contend with the Federalists.[3] To a striking extent the Anti-Federalist delegates in democratic Massachusetts were preoccupied with a rather undifferentiated fear of abuse of power and trickery from the propertied and educated classes.

When the ratifying convention met, there was, from all accounts, a majority opposed to ratification; yet after close to a month of debate a sufficient number of delegates changed their minds to give the Federalists a small majority. The Federalists, proceeding cautiously, succeeded in securing clause-by-clause consideration of the Constitution, fearing (and apparently with good reason) that an early vote would go against them. In this they were aided by Samuel Adams, who, although generally thought to be unfriendly to the Constitution, threw his considerable weight on the side of full deliberation and, in one of his few speeches at the convention, supported clause-by-clause consideration. John Hancock, governor of Massachusetts and president of the convention, also provided crucial support. Popular, vain, and extremely sensitive to currents of opinion, Hancock was prevented by a genuine but manageable illness from occupying the chair until the issues and the lines of division had begun to come into focus. When he did appear, Hancock proposed a group of amendments to the Constitution, which Samuel Adams endorsed. The statements of both men were, probably deliberately, somewhat ambiguous about whether the amendments were to be a condition of ratification or merely recommendatory. As debate continued, sentiment for ratification increased, with the Federalists supporting recommendatory amendments; and neither Hancock nor Adams pressed for conditional ratification. Whatever their motives (a much-canvassed question), Hancock's and Adams' actions were of the utmost importance in securing ratification in the crucial state of Massachusetts and in introducing recommendatory amendments. This proved to be the compromise used to secure ratification in other states, tempering the opposition of the Anti-Federalists while maintaining the integrity of the Constitution.

On 6 February 1788 the Constitution was adopted by the Massachusetts convention by the narrow margin of 187 to 168, and the recommendatory amendments were agreed upon. Several Anti-Federalists who had voted against the Constitution rose to express their acceptance of the majority determination.[4] In marked contrast to events in Pennsylvania, opposition largely ceased in Massachusetts once the Constitution was adopted.

1. See John A. Munroe, *Federalist Delaware, 1775–1815* (New Brunswick, N.J., 1954); Richard P. McCormick, *Experiment in Independence: New Jersey in the Critical Period, 1781–1789* (New Brunswick, N.J., 1950); William W. Abbot, "The Structure of Politics in Georgia, 1782–1789," *William and Mary Quarterly* January 1957; Kenneth Coleman, *The American Revolution in Georgia, 1763–1789* (Athens, Ga., 1958); Bernard C. Steiner, "Connecticut's Ratification of the Federal Constitution," *Proceedings of the American Antiquarian Society* n.s. 25 (1915): 70–127.

2. For background in Massachusetts, see Richard B. Morris, "Insurrection in Massachusetts," in *America in Crisis*, ed. Daniel Aaron (New York 1952); George R. Minot, *The History of the Insurrection of Massachusetts* (Boston 1810); Samuel Eliot Morison, "Struggle over the Adoption of the Constitution of Massachusetts, 1780," Massachusetts Historical Society, *Proceedings* 50 (1917): 353–411; Anson Ely Morse, *The Federalist Party in Massachusetts to the Year 1800* (Princeton 1909); David H. Fischer, "The Myth of the Essex Junto," *William and Mary Quarterly* April 1964.

3. Thus *Centinel* regrets that in Massachusetts "the cause of liberty has been so weakly, although zealously advocated—that its champions were so little illuminated." Centinel XV, 2.7.166. See generally Samuel Bannister Harding, *The Contest over the Ratification of the Federal Constitution in the State of Massachusetts* (New York 1896).

4. The New Hampshire convention met on 13 February; opposition was similar in character and strength to that in Massachusetts, and the Federalists, fearing defeat, succeeded in gaining a postponement of the convention until the middle of June. Joseph B. Walker, *Birth of the Federal Constitution* (Boston 1888).

Letters of Agrippa, I–XI

MASSACHUSETTS GAZETTE
November 1787–January 1788

The important *Agrippa* letters appear to have been written by James Winthrop.[1] The son of mathematics professor John Winthrop of Harvard, James
became librarian of Harvard in 1770 following his graduation from that
institution. He became register of probate in Middlesex in 1787 and Judge of
Common Pleas in 1791. While Harvard librarian, he fought in the Revolution, was postmaster of Cambridge, and served as a volunteer against the
Shays insurgents. Winthrop was twice passed over for his father's pro-
fessorship in mathematics because, it is reported, his "intemperate manner
and . . . eccentricities militated against him."[2] His chief literary effort was a
study and interpretation of biblical prophecies.

The letters of Agrippa are vigorously and well argued, but were not much
reprinted, probably because of their preoccupation with the interests of
Massachusetts. That preoccupation deserves the reader's close attention,
however, because it reflects the principled selfishness that is the ground of
Agrippa's argument (VII, 4.6.26–29). The letters fall into two distinct sets,
the first (I–XI, 4.6.1–47) addressed to the people of Massachusetts, the
second (XII–XVI, 4.6.48–79) to the Massachusetts Convention. This fact
explains much of the repetition and some of the variation in Agrippa's
arguments. In both sets there are highly theoretical arguments as well as
specific criticisms of the proposed Constitution and suggestions for action;
but the differences in form and focus are due partly to the different circumstances and audiences to which the papers were addressed.

Each of the sets of letters has its own plan or outline, although Agrippa
frequently allows the argument to stray, and indeed some of the most interesting and fruitful observations are made in the course of diversions or
secondary arguments. The overall theme concerns the connection between
freedom, commerce, and local institutions. The chief dangers of the proposed Constitution are, first, the destruction of the states, which are necessary because of the heterogeneity to be found in the United States, and,
second, the stifling of commerce by excessive regulation.

The first set of papers is particularly interesting on the question of the
small republic (IV, 4.6.14–17) and on commerce as the bond of Union (VIII,

4.6.30–33). Agrippa reveals here, in a particularly open way, a tension that is quite common in Anti-Federalist thought between the claims of civic virtue and of commerce as the bond of civil society. The second set of letters contains an extended and significant discussion of the Bill of Rights. A brief outline follows.

Part I—To the People
  I. Introduction and general sketch: Freedom is necessary to industry; great objective should be to encourage the spirit of commerce (I, 4.6.1–6).
  II. Advantages of present system: efficiency of states for internal regulation (II, III, 4.6.7–13).
  III. Disadvantages of the consolidation implicit in the proposed Constitution (IV–VII, 4.6.14–29).
    A. Impossibility of governing an extensive empire on republican principles except as a confederated republic because of the heterogeneity of the parts. Yet the new system is a consolidation (IV, 4.6.14–17).
    B. Proof that the new system is a consolidation (V–VI, 4.6.18–25).
    C. Harm of this consolidation for Massachusetts (VII, 4.6.26–29).
  IV. The true bond of Union is commerce (VIII–IX, 4.6.30–37).
    A. We are now a federal republic under that moderate political authority that is necessary to the peaceful operation of commercial intercourse (VIII, 4.6.30–33).
    B. Criticism of deficiencies of Articles of Confederation taken up:
      (1) regarding taxation (VIII, 4.6.30–33)
      (2) regarding regulation of intercourse with foreign nations (IX, 4.6.34–37).
  V. Summary and suggested amendments to Articles of Confederation (X, 4.6.38–44).
  (VI. P.S.—attack on Federalist Party [XI, 4.6.45–47]).

Part II—To the Massachusetts Convention
  This second set of papers consists of a long paper devoted to the subject of the Federal Republic, and retracing much of the ground of the first set of papers (but sometimes with interesting elaborations), together with a new discussion of the Bill of Rights, and a set of proposed amendments to the Constitution.
  I. Federal Republic is the form of government best suited to answer both internal and external needs. This is the system we now possess; it can be improved by modest amendments; it would be destroyed by the proposed Constitution (XII, 4.6.48–59).
  II. Bill of Rights and Constitution (XIII–XV, 4.6.60–71).
  III. Proposed Amendments to the Constitution (XVI, 4.6.72–79).

1. "It is said Winthrop writes under Agrippa. These pieces gain him no credit." C. Gore to R. King, 23 December 1787, *King, Life and Correspondence* I, 265; Ford, *Essays* 40, 51–52; Charles Warren, "Elbridge Gerry, James Warren, Mercy Warren, and the Ratification of the Federal Constitution in Massachusetts," Massachusetts Historical Society *Proceedings* 64 (1930–32):147, n. 6; Harding, *Contest over Ratification* 21, n.1.

Ford's reprinting of these letters (*Essays* 53–122) contains errors of numbering and dating and an omission, which are identified in the notes here. As Ford points out (p. 51), Agrippa's letters called forth a number of replies; but none of these seriously took up his arguments. See *Massachusetts Gazette* 30 November 1787 (Cassius, reprinted in Ford, *Essays* 22–23); 21 December 1787 ("Charles James Fox"); 28 December 1787, 4 January 1788 ("Kempis O'Flanagan"); 25 January 1788 (Janius).

2. Clifford K. Shipton, "James Winthrop," *Dictionary of American Biography* XX, 407. As evidence of Winthrop's eccentricity Shipton relates that in the *Memoirs* of the American Academy of Arts and Sciences he published "fallacious solutions" of certain problems in mathematics, "to the great mortification of the other members."

I

23 November 1787

To the People.

Many inconveniencies and difficulties in the new plan of government have been mentioned by different writers on that subject. Mr Gerry has given the publick his objections against it, with a manly freedom.[1] The seceding members from the Pennsylvania Assembly also published theirs.[2] Various anonymous writers have mentioned reasons of great weight. Among the many objections have been stated the unlimited right of taxation—a standing army—an inadequate representation of the people—a right to destroy the constitution of the separate states, and all the barriers that have been set up in defence of liberty—the right to try causes between private persons in many cases without a jury; without trying in the vicinity of either party; and without any limitation of the value which is to be tried. To none of these or any other objections has any answer been given, but such as have acknowledged the truth of the objection while they insulted the objector. This conduct has much the appearance of trying to force a general sentiment upon the people.

4.6.1

The idea of promoting the happiness of the people by opposing all their habits of business, and by subverting the laws to which they are habituated, appears to me to be at least a mistaken proceeding. If to this we add the limitations of trade, restraints on its freedom, and the alteration of its course, and *transfer of the market,* all under the pretence of regulation for *federal purposes,* we shall not find any additional reason to be pleased with the plan.

4.6.2

It is now conceded on all sides that the laws relating to civil causes were never better executed than at present. It is confessed by a warm federalist in answer to mr. Gerry's sensible letter, that the courts are so arranged at

4.6.3

present that no inconvenience is found, and that if the new plan takes place great difficulties may arise.[3] With this confession before him, can any reasonable man doubt whether he shall exchange a system, found by experience to be convenient, for one that is in many respects inconvenient, and dangerous? The expense of the new plan is terrifying, if there was no other objection. But they are multiplied. Let us consider that of the representation.

4.6.4   There is to be one representative for every thirty thousand people. Boston would nearly send one, but with regard to another there is hardly a county in the state which would have one. The representatives are to be chosen for two years. In this space, when it is considered that their residence is from two hundred to five [hundred?] miles from their constituents, it is difficult to suppose that they will retain any great affection for the welfare of the people. They will have an army to support them, and may bid defiance to the clamours of their subjects. Should the people cry aloud the representative may avail himself of the right to alter the *time of election* and postpone it for another year. In truth, the question before the people is, *whether they will have a limited government or an absolute one?*

4.6.5   It is a fact justified by the experience of all mankind from the earliest antiquity down to the present time, that freedom is necessary to industry. We accordingly find that in absolute governments, the people, be the climate what it may, are [in] general lazy, cowardly, turbulent, and vicious to an extreme. On the other hand, in free countries are found in general, activity, industry, arts, courage, generosity, and all the manly virtues.

Can there be any doubt which to choose? He that hesitates must be base indeed.

4.6.6   A favourite objection against a free government is drawn from the irregularities of the Greek and Roman republicks. But it is to be considered that war was the employment which they considered as most becoming freemen. Agriculture, arts, and most domestick employment were committed chiefly to slaves. But Carthage, the great commercial republick of antiquity, though resembling Rome in the form of its government, and her rival for power, retained her freedom longer than Rome, and was never disturbed by sedition during the long period of her duration.[4] This is a striking proof that the fault of the Greek and Roman republicks was not owing to the form of their government, and that the spirit of commerce is the great bond of union among citizens.[5] This furnishes employment for their activity, supplies their mutual wants, defends the rights of property, and producing reciprocal dependencies, renders the whole system harmonious and energetick. Our great object therefore ought to be to encourage this spirit. If we examine the present state of the world we shall find that most of the business is done in the freest states, and that industry decreases in proportion to the rigour of government.

Agrippa.

To the People of Massachusetts.

In the Gazette of the 23d instant, I ascertained from the state of other countries and the experience of mankind, that free countries are most friendly to commerce and to the rights of property. This produces greater internal tranquillity. For every man, finding sufficient employment for his active powers in the way of trade, agriculture and manufactures, feels no disposition to quarrel with his neighbour, nor with the government which protects him, and of which he is a constituent part.[6] Of the truth of these positions we have abundant evidence in the history of our own country. Soon after the settlement of Massachusetts, and its formation into a commonwealth, in the earlier part of the last century, there was a sedition at Hingham and Weymouth. The governour passing by at that time with his guard, seized some of the mutineers and imprisoned them. This was complained of as a violation of their rights, and the governour lost his election the next year; but the year afterwards was restored and continued to be re-elected for several years. The government does not appear to have been disturbed again till the revocation of the charter in 1686, being a period of about half a century.[7]

Connecticut set out originally on the same principles, and has continued uniformly to exercise the powers of government to this time.

During the last year, we had decisive evidences of the vigour of this kind of government.[8] In Connecticut, the treason was restrained while it existed only in the form of conspiracy. In Vermont, the conspirators assembled in arms, but were suppressed by the exertions of the militia, under the direction of their sheriffs. In New-Hampshire, the attack was made on the legislature, but the insurrection was in a very few hours suppressed, and has never been renewed. In Massachusetts, the danger was, by delay, suffered to increase. One judicial court after another was stopped, and even the capital trembled. Still, however, when the supreme executive gave the signal, a force of many thousands of active, resolute men, took the field, during the severities of winter, and every difficulty vanished before them. Since that time we have been continually coalescing. The people have applied with diligence to their several occupations, and the whole country wears one face of improvement. Agriculture has been improved, manufactures multiplied, and trade prodigiously enlarged. These are the advantages of freedom in a growing country. While our resources have been thus rapidly increasing, the courts have set in every part of the commonwealth, without any guard to defend them; have tried causes of every kind, whether civil or criminal, and the sheriffs, have in no case been interrupted in the execution of their office. In those cases indeed, where the government was more

4.6.7

4.6.8

particularly interested, mercy has been extended, but in civil causes, and in the case of moral offences, the law has been punctually executed. Damage done to individuals, during the tumults, has been repaired, by judgment of the courts of law, and the award has been carried into effect. This is the present state of affairs, when we are asked to relinquish that freedom which produces such happy effects.

4.6.9   The attempt has been made to deprive us of such a beneficial system, and to substitute a rigid one in its stead, by criminally alarming our fears, exalting certain characters on one side, and villifying them on the other.[9] I wish to say nothing of the merits or demerits of individuals; such arguments always do hurt. But assuredly my countrymen cannot fail to consider and determine who are the most worthy of confidence in a business of this magnitude.—Whether they will trust persons, who have, from their cradles, been incapable of comprehending any other principles of government, than those of absolute power, and who have, in this very affair, tried to deprive them of their constitutional liberty, by a pitiful trick. They cannot avoid prefering those who have uniformly exerted themselves to establish a limited government, and to secure to individuals all the liberty that is consistent with justice, between man and man, and whose efforts, by the smiles of Providence, have hitherto been crowned with the most splendid success. After the treatment we have received, we have a right to be jealous, and to guard our present constitution with the strictest care. It is the right of the people to judge, and they will do wisely to give an explicit instruction to their delegates in the proposed convention, not to agree to any proposition that will, in any degree, militate with that happy system of government under which Heaven has placed them.

Agrippa.

November 24, 1787.

III

30 November 1787

To the People.

4.6.10   It has been proved, from the clearest evidence, in two former papers, that a free government, I mean one in which the power frequently returns to the body of the people, is in principle the most stable and efficient of any kind; that such a government affords the most ready and effectual remedy for all injuries done to persons and the rights of property. It is true we have had a tender act. But what government has not some law in favour of debtors? The difficulty consists in finding one that is not more unfriendly to the creditors than ours. I am far from justifying such things. On the contrary I believe that it is universally true, that acts made to favour a part of the community are wrong in principle. All that is now intended is, to remark that we are not worse than other people in that respect which we most condemn. Probably the inquiry will be made, whence the complaints arise. This is easily answered. Let any man look round his own neighbourhood, and see if the people are not, with a very few exceptions, peaceable and attached to the government; if the country had ever within their knowledge more appearance of industry, improvement and tranquillity; if there was ever more of the produce of all kinds together for the market; if their stock does not rapidly increase; if there was ever a more ready vent for their surplus; and if the average of prices is not about as high as was usual in a plentiful year before the war. These circumstances all denote a general prosperity. Some classes of citizens indeed suffer greatly. Two descriptions I at present recollect. The publick creditors form the first of these classes and they ought to, and will be provided for. Let us for a moment consider their situation and prospects. The embarrassments consequent upon a war, and the usual reduction of prices immediately after a war, necessarily occasioned a want of punctuality in publick payments. Still however the publick debt has been very considerably reduced, not by the dirty and delusive scheme of depreciation, but the nominal sum. Applications are continually making for purchases in our eastern and western lands. Great exertions are making for clearing off the arrears of outstanding taxes, so that the certificates for interest on the state debt have considerably increased in value. This is a certain indication of returning credit. Congress this year disposed of a large tract of their lands towards paying the principal of their debt. Pennsylvania has discharged the whole of their part of the continental debt. New-York has nearly cleared its state debt, and has located a large part of their new lands towards paying the continental demands. Other states have made considerable payments. Every day from these considerations the publick ability and inclination to satisfy their creditors increases. The exertions of last winter were as much to support publick as private credit. The prospect therefore of the publick creditors is brightening under the present system. If the new system should take effect without amendments, which however is hardly probable, the increase of expense will be death to the hopes of all creditors both of the continental and of the state. With respect however to our publick delays of payment we have the precedent of the best established countries in Europe.

The other class of citizens to which I alluded was the ship-carpenters. All 4.6.11 agree that their business is dull; but as nobody objects against a system of commercial regulations for the whole continent, that business may be relieved without subverting all the ancient foundations and laws which have the respect of the people. It is a very serious question whether giving to Congress the unlimited right to regulate trade would not injure them still further. It is evidently for the interest of the state to encourage our own trade as much as possible. But in a very large empire, as the whole states consolidated must be, there will always be a desire of the government to increase the trade of the capital, and to weaken the extremes. We should in that case be one of the extremes, and should feel all the impoverishment incident to that situation. Besides, a jealousy of our enterprising spirit, would always be an inducement to cramp our exertions. We must then be impoverished or we must rebel. The alternative is dreadful.

4.6.12   At present this state is one of the most respectable and one of the most influential in the union. If we alone should object to receiving the system without amendments, there is no doubt but it would be amended. But the case is not quite so bad. New-York appears to have no disposition even to call a convention. If they should neglect, are we to lend our assistance to compel them by arms, and thus to kindle a civil war without any provocation on their part. Virginia has put off their convention till May, and appears to have no disposition to receive the new plan without amendments. Pennsylvania does not seem to be disposed to receive it as it is. The same objections are made in all the states, that the civil government which they have adopted and which secures their rights will be subverted. All the defenders of this system undertake to prove that the rights of the states and of the citizens are kept safe. The opposers of it agree that they will receive the least burdensome system which shall defend those rights.

4.6.13   Both parties therefore found their arguments on the idea that these rights ought to be held sacred. With this disposition is it not in every man's mind better to recommit it to a new convention, or to Congress, which is a regular convention for the purpose, and to instruct our delegates to confine the system to the general purposes of the union, than to *endeavour* to force it through in its present form, and with so many opposers as it must have in every state on the continent. The case is not of such pressing necessity as some have represented. Europe is engaged and we are tranquil. Never therefore was an happier time for deliberation. The supporters of the measure are by no means afraid of insurrections taking place, but they are afraid that the present government will prove superiour to their assaults.

Agrippa.

IV

3 December 1787

To the People.

4.6.14   Having considered some of the principal advantages of the happy form of government under which it is our peculiar good fortune to live, we find by experience, that it is the best calculated of any form hitherto invented, to secure to us the rights of our persons and of our property, and that the general circumstances of the people shew an advanced state of improvement never before known. We have found the shock given by the war in a great measure obliterated, and the publick debt contracted at that time to be considerably reduced in the nominal sum. The Congress lands are fully adequate to the redemption of the principal of their debt, and are selling and populating very fast. The lands of this state, at the west, are, at the moderate price of eighteen pence an acre, worth near half a million pounds in our money. They ought, therefore, to be sold as quick as possible. An application was made lately for a large tract at that price, and continual applications are made for other lands in the eastern part of the state. Our resources are daily augmenting.

We find, then, that after the experience of near two centuries our separate governments are in full vigour. They discover, for all the purposes of internal regulation, every symptom of strength, and none of decay. The new system is, therefore, for such purposes, useless and burdensome. 4.6.15

Let us now consider how far it is practicable consistent with the happiness of the people and their freedom. It is the opinion of the ablest writers on the subject, that no extensive empire can be governed upon republican principles, and that such a government will degenerate to a despotism, unless it be made up of a confederacy of smaller states, each having the full powers of internal regulation.[10] This is precisely the principle which has hitherto preserved our freedom. No instance can be found of any free government of considerable extent which has been supported upon any other plan. Large and consolidated empires may indeed dazzle the eyes of a distant spectator with their splendour, but if examined more nearly are always found to be full of misery. The reason is obvious. In large states the same principles of legislation will not apply to all the parts. The inhabitants of warmer climates are more dissolute in their manners, and less industrious, than in colder countries. A degree of severity is, therefore, necessary with one which would cramp the spirit of the other.[11] We accordingly find that the very great empires have always been despotick. They have indeed tried to remedy the inconveniences to which the people were exposed by local regulations; but these contrivances have never answered the end. The laws not being made by the people, who felt the inconveniences, did not suit their circumstances. It is under such tyranny that the Spanish provinces languish, and such would be our misfortune and degradation, if we should submit to have the concerns of the whole empire managed by one legislature. To promote the happiness of the people it is necessary that there should be local laws; and it is necessary that those laws should be made by the representatives of those who are immediately subject to the want of them. By endeavouring to suit both extremes, both are injured. 4.6.16

It is impossible for one code of laws to suit Georgia and Massachusetts. 4.6.17

They must, therefore, legislate for themselves. Yet there is, I believe, not one point of legislation that is not surrendered in the proposed plan. Questions of every kind respecting property are determinable in a continental court, and so are all kinds of criminal causes. The continental legislature has, therefore, a right to make rules *in all cases* by which their judicial courts shall proceed and decide causes. No rights are reserved to the citizens. The laws of Congress are in all cases to be the supreme law of the land, and paramount to the constitutions of the individual states. The Congress may institute what modes of trial they please, and no plea drawn from the constitution of any state can avail. This new system is, therefore, a consolidation of all the states into one large mass, however diverse the parts may be of which it is to be composed. The idea of an uncompounded republick, on an average, one thousand miles in length, and eight hundred in breadth, and containing six millions of white inhabitants all reduced to the same standard of morals, or habits, and of laws, is in itself an absurdity, and contrary to the whole experience of mankind. The attempt made by Great-Britain to introduce such a system, struck us with horrour, and when it was proposed by some theorist that we should be represented in parliament,[12] we uniformly declared that one legislature could not represent so many different interests for the purposes of legislation and taxation. This was the leading principle of the revolution, and makes an essential article in our creed. All that part, therefore, of the new system, which relates to the internal government of the states, ought at once to be rejected.

Agrippa.

V

11 December 1787

To the People.

4.6.18   In the course of inquiry it has appeared, that for the purposes of internal regulation and domestick tranquillity, our small and separate governments are not only admirably suited in theory, but have been remarkably successful in practice. It is also found, that the direct tendency of the proposed system, is to consolidate the whole empire into one mass, and, like the tyrant's bed, to reduce all to one standard. Though this idea has been stated in different parts of the continent, and is the most important trait of this draft, the reasoning ought to be extensively understood. I therefore hope to be indulged in a particular statement of it.

4.6.19   Causes of all kinds, between citizens of different states, are to be tried before a continental court. This court is not bound to try it according to the local laws where the controversies happen; for in that case it may as well be tried in a state court. The rule which is to govern the new courts, must, therefore, be made by the court itself, or by its employers, the Congress. If by the former, the legislative and judicial departments will be blended; and if by the Congress, though these departments will be kept separate, still the power of legislation departs from the state in all those cases. The Congress, therefore, have the right to make rules for trying *all kinds* of *questions* relating to property between citizens of different states. The sixth article of the new constitution provides, that the continental laws shall be the supreme law of the land, and that all judges in the separate states shall be bound thereby, any thing in the constitution or laws of any state to the contrary notwithstanding. All the state officers are also bound by oath to support this constitution. These provisions cannot be understood otherwise than as binding the state judges and other officers, to execute the continental laws in their own proper departments within the state. For all questions, other than those between citizens of the same state, are at once put within the jurisdiction of the continental courts. As no authority remains to the state judges, but to decide questions between citizens of the same state, and those judges are to be bound by the laws of Congress, it clearly follows, that all questions between citizens of the same state are to be decided by the general laws and not by the local ones.

Authority is also given to the continental courts, to try all causes between a state and its own citizens.[13] A question of property between these parties rarely occurs. But if such questions were more frequent than they are, the proper process is not to sue the state before an higher authority; but to apply to the supreme authority of the state, by way of petition. This is the universal practice of all states, and any other mode of redress destroys the sovereignty of the state over its own subjects. The only case of the kind in which the state would probably be sued, would be upon the state notes. The endless confusion that would arise from making the estates of individuals answerable, must be obvious to every one.

4.6.20

There is another sense in which the clause relating to causes between the state and individuals is to be understood, and it is more probable than the other, as it will be eternal in its duration, and increasing in its extent. This is the whole branch of the law relating to criminal prosecutions. In all such cases the state is plaintiff, and the person accused is defendant. The process, therefore, will be, for the attorney-general of the state to commence his suit before a continental court. Considering the state as a party, the cause must be tried in another, and all the expense of the transporting witnesses incurred. The individual is to take his trial among strangers, friendless and unsupported, without its being known whether he is habitually a good or a bad man; and consequently with one essential circumstance wanting by which to determine whether the action was performed maliciously or accidentally. All these inconveniences are avoided by the present

4.6.21

important restriction, that the cause shall be tried by a jury of the vicinity, and tried in the county where the offence was commited. But by the proposed *derangement*, I can call it by no softer name, a man must be ruined to prove his innocence. This is far from being a forced construction of the proposed form. The words appear to me not intelligible, upon the idea that it is to be a *system* of government, unless the construction now given, both for civil and criminal processes, be admitted. I do not say that it is intended that all these changes should take place within one year, but they probably will in the course of a half a dozen years, if this system is adopted. In the mean time we shall be subject to all the horrors of a divided sovereignty, not knowing whether to obey the Congress or the state. We shall find it impossible to please two masters. In such a state frequent broils will ensue. Advantage will be taken of a popular commotion, and even the venerable forms of the state be done away, while the new system will be enforced in its utmost rigour by an army. I am the more apprehensive of a standing army, on account of a clause in the new constitution which empowers Congress to keep one at all times; but this constitution is evidently such that it cannot stand any considerable time without an army. Upon this principle one is very wisely provided. Our present government knows of no such thing.

Agrippa.

VI

14 December 1787

To the People.

4.6.22

To prevent any mistakes, or misapprehensions of the argument, stated in my last paper, to prove that the proposed constitution is an actual consolidation of the separate states into one extensive commonwealth, the reader is desired to observe, that in the course of the argument, the new plan is considered as an intire system. It is not dependent on any other book for an explanation, and contains no references to any other book. All the defences of it, therefore, so far as they are drawn from the state constitutions, or from maxims of the common law, are foreign to the purpose. It is only by comparing the different parts of it together, that the meaning of the whole is to be understood. For instance—

4.6.23

We find in it, that there is to be a legislative assembly, with authority to constitute courts for the trial of all kinds of civil causes, between citizens of different states. The right to appoint such courts necessarily involves in it the right of defining their powers, and determining the rules by which their judgment shall be regulated; and the grant of the former of those rights is nugatory without the latter. It is vain to tell us, that a maxim of common law requires contracts to be determined by the law existing where the contract was made: for it is also a maxim, that the legislature has a right to alter the common law. Such a power forms an essential part of legislation. Here, then a declaration of rights is of inestimable value. It contains those principles which the government never can invade without an open violation of the compact between them and the citizens.[14] Such a declaration ought to have come to the new constitution in favour of the legislative rights of the several states, by which their sovereignty over their own citizens within the state should be secured. Without such an express declaration the states are annihilated in reality upon receiving this constitution—the forms will be preserved only during the pleasure of Congress.

The idea of consolidation is further kept up in the right given to regulate trade.[15] Though this power under certain limitations would be a proper one for the department of Congress; it is in this system carried much too far, and much farther than is necessary. This is, without exception, the most commercial state upon the continent. Our extensive coasts, cold climate, small estates, and equality of rights, with a variety of subordinate and concurring circumstances, place us in this respect at the head of the union. We must, therefore, be indulged if a point which so nearly relates to our welfare be rigidly examined. The new constitution not only prohibits vessels, bound from one state to another, from paying any duties, but even from entering and clearing. The only use of such a regulation is, to keep each state in complete ignorance of its own resources. It certainly is no hardship to enter and clear at the custom house, and the expense is too small to be an object. 4.6.24

The unlimitted right to regulate trade, includes the right of granting exclusive charters. This, in all old countries, is considered as one principal branch of prerogative. We find hardly a country in Europe which has not felt the ill effects of such a power. Holland has carried the exercise of it farther than any other state; and the reason why that country has felt less evil from it is, that the territory is very small, and they have drawn large revenues from their colonies in the East and West Indies. In this respect, the whole country is to be considered as a trading company, having exclusive privileges. The colonies are large in proportion to the parent state; so that, upon the whole, the latter may gain by such a system. We are also to take into consideration the industry which the genius of a free government inspires. But in the British islands all these circumstances together have not prevented them from being injured by the monopolies created there. Individuals have been enriched, but the country at large has been hurt. Some valuable branches of trade being granted to companies, who transact their business in London, that city is, perhaps, the place of the greatest trade in the world. But Ireland, under such influence, suffers exceedingly, and is impoverished; and Scotland is a mere bye-word. Bristol, the second city in 4.6.25

England, ranks not much above this town in population. These things must be accounted for by the incorporation of trading companies; and if they are felt so severely in countries of small extent, they will operate with tenfold severity upon us, who inhabit an immense tract; and living towards one extreme of an extensive empire, shall feel the evil, without retaining that influence in government, which may enable us to procure redress. There ought, then, to have been inserted a restraining clause which might prevent the Congress from making any such grant, because they consequentially defeat the trade of the out-ports, and are also injurious to the general commerce, by enhancing prices and destroying that rivalship which is the great stimulus to industry.

Agrippa.

VII
18 December 1787

To the People.

4.6.26　　There cannot be a doubt, that, while the trade of this continent remains free, the activity of our countrymen will secure their full share. All the estimates for the present year, let them be made by what party they may, suppose the balance of trade to be largely in our favour. The credit of our merchants is, therefore, fully established in foreign countries. This is a sufficient proof, that when business is unshackled, it will find out that channel which is most friendly to its course. We ought, therefore, to be exceedingly cautious about diverting or restraining it. Every day produces fresh proofs, that people, under the immediate pressure of difficulties, do not, at first glance, discover the proper relief. The last year, a desire to get rid of embarrassments induced many honest people to agree to a tender-act, and many others, of a different description, to obstruct the courts of justice. Both these methods only increased the evil they were intended to cure. Experience has since shewn, that, instead of trying to lessen an evil by altering the present course of things, every endeavour[16] should have been applied to facilitate the course of law, and thus to encourage a mutual confidence among the citizens, which increases the resources of them all, and renders easy the payment of debts. By this means one does not grow rich at the expense of another, but all are benefited. The case is the same with the states. Pennsylvania, with one port and a large territory, is less favourably situated for trade than the Massachusetts, which has an extensive coast in proportion to its limits of jurisdiction. Accordingly a much larger proportion of our people

are engaged in maritime affairs. We ought therefore to be particularly attentive to securing so great an interest. It is vain to tell us that we ought to
overlook local interests. It is only by protecting local concerns, that the
interest of the whole is preserved. No man when he enters into society, does
it from a view to promote the good of others, but he does it for his own good.
All men having the same view are bound equally to promote the welfare of
the whole. To recur then to such a principle as that local interests must be
disregarded, is requiring of one man to do more than another, and is subverting the foundation of a free government. The Philadelphians would be
shocked with a proposition to place the seat of general government and the
unlimited right to regulate trade in the Massachusetts. There can be no
greater reason for our surrendering the preference to them. Such sacrifices,
however we may delude ourselves with the form of words, always originate
in folly, and not in generosity.[17]

Let me now request your attention a little while to the actual state of   4.6.27
publick credit, that we may see whether it has not been as much misrepresented as the state of our trade.

At the beginning of the present year, the whole continental debt was
about twelve millions of pounds in our money. About one quarter part of
this sum was due to our foreign creditors. Of these France was the principal,
and called for the arrears of interest. A new loan of one hundred and twenty
thousand pounds was negotiated in Holland, at five per cent. to pay the
arrears due to France. At first sight this has the appearance of bad economy,
and has been used for the villainous purpose of disaffecting the people. But
in the course of this same year, Congress have negotiated the sale of as
much of their western lands on the Ohio and Missisippi, as amount nearly to
the whole sum of the foreign debt; and instead of a dead loss by borrowing
money at five per cent. to the amount of an hundred and twenty thousand
pounds, in one sum, they make a saving of the interest at six per cent. on
three millions of their domestick debt, which is an annual saving of an
hundred and eighty thousand pounds. It is easy to see how such an immense
fund as the western territory may be applied to the payment of the foreign
debt. Purchasers of the land would as willingly procure any kind of the
produce of the United States as they would buy loan office certificates to
pay for the land. The produce thus procured would easily be negotiated for
the benefit of our foreign creditors. I do not mean to insinuate that no other
provision should be made for our creditors, but only to shew that our credit
is not so bad in other countries as has been represented, and that our
resources are fully equal to the pressure.

The perfection of government depends on the equality of its operation, as   4.6.28
far as human affairs will admit, upon all parts of the empire, and upon all the
citizens. Some inequalities indeed will necessarily take place. One man will
be obliged to travel a few miles further than another man to procure justice.

But when he has travelled, the poor man ought to have the same measure of justice as the rich one. Small inequalities may be easily compensated. There ought, however, to be no inequality in the law itself, and the government ought to have the same authority in one place as in another. Evident as this truth is, the most plausible argument in favour of the new plan is drawn from the inequality of its operation in different states. In Connecticut, they have been told that the bulk of the revenue will be raised by impost and excise, and therefore they need not be afraid to trust Congress with the power of levying a dry tax at pleasure. New-York, and Massachusetts, are both more commercial states than Connecticut. The latter, therefore, hopes that the other two will pay the bulk of the continental expense. The argument is in itself delusive. If the trade is not over-taxed, the consumer pays it. If the trade is over-taxed, it languishes, and by the ruin of trade the farmer loses his market. The farmer has in truth no other advantage from imposts than that they save him the trouble of collecting money for the government. He neither gets or loses money by changing the mode of taxation. The government indeed finds it the easiest way to raise the revenue; and the reason is that the tax is by this means collected where the money circulates most freely. But if the argument was not delusive, it ought to conclude against the plan, because it would prove the unequal operation of it, and if any saving is to be made by the mode of taxing, the saving should be applied towards our own debt, and not to the payment of the part of a continental burden which Connecticut ought to discharge. It would be impossible to refute in writing all the delusions made use of to force this system through. Those respecting the publick debt, and the benefit of imposts, are the most important, and these I have taken pains to explain. In one instance indeed, the impost does raise money at the direct expense of the seaports. This is when goods are imported subject to a duty, and re-exported without a drawback. Whatever benefit is derived from this source, surely should not be transferred to another state, at least till our own debts are cleared.

4.6.29   Another instance of unequal operation is, that it establishes different degrees of authority in different states, and thus creates different interests. The lands in New-Hampshire having been formerly granted by this state, and afterwards by that state, to private persons, the whole authority of trying titles becomes vested in a continental court, and that state loses a branch of authority, which the others retain, over their own citizens.

I have now gone through two parts of my argument, and have proved the efficiency of the state governments for internal regulation, and the disadvantages of the new system, at least some of the principal. The argument has been much longer than I at first apprehended, or, possibly, I should have been deterred from it. The importance of the question has, however, prevented me from relinquishing it.

Agrippa.

VIII
25 December 1787

To the People.

It has been proved, by indisputable evidence, that power is not the grand principle of union among the parts of a very extensive empire; and that when this principle is pushed beyond the degree necessary for rendering justice between man and man, it debases the character of individuals, and renders them less secure in their persons and property. Civil liberty consists in the consciousness of that security, and is best guarded by political liberty, which is the share that every citizen has in the government. Accordingly all our accounts agree, that in those empires which are commonly called despotick, and which comprehend by far the greatest part of the world, the government is most fluctuating, and property least secure. In those countries insults are borne by the sovereign, which, if offered to one of our governours, would fill us with horrour, and we should think the government dissolving.

4.6.30

The common conclusion from this reasoning is an exceedingly unfair one, that we must then separate, and form distinct confederacies. This would be true if there was no principle to substitute in the room of power. Fortunately there is one. This is commerce.[18] All the states have local advantages, and in a considerable degree separate interests. They are, therefore, in a situation to supply each other's wants. Carolina, for instance, is inhabited by planters, while the Massachusetts is more engaged in commerce and manufactures. Congress has the power of deciding their differences. The most friendly intercourse may therefore be established between them. A diversity of produce, wants and interests, produces commerce, and commerce, where there is a common, equal and moderate authority to preside, produces friendship.

4.6.31

The same principles apply to the connection with the new settlers in the west. Many supplies they want, for which they must look to the older settlements, and the greatness of their crops enables them to make payments. Here, then, we have a bond of union which applies to all parts of the empire, and would continue to operate if the empire comprehended all America.

4.6.32

We are now, in the strictest sense of the terms, a federal republick. Each part has within its own limits the sovereignty over its citizens, while some of the general concerns are committed to Congress. The complaints of the deficiency of the Congressional powers are confined to two articles. They are not able to raise a revenue by taxation, and they have not a complete regulation of the intercourse between us and foreigners. For each of these complaints there is some foundation, but not enough to justify the clamour

4.6.33

which has been raised. Congress, it is true, owes a debt which ought to be paid. A considerable part of it has been paid. Our share of what remains would annually amount to about sixty or seventy thousand pounds. If, therefore, Congress were put in possession of such branches of the impost as would raise this sum in our state, we should fairly be considered as having done our part towards their debt; and our remaining resources, whether arising from impost, excise, or dry tax, might be applied to the reduction of our own debt. The principal of this last amounts to about thirteen hundred thousand pounds, and the interest to between seventy or eighty thousand. This is, surely, too much property to be sacrificed; and it is as reasonable that it should be paid as the continental debt. But if the new system should be adopted, the whole impost, with an unlimited claim to excise and dry tax, will be given to Congress. There will remain no adequate fund for the state debt, and the state will still be subject to be sued on their notes.—This is, then, an article which ought to be limited. We can, without difficulty, pay as much annually as shall clear the interest of our state debt, and our share of the interest on the continental one. But if we surrender the impost, we shall still, by this new constitution, be held to pay our full proportion of the remaining debt, as if nothing had been done. The impost will not be considered as being paid by this state, but by the continent. The federalists, indeed, tell us, that the state debts will all be incorporated with the continental debt, and all paid out of one fund. In this, as in all other instances, they endeavour to support their scheme of consolidation by delusion. Not one word is said in the book in favour of such a scheme, and there is no reason to think it true. Assurances of that sort are easily given, and as easily forgotten. There is an interest in forgetting what is false. No man can expect town debts to be united with that of the state; and there will be as little reason to expect, that the state and continental debts will be united together.

Agrippa.

IX

28 December 1787

To the People.

4.6.34   We come now to the second and last article of complaint against the present confederation, which is, that Congress has not the sole power to regulate the intercourse between us and foreigners. Such a power extends not only to war and peace, but to trade and naturalization. This last article ought never to be given them; for though most of the states may be willing for certain reasons to receive foreigners as citizens, yet reasons of equal weight may induce other states, differently circumstanced, to keep their blood pure. Pennsylvania has chosen to receive all that would come there. Let any indifferent person judge whether that state in point of morals, education, energy is equal to any of the eastern states; the small state of Rhode-Island only excepted. Pennsylvania in the course of a century has acquired her present extent and population at the expense of religion and good morals. The eastern states have, by keeping separate from the foreign mixtures, acquired, their present greatness in the course of a century and an half, and have preserved their religion and morals.[19] They have also preserved that manly virtue which is equally fitted for rendering them respectable in war, and industrious in peace.

The remaining power for peace and trade might perhaps be safely enough lodged with Congress under some limitations. Three restrictions appear to me to be essentially necessary to preserve the equality of rights to the states, which it is the object of the state governments to secure to each citizen. 1st. It ought not to be in the power of Congress either by treaty or otherwise to alienate part of any state without the consent of the legislature. 2d. They ought not to be able by treaty or other law to give any legal preference to one part above another. 3d. They ought to be restrained from creating any monopolies. Perhaps others may propose different regulations and restrictions. One of these is to be found in the old confederation, and another in the newly proposed plan. The third seems to be equally necessary.

4.6.35

After all that has been said and written on this subject, and on the difficulty of amending our old constitution so as to render it adequate to national purposes, it does not appear that any thing more was necessary to be done, than framing two new articles. By one a limited revenue would be given to Congress with a right to collect it, and by the other a limited right to regulate our intercourse with foreign nations. By such an addition we should have preserved to each state its power to defend the rights of the citizens, and the whole empire would be capable of expanding, and receiving additions without altering its former constitution. Congress, at the same time, by the extent of their jurisdiction, and the number of their officers, would have acquired more respectability at home, and a sufficient influence abroad. If any state was in such a case to invade the rights of the Union, the other states would join in defence of those rights, and it would be in the power of Congress to direct the national force to that object. But it is certain that the powers of Congress over the citizens should be small in proportion as the empire is extended; that, in order to preserve the balance, each state may supply by energy what is wanting in numbers. Congress would be able by such a system as we have proposed to regulate trade with foreigners by such duties as should effectually give the preference to the produce and manufactures of our own country. We should then have a friendly intercourse

4.6.36

established between the states, upon the principles of mutual interest. A moderate duty upon foreign vessels would give an advantage to our own people, while it would avoid all the [dis]advantages arising from a prohibition, and the consequent deficiency of vessels to transport the produce of the southern states.

4.6.37 Our country is at present upon an average a thousand miles long from north to south, and eight hundred broad from the Missisippi to the Ocean. We have at least six millions of white inhabitants, and the annual increase is about two hundred and fifty thousand souls, exclusive of emigrants from Europe. The greater part of our increase is employed in settling the new lands, while the older settlements are entering largely into manufactures of various kinds. It is probable, that the extraordinary exertions of this state in the way of industry for the present year only, exceed in value five hundred thousand pounds. The new settlements, if all made in the same tract of country, would form a large state annually; and the time seems to be literally accomplished when a nation shall be born in a day. Such an immense country is not only capable of yielding all the produce of Europe, but actually does produce by far the greater part of the raw materials. The restrictions on our trade in Europe, necessarily oblige us to make use of those materials, and the high price of labour operates as an encouragement to mechanical improvements. In this way we daily make rapid advancements towards independence in resources as well as in empire. If we adopt the new system of government we shall by one rash vote lose the fruit of the toil and expense of thirteen years, at the time when the benefits of that toil and expense are rapidly increasing. Though the imposts of Congress on foreign trade may tend to encourage manufactures, the excise and dry tax will destroy all the beneficial effects of the impost, at the same time that they diminish our capital. Be careful then to give only a limited revenue, and the limited power of managing foreign concerns. Once surrender the rights of internal legislation and taxation, and instead of being respected abroad, foreigners will laugh at us, and posterity will lament our folly.

Agrippa.

X
1 January 1788

To the People.

Friends and Brethren,

4.6.38 It is a duty incumbent on every man, who has had opportunities for inquiry, to lay the result of his researches on any matter of publick importance before the publick eye. No further apology will be necessary with the generality of my readers, for having so often appeared before them on the subject of the lately proposed form of government. It has been treated with that freedom which is necessary for the investigation of truth, and with no greater freedom. On such a subject, extensive in its nature, and important in its consequences, the examination has necessarily been long, and the topicks treated of have been various. We have been obliged to take a cursory, but not inaccurate view of the circumstances of mankind under the different forms of government to support the different parts of our argument. Permit me now to bring into one view the principal propositions on which the reasoning depends.

It is shewn from the example of the most commercial republick of antiquity, which was never disturbed by a sedition for above seven hundred years, and at last yielded after a violent struggle to a foreign enemy, as well as from the experience of our own country for a century and an half; that the republican, more than any other form of government is made of durable materials. It is shewn from a variety of proof, that one consolidated government is inapplicable to a great extent of country; is unfriendly to the rights both of persons and property, which rights always adhere together; and that being contrary to the interest of the extreme of an empire, such a government can be supported only by power, and that commerce is the true bond of union for a free state. It is shewn from a comparison of the different parts of the proposed plan, that it is such a consolidated government.

4.6.39

By article 3, section 2, Congress are empowered to appoint courts with authority to try civil causes of every kind, and even offences against particular states; by the last clause of article 1, section 8, which defines their legislative powers, they are authorized to make laws for carrying into execution all the "powers vested by this constitution in the government of the United States, or in *any department* or officer thereof;" and by article 6, the judges in every state are to be bound by the laws of Congress. It is therefore a complete consolidation of all the states into one, however diverse the parts of it may be. It is also shewn that it will operate unequally in the different states, taking from some of them a greater share of wealth; that in this last respect it will operate more to the injury of this commonwealth than of any state in the union; and that by reason of its inequality it is subversive of the principles of a free government, which requires every part to contribute an equal proportion. For all these reasons this system ought to be rejected, even if no better plan was proposed in the room of it. In case of a rejection we must remain as we are, with trade extending, resources opening, settlements enlarging, manufactures increasing, and publick debts diminishing by fair payment. These are mighty blessings, and not to be lost by the hasty adoption of a new system. But great as these benefits are, which we derive from our present system, it has been shewn, that they may be increased by giving Congress a limited power to regulate trade, and

4.6.40

assigning to them those branches of the impost on our foreign trade only, which shall be equal to our proportion of their present annual demands. While the interest is thus provided for, the sale of our lands in a very few years will pay the principal, and the other resources of the state will pay our own debt. The present mode of assessing the continental tax is regulated by the extent of landed property in each state. By this rule the Massachusetts has to pay one eighth. If we adopt the new system, we shall surrender the whole of our impost and excise, which probably amount to a third of those duties of the whole continent, and must come in for about a sixth part of the remaining debt. By this means we shall be deprived of the benefit arising from the largeness of our loans to the continent, shall lose our ability to satisfy the just demands on the state. Under the limitations of revenue and commercial regulation contained in these papers, the balance will be largely in our favour; the importance of the great states will be preserved, and the publick creditors both of the continent and state will be satisfied without burdening the people. For a more concise view of my proposal, I have thrown it into the form of a resolve supposed to be passed by the convention which is shortly to set in this town.

4.6.41   "Commonwealth of Massachusetts.

Resolved, That the form of government lately proposed by a federal convention, held in the city of Philadelphia, is so far injurious to the interests of this commonwealth, that we are constrained by fidelity to our constituents to reject it; and we do hereby reject the said proposed form and every part thereof. But in order that the union of these states may, as far as possible, be promoted, and the federal business as little obstructed as may be, we do agree on the part of this commonwealth, that the following addition be made to the present articles of confederation.

4.6.42   "XIV. The United States shall have power to regulate the intercou[r]se between these states and foreign dominions, under the following restrictions; viz 1st. No treaty, ordinance, or law shall alienate the whole or part of any state, without the consent of the legislature of such state. 2d. The United States shall not by treaty or otherwise give a preference to the ports of one state over those of another; Nor, 3d create any monopolies or exclusive companies; Nor, 4th, extend the privileges of citizenship to any foreigner. And for the more convenient exercise of the powers hereby and by the former articles given, the United S[t]ates shall have authority to constitute judicatories, whether supreme or subordinate, with power to try all piracies and felonies done on the high seas, and also all civil causes in which a foreign state, or subject thereof actually resident in a foreign country and not being British absentees, shall be one of the parties. They shall also have authority to try all causes in which ambassadours shall be concerned. All these trials shall be by jury and in some sea-port town. All imposts levied by Congress on trade shall be confined to foreign produce or foreign manufactures imported, and to foreign ships trading in our harbours, and all their absolute prohibitions shall be confined to the same articles. All imposts and confiscations shall be to the use of the state in which they shall accrue, excepting in such branches as shall be assigned by any state as a fund for defraying their proportion of the continental. And no powers shall be exercised by Congress but such as are expressly given by this and the former articles. And we hereby authorize our delegates in Congress to sign and ratify an article in the foregoing form and words, without any further act of this state for that purpose, provided the other states shall accede to this proposition on their part on or before the first day of January, which will be in the year of our Lord 1790. All matters of revenue being under the controul of the legislature, we reccommend to the general court of this common-wealth, to devise, as early as may be, such funds arising from such branches of foreign commerce, as shall be equal to our part of the current charges of the continent, and to put Congress in possession of the revenue arising therefrom, with a right to collect it, during such term as shall appear to be necessary for the payment of the principal of their debt, by the sale of the western lands.''

By such an explicit declaration of the powers given to Congress, we shall provide for all federal purposes, and shall at the same time secure our rights. It is easier to amend the old confederation, defective as it has been repre-sented, than it is to correct the new form. For with what ever view it was framed, truth constrains me to say, that it is insiduous in its form, and ruinous in its tendency. Under the pretence of different branches of the legislature, the members will in fact be chosen from the same general de-scription of citizens. The advantages of a check will be lost, while we shall be continually exposed to the cabals and corruption of a British election. There cannot be a more eligible mode than the present, for appointing members of Congress, nor more effectual checks provided than our separate state governments, nor any system so little expensive, in case of our adopt-ing the resolve just stated, or even continuing as we are. We shall in that case avoid all the inconvenience of concurrent jurisdictions, we shall avoid the expensive and useless establishments of the Philadelphia proposition, we shall preserve our constitution and liberty, and we shall provide for all such institutions as will be useful. Surely then you cannot hesitate, whether you will chuse freedom or servitude. The object is now well defined. By adopting the form proposed by the convention, you will have the derision of foreigners, internal misery, and the anathemas of posterity. By amending the present confederation, and granting limited powers to Congress, you secure the admiration of strangers, internal happiness, and the blessings and prosperity of all succeeding generations. Be wise then, and by preserving your freedom, prove, that Heaven bestowed it not in vain. Many will be the efforts to delude the convention. The mode of judging is itself suspicious, as being contrary to the antient and established usage of the commonwealth. But since this mode is adopted, we trust, that the numbers [members?] of

4.6.43

that venerable assembly will not so much regard the greatness of their power, as the sense and interest of their constituents. And they will do well to remember that even a mistake in adopting it, will be destructive, while no evils can arise from a total, and much less, probably, from such a partial rejection as we have proposed.

4.6.44   I have now gone through my reasonings on this momentous subject, and have stated the facts and deductions from them, which you will verify for yourselves. Personal interest was not my object, or I should have pursued a different line of conduct. Though I conceived that a man who owes allegiance to the state is bound, on all important occasions, to propose such inquiries as tend to promote the publick good; yet I did not imagine it to be any part of my duty to present myself to the fury of those, who appear to have other ends in view. For this cause, and for this only, I have chosen a feigned signature. At present all the reports concerning the writer of these papers are merely conjectural. I should have been ashamed of my system if it had needed such feeble support as the character of individuals. It stands on the firm ground of the experience of mankind. I cannot conclude this long disquisition better than with a caution derived from the words of inspiration. *Discern the things of your peace now in the days thereof, before they be hidden from your eyes.*[20]

Agrippa.

XI
8 January 1788

To the People. —

4.6.45   My last Address contained the outlines of a system fully adequate to all the useful purposes of the union. Its object is to raise a sufficient revenue from the foreign trade, and the sale of our publick lands, to satisfy all the publick exigencies, and to encourage, at the same time, our internal industry and manufactures. It also secures each state in its own separate rights, while the continental concerns are thrown into the general department. The only deficiencies that I have been able to discover in the plan, and in the view of federalists they are very great ones, are, that it does not allow the interference of Congress in the domestick concerns of the state, and that it does not render our national councils so liable to foreign influence. The first of these articles tends to guard us from that infinite multiplication of officers which the report of the Convention of Philadelphia proposes. With regard to the second, it is evidently not of much importance to any foreign nation to purchase, at a very high price, a majority of votes in an assembly, whose members are continually exposed to a recall. But give those members a right to sit six, or even two, years, with such extensive powers as the new system proposes, and their friendship will be well worth a purchase. This is the only sense in which the Philadelphia system will render us more respectable in the eyes of foreigners. In every other view they lose their respect for us, as it will render us more like their own degraded models. It is a maxim with them, that every man has his price. If, therefore we were to judge of what passes in the hearts of the federalists when they urge us, as they continually do, *to be like other nations*, and when they assign mercenary motives to the opposers of their plan, we should conclude very fairly, that themselves wish to be provided for at the publick expense. However that may be, if we look upon the men we shall find some of their leaders to have formed pretty strong attachments to foreign nations. Whether those attachments arose from their being educated under a royal government, from a former unfortunate mistake in politicks, or from the agencies for foreigners, or any other cause, is not in my province to determine. But certain it is, that some of the principal fomenters of this plan have never shewn themselves capable of that generous system of policy which is founded in the affections of freemen. Power and high life are their idols, and national funds are necessary to support them.

Some of the principal powers of Europe have already entered into treaties with us, and that some of the rest have not done it, is not owing, as is falsely pretended, to the want of power in Congress. Holland never found any difficulty of this kind from the multitude of sovereignties in that country, which must all be consulted on such an occasion. The resentment of Great Britain for our victories in the late war has induced that power to restrain our intercourse with their subjects. Probably an hope, the only solace of the wretched, that their affairs would take a more favourable turn on this continent, has had some influence on their proceedings. All their restrictions have answered the end of securing our independence by driving us into many valuable manufactures. Their own colonies in the mean time have languished for want of an intercourse with these states. The new settlement in Nova Scotia has miserably decayed, and the West India Islands have suffered for want of our supplies, and by the loss of our market. This has affected the revenue; and however contemptuously some men may affect to speak of our trade, the supply of six millions of people is an object worth the attention of any nation upon earth. Interest in such a nation as Britain will surmount their resentment. However their pride may be stung, they will pursue after wealth. Increase of revenue to a nation overwhelmed with a debt of near *two hundred and ninety millions* sterling is an object to which little piques must give way; and there is no doubt that their interest consists in securing as much of our trade as they can.

These are topicks from which are drawn some of the most plausible reasons that have been given by the federalists in favour of their plan, as

4.6.46

4.6.47

derived from the sentiments of foreigners. We have weighed them and found them wanting. That they had not themselves full confidence in their own reasons at Philadelphia is evident from the method they took to bias the state Convention. Mess'rs Wilson and M'Kean, two Scottish names, were repeatedly worsted in the argument. To make amends for their own incapacity, the gallery was filled with a rabble, who shouted their applause, and these heroes of aristocracy were not ashamed, though modesty is their national virtue, to vindicate such a violation of decency:[21] Means not less criminal, but not so flagrantly indecent, have been frequently mentioned among us to secure a majority. But those who vote for a price, can never sanctify wrong, and treason will still retain its deformity.

Agrippa.

1. See above, 2.1.

2. See above, 3.2.

3. See A Landholder (Oliver Ellsworth), *Connecticut Courant* 3 December 1787, Ford, *Essays* 159.

4. See XIII, 4.6.49–50. On the bearing of the examples of Greece and Rome, see *The Federalist* no. 8, 47; no. 9, 50–51; on Rome and Carthage, no. 6, 32.

5. *The Federalist* no. 9, 51. On commerce as the bond of union, see Agrippa VIII, 4.6.31 n. 18.

6. For an elaboration of this view, see Charles Pinckney's speech in the Philadelphia convention on 25 June 1787; and for a major forerunner of the *The Federalist* answer, see Madison's reply to Pinckney on the next day. Farrand I, 397–404, 421–23. It may be observed that Agrippa's examples, which follow, support the proposition that a republican government will be energetic enough to suppress sedition, not that it will be exempt from it.

7. See Thomas Hutchinson, *History of the Colony and Province of Massachusetts Bay* (Cambridge, Mass., 1936) I, 123 ff.

8. The reference is to the disturbances culminating in Shays' rebellion. On the issue of American conditions in the 1780s, see Federal Farmer I, 2.8.1 n. 4; Centinel IV, 2.7.91 n. 43; Plebeian 6.11.5 n. 6.

9. For a reply to this and the following remarks, see Cassius (James Sullivan), in the *Massachusetts Gazette* 30 November 1787, Ford, *Essays* 22–23.

10. For other Anti-Federalist arguments to this effect, see Cato III, 2.6.12–16 n. 8. For Federalist defenses of the extended republic, see, in addition to *The Federalist* (nos. 9, 10, 14, 51), Ford *Pamphlets* 203–6 (Fabius), 129–30 (Citizen of Philadelphia), 248 (Aristides); Ford, *Essays* 215–16 (A Countryman); McMaster and Stone 193 (Plain Truth); ibid. 336, 386, 395 (Wilson); Elliot II, 352–53 (Hamilton); Elliot III, 85, 125, 199 (Randolph); ibid. 107–8 (Corbin), 232 (Marshall); Elliot IV, 22 (Davis); ibid. 262, 326–327 (Pinckney); *Poughkeepsie Country Journal* 12 December 1787 (Cato).

11. On heterogeneity, and particularly differences between North and South, see IX, 4.6.34–35; XII, 4.6.48; Cato III, 2.6.18 n. 13.

12. See Resolution of Stamp Act Congress, 19 October 1765; Massachusetts Circular Letter, 11 February 1768; Declaration and Resolves of First Continental Congress, 14 October 1774. Nos. 38, 45, and 56 in Henry Steele Commager, *Documents of American History* (New York 1968).

13. This alleged authority, upon which a considerable part of Agrippa's proof of the consolidating tendency of the Constitution depends, is not of course given explicitly in the Constitution. Apparently Agrippa is referring to the comprehensive federal

jurisdiction that he says "clearly follows" from Article VI; but his contention is extremely dubious. See XIII, 4.6.52, for a slightly different version of this argument. Cf. Centinel II, 2.7.42;

14. On bills of rights as the standard by which rulers can be held to the terms of the contract and the people justified in their resistance, see XIII, 4.6.51, 71. For similar Anti-Federal arguments, see Old Whig IV, 3.3.21–30; Philadelphiensis IV, 3.9.21–22; DeWitt, 4.3.8; [Maryland] Farmer I, 5.1.15–16; Impartial Examiner 5.14.5, 10.

15. On the power to regulate commerce, see XIII, 4.6.53.

16. The original reads, "shewn, that instead of . . . course of things, that every endeavour . . ."

17. Cf. Monroe 5.21.12. See Agrippa·XII, 4.6.58 n. 31.

18. On commerce as the producer of friendship and peace, see *The Federalist* no. 6; and cf. no. 11, 72: "An unity of commercial, as well as political interests, can only result from an unity of government." See Candidus 4.9.13–15.

19. John Adams, in Philadelphia for the meetings of the first Continental Congress in 1774, observed: "Phyladelphia with all its Trade, and Wealth, and Regularity is not Boston. The Morals of our People are much better, their Manners are more polite, and agreeable—they are purer English. Our Language is better, our Persons are handsomer, our Spirit is greater, our Laws are wiser, our Religion is superiour, our Education is better. We exceed them in every Thing, but in a Markett, and in charitable public foundations." *Diary and Autobiography of John Adams*, ed. L. H. Butterfield (Cambridge 1961), 9 October 1774, II, 150. See Agrippa XII, 4.6.48.

20. Var. on Luke 19:42.

21. See McMaster and Stone 364–65.

Maryland: Introduction

By the spring of 1788 six states had ratified the Constitution, and the center of activity shifted to the South, where only Georgia had ratified. The great danger to the Constitution here lay in the possibility of concerted southern action under the leadership of Patrick Henry of Virginia. The Maryland and South Carolina conventions were to meet before Virginia's, and the strategy of their Anti-Federalists was to work for a postponement if they could not secure rejection and thus to invite Virginia, with its strong Anti-Federalist group, to take the lead in rejecting or drastically modifying the Constitution.

Maryland was one of the most aristocratic of the American states, being governed by a group of planters and merchants linked by interest, background, and marriage under a constitution that required fairly high property qualifications for political participation, especially for holding senatorial and executive office. Despite a relatively low level of political participation, however, there was an active opposition group, led by Samuel Chase, and there had been considerable controversy over paper money.[1] When the legislature took up the proposed new Constitution in 1787 the Federalists agreed to delay the convention until April 1788, and to eliminate the normal property qualifications for delegates. The Senate also accepted a proposal for a "convention of the people for their full and free investigation and decision" in the place of its own words, "for their assent and ratification."[2] But the Federalists compromised out of strength and a desire to get on with the business. The convention elected was overwhelmingly Federalist. For unknown reasons the Anti-Federalist leaders did not appear in the convention for the first few days. By the time Chase, Luther Martin, and William Paca arrived, three days after the convention opened, the Constitution had gone through two readings and the question to adopt was before the House. Chase gave a lengthy speech opposing ratification. Knowing they had a safe majority and favorable rules, the Federalists listened in silence, offering no rebuttal. After an unsuccessful attempt by Paca to introduce amendments, the vote was taken, and on 26 April the Constitution was adopted 63–11.[3] The Federalists refused to accept even recommendatory amendments, which, after several days of attempted compromise in committee, were rejected by a vote of 47–26. Maryland was the only state to ratify after Massachusetts that did not submit recommendatory amendments.

1. See Philip A. Crowl, *Maryland during and after the Revolution: A Political and Economic Study* (Baltimore 1943); Forrest McDonald, *We the People* 148–62.

2. Bernard Steiner, "Maryland's Adoption of the Federal Constitution," *American Historical Review* October 1899 and January 1900.

3. Paca voted with the majority. For accounts of the proceedings, see A. C. Hanson, "To the People of Maryland," *Documentary History of the Constitution* IV, 650–63, and the accounts of the Maryland Convention Minority 5.4 and John Francis Mercer 5.5.

A Farmer, Essay V

(BALTIMORE) MARYLAND GAZETTE
March 1788

Among the more penetrating and comprehensive Anti-Federalist essays are these written by A [Maryland] Farmer, printed in the *Maryland Gazette* during February, March, and April of 1788, and here reprinted for the first time. On the issues of a bill of rights, political parties, and especially representation and simple versus complex government, the argument of this Maryland writer is indispensable to the student of Anti-Federalist thought.

While no direct evidence of authorship has been found, it seems likely that A [Maryland] Farmer was John Francis Mercer, a non-signing member of the Constitutional Convention and an active Maryland Anti-Federalist.[1] Born in Virginia, Mercer was educated at William and Mary, studied law under Thomas Jefferson, performed extensive military service during the Revolutionary War, and represented Virginia in Congress. On his marriage in 1785, he removed to Maryland, from which state he was chosen to serve in the Federal Convention in 1787, which he left before its work was finished. He played an active part in the Maryland opposition to the Constitution. On the establishment of the new government, Mercer aligned himself with the Republicans and devoted himself largely to politics. He served as a member of the Maryland House of Delegates, briefly as a member of the federal House of Representatives, and as Governor of Maryland.[2] The attribution is inconclusive since it depends almost entirely on a similarity in argument between those of A Farmer and those known to have been made by Mercer. Yet the similarity is striking and goes well beyond ordinary parallels among Anti-Federalists. The chief source of Mercer's views is Madison's report of his speech in the Convention on 14 August. We have in addition a useful letter to Jefferson, written in 1804, and the "Address to the Members of the Conventions of New York and Virginia," which is printed below.[3]

Both Mercer and A Farmer find their central argument in the contention that the Constitution falls between the two stools of genuine simple government and genuine mixed or complex government. Like many Anti-Federalists, they are much concerned with representation, but their analyses of representation—as a system tending to lead to aristocratic domination and then to tyranny unless held in check by permanent and fixed orders—are very similar to one another and quite distinct from the more usual discussions by, for example, Samuel Chase of Maryland and Richard Henry Lee of Virginia.[4] Both Mercer and A Farmer are favorably impressed with England as an example of mixed government, and both argue for a strong executive in any stable complex government.[5] Their concern for the preservation of the states is less distinctive, but here too Mercer and A Farmer are unusual in their particular discussion of the federal system as a system of balance of power[6] and in their concern with party.[7]

References are provided to the main points of similarity, so that the reader can judge for himself the accuracy of the editor's opinion that Mercer was in all probability the author of this interesting and important series of essays.

A Farmer took up his pen to reply to a Federalist pamphlet by Aristides, the pseudonym of Alexander Contee Hanson, a Maryland legislator and judge.[8] First he replies to what Aristides had described as his attack on "the whole body of anti-federalists in their stronghold," the absence of a bill of rights. While making the usual arguments here, A Farmer also turns a common Federalist view on its head by contending that, whereas in a monarchy numbers are typically on the side of the individual, in a popular government the danger to the individual lies in the interests or heated passions of the majority and that, therefore, the freer or more democratic the government, the greater the need for clear expressions of individual rights. A Farmer concludes this essay with the question whether a national government is to be preferred for the United States to a league or a confederation.

In his second essay A Farmer postpones a promised discussion of consolidation and takes up the subject of representation. This is one of the four or five major Anti-Federalist discussions of this critical issue. Here and throughout there is a tension in the author's thought between a defense of simple government in principle and an objection to a *premature* adoption of a complex government for which America does not provide the materials. He begins with sharp sarcasm about the brash confidence of his opponents in their new knowledge and an unusually strong statement (even for the conservative Anti-Federalists) that "there is nothing solid or useful that is new" (II, 5.1.22). Far from being unknown in former times, government by representation is coeval with mankind but, being the government most liable to corruption, has always been of short duration. Broadly speaking, the argument in this important if somewhat loose essay is that representative government is aristocracy, which is corrupt and tyrannical and which leads the desperate people to hand themselves over to a single man. Normally, then, representative government leads to tyranny supported by a standing army; but A Farmer holds out a possibility of tempering the aristocracy with a strong and independent executive (unlike the union of Senate and Executive under the Constitution). The usual course of degeneration will be speeded and exaggerated in the United States, however, when thirteen complicated forms of government are bound in a single further complicated government to the complete destruction of "all responsibility (the only test of good government)" (II, 5.1.34). The question of standing armies, their effects on liberty, and guards against them, occupy the latter half of the essay (II, 5.1.35–53).

In the third essay, A Farmer takes up the question of whether a national or a federal government is to be preferred. While a national government will add to the dignity and splendor of the United States, true happiness lies in simple quiet government. However, A Farmer sees little in the present corrupted manners of his fellow citizens to suggest that they are now capable of sustaining self-government. So far as relations among the states and defense against foreign intrigue or corruption are concerned, a confederation of small popular governments is best. In the latter part of the essay, A Farmer provides a very interesting sketch of the three main classes in the United States, and their probable future (III, 5.1.56–60). He ends with the observation that "on the preservation of parties, public liberty depends," and that the aim of a free and wise people should be to balance parties so that from the weakness of all they may be governed by the moderation of the combined judgments of the whole (III, 5.1.60).

In the fourth essay A Farmer criticizes the absence of provision for trial by jury in civil cases and discusses the value of the jury as the democratic part of the judiciary—the people's check on government and their school in public affairs.

In his very important and complex fifth essay, A Farmer returns to his major theme of representation. The discussion begins with "governments of simplicity and equal right," which have not been dealt with faithfully in theory and practice (V, 5.1.69). For whatever reasons, we seem to be tending toward mixed government with permanent and fixed orders. If this is to be our direction, let us proceed slowly and carefully. Government by representation "sets all system at defiance" by inducing constant change (V, 5.1.71). A representative system can only succeed if based on fixed and permanent orders, but the only such order in America is the yeomanry, which is powerless. The Constitution tries to erect a republic on the ruins of a corrupt monarchy. A government for the United States founded on representation requires at least an executive for life and a senate also for life appointed by the executive. The problem is to prevent the executive from becoming hereditary, for which reason the vice presidency is important (V, 5.1.72–74).

Having considered the dangers of representation and the requirements of a representative system—if that is what the United States must have—A Farmer returns in the conclusion of this essay to the advantages of simple government (V, 5.1.75–82). The English system, although good of its kind, is undeservedly praised. It is a rational system; but it required the introduction of a ministerial system and corruption to support it, and it does not prevent poverty in the lower orders and disorder. England may be compared with Switzerland, whose government is simple and in the hands of the people personally, where every citizen is legislator and soldier and where liberty, peace, and prosperity reign. Government should be in the hands of the people, that is, those who hold the property of the soil. With government in the hands of the freeholders, with reasonable sumptuary laws, and with the institution of seminaries of useful learning, the people would cease abusing their governments and would "wade up to their knees in blood" to defend them (V, 5.1.82).

In his sixth essay A Farmer replies to Aristides on various minor points, chiefly the question of concurrent jurisdiction of federal and state courts.

A Farmer concludes with a long essay, extending over several numbers of the *Maryland Gazette,* in which he replies to some further criticisms of Aristides and summarizes his own argument. He traces the decline of government from its initial devotion to equal rights to its unavoidably (or so A Farmer seems to think) unequal operation. Oppressed by the few, the people call on one man to rule them (VII, 5.1.94–100). This monarchy, in turn, suffers its inevitable corruption, which in turn corrupts the whole society (VII, 5.1.101–3). At length, the people look to heaven for that solace and equality they are denied on earth, but religious tyranny and corruption support and are supported by civil tyranny and corruption (VII, 5.1.104–7). Despite the loss of civil and political liberty, Europe has at least preserved a degree of social happiness impossible in great empires, due to the moderating influence of a system of balance among national powers (VII, 5.1.108–11). A Farmer concludes with reflections on the American state governments, the imperfections of which have led to the present agitations. Yet the future seems likely to be worse than the past (VII, 5.1.112–13). "[T]he truth is that we aimed at, and still aim at premature public splendor and private luxury, forgetting that bodies politic, like natural bodies, have their duration of manly vigor and the decline of age. . . . We wanted to be every thing at once—that is what we now wish, and in the event we shall be nothing or worse than nothing, we strived to patch up the ruined fabric of the British constitution for our use, and . . . we never reflected, that we had none of the distinctions of ranks which preserve that government—that the state of our society was altogether different—and that we had only the wishes, but none of the means" (VII, 5.1.113).

(Indecipherable words or passages in the original are indicated here by brackets and space.)

1. If it is assumed that the author was a fairly prominent Maryland Anti-Federalist, a reasonable assumption especially given the somewhat aristocratic structure of Maryland politics, Mercer becomes one of a handful of possibilities, and some of these had expressed themselves publicly in other forms. Mercer probably was "retired in the country," as A Farmer says he was in his sixth essay (VI, 5.1.84), on his estate in Anne Arundel County. The last of A Farmer's pieces was published on 22 April 1788, the day after the opening of the Maryland Convention (where Mercer was present), and it may be that the promised continuation was cut off by the necessity to attend the convention. None of this proves more, of course, than that Mercer might have been the author. For an address of John Francis Mercer, see 5.5.

2. James Mercer Garnett, "John Francis Mercer," *Maryland Historical Magazine* September 1907, pp. 209–12; Mary W. Williams, "John Francis Mercer," *Dictionary of American Biography* XII, 543–44.

3. Mercer 5.5; *Farrand* II, 284–85 (14 August); *Maryland Historical Magazine* September 1907, pp. 209–12.

4. See II, 5.1.22–29; V, 5.1.72; VII, 5.1.113; Farrand II, 284; Mercer 5.5.5. Cf. Federal Farmer, II, 2.8.15 and n. 11. Despite the distinctiveness of the argument presented by Mercer and A Farmer, I have nevertheless contended that it is characteristic, in the sense of explicitly stating and examining a persistent but usually obscured Anti-Federalist theme or problem.

5. See II, 5.1.31; V, 5.1.74–75; Farrand II, 284–85; Mercer 5.5.11.

6. See III, 5.1.52; VI, 5.1.109; *Maryland Historical Magazine* September 1907, p. 210.

7. See III, 5.1.60; *Maryland Historical Magazine* September 1907.

8. See Ford, *Pamphlets* 217–57.

V

25 March 1788

I have been long since firmly persuaded, that there are no hidden sources of moral agency beyond the reach of investigation.—The all-wise and all-bountiful Author of Nature, could never have created *human reason* unequal to the happy regulation of *human conduct*.—The errors and misfortunes of mankind spring from obvious sources. Religious and political prejudices, formed by education, strengthened by habit, maintained by interest, and consecrated by fear, are forever arming the passions against the judgment.—The celebrated Blaise Pascal (the powers of whose understanding were rather miraculous than surprizing) closed his painful researches after religious truth, with this dogma, as pernicious as untrue,— *"That a religion purely spiritual, was never intended for mankind."*[44] There could be no judgment more unbiassed, for there was no mind so strong, no

5.1.68

heart more pure; but bred in the bosom of the church, even her idolatry impressed him with veneration and awe. Notwithstanding his conclusion, the doctrines of Calvin maintain their ground in their primitive simplicity, divested of the aid of ceremony and form. The thunders of the Vatican, which for ages deluged Europe with blood, have dissipated their force, and reason has resumed her spiritual empire. Would to God, that the history of temporal despotism had terminated as favourably for the happiness of mankind!—In the political world, the chains of civil power, upheld by the numerous links of private interest, have proved more equal and permanent in their effects; they have, and I fear forever must, shackle the human understanding; and it is much to be questioned whether the full and free political opinion of any one great luminary of science, has been fairly disclosed to the world—Even when the great and amiable Montesquieu had hazarded a panegyric on the English constitution, he shrinks back with terror into this degrading apostrophe—*"Think not that* I *mean to undervalue other governments*—I *who think an excess of liberty*[,] *an excess of all things, even of reason itself, a misfortune, and that the happiness of mankind is only to be found in a medium between two extremes."*[45]—The author of the Persian letters, at that moment recollected the afflicting presure he had felt from the hand of Gallic government, and his pen trembled as he wrote.

5.1.69   Is it then possible that governments of simplicity and equal right, can have been fairly dealt by in theory or practice? The votaries of tyranny and usurpation stand not alone—in bitter opposition; every man of enterprize, of superior talents and fortune, is interested to debase them; their banners have ever been deserted because they never can pay their troops.—The most amiable and sensible of mankind seem to have made a stand in favour of a mixed government founded on the permanent orders and objects of men.—Thither I suspect the American government is now tending. If it must be so—Let it go gently then—with slow and equal steps.—Let each gradation and experiment have a full and fair trial—Let there be no effect without a good, apparent and well considered cause—Let us live all the days of our lives, and as happily as circumstances will permit.—Finally, let moderation be our guide and the influence of manners will conduct us (I hope without injury) to some permanent, fixed establishment, where we may repose a while, unagitated by alteration or revolution—For in sudden and violent changes, how many of the most worthy of our fellow-citizens must get their bones crushed?

5.1.70   I cannot think that any *able and virtuous citizen,* would in his cool and dispationate moments, wish to blend or risque the fundamental rights of men, with any organization of society that the Americans can or will make for fifty years to come.—Let us keep these rights of individuals—these unalienable blessings[—]reserved and separated from every constitution and form—If they are unmingled, the attentive eyes of every citizen will be kept fixed upon them. We shall watch them as a sacred deposit, and we may carry them uninjured and unimpaired through every vicissitude and change, from the government we have left, into some other that may be established on the fixed and solid principles of reason.— Nor can there be, I imagine, any *prudent man*, who would trust the whimsical inventions of the day, with that dangerous weapon *a standing army*, in our present unsettled circumstances—striving to substantiate inefficient and unnatural forms—it would wield us into despotism in a moment, and we have surely had throat-cutting enough in our day.

Throughout the world government by representation, seems only to have been established to disgrace itself and be abolished—its very principle is change, and it sets all system at defiance—it perishes by speedy corruption.—The few representatives can always corrupt themselves by legislative speculations, from the pockets of their numerous constituents—quick rotation, like a succession of terms tenants on a farm, only encreases the evil by rendering them more rapacious. If the executive is changeable, he can never oppose large decided majorities of influential individuals—or enforce on those powerful men, who may render his next election [   ] the rigor of *equal law, which is the grand and only object of human society.*—If the executive is to be rendered ineligible for a certain period, he will either *not do his duty,* or he will retire into the unprotected situation of a private individual, with all the sworn animosities of a powerful majority—aristocracy—junto—the cry of the populace, or perhaps the whole combined to pursue him to the grave, or a public execution.[46] The considerate and good, who adorn private life, and such only can be safely trusted in high public station, will never commit themselves to a situation where a consciencious discharge of duty may embitter the evening of life, if not draw down ruin and infamy on themselves and families.—There never was but one man who stepped from the top to the bottom, without breaking his neck, and that was Sylla; and although it is true that whilst he was up, he broke the hearts of the Romans, yet his dying undisturbed in private life, is one of those miracles that must remain forever unexplained. If the aristocracy, or representation of wealth, (the principle of wh[i]ch order is to keep all things as they are, for by confusion they may lose more than they can gain) is also changeable, there then is nothing fixed and permanent in government.—Legislative tyranny commences, and exhibits a perpetual scene of plunder and confusion, fearlessly practised under the sanction of authority and law. It is true that the influence of manners may and will resist for a time; yet that must give way to a general and prevalent corruption—Those who are respectable at home and have permanent [   ] in life, and such only can give stability to government, will not suffer themselves to be mounted up on the wheel of fortune, to be let down again as it turns, the mockery of children and fools.—Where representation has been admitted as a component part of government, it has always proved defective, if not

5.1.71

destructive. What then must be the consequence where the whole government is founded on representation? Every American can now answer, it will be at best but—*representation of government*—with us the influence of manners has been great—it is indeed declining fast; but aided by the solidity of the judiciary establishments, and the wisest code of civil laws, that ever mankind were blessed with, it has hitherto supported the forms of society: But the people are now weary of their representatives and their governments.—We may trace the progress.—One candidate, to recommend his pretensions, discloses and descants on the errors of the preceding administration—The people believe him and are deceived—they change men; but measures are still the same, or injured by the sudden and violent alteration of system[47]—At least the next candidate asserts it is so—is again believed, and his constituents again deceived; a general disgust and sullen silence ensue; elections are deserted; government is first despised, and then cordially hated.

5.1.72   There can be no fixed and permanent government that does not rest *on the fixed and permanent orders and objects of mankind.*[48]—Government on *paper* may amuse, but we pay dear for the amusement, the only fixed and permanent *order* with us at present are the YEOMANRY, and they have no power whatever,—unless the right of changing masters at a certain period, and devolving on their changeable representatives their whole political existence—may be called power—The order of GENTRY, with us, is not a fixed and permanent order at all, and if they attempt to erect themselves into one at present, it is usurpation, and they will be pulled down; and yet, in my opinion, such an order is essential to a perfect government, founded on representation.—Every other mode of introducing wealth into power, has proved vicious and abominable.—With us delegates become by selection, themselves a species of subaltern aristocracy—they intrigue with the senates, who by a refined mode of election are a misbegotten, side blow, representation of wealth, and they both form an imperfect aristocracy, on the worst principles on which that order can be admitted into government—and the democratic influence which is thus amalgomated and not divided, but unformed becomes vicious from its impotence.

5.1.73   These defects spring from our attempting to erect republican fabrics on the ruined and imperfect pillars of an old corrupt monarchy—not less absurd, than to expect the limbs to perform the functions of life, after cutting off the head.—The opposition which brought Charles the first to the block, was composed of some of the ablest and most virtuous characters that ever adorned any age or clime—Hampden, Pym, Selden, Sir Harry Vane, Sydney, Marvell and many others.—They pursued their old model—attempted to form a government by representation which was at first steadied and restrained by the best senate in the world, (the English House of Lords)— the two houses soon disagreed, and there being no third power to interpose, the representatives, voted the House of Lords useless—new modelled the government into a single branch, and then began to plunder most unmercifully—At last Cromwell kicked them all out of doors, and after his tyrannical usurpation and death, the nation were very happy to take shelter again under the regal government, and even restored an unworthy family (which they had irritated beyond forgiveness) to the throne.

A Farmer.

(To be continued.)

28 March 1788

(Continued from our last.)

After every consideration I can give this subject, I am satisfied, that *government founded on representation*, indispensibly requires, at least an executive for life, whose person must be sacred from impeachment, and only his ostensible ministers responsible—A senate for life, the vacancies to be filled up and the number occasionally encreased but under a limitation, by the executive—the hand that holds the balance must have the power of adding weight and influence to the lightest scale, and of frequently removing turbulent men into an higher and inoffensive situation:—I am inclined to think that an important portion of American opinion leans that way at this moment—My fear is, that our general government may ultimate in an hereditary authority—if not despotism—to avoid the former, great attention should be paid to the important office of Vice-President—at present but little understood:—A Vice-President to succeed on a vacancy prevents those evils which have ruined Poland and all the northern kingdoms—thus we see the King of the Romans has secured Germany from every evil of elective monarchy, and had the golden bull prevented one of the family or kindred of the reigning Emperor from filling the office of the King of the Romans, this part of the Germanic constitution would have been perfect, and the house of Austria would never have been enabled to usurp the imperial crown as a patrimony and desolate Europe with her ambitious views; she would have continued in that beggarly condition from which Rodolph of Hapsburg raised it—The American constitution is much better guarded but not by any means completely so.

5.1.74

If this is the best we can hope for—if this is the best reward we can expect for the sons of America slain, and the distresses we shall long continue to feel—is it not incumbent on us to examine minutely all its consequences?—Let us view government by representation in its favorite form—The constitution of England—its uncommon success and length of duration there, has drawn on it very unmerited encomiums from the enlightened Genevan[,] Delolme—the only great political writer who does not

5.1.75

seem to hold representation in contempt,[49]—indeed the viewing it through this favorable medium has always animated our hopes, and led many sensible Americans to imagine, this old and universal experiment, to be peculiar to that isle—In pursuing my inquiry into the principles and effects of the British government, I shall first grant that it is a rational system, founded on solid, safe principles—and one of the best governments for the higher ranks of mankind in the world—but then I must insist that it was hardly a government at all, until it became simplified by the introduction and regular formation of the effective administration of responsible ministers, on its present system—which we cannot date higher up, than the appointment of Lord Strafford and others by Charles 1st.*—Moreover I do not know how far the system of bribery introduced by Sir Robert Walpole, and the influence of the numerous body of public creditors, are not now absolutely necessary to its present stability—and after all, I am not satisfied how such a simplification as would produce a responsibility, can be effected in a government, complicated by so many subordinate and powerful corporations as the American States will be—and yet responsibility must be attained and an easy and certain mode adopted, of changing measures and men without commotion, or liberty will be lost in the attempt—I am confused and bewildered when I arrive at this point of reflection, and despotism meets me at every turn.—There are but *two* modes of governing mankind, by just and equal law, enforced impartially on all ranks of society, or by the sword:—If such laws cannot be obtained, or the attainment is attended with too much difficulty, the sword will supply their place; *et inter arma leges silent. When arms command the laws are disobeyed.* Shall we have patience, with the disorders of our complicated machine? As Alexander dissolved the gordian knot with the sword—so I fear a standing army will simplify the governments of America—I have said that the government of England afforded firm protection of property—it certainly does so, comparatively speaking—yet the history of its frequent revolutions, will discover that even property is insecure there. During the civil wars, in which the Stuarts involved this nation, two-thirds of the property of the kingdom changed masters; and in those between Lancaster and York, and before the firm establishment of the line of Tuder, almost all the old families perished and their property became dissipated:—And yet its protection of property is its favorable side; turn your eyes to the lower order of citizens, and they are pressed into the earth by taxation and imposition—very rarely will industry enable the husbandman to rear a family—where the sons of agriculture are so poorly rewarded, government must be ulcerated to the heart—the miserable poor who pursue the dictates of nature and religion, in that connection which is destined to sweeten the bitter draught of life, are commonly handed

---

*Before that period they were minions and favorites, who by plundering and oppressing the people excited constant commotion, and were seldom changed but with their masters, and by the axe or halter.

from constable to constable, until their unfortunate birth compels some parish to own them.—The people of England have always and forever will emigrate—The people of England never repair to arms to repel foreign invasion—and they never will unless compelled—to conquer England, it would only seem necessary from past example, to escape their floating defences and land on the island; passing by former invasions and conquests. As late as the year 1745, Prince Charles Edward, at the head of an undisciplined rabble, belonging to some Highland clans attached to his family, marched undisturbed, through the most populous counties into the heart of the kingdom, and the capital containing 200,000 fighting men trembled for its safety at the approach of an unexperienced boy, followed by 4 or 5000 half armed peasants—scarcely a man in the kingdom shouldered a musquet until the danger disappeared, and government owed its safety to the protection of foreign mercenaries, or rather the weakness and irresolution of the assailant—The fact is, the people will never fight (if they can help it) for representatives, taxes and rags.

Let us now contrast this scene with one, where the people *personally* exercise the powers of government[50]—The three small democratic Cantons of Uri, Schuitz and Underwald, broke the chains of their former servitude, and laid the foundation of the Swiss confederacy—they effected the revolution, and in conjunction with the other democratic Cantons and their democratic allies the Grisons, have supported the grand fabric of Helvetic liberty to this day. Every Swiss farmer is by birth a legislator, and he becomes a voluntary soldier to defend his power and his property; their fathers have been so before them for near 500 years, without revolution, and almost without commotion—they have been the secure spectators of the constant and universal destruction of the human species, which the usurpations of the *few* have ever created, and must I fear forever perpetuate:— Whilst all Europe were butchering each other for the love of God, and defending the usurpations of the clergy, under the masque of religion, the malignant evil crept into this sacred asylum of liberty; (but where the government resides in the body of the people, they can never be corrupted by the artifice or the wealth of the *few*) they soon banished the daemon of discord, and Protestant and Papist sat down under the peaceful shade of the same tree, whilst in every surrounding State and kingdom, the son was dragging the father, and brothers, their brothers, to the scaffold, under the sanction of those distinctions:—Thus these happy Helvetians have in peace and security beheld all the rest of Europe become a common slaughterhouse.—A free Swiss acquires from his infancy, a knowledge of the fundamental laws of his country, and the leading principles of their national policy are handed down by tradition from father to son—the first of these is never to trust power to representatives, or a national government. A free Swiss pays no taxes, on the contrary he receives taxes; every male of 16 years, shares near ten shillings sterling annually, which the rich and powerful

5.1.76

surrounding monarchies pay for the friendship of these manly farmers. Whenever their societies become too large, as government belongs to the citizens and the citizens are the property of no government, they divide amicably, and each separate part pursues the simple form, recommended by their ancestors and become venerable, by the glorious and happy experience of ages of prosperity—Their frugal establishments are chiefly supported by the pay which the officers of government receive for the services they render individuals. With a country the most unfriendly to industry in the world, they have become in a series of years, passed in uninterrupted but moderate labor, frugality, peace and happiness, the richest nation under the sun. I have seen a computation, by which it appeared, that the interest of the money they have before hand, and that which is due them from the rich nations of Europe, would support themselves and their posterity forever, without farther exertion; and this whilst every other government is actually as much or more in debt than it is worth.

5.1.77   An intelligent author has remarked, that passing from a democratic to an aristocratic Canton of Swisserland, you quit the society of men to contemplate the regular labor of brutes;[51] they are compelled indeed in the aristocratic Cantons to be extremely moderate in their government, and to lay few or no taxes, or they would drive their subjects into the neighboring free States—as it is, they are well cloathed, well fed and taken good care of—The same author remarks, that the line which separates all Swisserland, from the countries around (where men like cattle are the property of their proud Lords and kept chained to the soil) is the line of division between light and darkness—between happiness and horror.

5.1.78   The love of the Switzers for their country is altogether romantic and surpasses the bounds of credibility—those memorable relations authenticated by the common consent of all historians, of their beating on all occasions the flower of the Austrian and French troops (who have invaded them) with numbers so unequal and trifling as scarce to exceed their enemies out-guards; the instances of hundreds of citizens devoting their lives for the safety of their country; of their frequently disdaining life and refusing quarter when overpowered by numbers, have astonished and terrified the neighbouring powers, and seem incomprehensible to a people dispirited by taxes, overloaded with debts and disgusted with government. I cannot omit a striking characteristic, authenticated by Coxe and others, whose authority will not be questioned; they relate that there is a rustic tune familiar in the mountains of Swisserland—it is called the *Rantz des vacques*—it consists of a few simple notes of native wild melody. The French and Dutch governments have been compelled to forbid under very severe penalties, the playing this woodland music, to those Swiss troops, which they hire for a limited time; the well-known notes revive instantly all the fond images, which were impressed on their youthful bosoms, their friends, their parents, their relations and their beloved country, rush into their imaginations in a full tide of affection—no persuasion can detain them, they desert home in regiments, or if retained by force, they pine away in the deepest melancholy—no instance has yet occurred of Swiss troops serving in any part of Europe, who have not returned, with the diligence and anxiety of affectionate children, on the first appearance of danger to their parent country:[52]—The same amor-patriae, the same divine love of their country, universally pervades the bosom of every citizen, who in right of his birth, legislates for himself:—Grosley relates that he saw in Rome a poor fellow (who had travelled through great part of Europe and Asia afoot) declaiming to a crowd with the most passionate zeal, in praise of his own country, boasting of her happiness and prefering San Marino to all the world besides[53]—This democratic republic, is a little bee-hive of free citizens, who have made a delicious garden of the top of a bleak barren mountain, situated in the midst of the finest and most fruitful plains of Italy, which tyranny has depopulated around them.—Look into the human breast—We love that power, which we exercise ourselves, but we detest that which others exercise over us, be they Representatives, Lords, or Kings; and to this source we may trace the abuse, which the Americans bestow on their country and their governments.

But we are told that Swisserland, *should be no example for us*—I am very sorry for it—they are the only, the only part of the human species that sustain the dignity of character, belonging to the divine resemblance we bear,—*they are few in number it is said*—This is not true—they are more numerous than we are—*They cover a small spot of territory*—this is also not true—they possess a large tract of country in the very heart of Europe—but this is not all—The Helvetic confederacy, including the three leagues of the Grisons comprehends one hundred perhaps two hundred, independent governments and States—nor is there any reason from their history or present state to doubt, that the same plan of confederation might not be extended with as lasting and happy effects to one thousand independent governments—But it is also said *they are a poor, frugal* people—As to their poverty that is likewise untrue—they have great sums of money before hand and owe not a six-pence—they indeed are a wise and consequently a frugal people—though they still have great estates and even luxury among them too—But should we despise their poverty or their frugality? We who are so many millions worse than nothing? *But still we are told we must not take example from them—we must take example from Holland and Germany—* They had better at once tell us, that we must desert the worship of God and follow that of the devil.

From the first dawn of light, that broke in upon my reason, I became devoted to governments of simplicity and equal right—The names of heroes, whose blood has bedewed the altars of freedom, vibrate like the shock of electricity, on my frame; and when I read the story of Brutus and of Cassius, the most noble and the last of the Romans, tears of admiration gush from my

5.1.79

5.1.80

eyes.—Under these impressions which only the grave can erase, I feel unspeakable horror at every step, which removes power and rights, at a greater distance from the body of the people, to whom they belong, and confines them to the hands of *the few*. I have proposed to myself this question: If representatives cannot govern the people—If they abuse the power entrusted to them, shall they devolve this power on a still smaller number, who must be more liable to corruption from the encrease of temptation? Or should they restore it into the hands of the people, from whom they received it? who alone are incorruptible, because the wealth of the few can never bribe the many, against the duty they owe to themselves. If I am told that the people are incapable of governing themselves—I shall answer that they have never been tried in America, except among the native Indians, who are free and happy, and who prove that self-government is the growth of our soil—And I also answer that they are more fit for self-government, than they are at present for any of the safe and solid governments, founded on representation.—When I see all these principles established by the example of the Swiss, who have remained under the simplest of all forms of government for near five hundred years, in uninterrupted tranquility and happiness—whilst every other invention of genius, devise of art, or imposition of force, has been torn up by the roots, with every aggravated circumstance of horror—I can no longer doubt—All the mists of theory and speculation vanish before an experiment like this.

5.1.81   The greatest human discernment, ever concentrated in the mind of one man, was the portion of the celebrated Nicholas Machiavelli—a name loaded with abuse by tyrants, flatterers and the mushrooms of science, because he told the truth; because he was a republican and the friend of mankind in times of usurpation; or because, they have never read or do not understand his works. After every inquiry which the most unbounded information and reflection, with a long experience in high public office afforded, Machiavelli, delivers his deliberate opinion in favour of the body of the people, as the only safe depository of liberty and power—He prefers it to the aristocracy and the Prince; but he does not disgrace the inquiry by mentioning representation.[54] If this was the opinion of Machiavelli, a citizen of Florence, where a numerous populace confined and crowded within the walls of a city, formed the most turbulent republic, that ever disgraced the cause of freedom by cruelty and anarchy—How much more favourably must his decision apply to the yeomanry of America—Landholders and consequently the most independent of mankind, mild by nature, moderate by manners, and persevering in every honest pursuit:—Surely if ever men were worthy of being entrusted with their own rights, the freeholders of America are—*Make them then and their posterity legislators by birth*—I mean not the lowest populace—I mean that class of citizens to whom this country belongs:—Numbers unqualified by property, should have their influence—they should be protected—they might preserve the right of election—But they who hold the property of the soil, are alone entitled to govern it:—To effect this there would need but little change in the present forms—They might all stand—But the laws which pass the legislature before they become binding, should be referred to the different counties and cities—printed reasons drawn by committees, might if necessary, accompany each, together with an annual estimate of public wants and a detail of the expenditures of the former sums granted. Let these laws then be submitted to the free deliberation of the *freeholders* of the counties and cities—the numbers of the yeas and nays be taken on each by the presiding magistrate, and transmitted to the executive, who may then upon comparing the returns from the several counties and corporations, declare what laws are the will of the people. On the appearance of any sudden danger the two houses or indeed a majority of one house, might invest the Executive with that authority, exigency might require for the safety of the republic, until remedy should be provided by law.

The number of representatives might be decreased and an expence saved—this would at one blow destroy all legislative speculations—the influence of demagogues, or oligarchic juntos must then cease—The assemblage of the freeholders, separate in different counties would prevent disturbance—As no new law could be made in them, little confusion could ensue—After some years, or even immediately if confined to future cases—the celebrated law of Geneva might be introduced, and no freeholder admitted to the assembly until he had paid his father's debts. Sumptuary laws, permitting the use, but prohibiting the abuse of wealth, might be interposed to guard the public manners.—The Governor and two members of the senate might constitute a council of censors, to punish offenders against the sumptuary laws and the laws of morality, by a removal from office, and even disfranchisement, if necessary, with an appeal to the people of the county where the offender resided, in the latter case, and to the people of the State in the former.—Seminaries of useful learning, with professorships of political and domestic œconomy might be established in every county, discarding the philosophy of the moon and skies, we might descend to teach our citizens what is useful in this world—the principles of free government, illustrated by the history of mankind—the sciences of morality, agriculture, commerce, the management of farms and household affairs—The light would then penetrate, where mental darkness now reigns.—Do these things and in a very few years, the people instead of abusing, would wade up to their knees in blood, to defend their governments.

For some years past this has been the darling object of my life—to which all my views have tended—And I now think that nothing intermediate would be lasting or worthy the pursuit—Whenever I fairly lose sight of this—As soon as I turn my back forever on these dear illusions, which will be as soon as the proposed fœderal government is adopted—I shall turn all my wishes

5.1.82

5.1.83

to that social state, whither that government will lead us, and I both hope and expect that with those amendments and guards, which it seems to be the general disposition to provide—it will gradually maturate in a safe and reasonable government.—Until that adoption I speak to my fellow citizens in the words of the proverb—*Do not that by others, which you can do yourselves.*

A Farmer.

44. Blaise Pascal, *Pensées,* La Fuma, no. 413.
45. *The Spirit of Laws* XI, ch. 6.
46. Cf. *The Federalist* nos. 71–72.
47. Farrand II, 284.
48. Cf. Mercer 5.5.11. See Centinel I, 2.7.7 n. 4.
49. DeLolme, *The Constitution of England* II, chs. 5–8. See Centinel I, 2.7.7 n. 4.
50. Cf. references to Switzerland noted in Old Whig IV, 3.3.30 n. 22.
51. This reference has not been identified.
52. William Coxe, *Sketches of the Natural, Civil, and Political State of Swisserland,* 2d ed. (London 1780) 274–75; cf. 51–53, 124–25.
53. Cf. John Adams' less favorable view of San Marino, in his *Defence* I, letter 3 (*Works* IV, 308–10).
54. See Machiavelli, *Discourses* I, ch. 6.

Virginia: Introduction

Following the ratification on 23 May of South Carolina, where the opposition of Anti-Federalists like Rawlins Lowndes, Aedanus Burke, and Thomas Sumpter was easily brushed aside, the debate over the Constitution came to a focus in Virginia. The Federalists still feared concerted Southern action under the leadership of Patrick Henry, and they distrusted Henry's motives and aims. Despite Henry's denials, many Federalists believed that he desired a separate Southern confederacy. "You are better acquainted with Mr. Henry's politics than I can be," Madison wrote to Edmund Randolph in January 1788, "but I have for some time considered him as driving at a Southern Confederacy and not further concurring in the plan of amendments than as he hopes to render it subservient to his real designs."[1] Madison was probably wrong about Henry's real design, and the Federalists unquestionably found a rhetorical advantage in accusing their opponents of wanting to break up the Union;[2] but a separate Southern confederacy was surely considered by the Southern Anti-Federalists as a possible outcome, as well as a bargaining point, and it was objectively a genuine possibility.

Still aristocratic in significant respects, Southern politics tended to be based on established and respected individual leaders, rather than on economic interests or on the political parties developing elsewhere in the country.[3] This was particularly true in Virginia which George Ticknor Curtis aptly described as being "filled with the spirit of republican freedom, although its polity and manners were marked by several aristocratic features."[4] This combination of qualities helped to make the Virginia ratifying convention debates the best and most thorough of all the states. As nowhere else on the continent, the political elite in Virginia was divided. The Virginia Anti-Federalists led by such men as Patrick Henry, George Mason, and Richard Henry Lee were more capable and commanded more respect than any other group of Anti-Federalists in the country. A searching debate in convention lasted more than three weeks; and when the vote was finally taken on 25 June, Virginia ratified the Constitution by a vote of 89 to 79, submitting a list of recommendatory amendments.[5]

1. Madison, *Writings* (ed. Hunt) V, 80–81. Six months later John R. Smith wrote to Madison that "the idea of Virginia standing independent of other States, or forming a partial confederacy or a foreign alliance is more openly avowed by some people in

this quarter, than anywhere else, and I am certain the sentiment originates with the old Governor." *Documentary History of the Constitution* IV, 703. On the question of separate confederacies see above, vol. 1, ch. 4, n. 2.

2. This is of course basic to the rhetorical design of *The Federalist*. See *Observer* 6.4.3.

3. Thus Anti-Federalist Henrico county elected John Marshall, a known Federalist, to represent it in the state ratifying convention. John Marshall, *An Autobiographical Sketch*, ed. John Stokes Adams (Ann Arbor 1937) 7.

4. Curtis, *Constitutional History of the United States* I, 632.

5. In the meantime, however, and unknown to the Virginians, New Hampshire had ratified the Constitution on 21 June by a vote of 57–47; New Hampshire was thus the ninth state to ratify, and Virginia the tenth.

The Impartial Examiner, Essay I

VIRGINIA INDEPENDENT CHRONICLE
February 1788

The five essays of the Impartial Examiner appeared in the *Virginia Independent Chronicle,* the first during February and March of 1788, and the remainder in successive weeks in May and June. They constitute another important and interesting Anti-Federal statement reprinted here for the first time. The Impartial Examiner begins the first, long essay with a good statement of the dangers of ill-considered innovation (5.14.1). He makes and elaborates a distinction between arbitrary and free governments, on which the whole argument rests: "in [arbitrary governments] the governors are invested with powers of acting according to their own wills, without any other limits than what they themselves may understand to be necessary for the general good; whereas in [free goverments] they are intrusted with no such unlimited authority, but are restrained in their operations to conform to certain fundamental principles, the preservation whereof is expressly stipulated for in the *civil compact:* and whatever is not so stipulated for is virtually and impliedly given up" (5.14.2). Judged by this criterion, the author finds the proposed Constitution arbitrary: it provides for unlimited supremacy of the federal government, despite the absence among the different parts of the United States of that union of interest that must be the basis of union of counsels (5.14.4, 5, 10). There is no declaration of rights, without which civil liberty cannot exist, there being no standard to appeal to in cases of governmental oppression (5.14.5, 10). The Constitution grants dangerous and unlimited powers in the areas of taxation (5.14.6–7), standing armies (5.14.8), and the judiciary (5.14.9). While respecting the intentions of the framers, the author insists that the people must exercise an independent judgment (5.14.10–12). He contends that a more moderate revision is feasible, and (in a balanced and penetrating statement) he emphasizes the nobility of true confederation (5.14.13). The Impartial Examiner concludes the first essay with a good statement of the dangers of loose and extensive powers that goes well beyond the usual Anti-Federal cautions. The problem is to perpetuate the free republic as "the ardent glow of freedom" evaporates—as the leaders grow restless for exercise of ambition, as the advantages of the new government "grow stale with use," and as the people grow fat with prosperity. To avoid these dangers the principles of the political order must be firmly fixed in the Constitution (5.14.14–16).

In the remaining essays, the Impartial Examiner mainly elaborates the themes already laid down. He argues in the second essay that arbitrary government is inherently despotic (5.14.17–22). The first question to be raised is whether the system proposed is "coincident with [American] standing maxims of liberty" and the second whether it is "conducive to good policy" (5.14.24). Having shown in the first essay that the system fails with respect to the former, Impartial Examiner argues that no examination of the latter is strictly necessary; but he follows the many writers who proceed to the question of policy, concluding this essay with an argument that the so-called Anti-Federalists are the true Federalists (5.14.25–26).

In essay III the Impartial Examiner takes up the question of representation, contending (in one of the good Anti-Federalist discussions of this matter) that representation must be both ample and complete and that the representation in the House of Representatives is not sufficiently numerous to be either (5.14.28–32). The Senate is elected not by the people but by the state legislatures and is open to even stronger objections (5.14.33–34).

The executive proposed by the new Constitution, discussed in essay IV, ought not to have a negative on legislation, this power being an imitation of the British system, whose circumstances are very different. The executive veto will destroy rather than maintain the balance in the American republican system (5.14.35–40).

In conclusion (essay V) the Impartial Examiner argues that the evils experienced under the Articles of Confederation spring not from vicious principles pervading the whole system (which would admittedly require radical change) but from certain weaknesses in some of the parts. The weaknesses may therefore be remedied by strengthening these parts, in particular by investing Congress with sufficient power to regulate commerce and to procure the necessary revenue for the common defense or general welfare.

I

20 February 1788

To the free people of Virginia.

Countrymen and Fellow-Citizens,

5.14.1   That the subject, which has given rise to the following observations, is of the highest consequence to this country, requires not the aid of logical proof; that it merits the most serious attention of every member of this community, is a fact not to be controverted. Will not a bare mention of the new Fœderal Constitution justify this remark? To foreigners or such, whose local connections form no permanent interest in America, this may be totally indifferent; and to them it may afford mere matter of speculation and private amusement. When such advert to the high and distinguished characters, who have drawn up, and proposed a set of articles to the people of an extensive continent as a form of their future government, an emotion of curiosity may induce them to examine the contents of those articles: and they may, perhaps, from having contemplated on a former situation of those people—that they had struggled against a potent enemy—that they had by their virtuous and patriotic exertions rescued themselves from impending danger—that they had used the like endeavors to establish for themselves a system of government upon free and liberal principles—that they had in pursuance of those endeavors chosen a system, as conducive to the great ends of human happiness, the preservation of their *natural rights* and *liberties*—that this system has prevailed but a few years; and now already a change, a fundamental change therein is meditated:—strangers, I say, having contemplated on these circumstances, may be led to consider this nation, as a restless and dissatisfied people, whose fickle inconsistent minds suffer them not to abide long in the same situation; who perpetually seeking after new things throw away one blessing in pursuit of another: and while they are thus indulging their caprice—lose all, ere any can ripen into maturity. If the unconcerned part of those among us entertain themselves in this manner, can any good American be content to deserve such reflections? Will not all rather feel an honest indignation, if they once perceive their country stamped with a character like this? And yet, may we not justify such conceptions, if we thus precipitate ourselves into a new government before we have sufficiently tried the virtues of the old?[1] So incident is error to the human mind, that it is not to be wondered at indeed, if our present Constitution is incomplete. The best regulated governments have their defects, and might perhaps admit of improvement: but the great difficulty consists in clearly discovering the most exceptionable parts and judiciously applying the amendments. A wise nation will, therefore, attempt innovations of this kind with much circumspection. They will view the political fabric, which they have once reared, as the sacred *palladium* of their happiness;—they will touch it, as a man of tender sensibility toucheth the apple of his own eye,—they will touch it with a light, with a trembling—with a cautious hand,—lest they injure the whole structure in endeavoring to reform any of its parts. In small and trivial points alterations may be attempted with less danger; but—where the very nature, the essence of the thing is to be changed: when the foundation itself is to be transformed, and the whole plan entirely new modelled;—should you not hesitate, O Americans? Should you not pause—and reflect a while on the the important step, you are about to take? Does it not behove you to examine well into the nature and tendency of the Constitution now proposed for your adoption? And by comparing it with your present mode of government, endeavor to distinguish which of the two is most eligible? Whether *this* or *that* is best calculated for promoting your happiness? for obtaining and securing those benefits, which are the great object of civil society? Will it be consistent with the duty, which you owe to yourselves, as a nation, or with the affection, which you ought to bear for your posterity, if you rashly or inconsiderately adopt a measure, which is to influence the fate of this country for ages yet to come? How will it accord with your dignity and reputation, as an independent people, if either through an over-weaning fondness for novelty you are suddenly transported on the wings of imagination, and too hastily make up your thoughts on this great subject; or by sinking into a listless inactivity of mind, view it as an indifferent matter unworthy of any deliberate consideration? Will any respect? Will any honor? Will any veneration be due to the memory of yourselves, as ancestors, if millions of beings, who have not yet received their birth, when you are all mouldered into dust, should find themselves fixed in a miserable condition by one injudicious determination of your's at this period? If you see no impropriety in these questions, the suggestions contained in them will not appear altogether unworthy of attention. One moment's reflection, it is humbly presumed, will render it obvious that on this occasion they are not impertinently propounded.

5.14.2　　In pursuing this address I beg leave to premise that the only true point of distinction between arbitrary and free governments seems to be, that in the former the governors are invested with powers of acting according to their own wills, without any other limits than[2] what they themselves may understand to be necessary for the general good; whereas in the latter they are intrusted with no such unlimited authority, but are restrained in their operations to conform to certain fundamental principles, the preservation whereof is expressly stipulated for in the *civil compact:* and whatever is not so stipulated for is virtually and impliedly given up. Societies so constituted invest their supreme governors with ample powers of exerting themselves according to their own judgment in every thing not inconsistent with or derogatory to those principles; and so long as they adhere to such restrictions, their deeds ought not to be rescinded or controuled by any other power whatsoever. Those principles are certain inherent rights pertaining to all mankind in a state of natural liberty, which through the weakness, imperfection, and depravity of human nature cannot be secured in that state. Men, therefore, agree to enter into society, that by the united force of *many* the rights of *each* individual may be protected and secured. These are in all just governments laid down as a foundation to the *civil compact,* which contains a *covenant* between *each* with *all,* that they shall enter into one society to be governed by the same powers; establishes for that purpose the *frame* of government; and consequently creates a *Convention* between *every* member, binding those, who shall at any time be intrusted with power, to a faithful administration of their trust according to the form of the *civil policy,* which they have so constituted, and obliging all to a due obedience therein. There can be no other just origin of civil power, but some such mutual contract of all the people: and although their great object in forming society is an intention to secure their natural rights; yet the relations arising from this *political union* create certain duties and obligations to the state, which require a sacrifice of some portion of those rights and of that exuberance of liberty, which obtains in a state of nature.—This, however, being compensated by certain other adventitious rights and privileges, which are acquired by the social connection; it follows that the advantages derived from a government are to be estimated by the *strength* of the *security,* which is attended at once with the *least sacrifice* and the *greatest acquired benefits.* That government, therefore, which is best adapted for promoting these three *great ends,* must certainly be the best constituted scheme of *civil policy.* Here, then, it may not be improper to remark that persons forming a social community cannot take too much precaution when they are about to establish the plan of their government. They ought to construct it in such a manner as to procure the best possible security for their rights;—in doing this they ought to give up no greater share than what is understood to be absolutely necessary:—and they should endeavor so to organize, arrange and connect it's several branches, that when duly exercised it may tend to promote the *common good* of all, and contribute as many advantages, as the civil institution is capable of. It has been before observed that the only just origin of civil power is a contract entered into by all the people for that purpose.—If this position be true (and, I dare presume, it is not controverted, at least in this country) right reason will always suggest the expediency of adhering to the essential requisites in forming that contract upon true principles. A cautious people will consider all the inducements to enter into the *social state,* from the most important object down to the minutest prospect of advantage. Every motive with them will have its due weight. They will not pay a curious attention to trifles and overlook matters of great consequence:—and in pursuing these steps they will provide for the attainment of *each* point in view with a care—with an earnestness proportionate to its dignity, and according as it involves a *greater* or a *lesser* interest. It is evident, therefore that they should attend most diligently to those sacred rights, which they have received with their birth, and which can neither be retained to themselves, nor transmitted to their posterity, unless they are *expressly reserved:* for it is a maxim, I dare say, universally acknowledged, that when men establish a system of government, in granting the powers therein they are always understood to surrender whatever they do not so expressly reserve.[3] This is obvious from the very design of the civil institution, which is adopted in lieu of the state of natural liberty, wherein each individual, being equally intitled to the enjoyment of all natural rights, and having equally a just authority to exercise full powers of acting, with relation to other individuals, in any manner not injurious to their rights, must, when he enters into society, be presumed to give up all those powers into the hands of the state by submitting his whole conduct to the direction thereof. This being done by every member, it follows, as a regular conclusion, that all such powers, whereof the whole were possessed, so far as they related to each other individually, are of course given up by the mere act of union. If this surrender be made without any reservation, the conclusion is equally plain and regular, that *each* and *all* have given up not only those powers, which relate to others, but likewise every claim, which pertained to themselves, as individuals. For the universality of the grant in this case must necessarily include every *power* of acting, and every *claim* of possessing or obtaining any thing—except according to the regulations of the state. Now a right being properly defined, "a power or claim established by law, to act, or to possess, or to obtain something from others,"[4] every natural right is such *power* or *claim* established by the law of nature. Thus, it is manifest, that in a society constituted after this manner, every right whatsoever will be under the power and controul of the civil jurisdiction. This is the leading characteristic of an arbitrary government, and whenever any people establish a system like this, they subject themselves to one, which has not a single property of a free constitution. Hence results the necessity of an *express stipulation* for all such rights as are intended to be exempted from the civil authority.

5.14.3   Permit me now, my country men, to make a few observations on the proposed Fœderal Constitution. In this attempt the subject, as it is arduous and difficult, naturally impresses the modest mind with diffidence: yet being of the last importance, as involving in it the highest interest, that freemen can have—all that is dear and valuable to the citizens of these United States; a consciousness of the strong claim, which this subject has, to a free and general discussion, has prevailed over that discouraging idea so far as to produce the present address to you. This is done with a reliance on that benevolence and liberality of sentiment, with which you have hitherto been actuated. From these benign qualities, it is hoped, the most favorable indulgence will be granted, and that the zeal, with which this is written, will be allowed in some measure an excuse for its defects. However imperfect, therefore this may be, however inadequate to your own ideas, or to the wishes of him, who offers it to your consideration; you are hereby intreated to let the perusal, with which you may think proper to favor it, be serious, candid, dispassionate—as it relates to a common cause, in which all are alike concerned.

5.14.4   Suffer me, then, in the first place to advert to a part of the sixth article in this constitution. It may, perhaps, appear somewhat irregular, to begin with this article, since it is almost the last proposed: yet, if it be considered that this at once defines the extent of Congressional authority, and indisputably fixes its supremacy, every idea of impropriety on this head will probably vanish. The clause alluded to contains the following words, "This constitution, and the laws of the United States, which shall be made in pursuance thereof, and all treaties made, or which shall be made, under the authority of the United States, shall be the supreme law of the land; and the judges in every state shall be bound thereby; any thing in the constitution or laws of any state to the contrary, notwithstanding." If this constitution should be adopted, here the sovereignty of America is ascertained and fixed in the fœderal body at the same time that it abolishes the present independent sovereignty of each state. Because this government being general, and not confined to any particular part of the continent; but pervading every state and establishing its authority equally in all, its superiority will consequently be recognized in each; and all other powers can operate only in a secondary subordinate degree. For the idea of two sovereignties existing within the same community is a perfect solecism. If they be supposed equal, their operation must be commensurate, and like two mechanical powers of equal *momenta* counteracting each other;—there the force of the one will be destroyed by the force of the other: and so there will be no efficiency in either. If one be greater than the other, they will be similar to two unequal bodies in motion with a given degree of velocity, and impinging each other from opposite points;—the motion of the lesser in this case will necessarily be destroyed by that of the greater: and so there will be efficiency only in the greater. But what need is there for a mathematical deduction to shew the impropriety of two such distinct co-existing sovereignties? The natural understanding of all mankind perceives the apparent absurdity arising from such a supposition: since, if the word means any thing at all, it must mean that *supreme power,* which must reside somewhere instate; or, in other terms, it is the united powers of each individual member of the state collected and consolidated into *one body.* This collection, this union, this supremacy of power can, therefore, exist only in one body. This is obvious to every man: and it has been very properly suggested that under the proposed constitution each state will dwindle into "the insignificance of a town corporate."[5] This certainly will be their utmost consequence; and, as such, they will have no authority to make laws, even for their own private government any farther than the permissive indulgence of Congress may grant them leave. This, Virginians, will be your mighty, your enviable situation after all your struggles for independence! and, if you will take the trouble to examine, you will find that the great, the supereminent authority, with which this instrument of union proposes to invest the fœderal body, is to be created without a single check—without a single article of covenant for the preservation of those inestimable rights, which have in all ages been the glory of freemen. It is true, "the United States shall guarantee to every state in this union a republican form of government": yet they do not guarantee to the different states their present forms of government, or the bill of rights thereto annexed, or any of them; and the expressions are too vague, too indefinite to create such a compact by implication. It is possible that a "republican form" of government may be built upon as absolute principles of despotism as any oriental monarchy ever yet possessed. I presume that the liberty of a nation depends, not on planning the frame of government, which consists merely in fixing and delineating the powers thereof; but on prescribing due limits to those powers, and establishing them upon just principles.

5.14.5   It has been held in a northern state by a zealous advocate for this constitution that there is no necessity for "a bill of rights" in the fœderal government; although at the same time he acknowledges such necessity to have existed when the constitutions of the separate governments were established.[6] He confesses that in these instances the people "invested their representatives with every power and authority, which they did not in explicit terms reserve": but "in delegating fœderal powers," says he, "every thing, which is not given, is reserved." Here is a distinction, I humbly conceive, without a difference, at least in the present enquiry. How far such a discrimination might prevail with respect to the present system of union, it is immaterial to examine: and had the observation been restrained to that alone, perhaps it might be acknowledged to contain some degree of propriety. For under the confederation it is well known that the authority of Congress cannot extend so far as to interfere with, or exercise any kind of coercion on, the powers of legislation in the different states; but the internal police of each is left free, sovereign and independent: so that the liberties of the people being secured as well as the nature of their constitution will admit; and the declaration of rights, which they have laid down as the *basis* of government, having their full force and energy, any farther stipulation on that head might be unnecessary. But, surely, when this doctrine comes to be applied to the *proposed* fœderal constitution, which is framed with such large and extensive powers, as to transfer the individual sovereignty from each state to the *aggregate body,*—a constitution, which delegates to Congress an authority to interfere with, and restrain the legislatures of every state—invests them with supreme powers of legislation throughout all the states—annihilates the separate independency of each; and, in short—swallows up and involves in the plenitude of its jurisdiction all other powers whatsoever:—I shall not be taxed with arrogance in declaring such an argument to be fallacious; and insisting on the necessity of a positive unequivocal declaration in favor of the rights of freemen in this case even more strongly than in the case of their separate governments. For it seems to me that when any civil establishment is formed, the more general its influence, the more extensive the powers, with which it is invested, the greater reason there is to take the necessary precaution for securing a due administration, and guarding against unwarrantable abuses.

(To be continued.)

27 February 1788

(Continued from our last)

Section 8th of the first article gives the Congress a power "to lay and collect, taxes, duties, imposts and excises." If it be a true maxim that those, who are entrusted with the exercise of the higher powers of government, ought to observe two essential rules: first in having no other view than the general good of all without any regard to private interest; and secondly, to take equal care of the whole body of the community, so as not to favor one part more than another: it is apparent that under the proposed constitution, this general confederated society, made up of thirteen different states, will have very little security for obtaining an observance, either of the one, or of the other, rule. For being different societies, though blended together in legislation, and having as different interests; no uniform rule for the whole seems to be practicable; and hence, it is to be feared, that the general good may be lost in a mutual attention to private views. From the same causes we may lament the probability of losing the advantage of the second rule; for it may be expected, in like manner, that the general care of the whole will be lost by the separate endeavors of different legislators to favor their own states. So long as mankind continues to be influenced by interest, the surest means of effecting an union of counsels in any assembly is by an union of interests.[7] Now, if it be considered that it is this concert, that it is this union in promoting the *general good,* which alone can preserve concord in this great republic, and secure it success and glory,—unhappy will be the situation of America, if she once precludes the beneficial effects of such a good understanding. Yet, I apprehend that these evils may result in a great measure from an exercise of that branch of legislative authority, which respects internal direct taxation. For in this, it is scarcely probable that the interest, ease or convenience of the several states can be so well consulted in the fœderal assembly, as in their own respective legislatures. So different are many species of property, so various the productions, so unequal the profits arising, even from the same species of property, in different states, that no general mode of contribution can well be adopted in such a manner as at once to affect all in an equitable degree. Hence may arise disagreeable objects of contention. A diversity of interests will produce a diversity of schemes. Thus each state, as it is natural, will endeavor to raise a revenue by such means, as may appear least injurious to its own interest: a source of dissention manifestly detrimental to that harmony, which is necessary to support the confederation. I cannot conceive it impracticable to reform the fœderal system in such a manner as to ensure a compliance with the necessary requisitions of Congress from the different state legislatures. Then all the several states being left to raise their own share of the revenue, and being the only proper judges of the mode most convenient to themselves, it is highly probable that this important branch of government would be car-

5.14.6

ried on more generally to the satisfaction of each state; and would tend to promote a spirit of concord between all the parts of this great community. Because *each* being thus accomodated, and participating the advantages of the union,—*none* subjected to any inconvenience thereby,—*all* would consequently concur in nourishing an affection for the government, which so cemented them.

5.14.7 I believe, it is acknowledged that the establishment of excises has been one of the greatest grievances, under which the English nation has labored for almost a century and an half. Although this may seem an œconomical tax, as arising out of manufactures, from which the *industrious* may derive advantages; and whereof the *wealthy* by consuming the greatest share, will of course contribute the largest proportion of the tax: yet the nature of it being such, as requires severe laws for its execution, it has justly become an object of general detestation. This has induced Judge Blackstone to declare that "the rigour and arbitrary proceedings of excise laws seem hardly compatible with the temper of a free nation."[8] While, therefore, you are freemen—while you are unused to feel any other power, but such as can be exercised within the bounds of moderation and decency, it, doubtless, behoves you to consider whether it is an eligible step to subject yourselves to a new species of authority, which may warrant the most flagrant violations of the sacred rights of habitation. If this branch of revenue takes place, all the consequent rigour of excise laws will necessarily be introduced in order to enforce a due collection. On any charges or offence in this instance you will see yourselves deprived of your boasted trial by jury. The much admired common law process will give way to some quick and summary mode, by which the unhappy defendant will find himself reduced, perhaps to ruin, in less time than a charge could be exhibited against him in the usual course.

5.14.8 It has ever been held that standing armies in times of peace are dangerous to a free country; and no observation seems to contain more reason in it. Besides being useless, as having no object of employment, they are inconvenient and expensive. The soldiery, who are generally composed of the dregs of the people, when disbanded, or unfit for military service, being equally unfit for any other employment, become extremely burthensome. As they are a body of men exempt from the common occupations of social life, having an interest different from the rest of the community, they wanton in the lap of ease and indolence, without feeling the duties, which arise from the political connection, though drawing their subsistence from the bosom of the state. The severity of discipline necessary to be observed reduces them to a degree of slavery; the unconditional submission to the commands of their superiors, to which they are bound, renders them the fit instruments of tyranny and oppression.—Hence they have in all ages afforded striking examples of contributing, more or less, to enslave mankind;—and whoever will take the trouble to examine, will find that by far the greater part of the different nations, who have fallen from the glorious state of liberty, owe their ruin to standing armies. It has been urged that they are necessary to provide against sudden attacks.[9] Would not a well regulated militia, duly trained to discipline, afford ample security? Such, I conceive, to be the best, the surest means of protection, which a free people can have when not actually engaged in war. This kind of defence is attended with two advantages superior to any others; first, when it is necessary to embody an army, they at once form a band of soldiers, whose interests are uniformly the same with those of the whole community, and in whose safety they see involved every thing that is dear to themselves: secondly, if one army is cut off, another may be immediately raised already trained for military service. By a policy, somewhat similar to this, the Roman empire rose to the highest pitch of grandeur and magnificence.

The supreme court is another branch of fœderal authority, which wears the aspect of imperial jurisdiction, clad in a dread array, and spreading its wide domain into all parts of the continent. This is to be co-extensive with the legislature, and, like that, is to swallow up all other courts of judicature.—For what is that judicial power which "shall extend to all cases in law and equity" in some having "original," in all others "appellate jurisdiction," but an establishment universal in its operation? And what is that "appellate jurisdiction both as to law and fact," but an establishment, which may in effect operate as original jurisdiction?[10]—Or what is an appeal to enquire into facts after a solemn adjudication in any court below, but a trial *de novo*? And do not such trials clearly imply an incompetency in the inferior courts to exercise any kind of judicial authority with rectitude? Hence, will not this eventually annihilate their whole jurisdiction? Here is a system of jurisprudence to be erected, no less surprising than it is new and unusual. Here is an innovation, which bears no kind of analogy to any thing, that Englishmen, or Americans, the descendants of Englishmen, have ever yet experienced. Add to all, that this high prerogative court establishes no fundamental rule of proceeding, except that the trial by jury is allowed in some criminal cases. All other cases are left open—and subject "to such regulations as the Congress shall make."—Under these circumstances I beseech you all, as citizens of Virginia, to consider seriously whether you will not endanger the solemn trial by jury, which you have long revered, as a sacred barrier against injustice—which has been established by your ancestors many centuries ago, and transmitted to you, as one of the greatest bulwarks of civil liberty—which you have to this day maintained inviolate:—I beseech you, I say, as members of this commonwealth, to consider whether you will not be in danger of losing this inestimable mode of trial in all those cases, wherein the constitution does not provide for its security.[11] Nay, does not that very provision, which is made, by being confined to a few particular cases, almost imply a total exclusion of the rest? Let it, then, be a reflection deeply impressed on your minds—that if this noble privilege, which by long experience has been found the most exquisite

5.14.9

method of determining controversies according to the scale of equal liberty, should once be taken away, it is unknown what new species of trial may be substituted in its room. Perhaps you may be surprised with some strange piece of judicial polity,—some arbitrary method, perhaps confining all trials to the entire decision of the magistracy, and totally excluding the great body of the people from any share in the administration of public justice.

(*To be continued*)

5 March 1788

(*Concluded from our last.*)

5.14.10   After the most deliberate reflections on this important matter, permit me, my dear countrymen, to declare to you in the most unfeigned manner, that not perceiving any thing in the proposed plan of government, which seems calculated to ensure the happiness of America—I could not, as a fellow-citizen, resist the inclination to impart these sentiments to you. Unmoved by party—rage—unassailed by passion—uninfluenced by any other interest, but the genuine effusion of zeal for this, our common country, I confess to you in the language of sincerity and candor, that after the first reading of this new code, I could not behold it, but with an eye of disapprobation. Unwilling, however, to reject at first sight an object of such high moment, I resolved to distrust the propriety of a construction passed at so early a period.—This led me to peruse it with the utmost diligence I was capable of; and believe me, the foregoing observations have arisen from the fullest conviction that the system involves in it the most dangerous principles; and—so far from exalting the *standard* of American liberty, I fear indeed that, should it be adopted, this glorious *work,* which already has cost the lives of many worthy patriots, will ere long be leveled with the dust. Let it not be conjectured from hence that any illiberal conceptions are formed by the writer hereof respecting the intentions of those gentlemen, who have offered this plan of fœderal government.[12] He knows no circumstance inducing him to suppose they had any other object in view but the good of their country.—When we contemplate the great—the magnanimous HERO, who has conducted our armies through all the trying vicissitudes of danger and difficulty,—there is no man so disingenuous—there is no man so ungrateful, as to impute any transactions of his to sinister motives. Every true American is well assured that steadiness of virtue—that benignity of soul have the chief rule in all his actions.—Yet every American, and every other person, are satisfied also that there is no infallibility in human nature.—To be man is to be subject to error. The best, the greatest, the wisest are liable to commit mistakes.—Let it be remembered, then, that this code of gov-

ernment is solemnly proposed to every freeman in America. For what?—
For the purpose of binding them without their approbation? No.—For an
implicit acceptance? No.—For their adoption merely in compliment to the
general convention? No.—What then?—Every man's duty to his country
points out to him the end of this proposition. Every man knows that it is for
a free, a candid, and impartial discussion and determination thereon;
whether they will approve and adopt it; or whether they will disapprove and
reject it. Can any citizen, therefore, be so weak? can any be so timid? so
pusillanimous, as to acknowledge that he has no right to exercise his own
judgement with regard to this matter? If there should be any haughty spirits
among us, who think that this subject ought to be handled by none but a few
persons of eminent characters, let such recollect that the dignity, the importance of their country should inspire sentiments more exalted than the
highest characters—sentiments, that should correspond with the worth of
America, not with the consequence of any mere individuals. Will you, then,
Virginians, arrogate too much by boldly asserting the privilege to judge for
yourselves in what so nearly concerns the cause of liberty? No, no, my
countrymen, you will not arrogate too much; you will not: I avow it by the
souls of those brave patriots, who fought for the same cause in the late war.
You will in this affair act as becomes you. The rank, you hold amongst the
nations of the earth, requires this of you. And you will forfeit that rank: you
will forfeit the character of *freemen;* and shew that you deserve to be enslaved, if you decline that privilege. The happiness of a multitude of people
is certainly the highest advantage, which can be conferred on any society:
and if you will contribute a full share of duty to effect this, so shall you
obtain a due share of glory. No pomp of character, no sound of names, no
distinction of birth—no pre-eminence of any kind, should dispose you to
hoodwink your own understandings; and in that state suffer yourselves to be
led at the will of any order of men whatsoever. The part you have acted
heretofore,—the brave, the noble efforts, you have made, are proof enough
of your fortitude, and totally exclude every idea of pusillanimity. Herein
you have evinced the highest sense of public virtue: herein you have manifested to the whole world that the cause of liberty has hitherto had the
prevailing influence over your hearts. And shall men possessed of these
sentiments? shall those valiant defenders of their country, who have not
feared to encounter toil and danger in a thousand shapes, who have not
startled, even at the prospect of death itself? Shall you, O Virginians; shall
you, I say, after exhibiting such bright examples of true patriotic heroism,
suddenly become inconsistent with yourselves; and were [fail?] to maintain
a privilege so incontestibly your due?—No, my countrymen;—by no means
can I conceive that the laudable vigor, which flamed so high in every breast,
can have so far evaporated in the space of five years. I doubt not, but you
will in this trying instance acquit yourselves in a manner worthy of your
former conduct. It is not to be feared that you need the force of persuasion,

to exercise a proper freedom of enquiry into the merits of this proposed plan of government: or that you will not pay a due attention to the welfare of that country, for which you have already so bravely exerted yourselves. Of this I am well assured; and do not wonder when imagination presents to my view the idea of a numerous and respectable body of men reasoning on the principles of this fœderal constitution. If herein I conceive that you are alarmed at the exceedingly high and extensive authority, which it is intended to establish, I cannot but see the strongest reasons for such apprehensions. For a system, which is to supercede the present different governments of the states, by ordaining that "laws made in pursuance thereof shall be supreme, and shall bind the judges in every state, any thing in the constitution or laws of any state to the contrary notwithstanding," must be alarming indeed! What cannot this omnipotence of power effect? How will your bill of rights avail you any thing? By this authority the Congress can make laws, which shall bind all, repugnant to your present constitution—repugnant to every article of your rights; for they are a part of your constitution,—they are the basis of it. So that if you pass this new constitution, you will have a naked plan of government unlimited in its jurisdiction, which not only expunges your bill of rights by rendering ineffectual, all the state governments; but is proposed without any kind of stipulation for any of those natural rights, the security whereof ought to be the end of all governments. Such a stipulation is so necessary, that it is an absurdity to suppose any civil liberty can exist without it. Because it cannot be alledged in any case whatsoever, that a breach has been committed—that a right has been violated; as there will be no standard to resort to—no criterion to ascertain the breach, or even to find whether there has been any violation at all.[13] Hence it is evident that the most flagrant acts of oppression may be inflicted; yet, still there will be no apparent object injured: there will be no unconstitutional infringement. For instance, if Congress should pass a law that persons charged with capital crimes shall not have a *right to demand the cause or nature of the accusation,* shall not be *confronted with the accusers or witnesses, or call for evidence in their own favor;* and a question should arise respecting their authority therein,—can it be said that they have exceeded the limits of their jurisdiction, when *that* has no limits; when no provision has been made for such a right?—When no responsibility on the part of Congress has been required by the constitution? The same observation may be made on any arbitrary or capricious imprisonments *contrary to the law of the land.* The same may be made, if *excessive bail should be required;* if *excessive fines should be imposed;* if *cruel and unusual punishments should be inflicted;* if *the liberty of the press should be restrained:* in a word—if laws should be made totally derogatory to the whole catalogue of rights, which are now secured under your present form of government.

5.14.11   You will, doubtless, consider whether the inconveniences may not be very disagreeable, and perhaps injurious, to which this country may be subjected by excise laws,—by direct taxation of every kind,—by the establishment of fœderal courts. You will advert to the dangerous and oppressive consequences, that may ensue from the introduction of standing armies in times of peace; those baneful engines of ambition, against which free nations have always guarded with the greatest degree of caution. You will determine likewise as to the propriety of being excluded from keeping ships of war without the consent of Congress. The situation of these states renders a naval force extremely desirable. Being bounded on one side by the sea, their coasts are accessible to every lawless adventurer: and without ships to guard them, they are subject to continual depredations. The expediency of this species of defence is manifest. The great advantages to be derived from it,—the strength,—the consequence, which it adds to a nation, are such, that every well-wisher to this country would rejoice to see as large a navy established, as the circumstances of the state can at any time admit of. This, therefore, seems to be a very improper restraint upon the states,—a restraint, which may perhaps eventually prove very injurious.

Upon the whole, my fellow-citizens, if you judge this proposed constitution to be eligible or ineligible, you will accordingly instruct your delegates when they are about to meet in convention. The wisdom of the legislature has judged it advisable to fix the time for deciding on this momentous business at the distance of several months, that you may become thoroughly acquainted with a subject, which so nearly concerns your greatest interests. 5.14.12

I know it is a favorite topic with the advocates for the new government—that it will advance the dignity of Congress; and that the energy, which is now wanting in the fœderal system, will be hereby rendered efficient. Nobody doubts, but the government of the union is susceptible of amendment. But can any one think that there is no medium between want of power, and the possession of it in an unlimited degree? Between the imbecility of mere recommendatory propositions, and the sweeping jurisdiction of exercising every branch of government over the United States to the greatest extent? Between the present feeble texture of the confœderation, and the proposed nervous ligaments? Is it not possible to strengthen the hands of Congress so far as to enable them to comply with all the exigencies of the union—to regulate the great commercial concerns of the continent,—to superintend all affairs, which relate to the United States in their aggregate capacity, without devolving upon that body the supreme powers of government in all its branches?[14] The original institution of Congressional business,—the nature, the end of that institution evince the practicability of such a reform; and shew that it is more honorable, more glorious—and will be more happy for each American state to retain its independent sovereignty. For what can be more truly great in any country than a number of different states in the full enjoyment of liberty—exercising distinct powers of government; yet associated by *one general head,* and under the 5.14.13

influence of a mild, just and well-organized confederation duly held in *equilibrio;*—whilst all derive those external advantages, which are the great purposes of the union? This separate independency existing in each—this harmony pervading the whole—this due degree of energy in the fœderal department, all together, will form a beautiful *species* of national grandeur. These will add lustre to every member, and spread a glory all around. These will command the admiration of mankind. These will exhibit a bright *specimen* of real dignity, far superior to that immense devolution of power, under which the sovereignty of each state shall shrink to nothing.

5.14.14   It requires no great degree of knowledge in history to learn what dangerous consequences generally result from large and extensive powers. Every man has a natural propensity to power; and when one degree of it is obtained, *that* seldom fails to excite a thirst for more:—an higher point being gained, still the soul is impelled to a farther pursuit. Thus step by step, in regular progression, she proceeds onward, until the lust of domination becomes the ruling passion, and absorbs all other desires. When any man puts himself under the influence of such a passion, it is natural for him to seek after every opportunity, and to employ every means within reach, for obtaining his purpose. There is something so exceedingly bewitching in the possession of power that hardly a man can enjoy it, and not be affected after an unusual manner. The pomp of superiority carries with it charms, which operate strongly on the imagination. Nay, it is a melancholy reflection that too often the very disposition itself is transformed,—and for the gratification of ambitious views, the mild, the gentle, humane—the virtuous becomes cruel and violent, losing all sense of honor, probity, humanity and gratitude.[15]—Hence, should it not be a *maxim,* never to be forgotten—that a free people ought to intrust no set of men with powers, that may be abused without controul, or afford opportunities to designing men to carry dangerous measures into execution, without being responsible for their conduct? And as no human foresight can penetrate so far into future events, as to guard always against the effects of vice,—as the securest governments are seldom secure enough;—is it not the greatest imprudence to adopt a system, which has an apparent tendency to furnish ambitious men with the means of exerting themselves—perhaps to the destruction of American liberty?

5.14.15   It is next to impossible to enslave a people immediately after a firm struggle against oppression, while the sense of past injury is recent and strong. But after some time this impression naturally wears off;—the ardent glow of freedom gradually evaporates;—the charms of popular equality, which arose from the *republican plan,* insensibly decline;—the pleasures, the advantages derived from the new kind of government grow stale through use.[16] Such declension in all these vigorous springs of action necessarily produces a supineness. The altar of liberty is no longer watched with such attentive assiduity;—a new train of passions succeeds to the empire of the mind;—different objects of desire take place:—and, if the nation happens to enjoy a series of prosperity, voluptuousness, excessive fondness for riches, and luxury gain admission and establish themselves—these produce venality and corruption of every kind, which open a fatal avenue to bribery. Hence it follows, that in the midst of this general contageon a few men—or one—more powerful than all others, industriously endeavor to obtain all authority; and by means of great wealth—or embezzling the public money,—perhaps totally subvert the government, and erect a system of aristocratical or monarchic tyranny in its room. What ready means for this *work of evil* are numerous standing armies, and the disposition of the great revenue of the United States! Money can purchase soldiers;—soldiers can produce money; and both together can do any thing. It is this depravation of manners, this wicked propensity, my dear countrymen, against which you ought to provide with the utmost degree of prudence and circumspection. All nations pass this *parokism* of vice at some period or other;—and if at that dangerous juncture your government is not secure upon a solid foundation, and well guarded against the machinations of evil men, the liberties of this country will be lost—perhaps forever!

Let us establish a strong fœderal government, which shall render our Congress a great and eminent body, says one. By all means, replies another; and then they will command the attention of all Europe.—Why, pray, what will it avail you in the hour of distress—in the midst of calamity, though all Europe should pay attention to the Congress? What advantage will it be to the citizens of America, should they elevate Congress to the highest degree of grandeur;—should the sound of that grandeur be wafted across the Atlantic, and echoe through every town in Europe? What will the pomp—the splendor of that *dignified body* profit you, I say, if you place yourselves in a situation, which may terminate in wretchedness? Of what consequence will that state of congressional pre-eminence be to you, or to your posterity, if either the one, or the other should thereby be reduced to a mere herd of——? O great GOD, avert that dreadful catastrophe.—Let not the day be permitted to dawn, which shall discover to the world that America remains no longer a free nation!—O let not this last sacred asylum of persecuted *liberty* cease to afford a resting place for that fair goddess!—Re-animate each spirit, that languishes in this glorious cause! Shine in upon us, and illumine all our counsels!—Suffer thy bright ministers of grace to come down and direct us;—and hovering for awhile on the wings of affection, breathe into our souls true sentiments of wisdom!—that in this awful, this important moment we may be conducted safely through the maze of error;—that a firm basis of national happiness may be established, and flourish in undiminished glory through all succeeding ages!

5.14.16

P.P.

December 17, 1787.

1. See Republican Federalist 4.13.15 n. 11.
2. The original reads, "them."
3. See Federal Farmer IV, 2.8.50 n. 40.
4. The source of this quotation has not been found.
5. See Pennsylvania House Minority 3.2.7.
6. James Wilson, "Address to the Citizens of Philadelphia," 6 October 1787, McMaster and Stone 143–44. See references in Federal Farmer IV, 2.8.50 n. 38; cf. [New Hampshire], Farmer 4.17.14 n. 9. On the general question of the need for a bill of rights see Mason 2.2.1. n. 1.
7. This argument should be contrasted with that of Publius in *The Federalist* no. 10 and with Publius' discussion of the causes of dissention among the states in nos. 6–8; see also Brutus I, 2.9.16.
8. *Commentaries* I, 318.
9. See Brutus VIII, 2.9.97 n. 67.
10. See Democratic Federalist 3.5.6 n. 6.
11. On trial by jury see references in Plebeian 6.11.15 n. 13.
12. See references in Federal Republican 3.6.5 n. 4; Centinel I, 2.7.5 n. 2.
13. See Agrippa VI, 4.6.23 n. 14.
14. On Anti-Federalist opposition to consolidation see Plebeian 6.11.15 n. 9.
15. The Impartial Examiner here reveals both the keen Anti-Federal insight into the problem of perpetuating the free republic and the rather narrow Anti-Federal solution to this problem. See Columbian Patriot 4.28.12–13; Warren 6.14.157. On the Federalist side compare *The Federalist* no. 49 with the views of Fabius (Ford, *Pamphlets* 183, 188, 213–15) and James Wilson's Fourth of July Oration, *Boston Gazette and the Country Journal* 28 July 1788. Cf. Abraham Lincoln, "Address before the Young Men's Lyceum of Springfield Illinois," 27 January 1838, *Collected Works* I, 108–15; and Harry V. Jaffa's interpretation of Lincoln's argument in his *Crisis of the House Divided* 183–232.
16. The original text has a semicolon at this point.

Speeches of
Patrick Henry in the
Virginia State Ratifying Convention

June 1788

Although he wrote no Anti-Federalist pamphlet or essay, Patrick Henry argued mightily against the Constitution in the Virginia Ratifying convention. The Virginia convention contained the most distinguished Anti-Federalist group in the country; yet Henry carried the opposition argument for the first week almost alone, in a series of six speeches covering the whole Anti-Federal ground, an exhibition of stamina, argument, and rhetoric unmatched on either side during the ratification debate. Henry's forensic skill;[1] his exploitation of his popularity with the independent yeomanry, with whom he shared a common origin; the maintenance of a simple, common manner and, some said, even an affected vulgarized pronunciation, contributed to his reputation as a demagogue, a reputation reenforced by his subsequent reentry into politics in 1799 as a Federalist.[2] It is doubtless true, as Nevins said, that he was not a "great constructive statesman,"[3] but that he was a man of substance as well as talent is demonstrated by his performance at the Virginia ratification convention.

Unfortunately Henry left no written record elucidating his political opinions, and his biographies do not so much discuss underlying guiding principles as enumerate specific positions.[4] George Ticknor Curtis, whose judgment is more favorable than that of many historians, described with approval Henry's contemporaries' opinion that, although wise, he lacked comprehensiveness, "and that the mere intensity with which he regarded the ends of public liberty was likely to mislead his judgment as to the means by which it was to be secured and upheld."[5] He was a Union man; indeed, it was he who at the First Continental Congress—his only public service outside Virginia—stated the fundamental principle of the nationalist position, words echoed in 1787 by James Wilson at Philadelphia. "The Distinctions between Virginians, Pennsylvanians, New Yorkers and New Englanders are no more. I am not a Virginian, but an American."[6] It was, however, as a Virginian that he performed most of his public service, as governor of Virginia and member of its House of Delegates, and it was through the eyes of a Virginian that he viewed American concerns. He declined an invitation to serve as one of Virginia's delegates to the Federal Convention in 1787, to a considerable extent at least because of his opposition to the Jay negotiations with Spain, in which he saw a willingness on the part of the Northern States to barter the United States claim to the Mississippi for commercial advantage.[7]

Henry's brilliant, turbulent, repetitious argument before the Virginia convention is unusually difficult to edit. Printed here in their entirety are his first two speeches (4 and 5 June) and two later, shorter speeches on a bill of rights (16 and 17 June). Other important speeches or statements are given in briefer form (9 and 12 June) or as interpolations, enclosed in braces { }, in the main statements (7 and 14 June). Bracketed (or sometimes parenthetical) interpolations summarizing omitted passages are from the original. It should be noted that Henry's discussions of the Mississippi negotiations and the peculiar interests of the South—for example, in regard to commercial regulations—are largely omitted here. While this great "contest for empire," as Anti-Federalist Grayson called it,[8] was an important concern of the Southern Anti-Federalists, it was subordinate to more general questions of principle and was only discussed at length, after the ground of principle had been covered.

The thread on which Henry's arguments against the Constitution are strung is the spirit of true federalism and Virginia patriotism. The Constitution, speaking the language of "We the People," destroys the confederation and, with it, Virginia (5.16.1–2, 6, 8, 9, 22–23). Although the connection is not always explicitly made, Henry's advocacy of federalism is tied to several further arguments. He contends that the Constitution represents a hankering after glory and riches rather than liberty, the true object of government and the object associated with the individual states and their federal union under the Articles of Confederation (5.16.2, 6). He denies that he favors secession or separate confederacies (5.16.11), insisting that only liberty is dearer to him than Union (5.16.6). Although Henry does not make any extensive use of the small republic argument, he indicates his acceptance of it (5.16.11). He contends that under the new Constitution the representation is grossly inadequate (5.16.2, 8, 19, 29); that, unlike the British system, there are no real checks or true responsibility (5.16.2, 7–8, 17), and that the only reliance is on the virtue of the rulers (5.16.7, 11, 17). The Constitution is not sufficiently hard-headed. "Tell me not of checks on paper; but tell me of checks founded on self-love" (5.16.14, 17).

Henry defends the system of requisitions (5.16.15–19) and sees the power to tax under the Constitution as especially dangerous, as the end of the states in any significant form, and as the source of excessive burdens on the people. Under the Constitution the people give up everything and lose all their capacity to check the government and preserve their liberty (5.16.2, 6, 7).

The advocates for the Constitution pretend external dangers and internal turbulence where none exist (5.16.1, 2–4). So far as there are dangers, Henry relies on the American spirit to preserve us (5.16.2, 12). It is not new constitutions but industry and economy that are needed to solve America's economic problems (5.16.10). Republican simplicity and the love of freedom are the rocks on which American liberty rests, and American laws must be conducive to and protective of this spirit (5.16.12–13). The absence of a bill of rights, will all its implications, indicates how far the Constitution is from the true American spirit of liberty (5.16.24–25, 34–41).

The text is taken from *Debates and Other Proceedings of the Convention of Virginia, Convened at Richmond, on Monday the 2d day of June, 1788, for the purpose of deliberating on the Constitution recommended by the Grand Federal Convention* (Petersburg 1788–89), 3 vols. Elliot's report of the Virginia debate is taken from this edition; and although Elliot makes frequent minor changes and mistakes (e.g., in his dates), it has been thought more convenient for the reader to give footnote references to Elliot rather than to the inaccessible 1788 edition.

1. "He appeared to me to speak," Jefferson wrote on first hearing Henry, "as Homer wrote." *Autobiography*, in *The Writings of Thomas Jefferson*, ed. P. L. Ford (New York 1892) I, 6.

2. Henry championed unpopular causes, such as the rights of Tories and assimilation of Indians, as well as popular ones, and he presented a solid case for his 1799 Federalism. See Jefferson to Madison, 7 May 1783, *The Writings of Thomas Jefferson* (ed. Ford) III, 318; Nevins, *The American States before and after the Revolution* 324; Moses Coit Tyler, *Patrick Henry* (Boston 1887) 417–19.

3. Nevins, *The American States before and after the Revolution* 135.

4. Among the more prominent biographers of Henry are William Wirt Henry, *Patrick Henry: Life, Correspondence, and Speeches*, 3 vols. (New York 1891); Robert D. Meade, *Patrick Henry: Patriot in the Making* (Philadelphia 1957), volume one of a projected two-volume biography; Tyler, *Patrick Henry* (see note 2 above); William Wirt, *Sketches of the Life and Character of Patrick Henry* (Philadelphia 1818).

5. Curtis, *Constitutional History* I, 663.

6. *Diary and Autobiography of John Adams*, ed. L. H. Butterfield (1961) II, 125 (6 September 1774). See Farrand I, 166 (8 June).

7. See Tyler, *Patrick Henry* 310–11.

8. Elliot III, 365.

4 June 1788

Mr. Chairman.—The public mind, as well as my own, is extremely uneasy   5.16.1 at the proposed change of Government. Give me leave to form one of that number of those who wish to be thoroughly acquainted with the reasons of this perilous and uneasy situation—and why we are brought hither to decide on this great national question. I consider myself as the servant of the people of this Commonwealth, as a centinel over their rights, liberty, and happiness. I represent their feelings when I say, that they are exceedingly uneasy, being brought from the state of full security, which they enjoyed, to the present delusive appearance of things. A year ago the minds of our citizens were at perfect repose. Before the meeting of the late Federal Convention at Philadelphia, a general peace, and an universal tranquility prevailed in this country;—but since that period they are exceedingly uneasy and disquieted. When I wished for an appointment to this Convention, my mind was extremely agitated for the situation of public affairs. I conceive the republic to be in extreme danger. If our situation be thus uneasy, whence has arisen this fearful jeopardy? It arises from this fatal system—it arises from the proposal to change our government:—A proposal that goes to the utter annihilation of the most solemn engagements of the States. A proposal of establishing 9 States into a confederacy, to the eventual exclusion of 4 States. It goes to the annihilation of those solemn treaties we have formed with foreign nations. The present circumstances of France—the good offices rendered us by that kingdom, require our most faithful and most punctual adherence to our treaty with her. We are in alliance with the Spaniards, the Dutch, the Prussians: Those treaties bound us as thirteen States, confederated together—Yet, here is a proposal to sever this confederacy. Is it possible that we shall abandon all our treaties and national engagements?—And for what? I expected to have heard the reasons of an event so unexpected to my mind, and many others. Was our civil polity, or public justice, endangered or saped? Was the real existence of the country threatened—or was this preceded by a mournful progression of events? This proposal of altering our Federal Government is of a most alarming nature: Make the best of this new Government—say it is composed by any thing but inspiration—you ought to be extremely cautious, watchful, jealous of your liberty; for instead of securing your rights you may lose them forever. If a wrong step be now made, the Republic may be lost forever. If this new Government will not come up to the expectation of the people, and they should be disappointed—their liberty will be lost, and tyranny must and will arise. I repeat it again, and I beg Gentlemen to consider, that a wrong step made now will plunge us in misery, and our Republic will be lost. It will be necessary for this Convention to have a faithful historical detail of the facts, that preceded the session of the Federal Convention, and the reasons that actuated its members in proposing an entire alteration of Government—and demonstrate the dangers that awaited us: If they were of such awful magnitude, as to warrant a proposal so extremely perilous as this, I must assert, that this Convention has an absolute right to a thorough discovery of every circumstance relative to this great event. And here I would make this enquiry of those worthy characters who composed a part of the late Federal Convention. I am sure they were fully impressed with the necessity of forming a great consolidated Government, instead of a confederation. That this is a consolidated Government is demonstrably clear, and the danger of

such a Government, is, to my mind, very striking. I have the highest veneration of those Gentlemen,—but, Sir, give me leave to demand, what right
had they to say, *We, the People*. My political curiosity, exclusive of my
anxious solicitude for the public welfare, leads me to ask who authorised
them to speak the language of, *We, the People,* instead of *We, the States*?
States are the characteristics, and the soul of a confederation.[1] If the States
be not the agents of this compact, it must be one great consolidated National
Government of the people of all the States. I have the highest respect for
those Gentlemen who formed the Convention, and were some of them not
here, I would express some testimonial of my esteem for them. America had
on a former occasion put the utmost confidence in them: A confidence
which was well placed: And I am sure, Sir, I would give up any thing to
them; I would chearfully confide in them as my Representatives. But, Sir,
on this great occasion, I would demand the cause of their conduct.—Even
from that illustrious man, who saved us by his valor, I would have a reason
for his conduct—that liberty which he has given us by his valor, tells me to
ask this reason,—and sure I am, were he here, he would give us that reason:
But there are other Gentlemen here, who can give us this information. The
people gave them no power to use their name. That they exceeded their
power is perfectly clear. It is not mere curiosity that actuates me—I wish to
hear the real actual existing danger, which should lead us to take those steps
so dangerous in my conception. Disorders have arisen in other parts of
America, but here, Sir, no dangers, no insurrection or tumult, has
happened—every thing has been calm and tranquil. But notwithstanding
this, we are wandering on the great ocean of human affairs. I see no land-
mark to guide us. We are running we know not whither. Difference in
opinion has gone to a degree of inflammatory resentment in different parts of
the country—which has been occasioned by this perilous innovation. The
Federal Convention ought to have amended the old system—for this purpose they were solely delegated: The object of their mission extended to no
other consideration. You must therefore forgive the solicitation of one unworthy member, to know what danger could have arisen under the present
confederation, and what are the causes of this proposal to change our Government.

5 June 1788

Mr. Chairman—I am much obliged to the very worthy Gentleman [Henry
Lee] for his encomium. I wish I was possessed of talents, or possessed of
any thing, that might enable me to elucidate this great subject. I am not free
from suspicion: I am apt to entertain doubts: I rose yesterday to ask a
question, which arose in my own mind. When I asked the question, I

5.16.2

thought the meaning of my interrogation was obvious: The fate of this question and America may depend on this: Have they said, we the States? Have they made a proposal of a compact between States? If they had, this would be a confederation: It is otherwise most clearly a consolidated government. The question turns, Sir, on that poor little thing—the expression, *We, the people,* instead of the States of America. I need not take much pains to show, that the principles of this system, are extremely pernicious, impolitic, and dangerous. Is this a Monarchy, like England—a compact between Prince and people; with checks on the former, to secure the liberty of the latter? Is this a Confederacy, like Holland—an association of a number of independent States, each of which retain its individual sovereignty? It is not a democracy, wherein the people retain all their rights securely. Had these principles been adhered to, we should not have been brought to this alarming transition, from a Confederacy to a consolidated Government.[2] We have no detail of those great considerations which, in my opinion, ought to have abounded before we should recur to a government of this kind. Here is a revolution as radical as that which separated us from Great Britain. It is as radical, if in this transition our rights and privileges are endangered, and the sovereignty of the States be relinquished: And cannot we plainly see, that this is actually the case? The rights of conscience, trial by jury, liberty of the press, all your immunities and franchises, all pretensions to human rights and privileges, are rendered insecure, if not lost, by this change so loudly talked of by some, and inconsiderately by others. Is this same relinquishment of rights worthy of freemen? Is it worthy of that manly fortitude that ought to characterize republicans: It is said eight States have adopted this plan. I declare that if twelve States and an half had adopted it, I would with manly firmness, and in spite of an erring world, reject it. You are not to inquire how your trade may be increased, nor how you are to become a great and powerful people, but how your liberties can be secured; for liberty ought to be the direct end of your Government.[3] Having premised these things, I shall, with the aid of my judgment and information, which I confess are not extensive, go into the discussion of this system more minutely. Is it necessary for your liberty, that you should abandon those great rights by the adoption of this system? Is the relinquishment of the trial by jury, and the liberty of the press, necessary for your liberty? Will the abandonment of your most sacred rights tend to the security of your liberty? Liberty the greatest of all earthly blessings—give us that precious jewel, and you may take every thing else: But I am fearful I have lived long enough to become an old fashioned fellow: Perhaps an invincible attachment to the dearest rights of man, may, in these refined enlightened days, be deemed *old fashioned:* If so, I am contended to be so: I say, the time has been, when every pore of my heart beat for American liberty, and which, I believe, had a counterpart in the breast of every true American: But suspicions have gone forth—suspicions of my integrity—publicly reported that my professions are not real—23 years ago was I supposed a traitor to my country; I was then said to be a bane of sedition, because I supported the rights of my country: I may be thought suspicious when I say our privileges and rights are in danger: But, Sir, a number of the people of this country are weak enough to think these things are too true: I am happy to find that the Honorable Gentleman on the other side, declares they are groundless: But, Sir, suspicion is a virtue, as long as its object is the preservation of the public good, and as long as it stays within proper bounds: Should it fall on me, I am contented: Conscious rectitude is a powerful consolation: I trust, there are many who think my professions for the public good to be real. Let your suspicion look to both sides: There are many on the other side, who, possibly may have been persuaded of the necessity of these measures, which I conceive to be dangerous to your liberty. Guard with jealous attention the public liberty. Suspect every one who approaches that jewel. Unfortunately, nothing will preserve it, but downright force: Whenever you give up that force, you are inevitably ruined. I am answered by Gentlemen, that though I might speak of terrors, yet the fact was, that we were surrounded by none of the dangers I apprehended. I conceive this new Government to be one of those dangers: It has produced those horrors, which distress many of our best citizens. We are come hither to preserve the poor Commonwealth of Virginia, if it can be possibly done: Something must be done to preserve your liberty and mine: The Confederation; this same despised Government, merits, in my opinion, the highest encomium: It carried us through a long and dangerous war: It rendered us victorious in that bloody conflict with a powerful nation: It has secured us a territory greater than any European Monarch possesses: And shall a Government which has been thus strong and vigorous, be accused of imbecility and abandoned for want of energy?[4] Consider what you are about to do before you part with this Government. Take longer time in reckoning things: Revolutions like this have happened in almost every country in Europe: Similar examples are to be found in ancient Greece and ancient Rome: Instances of the people loosing their liberty by their own carelessness and the ambition of a few. We are cautioned by the Honorable Gentleman who presides, against faction and turbulence: I acknowledge that licentiousness is dangerous, and that it ought to be provided against: I acknowledge also the new form of Government may effectually prevent it: Yet, there is another thing it will as effectually do: it will oppress and ruin the people. There are sufficient guards placed against sedition and licentiousness: For when power is given to this Government to suppress these, or, for any other purpose, the language it assumes is clear, express, and unequivocal, but when this Constitution speaks of privileges, there is an ambiguity, Sir, a fatal ambiguity;—an ambiguity which is very astonishing: In the clause under consideration, there is the strangest that I can conceive. I mean, when it says, that there shall not be more Representatives, than one for every 30,000. Now, Sir, how easy is it to evade this privilege? "The number shall not exceed one for every 30,000." This may be satisfied by one Representative from each State. Let our numbers be ever so great, this immence continent, may, by this artful expression, be reduced to have but 13 Representatives: I confess this construction is not natural; but the ambiguity of the expression lays a good ground for a quarrel. Why was it not clearly and unequivocally expressed, that they *should* be entitled, to have one for every 30,000? This would have obviated all disputes; and was this difficult to be done? What is the inference? When population increases, and a State shall send Representatives in this proportion, Congress *may* remand them, because the right of having one for every 30,000 is not clearly expressed: This possibility of reducing the number to one for each State, approximates to probability by that other expression, "but each State shall at least have one Representative." Now is it not clear that from the first expression, the number might be reduced so much, that some States should have no Representative at all, were it not for the insertion of this last expression? And as this is the only restriction upon them, we may fairly conclude that they *may* restrain the number to one from each State: Perhaps the same horrors may hang over my mind again. I shall be told I am continually afraid: But, Sir, I have strong cause of apprehension: In some parts of the plan before you, the great rights of freemen are endangered, in other parts absolutely taken away. How does your trial by jury stand? In civil cases gone—not sufficiently secured in criminal—this best privilege is gone: But we are told that we need not fear, because those in power being our Representatives, will not abuse the powers we put in their hands: I am not well versed in history, but I will submit to your recollection, whether liberty has been destroyed most often by the licentiousness of the people, or by the tyranny of rulers? I amagine, Sir, you will find the balance on the side of tyranny:[5] Happy will you be if you miss the fate of those nations, who, omitting to resist their oppressors, or negligently suffering their liberty to be wrested from them, have groaned under intolerable despotism. Most of the human race are now in this deplorable condition: And those nations who have gone in search of grandeur, power and splendor, have also fallen a sacrifice, and been the victims of their own folly: While they acquired those visionary blessings, they lost their freedom. My great objection to this Government is, that it does not leave us the means of defending our rights; or, of waging war against tyrants: It is urged by some Gentlemen, that this new plan will bring us an acquisition of strength, an army, and the militia of the States: This is an idea extremely ridiculous: Gentlemen cannot be in earnest. This acquisition will trample on your fallen liberty: Let my beloved Americans guard against that fatal lethargy that has pervaded the universe: Have we the means of resisting disciplined armies, when our only defence, the militia is put into the hands of Congress? The Honorable Gentleman said, that great danger would ensue if the Convention rose without adopting this system: I ask, where is that danger? I see none:

Other Gentlemen have told us within these walls, that the Union is gone—or, that the Union will be gone: Is not this trifling with the judgment of their fellow-citizens? Till they tell us the ground of their fears, I will consider them as imaginary: I rose to make enquiry where those dangers were; they could make no answer: I believe I never shall have that answer: Is there a disposition in the people of this country to revolt against the dominion of laws? Has there been a single tumult in Virginia? Have not the people of Virginia, when labouring under the severest pressure of accumulated distresses, manifested the most cordial acquiescence in the execution of the laws? What could be more awful than their unamious acquiescence under general distresses? Is there any revolution in Virginia? Whither is the spirit of America gone? Whither is the genius of America fled? It was but yesterday, when our enemies marched in triumph through our country: Yet the people of this country could not be appalled by their pompous armaments: They stopped their career, and victoriously captured them: Where is the peril now compared to that? Some minds are agitated by foreign alarms: Happily for us, there is no real danger from Europe: that country is engaged in more arduous business; from that quarter there is no cause of fear: You may sleep in safety forever for them. Where is the danger? If, Sir, there was any, I would recur to the American spirit to defend us;—that spirit which has enabled us to surmount the greatest difficulties:[6] To that illustrious spirit I address my most fervent prayer, to prevent our adopting a system destructive to liberty. Let not Gentlemen be told, that it is not safe to reject this Government. Wherefore is it not safe? We are told there are dangers; but those dangers are ideal; they cannot be demonstrated: To encourage us to adopt it, they tell us, that there is a plain easy way of getting amendments: When I come to contemplate this part, I suppose that I am mad, or, that my countrymen are so: The way to amendment, is, in my conception, shut. Let us consider this plain easy way: "The Congress, whenever two-thirds of both Houses shall deem it necessary, shall propose amendments to this Constitution, or, on the application of the Legislatures of two-thirds of the several States, shall call a Convention for proposing amendments, which, in either case, shall be valid to all intents and purposes, as part of this Constitution, when ratified by the Legislatures of three-fourths of the several States, or by Conventions in three-fourths thereof, as the one or the other mode of ratification may be proposed by the Congress. Provided, that no amendment which may be made prior to the year 1808, shall in any manner affect the first and fourth clauses in the ninth section of the first article; and that no State, without its consent, shall be deprived of its equal suffrage in the Senate." Hence it appears that three-fourths of the States must ultimately agree to any amendments that may be necessary. Let us consider the consequences of this: However uncharitable it may appear, yet I must tell my opinion, that the most unworthy characters may get into power and prevent the introduction of amendments: Let us suppose (for the case is supposeable, possible, and probable) that you happen to deal these powers to unworthy hands; will they relinquish powers already in their possession, or, agree to amendments? Two-thirds of the Congress, or, of the State Legislatures, are necessary even to propose amendments: If one-third of these be unworthy men, they may prevent the application for amendments; but what is destructive and mischievous is, that three-fourths of the State Legislatures, or of State Conventions, must concur in the amendments when proposed: In such numerous bodies, there must necessarily be some designing bad men: To suppose that so large a number as three-fourths of the States will concur, is to suppose that they will possess genius, intelligence, and integrity, approaching to miraculous. It would indeed be miraculous that they should concur in the same amendments, or, even in such as would bear some likeness to one another. For four of the smallest States, that do not collectively contain one-tenth part of the population of the United States, may obstruct the most salutary and necessary amendments: Nay, in these four States, six tenths of the people may reject these amendments; and suppose, that amendments shall be opposed to amendments (which is highly probable) is it possible, that three-fourths can ever agree to the same amendments? A bare majority in these four small States may hinder the adoption of amendments; so that we may fairly and justly conclude, that one-twentieth part of the American people, may prevent the removal of the most grievous inconveniences and oppression, by refusing to accede to amendments. A trifling minority may reject the most salutary amendments. Is this an easy mode of securing the public liberty? It is, Sir, a most fearful situation, when the most contemptible minority can prevent the alteration of the most oppressive Government; for it may in many respects prove to be such: Is this the spirit of republicanism? What, Sir, is the genius of democracy? Let me read that clause of the Bill of Rights of Virginia, which relates to this: 3d cl. "That Government is or ought to be instituted for the common benefit, protection, and security of the people, nation, or community: Of all the various modes and forms of Government, that is best which is capable of producing the greatest degree of happiness and safety, and is most effectually secured against the danger of mal-administration, and *that whenever any Government shall be found inadequate, or contrary to these purposes, a majority of the community hath, an undubitable, unalienable and indefeasible right to reform, alter, or abolish it, in such manner as shall be judged most conducive to the public weal.*"[7] This, Sir, is the language of democracy; that a majority of the community have a right to alter their Government when found to be oppressive: But how different is the genius of your new Constitution from this? How different from the sentiments of freemen, that a contemptible minority can prevent the good of the majority? If then Gentlemen standing on this ground, are come to that point, that they are willing to bind themselves and their posterity to be oppressed, I am amazed and inexpressibly astonished. If this be the opinion of the majority, I must submit; but to me, Sir, it appears perilous and destructive: I cannot help thinking so: Perhaps it may be the result of my age; these may be feelings natural to a man of my years, when the American spirit has left him, and his mental powers, like the members of the body, are decayed. If, Sir, amendments are left to the twentieth or the tenth part of the people of America, your liberty is gone forever. We have heard that there is a great deal of bribery practiced in the House of Commons in England; and that many of the members raised themselves to preferments, by selling the rights of the people: But, Sir, the tenth part of that body cannot continue oppressions on the rest of the people. English liberty is in this case, on a firmer foundation than American liberty. It will be easily contrived to procure the opposition of one tenth of the people to any alteration, however judicious. The Honorable Gentleman who presides, told us, that to prevent abuses in our Government, we will assemble in Convention, recall our delegated powers, and punish our servants for abusing the trust reposed in them.[8] Oh, Sir, we should have fine times indeed, if to punish tyrants, it were only sufficient to assemble the people. Your arms wherewith you could defend yourselves, are gone; and have no longer a aristocratical; no longer democratical spirit. Did you ever read of any revolution in any nation, brought about by the punishment of those in power, inflicted by those who had no power at all? You read of a riot act in a country which is called one of the freest in the world, where a few neighbours cannot assemble without the risk of being shot by a hired soldiery, the engines of despotism. We may see such an act in America. A standing army we shall have also, to execute the execrable commands of tyranny: And how are you to punish them? Will you order them to be punished? Who shall obey these orders? Will your Mace-bearer be a match for a disciplined regiment? In what situation are we to be? The clause before you gives a power of direct taxation, unbounded and unlimited: Exclusive power of Legislation in all cases whatsoever, for ten miles square; and over all places purchased for the erection of forts, magazines, arsenals, dock-yards, &c. What resistance could be made? The attempt would be madness. You will find all the strength of this country in the hands of your enemies: Those garrisons will naturally be the strongest places in the country. Your militia is given up to Congress also in another part of this plan: They will therefore act as they think proper: All power will be in their own possession: You cannot force them to receive their punishment: Of what service would militia be to you, when most probably you will not have a single musket in the State; for as arms are to be provided by Congress, they may or may not furnish them. Let me here call your attention to that part which gives the Congress power, "To provide for organizing, arming, and disciplining the militia, and for governing such part of them as may be employed in the service of the United States, reserving to the States respectively, the appointment of the officers, and the authority of training the militia, according to the discipline pre-

scribed by Congress.'' By this, Sir, you see that their controul over our last
and best defence, is unlimited. If they neglect or refuse to discipline or arm
our militia, they will be useless: The States can do neither, this power being
exclusively given to Congress: The power of appointing officers over men
not disciplined or armed, is ridiculous: So that this pretended little remains
of power left to the States, may, at the pleasure of Congress, be rendered
nugatory. Our situation will be deplorable indeed: Nor can we ever expect
to get this government amended, since I have already shewn, that a very
small minority may prevent it; and that small minority interested in the
continuance of the oppression: Will the oppressor let go the oppressed? Was
there ever an instance? Can the annals of mankind exhibit one single example, where rulers overcharged with power, willingly let go the oppressed,
though solicited and requested most earnestly? The application for amendments will therefore be fruitless. Sometimes the oppressed have got loose
by one of those bloody struggles that desolate a country. A willing relinquishment of power is one of those things which human nature never was,
nor ever will be capable of: The Honorable Gentleman's observations respecting the people's right of being the agents in the formation of this Government, are not accurate in my humble conception.[9] The distinction between a National Government and a Confederacy is not sufficiently discerned. Had the delegates who were sent to Philadelphia a power to propose
a Consolidated Government instead of a Confederacy? Were they not deputed by States, and not by the people? The assent of the people in their
collective capacity is not necessary to the formation of a Federal Government. The people have no right to enter into leagues, alliances, or con-
federations: They are not the proper agents for this purpose: States and
sovereign powers are the only proper agents for this kind of Government:
Shew me an instance where the people have exercised this business: Has it
not always gone through the Legislatures? I refer you to the treaties with
France, Holland, and other nations: How were they made? Were they not
made by the States? Are the people therefore in their aggregate capacity, the
proper persons to form a Confederacy? This, therefore, ought to depend on
the consent of the Legislatures; the people having never sent delegates to
make any proposition of changing the Government. Yet I must say, at the
same time, that it was made on grounds the most pure, and perhaps I might
have been brought to consent to it so far as to the change of Government;
but there is one thing in it which I never would acquiesce in. I mean the
changing it into a Consolidated Government; which is so abhorent to my
mind. The Honorable Gentleman then went on to the figure we make with
foreign nations; the contemptible one we make in France and Holland;
which, according to the system of my notes, he attributes to the present
feeble Government.[10] An opinion has gone forth, we find, that we are a
contemptible people: The time has been when we were thought otherwise:
Under this same despised Government, we commanded the respect of all

Europe: Wherefore are we now reckoned otherwise? The American spirit has fled from hence: It has gone to regions, where it has never been expected: It has gone to the people of France in search of a splendid Government—a strong energetic Government. Shall we imitate the example of those nations who have gone from a simple to a splendid Government. Are those nations more worthy of our imitation? What can make an adequate satisfaction to them for the loss they suffered in attaining such a Government for the loss of their liberty? If we admit this Consolidated Government it will be because we like a great splendid one. Some way or other we must be a great and mighty empire; we must have an army, and a navy, and a number of things: When the American spirit was in its youth, the language of America was different: Liberty, Sir, was then the primary object. We are descended from a people whose Government was founded on liberty: Our glorious forefathers of Great-Britain, made liberty the foundation of every thing. That country is become a great, mighty, and splendid nation; not because their Government is strong and energetic; but, Sir, because liberty is its direct end and foundation: We drew the spirit of liberty from our British ancestors; by that spirit we have triumphed over every difficulty: But now, Sir, the American spirit, assisted by the ropes and chains of consolidation, is about to convert this country to a powerful and mighty empire: If you make the citizens of this country agree to become the subjects of one great consolidated empire of America, your Government will not have sufficent energy to keep them together: Such a Government is incompatible with the genius of republicanism: There will be no checks, no real balances, in this Government: What can avail your specious imaginary balances, your rope-dancing, chain-rattling, ridiculous ideal checks and contrivances? But, Sir, we are not feared by foreigners: we do not make nations tremble: Would this, Sir, constitute happiness, or secure liberty?[11] I trust, Sir, our political hemisphere will ever direct their operations to the security of those objects. Consider our situation, Sir: Go to the poor man, ask him what he does; he will inform you, that he enjoys the fruits of his labour, under his own fig-tree, with his wife and children around him, in peace and security. Go to every other member of the society, you will find the same tranquil ease and content; you will find no alarms or disturbances: Why then tell us of dangers to terrify us into an adoption of this new Government? and yet who knows the dangers that this new system may produce; they are out of the sight of the common people: They cannot foresee latent consequences: I dread the operation of it on the middling and lower class of people: It is for them I fear the adoption of this system. I fear I tire the patience of the Committee, but I beg to be indulged with a few more observations: When I thus profess myself an advocate for the liberty of the people, I shall be told, I am a designing man, that I am to be a great man, that I am to be a demagogue; and many similar illiberal insinuations will be thrown out; but, Sir, conscious rectitude, out-weighs these things with me: I see great jeopardy in this new Government. I see none from our present one: I hope some Gentleman or other will bring forth, in full array, those dangers, if there be any, that we may see and touch them.

5.16.3 {[7 June] I have thought, and still think, that a full investigation of the actual situation of America, ought to precede any decision on this great and important question. That Government is no more than a choice among evils, is acknowledged by the most intelligent among mankind, and has been a standing maxim for ages. If it be demonstrated that the adoption of the new plan is a little or a trifling evil, then, Sir, I acknowledge that adoption ought to follow: But, Sir, if this be a truth that its adoption may entail misery on the free people of this country, I then insist, that rejection ought to follow. Gentlemen strongly urge its adoption will be a mighty benefit to us: But, Sir, I am made of such incredulous materials that assertions and declarations, do not satisfy me. I must be convinced, Sir. I shall retain my infidelity on that subject, till I see our liberties secured in a manner perfectly satisfactory to my understanding. . . .

5.16.4 { . . . You are told [by Governor Randolph] there is no peace,[12] although you fondly flatter yourselves that all is peace—No peace—a general cry and alarm in the country—Commerce, riches, and wealth vanished—Citizens going to seek comforts in other parts of the world—Laws insulted—Many instances of tyrannical legislation. These things, Sir, are new to me. He has made the discovery—As to the administration of justice, I believe that failures in commerce, &c. cannot be attributed to it. My age enables me to recollect its progress under the old Government. I can justify it by saying, that it continues in the same manner in this State, as it did under former Government. As to other parts of the Continent, I refer that to other Gentlemen. As to the ability of those who administer it, I believe they would not suffer by a comparison with those who administered it under the royal authority. Where is the cause of complaint if the wealthy go away? Is this added to the other circumstances, of such enormity, and does it bring such danger over this Commonwealth as to warrant so important, and so awful a change in so precipitate a manner? As to insults offered to the laws, I know of none. In this respect I believe this Commonwealth would not suffer by a comparison with the former Government. The laws are as well executed, and as patiently acquiesced in, as they were under the royal administration. Compare the situation of the country—Compare that of our citizens to what they were then, and decide whether persons and property are not as safe and secure as they were at that time. Is there a man in this Commonwealth, whose person can be insulted with impunity? Cannot redress be had here for personal insults or injuries, as well as in any part of the world—as well as in those countries where Aristocrats and Monarchs triumph and reign? Is not the protection of property in full operation here? The contrary cannot with truth be charged on this Commonwealth. Those severe charges which are exhibited against it, appear to me totally groundless. On a fair investigation, we shall be found to be surrounded by no real dangers. We have the animating fortitude and persevering alacrity of republican men, to carry us through misfortunes and calamities. 'Tis the fortune of a republic to be able to withstand the stormy ocean of human vicissitudes. I know of no danger awaiting us. Public and private security are to be found here in the highest degree. Sir, it is the fortune of a free people, not to be intimidated by imaginary dangers. Fear is the passion of slaves. Our political and natural hemisphere are now equally tranquil. Let us recollect the awful magnitude of the subject of our deliberation. Let us consider the latent consequences of an erroneous decision—and let not our minds be led away by unfair misrepresentations and uncandid suggestions. There have been many instances of uncommon lenity and temperance used in the exercise of power in this Commonwealth. I could call your recollection to many that happened during the war and since—But every Gentleman here must be apprized of them.

{The Honorable member has given you an elaborate account of what he 5.16.5 judges tyrannical legislation, and an *ex post facto law* (in the case of Josiah Philips.)[13] He has misrepresented the facts. That man was not executed by a tyrannical stroke of power. He was a fugitive murderer and an out-law—a man who commanded an infamous banditti, at a time when the war was at the most perilous stage. He committed the most cruel and shocking barbarities. He was an enemy to the human name.—Those who declare war against the human race, may be struck out of existence as soon as they are apprehended. He was not executed according to those beautiful legal ceremonies which are pointed out by the laws, in criminal cases. The enormity of his crimes did not entitle him to it. I am truly a friend to legal forms and methods; but, Sir, the occasion warranted the measure. A pirate, an outlaw, or a common enemy to all mankind, may be put to death at any time. It is justified by the laws of nature and nations. The Honorable member tells us then, that there are burnings and discontents in the hearts of our citizens in general, and that they are dissatisfied with their Government.[14] I have no doubt the Honorable member believes this to be the case, because he says so. But I have the comfortable assurance, that it is a certain fact, *that it is not so*. The middle and lower ranks of people have not those illumined ideas, which the well-born are so happily possessed of—They cannot so readily perceive latent objects. The microscopic eyes of modern States-men can see abundance of defects in old systems; and their illumined imaginations discover the necessity of change.}

. . . I have said that I thought this a Consolidated Government: I will now 5.16.6 prove it. Will the great rights of the people be secured by this Government? Suppose it should prove oppressive, how can it be altered? Our Bill of Rights declares, "That a majority of the community hath an *undubitable, unalienable,* and *indefeasible right* to reform, alter, or abolish it, in such manner as shall be judged most conducive to the public weal."[15] I have just proved that one tenth, or less, of the people of America, a most despicable minority may prevent this reform or alteration. Suppose the people of Virginia should wish to alter their Government, can a majority of them do it? No, because they are connected with other men; or, in other words, consolidated with other States: When the people of Virginia at a future day shall wish to alter their Government, though they should be unanimous in this desire, yet they may be prevented therefrom by a despicable minority at the extremity of the United States: The founders of your own Constitution made your Government changeable: But the power of changing it is gone from you! Whither is it gone? It is placed in the same hands that hold the rights of twelve other States; and those who hold those rights, have right and power to keep them: It is not the particular Government of Virginia: One of the leading features of that Government is, that a majority can alter it, when necessary for the public good. This Government is not a Virginian but an American Government. Is it not therefore a Consolidated Government? The sixth clause of your Bill of Rights tells you, "That elections of members to serve as Representatives of the people in Assembly, ought to be free, and that all men having sufficient evidence of permanent common interest with, and attachment to the community, have the right of suffrage, and *cannot* be *taxed* or *deprived* of *their property* for public uses, without their own consent, or that of their Representatives so elected, nor bound by any law to which they have not in like manner assented for the public good."[16] But what does this Constitution say? The clause under consideration gives an unlimitted and unbounded power of taxation: Suppose every delegate from Virginia opposes a law laying a tax, what will it avail? They are opposed by a majority: Eleven members can destroy their efforts: Those feeble ten cannot prevent the passing the most oppressive tax law. So that in direct opposition to the spirit and express language of your Declaration of Rights, you are taxed not by your own consent, but by people who have no connection with you. The next clause of the Bill of Rights tells you, "That all power of suspending law, or the execution of laws, by any authority without the consent of the Representatives of the people, is injurious to their rights, and ought not to be exercised."[17] This tells us that there can be no suspension of Government, or laws without our own consent: Yet this Constitution can counteract and suspend any of our laws, that contravene its oppressive operation; for they have the power of direct taxation; which suspends our Bill of Rights; and it is expressly provided, that they can make all laws necessary for carrying their powers into execution; and it is declared paramount to the laws and constitutions of the States. Consider how the only remaining defence we have left is destroyed in this manner: Besides the expences of maintaining the Senate and other House in as much splendor as they please, there is to be a great and mighty President, with very extensive powers; the powers of a King: He is to be supported in extravagant magnificence: So that the whole of our property may be taken by this American Government, by laying what taxes they please, giving themselves what salaries they please, and suspending our laws at their pleasure: I might be thought too inquisitive, but I believe I should take up but very little of your time in enumerating the little power that is left to the Government of Virginia; for this power is reduced to little or nothing: Their garrisons, magazines, arsenals, and forts, which will be situated in the strongest places within the States: Their ten miles square, with all the fine ornaments of human life, added to their powers, and taken from the States, will reduce the power of the latter to nothing. The voice of tradition, I trust, will inform posterity of our struggles for freedom: If our descendants be worthy the name of Americans, they will preserve and hand down to their latest posterity, the transactions of the present times; and though, I confess, my exclamations are not worthy the hearing, they will see that I have done my utmost to preserve their liberty: For I never will give up the power of direct taxation, but for a scourge: I am willing to give it conditionally; that is, after non-compliance with requisitions: I will do more, Sir, and what I hope will convince the most sceptical man, that I am a lover of the American Union, that in case Virginia shall not make punctual payment, the controul of our custom houses, and the whole regulation of trade, shall be given to Congress, and that Virginia shall depend on Congress even for passports, till Virginia shall have paid the last farthing; and furnished the last soldier: Nay, Sir, there is another alternative to which I would consent: Even that they should strike us out of the Union, and take away from us all federal privileges till we comply with federal requisitions; but let it depend upon our own pleasure to pay our money in the most easy manner for our people. Were all the States, more terrible than the mother country, to join against us, I hope Virginia could defend herself; but, Sir, the dissolution of the Union is most abhorent to my mind: The first thing I have at heart is American *liberty;* the second thing is American Union;[18] and I hope the people of Virginia will endeavor to preserve that Union: The increasing population of the southern States, is far greater than that of New-England: Consequently, in a short time, they will be far more numerous than the people of that country: Consider this, and you will find this State more particularly interested to support American liberty, and not bind our posterity by an improvident relinquishment of our rights. I would give the best security for a punctual compliance with requisitions; but I beseech Gentlemen, at all hazards, not to give up this unlimited power of taxation: The Honorable Gentleman has told us these powers given to Congress, are accompanied by a Judiciary which will connect all:[19] On examination you will find this very Judiciary oppressively constructed; your jury trial destroyed, and the Judges dependent on Congress. In this scheme of energetic Government, the people will find two sets of tax-gatherers—the State and the Federal Sheriffs. This it seems to me will produce such dreadful oppression, as the people cannot possibly bear: The Federal Sheriff may commit what oppression, make what distresses he pleases, and ruin you with impunity: For how are you to tie his hands? Have you any sufficient decided means of preventing him from sucking your blood by speculations, commissions and fees? Thus thousands of your people will be most shamefully robbed: Our State Sheriffs, those unfeeling blood-suckers, have, under the watchful eye of our Legislature, committed the most horrid and barbarous ravages on our people: It has required the most constant vigilance of the Legislature to keep them from totally ruining the people: A repeated succession of laws has been made to suppress their inequitous speculations and cruel extortions; and as often have their nefarious ingenuity devised methods of evading the force of those laws: In the struggle they have generally triumphed over the Legislature. It is fact that lands have sold for five shillings, which were worth one hundred pounds: If Sheriffs thus immediately under the eye of our State Legislature and Judiciary, have dared to commit these outrages, what would they not have done if their masters had been at Philadelphia or New-York? If they perpetrate the most unwarrantable outrage on your persons or property, you cannot get redress on this side of Philadelphia or New-York: And how can you get it there? If your domestic avocations could permit you to go thither, there you must appeal to Judges sworn to support this Constitution, in opposition to that of any State, and who may also be inclined to favor their own officers: When these harpies are aided by excise men, who may search at any time your houses and most secret recesses, will the people bear it? If you think so you differ from me: Where I thought there was a possibility of such mischiefs, I would grant power with a niggardly hand; and here there is strong probability that these oppressions shall actually happen. I may be told, that it is safe to err on that side; because such regulations *may* be made by Congress, as shall restrain these officers, and because laws are made by our Representatives, and judged by righteous Judges: But, Sir, as these regulations may be made, so they may not; and many reasons there are to induce a belief that they will not: I shall therefore be an infidel on that point till the day of my death.

5.16.7   This Constitution is said to have beautiful features; but when I come to examine these features, Sir, they appear to me horridly frightful: Among other deformities, it has an awful squinting; it squints towards monarchy: And does not this raise indignation in the breast of every American? Your President may easily become King: Your Senate is so imperfectly constructed that your dearest rights may be sacrificed by what may be a small minority; and a very small minority may continue forever unchangeably this Government, although horridly defective: Where are your checks in this Government? Your strong holds will be in the hands of your enemies: It is on a supposition that our American Governors shall be honest, that all the good qualities of this Government are founded: But its defective, and imperfect construction, puts it in their power to perpetrate the worst of mischiefs, should they be bad men: And, Sir, would not all the world, from the Eastern to the Western hemisphere, blame our distracted folly in resting our rights upon the contingency of our rulers being good or bad. Shew me that age and country where the rights and liberties of the people were placed on the sole chance of their rulers being good men, without a consequent loss of liberty? I say that the loss of that dearest privilege has ever followed with absolute certainty, every such mad attempt. If your American chief, be a man of ambition, and abilities, how easy is it for him to render himself absolute: The army is in his hands, and, if he be a man of address, it will be attached to him; and it will be the subject of long meditation with him to seize the first auspicious moment to accomplish his design; and, Sir, will the American spirit solely relieve you when this happens? I would rather infinitely, and I am sure most of this Convention are of the same opinion, have a King, Lords, and Commons, than a Government so replete with such insupportable evils. If we make a King, we may prescribe the rules by which he shall rule his people, and interpose such checks as shall prevent him from infringing them: But the President, in the field, at the head of his army, can prescribe the terms on which he shall reign master, so far that it will puzzle any American ever to get his neck from under the galling yoke. I cannot with patience, think of this idea. If ever he violates the laws, one of two things will happen: He shall come to the head of his army to carry every thing before him; or, he will give bail, or do what Mr. Chief Justice will order him. If he be guilty, will not the recollection of his crimes teach him to make one bold push for the American throne? Will not the immense difference between being master of every thing, and being ignominiously tried and punished, powerfully excite him to make this bold push? But, Sir, where is the existing force to punish him? Can he not at the head of his army beat down every opposition? Away with your President, we shall have a King: The army will salute him Monarch; your militia will leave you and assist in making him King, and fight against you: And what have you to oppose this force? What will then become of you and your rights? Will not absolute despotism ensue? [Here Mr. Henry strongly and pathetically expatiated on the probability of the President's enslaving America and the horrible consequences that must result.]

What[20] can be more defective than the clause concerning the elections?—The controul given to Congress over the time, place, and manner of holding elections, will totally destroy the end of suffrage. The elections may be held at one place, and the most inconvenient in the State; or they may be at remote distances from those who have a right of suffrage: Hence nine out of ten must either not vote at all, or vote for strangers: For the most influential characters will be applied to, to know who are the most proper to be chosen. I repeat that the controul of Congress over the *manner,* &c. of electing, well warrants this idea. The natural consequence will be, that this democratic branch, will possess none of the public confidence: The people will be prejudiced against Representatives chosen in such an injudicious manner. The proceedings in the northern conclave will be hidden from

5.16.8

the yeomanry of this country: We are told that the yeas and nays shall be taken and entered on the journals: This, Sir, will avail nothing: It may be locked up in their chests, and concealed forever from the people; for they are not to publish what parts they think require secrecy: They *may* think, and *will think,* the whole requires it. Another beautiful feature of this Constitution is the publication from time to time of the receipts and expenditures of the public money. This expression, from time to time, is very indefinite and indeterminate: It may extend to a century. Grant that any of them are wicked, they may squander the public money so as to ruin you, and yet this expression will give you no redress. I say, they may ruin you;—for where, Sir, is the responsibility? The yeas and nays will shew you nothing, unless they be fools as well as knaves: For after having wickedly trampled on the rights of the people, they would act like fools indeed, were they to publish and devulge their iniquity, when they have it equally in their power to suppress and conceal it.—Where is the responsibility—that leading principle in the British government? In that government a punishment, certain and inevitable, is provided: But in this, there is no real actual punishment for the grossest maladministration. They may go without punishment, though they commit the most outrageous violation on our immunities. That paper may tell me they will be punished. I ask, by what law? They must make the law—for there is no existing law to do it. What—will they make a law to punish themselves? This, Sir, is my great objection to the Constitution, that there is no true responsibility—and that the preservation of our liberty depends on the single chance of men being virtuous enough to make laws to punish themselves.[21] In the country from which we are descended, they have real, and not imaginary, responsibility—for there, maladministration has cost their heads, to some of the most saucy geniuses that ever were. The Senate, by making treaties may destroy your liberty and laws for want of responsibility. Two-thirds of those that shall happen to be present, can, with the President, make treaties, that shall be the supreme law of the land: They may make the most ruinous treaties; and yet there is no punishment for them. Whoever shews me a punishment provided for them, will oblige me. So, Sir, notwithstanding there are eight pillars, they want another. Where will they make another? I trust, Sir, the exclusion of the evils wherewith this system is replete, in its present form, will be made a condition, precedent to its adoption, by this or any other State. The transition from a general unqualified admission to offices, to a consolidation of government, seems easy; for though the American States are dissimilar in their structure, this will assimilate them: This, Sir, is itself a strong consolidating feature, and is not one of the least dangerous in that system. Nine States are sufficient to establish this government over those nine: Imagine that nine have come into it. Virginia has certain scruples. Suppose she will consequently, refuse to join with those States:—May not they still continue in friendship and union with her? If she sends her annual requisitions in dollars, do you think their stomachs will be so squeamish that they will refuse her dollars? Will they not accept her regiments? They would intimidate you into an inconsiderate adoption, and frighten you with ideal evils, and that the Union shall be dissolved. 'Tis a bugbear, Sir:—The fact is, Sir, that the eight adopting States can hardly stand on their own legs. Public fame tells us, that the adopting States have already heart-burnings and animosity, and repent their precipitate hurry: This, Sir, may occasion exceeding great mischief. When I reflect on these and many other circumstances, I must think those States will be fond to be in confederacy with us. If we pay our quota of money annually, and furnish our rateable number of men, when necessary, I can see no danger from a rejection. The history of Switzerland clearly proves, we might be in amicable alliance with those States without adopting this Constitution. Switzerland is a Confederacy, consisting of dissimilar Governments. This is an example which proves that Governments of dissimilar structure may be Confederated; that Confederate Republic has stood upwards of 400 years; and although several of the individual republics are democratic, and the rest aristocratic, no evil has resulted from this dissimilarity, for they have braved all the power of France and Germany during that long period. The Swiss spirit, Sir, has kept them together: They have encountered and overcome immense difficulties with patience and fortitude. In this vicinity of powerful and ambitious monarchs, they have retained their independence, republican simplicity and valour. [Here he makes a comparison of the people of that country, and those of France, and makes a quotation from Addison, illustrating the subject.] Look at the peasants of that country and of France, and mark the difference. You will find the condition of the former far more desirable and comfortable. No matter whether a people be great, splendid, and powerful, if they enjoy freedom. The Turkish Grand Seignior, along-side of our President, would put us to disgrace: But we should be abundantly consoled for this disgrace, when our citizen should be put in contrast with the Turkish slave. The most valuable end of government, is the liberty of the inhabitants. No possible advantages can compensate for the loss of this privilege. Shew me the reason why the American Union is to be dissolved. Who are those eight adopting States? Are they averse to give us a little time to consider, before we conclude? Would such a disposition render a junction with them eligible; or is it the genius of that kind of government, to precipitate people hastily into measures of the utmost importance, and grant no indulgence? If it be, Sir, is it for us to accede to such a government? We have a right to have time to consider—We shall therefore insist upon it. Unless the government be amended, we can never accept it. The adopting States will doubtless accept our money and our regiments—And what is to be the consequence, if we are disunited? I believe that it is yet doubtful, whether it is not proper to stand by a while, and see the effect of its adoption in other States. In forming a government, the utmost care should be taken to prevent its becoming oppressive; and this government is of such an intricate and complicated nature, that no man on this earth can know its real operation. The other States have no reason to think, from the antecedent conduct of Virginia, that she has any intention of seceding from the Union, or of being less active to support the general welfare: Would they not therefore acquiesce in our taking time to deliberate? Deliberate whether the measure be not perilous, not only for us, but the adopting States. Permit me, Sir, to say, that a great majority of the people even in the adopting States, are averse to this government. I believe I would be right to say, that they have been egregiously misled. Pennsylvania has *perhaps* been tricked into it. If the other States who have adopted it, have not been tricked, still they were too much hurried into its adoption. There were very respectable minorities in several of them; and if reports be true, a clear majority of the people are averse to it. If we also accede, and it should prove grievous, the peace and prosperity of our country, which we all love, will be destroyed. This government has not the affection of the people, at present. Should it be oppressive, their affection will be totally estranged from it—and, Sir, you know that a Government without their affections can neither be durable nor happy. I speak as one poor individual—but when I speak, I speak the language of thousands. But, Sir, I mean not to breath the spirit nor utter the language of secession. I have trespassed so long on your patience, I am really concerned that I have something yet to say. The honorable member has said that we shall be properly represented: Remember, Sir, that the number of our Representatives is but ten, whereof six is a majority. Will these men be possessed of sufficient information? A particular knowledge of particular districts will not suffice. They must be well acquainted with agriculture, commerce, and a great variety of other matters throughout the Continent: They must know not only the actual state of nations in Europe, and America, the situation of their farmers, cottagers, and mechanics, but also the relative situation and intercourse of those nations. Virginia is as large as England. Our proportion of Representatives is but ten men. In England they have 530. The House of Commons in England, numerous as they are, we are told, is bribed, and have bartered away the rights of their constituents: What then shall become of us? Will these few protect our rights? Will they be incorruptible? You say they will be better men than the English Commoners. I say they will be infinitely worse men, because they are to be chosen blindfolded: Their election (the term, as applied to their appointment, is inaccurate) will be an involuntary nomination, and not a choice. I have, I fear, fatigued the Committee, yet I have not said the one hundred thousandeth part of what I have on my mind, and wish to impart. On this occasion I conceived myself bound to attend strictly to the interest of the State; and I thought her dearest rights at stake: Having lived so long—been so much honored—my efforts, though small, are due to my country. I have found my mind hurried on from subject to subject, on this very great occasion. We have been all out of order from the Gentleman who opened to-day, to myself. I did not come prepared to speak on so multifarious a subject, in so general a manner. I trust you will indulge me another time.—Before you abandon the present system, I hope you will consider not only its defects, most maturely, but likewise those of that which you are to substitute to it. May you be fully apprised of the dangers of the latter, not by fatal experience, but by some abler advocate than me.

9 June 1788

. . . A number of characters of the greatest eminence in this country, object to this Government, for its consolidating tendency. This is not imaginary. It is a formidable reality. If consolidation proves to be as mischievous to this country, as it has been to other countries, what will the poor inhabitants of this country do? This Government will operate like an ambuscade. It will destroy the State Governments, and swallow the liberties of the people, without giving them previous notice. If Gentlemen are willing to run the hazard, let them run it; but I shall exculpate myself by my opposition, and monitory warnings within these walls. But, then comes paper money. We are at peace on this subject. Though this is a thing which that mighty Federal Convention had no business with, yet I acknowledge that paper money would be the bane of this country. I detest it. Nothing can justify a people in resorting to it, but extreme necessity. It is at rest however in this Commonwealth. It is no longer solicited or advocated. Sir, I ask you, and every other Gentleman who hears me, if he can retain his indignation, at a system, which takes from the State Legislatures the care and preservation of the interests of the people; 180 Representatives, the choice of the people of Virginia cannot be trusted with their interests. They are a mobbish suspected *herd*.[22] This country has not virtue enough to manage its own internal interests. These must be referred to the chosen few. If we cannot be trusted with the private contracts of the citizens, we must be depraved indeed. If he can prove that by one uniform system of abandoned principles, the Legislature has betrayed the rights of the people, then let us seek another shelter. So degrading an indignity—so flagrant an out-rage to the States—so vile a suspicion is humiliating to my mind, and many others.

5.16.9

Will the adoption of this new plan pay our debts? This, Sir, is a plain question. It is inferred, that our grievances are to be redressed, and the evils of the existing system to be removed by the new Constitution. Let me inform the Honorable Gentleman, that no nation ever paid its debts by a change of Government, without the aid of industry. You never will pay your debts but by a radical change of domestic œconomy. At present you buy too much, and make too little to pay. Will this new system promote manufac-

5.16.10

tures, industry and frugality? If instead of this, your hopes and designs will be disappointed; you relinquish a great deal, and hazard infinitely more, for nothing. Will it enhance the value of your lands? Will it lessen your burthens? Will your looms and wheels go to work by the act of adoption? If it will in its consequence produce these things, it will consequently produce a reform, and enable you to pay your debts. Gentlemen must prove it. I am a sceptic—an infidel on this point. I cannot conceive that it will have these happy consequences. I cannot confide in assertions and allegations. The evils that attend us, lie in extravagance and want of industry, and can only be removed by assiduity and œconomy. Perhaps we shall be told by Gentlemen, that these things will happen, because the administration is to be taken from us, and placed in the hands of the luminous few, who will pay different attention, and be more studiously careful than we can be supposed to be.[23] . . .

5.16.11   . . . This Government is so new it wants a name. I wish its other novelties were as harmless as this. He told us, we had an American Dictator in the year 1781[24]—We never had an American President. In making a Dictator, we follow the example of the most glorious, magnanimous and skilful nations. In great dangers this power has been given.—Rome had furnished us with an illustrious example.—America found a person worthy of that trust: She looked to Virginia for him. We gave a dictatorial power to hands that used it gloriously; and which were rendered more glorious by surrendering it up. Where is there a breed of such Dictators? Shall we find a set of American Presidents of such a breed? Will the American President come and lay prostrate at the feet of Congress his laurels? I fear there are few men who can be trusted on that head. The glorious republic of Holland has erected monuments of her warlike intrepidity and valor: Yet she is now totally ruined by a Stadtholder—a Dutch President. The destructive wars into which that nation has been plunged, has since involved her in ambition. The glorious triumphs of Blenheim and Ramillies were not so conformable to the genius, nor so much to the true interest of the republic, as those numerous and useful canals and dykes, and other objects at which ambition spurns. That republic has, however, by the industry of its inhabitants, and policy of its magistrates, suppressed the ill effects of ambition.—Notwithstanding two of their provinces have paid nothing, yet I hope the example of Holland will tell us, that we can live happily without changing our present despised Government. Cannot people be as happy under a mild, as under an energetic Government? Cannot content and felicity be enjoyed in a republic, as well as in a monarchy, because there are whips, chains and scourges used in the latter? If I am not as rich as my neighbour, if I give my mite—my all— republican forbearance will say, that it is sufficient—So said the honest confederates of Holland.—*You are poor—We are rich.—We will go on and do better, far better, than be under an oppressive Government.*—For better will it be for us to continue as we are, than go under that tight energetic

Government.—I am persuaded of what the Honorable Gentleman says, that separate confederacies will ruin us.[25] In my judgment, they are evils never to be thought of till a people are driven by necessity.—When he asks my opinion of consolidation—of one power to reign over America, with a strong hand; I will tell him, I am persuaded, of the rectitude of my honorable friend's opinion (Mr. *Mason*) that one Government cannot reign over so extensive a country as this is, without absolute despotism.[26] Compared to such a consolidation, small Confederacies are little evils; though they ought to be recurred to, but in case of necessity.—Virginia and North-Carolina are despised. They could exist separated from the rest of America. Maryland and Vermont were not over-run when out of the Confederacy. Though it is not a desirable object, yet I trust, that on examination it will be found, that Virginia and North-Carolina would not be swallowed up in case it was necessary for them to be joined together.

When we come to the spirit of domestic peace—The humble genius of Virginia has formed a Government, suitable to the genius of her people. I believe the hands that formed the American Constitution triumph in the experiment. It proves, that the man who formed it, and perhaps by accident, did what design could not do in other parts of the world. After all your reforms in Government, unless you consult the genius of the inhabitants, you will never succeed—your system can have no duration. Let me appeal to the candour of the Committee, if the want of money be not the source of all our misfortunes. We cannot be blamed for not making dollars. This want of money cannot be supplied by changes in Government. The only possible remedy, as I *have before* asserted, is industry aided by œconomy.[27] Compare the genius of the people with the Government of this country. Let me remark, that it stood the severest conflict, during the war, to which ever human virtue has been called. I call upon every Gentleman here to declare, whether the King of England had any subjects so attached to his family and Government—so loyal as we were. But the genius of Virginia called us for liberty.—Called us from those beloved endearments, which from long habits we were taught to love and revere. We entertained from our earliest infancy, the most sincere regard and reverence for the mother country. Our partiality extended to a predilection for her customs, habits, manners and laws. Thus inclined, when the deprivation of our liberty was attempted, what did we do? What did the genius of Virginia tell us? *Sell all and purchase liberty.* This was a severe conflict. Republican maxims were then esteemed—Those maxims, and the genius of Virginia, landed you safe on the shore of freedom. On this awful occasion, did you want a Federal Government? Did federal ideas possess your minds? Did federal ideas lead you to the most splendid victories? I must again repeat the favorite idea, that the genius of Virginia did, and will again lead us to happiness. To obtain the most splendid prize, you did not consolidate. You accomplished the most glorious ends, by the assistance of the genius of your country. Men were then taught

5.16.12

by that genius, that they were fighting for what was most dear to them. View the most affectionate father—the most tender mother—operated on by liberty, nobly stimulating their sons—their dearest sons—sometimes their only son, to advance to the defence of his country. We have seen sons of Cincinnatus, without splendid magnificence or parade, going, with the genius of their great progenitor Cincinnatus, to the plough—Men who served their country without ruining it—Men who had served it to the destruction of their private patrimonies—Their country owing them amazing amounts, for the payment of which no adequate provision was then made. We have seen such men, throw prostrate their arms at your feet. They did not call for those emoluments, which ambition presents to some imaginations. The soldiers, who were able to command every thing, instead of trampling on those laws, which they were instituted to defend, most strictly obeyed them. The hands of justice have not been laid on a single American soldier. Bring them into contrast with European veterans. You will see an astonishing superiority over the latter. There has been a strict subordination to the laws. The Honorable Gentleman's office gave him an opportunity of viewing if the laws were administered so as to prevent riots, routs, and unlawful assemblies. From his then situation, he could have furnished us with the instances in which licentiousness trampled on the laws.—Among all our troubles we have paid almost to the last shilling, for the sake of justice. We have paid as well as any State: I will not say better. To support the General Government, our own Legislature, to pay the interest of the public debts, and defray contingencies, we have been heavily taxed. To add to these things, the distresses produced by paper money, and by tobacco contracts, were sufficient to render any people discontented. These, Sir, were great temptations; but in the most severe conflict of misfortunes, this code of laws—this genius of Virginia, call it what you will, triumphed over every thing.

5.16.13   Why did it please the Gentleman (Mr. *Corbin*)[28] to bestow such epithets on our country? Have the worms taken posession of the wood, that our strong vessel—our political vessel, has sprung a-leak? He may know better than me, but I consider such epithets to be the most illiberal and unwarrantable aspersions on our laws. The system of laws under which we have lived, has been tried and found to suit our genius. I trust we shall not change this happy system. I cannot so easily take leave of an old friend. Till I see him following after and pursuing other objects, which can pervert the great objects of human legislation, pardon me if I withhold my assent.

5.16.14   Some here speak of the difficulty in forming a new code of laws. Young as we were, it was not wonderful if there was a difficulty in forming and assimilating one system of laws. I shall be obliged to the Gentleman, if he would point out those glaring, those great faults. The efforts of assimilating our laws to our genius has not been found altogether vain.—I shall pass over some other circumstances which I intended to mention, and endeavor to come to the capital objection, which my Honorable friend made. My worthy friend said, that a republican form of Government would not suit a very extensive country; but that if a Government were judiciously organized and limits prescribed to it; an attention to these principles might render it possible for it to exist in an extensive territory.[29] Whoever will be bold to say, that a Continent can be governed by that system, contradicts all the experience of the world. It is a work too great for human wisdom. Let me call for an example. Experience has been called the best teacher. I call for an example of a great extent of country, governed by one Government, or Congress, call it what you will. I tell him, that a Government may be trimmed up according to Gentlemen's fancy, but it never can operate—It will be but very short-lived. However disagreeable it may be to lengthen my objections, I cannot help taking notice of what the Honorable Gentleman said. To me it appears that there is no check in that Government. The President, Senators, and Representatives all immediately, or mediately, are the choice of the people. Tell me not of checks on paper; but tell me of checks founded on self-love. The English Government is founded on self-love. This powerful irresistible stimulous of self-love has saved that Government. It has interposed that hereditary nobility between the King and Commons. If the House of Lords assists or permits the King to overturn the liberties of the people, the same tyranny will destroy them; they will therefore keep the balance in the democratic branch. Suppose they see the Commons incroach upon the King; self-love, that great energetic check, will call upon them to interpose: For, if the King be destroyed, their destruction must speedily follow. Here is a consideration which prevails, in my mind, to pronounce the British Government, superior in this respect to any Government that ever was in any country. Compare this with your Congressional checks. I beseech Gentlemen to consider, whether they can say, when trusting power, that a mere patriotic profession will be equally operative and efficatious, as the check of self-love. In considering the experience of ages, is it not seen, that fair disinterested patriotism, and professed attachment to rectitude have never been solely trusted to by an enlightened free people?—If you depend on your President's and Senators patriotism, you are gone. Have you a resting place like the British Government? Where is the rock of your salvation? The real rock of political salvation is *self-love* perpetuated from age to age in every human breast, and manifested in every action. If they can stand the temptations of human nature, you are safe. If you have a good President, Senators and Representatives, there is no danger.—But can this be expected from human nature? Without real checks it will not suffice, that some of them are good. A good President, or Senator, or Representative, will have a natural weakness.—Virtue will slumber. The wicked will be continually watching:[30] Consequently you will be undone. Where are your checks? You have no hereditary Nobility—An order of men, to whom human eyes can be cast up for relief: For, says the Constitution, there is no title of nobility to be granted; which, by the bye, would not have been so dangerous, as the perilous cession of powers contained in that paper: Because, as Montesquieu says, when you give titles of Nobility, you know what you give; but *when you give power, you know not what you give*.[31]—If you say, that out of this depraved mass, you can collect luminous characters, it will not avail, unless this luminous breed will be propagated from generation to generation; and even then, if the number of vicious characters will preponderate, you are undone. And that this will certainly be the case, is, to my mind, perfectly clear.—In the British Government there are real balances and checks—In this system, there are only ideal balances. Till I am convinced that there are actual efficient checks, I will not give my assent to its establishment. The President and Senators have nothing to lose. They have not that interest in the preservation of the Government, that the King and Lords have in England. They will therefore be regardless of the interests of the people. The Constitution will be as safe with one body, as with two. It will answer every purpose of human legislation. How was the Constitution of England when only the Commons had the power? I need only remark, that it was the most unfortunate æra when that country returned to King, Lords and Commons, without sufficient responsibility in the King. When the Commons of England, in the manly language which became freemen, said to their King, *you are our servant*, then the temple of liberty was complete. From that noble source, have we derived our liberty:—That spirit of patriotic attachment to one's country:—That zeal for liberty, and that enmity to tyranny which signalized the then champions of liberty, we inherit from our British ancestors. And I am free to own, that if you cannot love a Republican Government, you may love the British Monarchy;[32] for, although the King is not sufficiently responsible, the responsibility of his agents, and the efficient checks interposed by the British Constitution, render it less dangerous than other Monarchies, or oppressive tyrannical Aristrocracies. What are their checks of exposing accounts?—Their checks upon paper are inefficient and nugatory.—Can you search your President's closet? Is this a real check? We ought to be exceeding cautious, in giving up this life—this soul—of money—this power of taxation to Congress. What powerful check is there here to prevent the most extravagant and profligate squandering of the public money? What security have we in money matters? Enquiry is precluded by this Constitution. I never wish to see Congress supplicate the States. But it is more abhorent to my mind to give them an unlimited and unbounded command over our souls—our lives—our purses, without any check or restraint. How are you to keep enquiry alive? How discover their conduct? We are told by that paper, that a regular statement and account of the receipts and expenditures of all public money, shall be published from time to time. Here is a beautiful check! What time? Here is the utmost latitude left. If those who are in Congress please to put that construction upon it, the words of the Constitution will be satisfied by publishing those accounts once in 100 years. They may publish or not as they please. Is this like the present despised system, whereby the accounts are to be published monthly?[33]

I come now to speak something of requisitions, which the Honorable Gentleman thought so truly contemptible and disgraceful.[34] That Honorable Gentleman being a child of the revolution, must recollect with gratitude the glorious effects of requisitions. It is an idea that must be grateful to every American. An English army was sent to compel us to pay money contrary to our consent. To force us by arbitrary and tyrannical coercion to satisfy their unbounded demands. We wished to pay with our own consent.—Rather than pay against our consent, we engaged in that bloody contest, which terminated so gloriously. By requisitions we pay with our own consent; by their means we have triumphed in the most arduous struggle, that ever tried the virtue of man. We fought then, for what we are contending now: To prevent an arbitrary deprivation of our property, contrary to our consent and inclination.

{[7 June 1788] I never will give up that *darling* word requisitions—My country may give it up—A majority may wrest it from me, but I will never give it up till my grave. Requisitions are attended with one singular advantage. They are attended by deliberation.—They secure to the States the benefit of correcting oppressive errors.[35] If our Assembly thought requisitions erroneous—If they thought the demand was too great, they might at least supplicate Congress to reconsider,—that it was a little too much. The power of direct taxation was called by the Honorable Gentlemen the soul of the Government:[36] Another Gentleman, called it the lungs of the Government.[37] We all agree, that it is the most important part of the body politic. If the power of raising money be necessary for the General Government, it is no less so for the States. If money be the vitals of Congress, is it not precious for those individuals from whom it is to be taken? Must I give my soul—my lungs, to Congress? Congress must have our souls. The State must have our souls. This is dishonorable and disgraceful. These two co-ordinate, interferring unlimited powers of harrassing the community, is un-exampled: It is unprecedented in history: They are the visionary projects of modern politicians: Tell me not of imaginary means, but of reality; This political solecism will never tend to the benefit of the community. It will be as oppressive in practice as it is absurd in theory. If you part with this which the Honorable Gentleman tells you is the soul of Congress, you will be inevitably ruined. I tell you, they shall not have the soul of Virginia. They tell us, that one collector may collect the Federal and State taxes. The General Government being paramount to the State Legislatures; if the Sheriff is to collect for both; his right hand for the Congress, his left for the State; his right hand being paramount over the left, his collections will go to Congress. We will have the rest. Defficiencies in collections will always operate against the States. Congress being the paramount supreme power,

5.16.15

5.16.16

must not be disappointed. Thus Congress will have an unlimited, un-bounded command over the soul of this Commonwealth. After satisfying their uncontrouled demands, what can be left for the States? Not a suffi-ciency even to defray the expence of their internal administration. They must therefore glide imperceptibly and gradually out of existence. This, Sir, must naturally terminate in a consolidation. If this will do for other people, it never will do for me.}

5.16.17   . . . I shall be told in this place, that those who are to tax us are our Representatives. To this I answer, that there is no real check to prevent their ruining us. There is no actual responsibility. The only semblance of a check is the negative power of not re-electing them. This, Sir, is but a feeble barrier when their personal interest, their ambition and avarice come to be put in contrast with the happiness of the people. All checks founded on any thing but self-love, will not avail. This constitution reflects in the most degrading and mortifying manner on the virtue, integrity, and wisdom of the State Legislatures: It presupposes that the chosen few who go to Congress will have more upright hearts, and more enlightened minds, than those who are members of the individual Legislatures. To suppose that ten Gentlemen shall have more real substantial merit, than 170 is humiliating to the last degree.[38] If, Sir, the diminution of numbers be an augmentation of merit, perfection must centre in one. If you have the faculty of discerning spirits, it is better to point out at once the man who has the most illumined qualities. If 10 men be better than 170, it follows of necessity, that one is better than 10—The choice is more refined. . . .

5.16.18   Congress by the power of taxation—by that of raising an army, and by their controul over the militia, have the sword in one hand, and the purse in the other. Shall we be safe without either? Congress have an unlimited power over both: They are entirely given up by us. Let him candidly tell me, where and when did freedom exist, when the sword and purse were given up from the people? Unless a miracle in human affairs interposed, no nation ever retained its liberty after the loss of the sword and purse. Can you prove by any argumentative deduction, that it is possible to be safe without re-taining one of these? If you give them up you are gone.

5.16.19   {[14 June] The means, says the Gentleman, must be commensurate to the end. How does this apply?[39]—All things in common are left with this Gov-ernment. There being an infinitude in the Government, there must be an infinitude of means to carry it on. This is a sort of mathematical Government that may appear well on paper, but cannot sustain examination, or be safely reduced to practice. The delegation of power to an adequate number of Representatives; and an unimpeded reversion of it back to the people at short periods, form the principal traits of a Republican Government. The idea of a Republican Government in that paper, is something superior to the poor people. The governing persons are the servants of the people. There the servants are greater than their masters; because it includes infinitude, and infinitude excludes every idea of subordination. In this the creature has destroyed, and soared above the creator. For if its powers be infinite, what rights have the people remaining? By that very argument despotism has made way in all countries, where the people unfortunately have been enslaved by it. We are told the sword and purse are necessary for the national defence. The junction of these without limitation in the same hands, is, by logical and mathematical conclusions, the description of despotism.}

. . . Give us at least a plausible apology why Congress should keep their proceedings in secret. They have the power of keeping them secret as long as they please; for the provision for a periodical publication is too inexplicit and ambiguous to avail any thing. The expression *from time to time* as I have more than once observed, admits of any extension. They may carry on the most wicked and pernicious of schemes, under the dark veil of secrecy. The liberties of a people never were nor ever will be secure, when the transactions of their rulers may be concealed from them. The most iniquitous plots may be carried on against their liberty and happiness. I am not an advocate for divulging indiscriminately all the operations of Government, though the practice of our ancestors in some degree justifies it. Such transactions as relate to military operations, or affairs of great consequence, the immediate promulgation of which might defeat the interests of the community, I would not wish to be published, till the end which required their secrecy should have been effected. But to cover with the veil of secrecy, the common rotine of business, is an abomination in the eyes of every intelligent man, and every friend to his country.

[Mr. *Henry* then, in a very animated manner, expatiated on the evil and pernicious tendency of keeping secret the common proceedings of Government; and said that it was contrary to the practice of other free nations. The people of England, he asserted, had gained immortal honor by the manly boldness wherewith they divulged to all the world, their political disquisitions and operations; and that such a conduct inspired other nations with respect. He illustrated his argument by several quotations.]—He then continued,—I appeal to this Convention if it would not be better for America to take off the veil of secrecy. *Look at us—hear our transactions.* If this had been the language of the Federal Convention, what would have been the result? Such a Constitution would not have come out to your utter astonishment, conceding such dangerous powers, and recommending secrecy in the future transactions of Government. I believe it would have given more general satisfaction, if the proceedings of that Convention had not been concealed from the public eye. This Constitution authorizes the same conduct. There is not an English feature in it. The transactions of Congress may be concealed a century from the public, consistently with the Constitution. This, Sir, is a laudable imitation of the transactions of the Spanish treaty. We have not forgotten with what a thick veil of secrecy those transactions were covered.

5.16.20

5.16.21

5.16.22   We are told that this Government collectively taken, is without an example—That it is national in this part, and federal in that part, &c.[40] We may be amused if we please, by a treatise of political anatomy. In the brain it is national: The stamina are federal—some limbs are federal—others national. The Senators are voted for by the State Legislatures, so far it is federal.—Individuals choose the members of the first branch; here it is national. It is federal in conferring general powers; but national in retaining them. It is not to be supported by the States—The pockets of individuals are to be searched for its maintenance. What signifies it to me, that you have the most curious anatomical description of it in its creation? To all the common purposes of Legislation it is a great consolidation of Government. You are not to have a right to legislate in any but trivial cases: You are not to touch private contracts: You are not to have the right of having arms in your own defence: You cannot be trusted with dealing out justice between man and man. What shall the States have to do? Take care of the poor—repair and make high-ways—erect bridges, and so on, and so on. Abolish the State Legislatures at once. What purposes should they be continued for? Our Legislature will indeed be a ludicrous spectacle—180 men marching in solemn farcical procession, exhibiting a mournful proof of the lost liberty of their country—without the power of restoring it. But, Sir, we have the consolation that it is a mixed Government: That is, it may work sorely on your neck; but you will have some comfort by saying, that it was a Federal Government in its origin.

5.16.23   I beg Gentlemen to consider—lay aside your prejudices—Is this a Federal Government? Is it not a Consolidated Government for every purpose almost? Is the Government of Virginia a State Government after this Government is adopted? I grant that it is a Republican Government—but for what purposes? For such trivial domestic considerations, as render it unworthy the name of a Legislature. I shall take leave of this political anatomy, by observing that it is the most extraordinary that ever entered into the imagination of man. If our political diseases demand a cure—this is an unheard of medicine. The Honorable member, I am convinced, wanted a name for it.[41] Were your health in danger, would you take new medicine? I need not make use of these exclamations; for every member in this Committee must be alarmed at making new and unusual experiments in Government. Let us have national credit and a national treasury in case of war. You never can want national resources in time of war; if the war be a national one; if it be necessary, and this necessity obvious to the meanest capacity. The utmost exertions will be used by the people of America in that case. A republic has this advantage over a monarchy, that its wars are generally founded on more just grounds. A republic can never enter into a war, unless it be a national war—unless it be approved of, or desired by the whole community. Did ever a republic fail to use the utmost resources of the community when a war was necessary? I call for an example. I call also for an example, when a republic has been engaged in a war contrary to the wishes of its people. There are thousands of examples, where the ambition of its Prince precipitated a nation into the most destructive war. No nation ever withheld power when its object was just and right. I will hazard an observation; I find fault with the paper before you, because the same power that declares war, has the power to carry it on. Is it so in England? The King declares war: The House of Commons gives the means of carrying it on. This is a strong check on the King. He will enter into no war that is unnecessary; for the Commons having the power of withholding the means, will exercise that power, unless the object of the war be for the interest of the nation. How is it here? The Congress can both declare war, and carry it on; and levy your money, as long as you have a shilling to pay. . . .

1. Cf. *The Federalist* no. 15, 92–98; Pennsylvania Convention Minority 3.11.30 n. 15.

2. See 5.16.1. On consolidation see Plebeian 6.11.15 n. 9.

3. See 5.16.2. Cf. Brutus VII, 2.9.86.

4. See Lowndes 5.12.1–2 and n. 7.

5. James Madison replied that "on a candid examination of history, we shall find that turbulence, violence, and abuse of power, by the majority trampling on the rights of the minority, have produced factions and commotions, which, in republics, have, more frequently than any other cause, produced despotism." The United States is not immune from this danger, which must be guarded against. "Perhaps, in the progress of this discussion, it will appear that the only possible remedy for those evils, and means of preserving and protecting the principles of republicanism will be found in that very system which is now exclaimed against as the parent of oppression." Elliot III, 87–88. See *The Federalist* no. 10 and Madison's speeches in the Constitutional Convention on 6 June and 26 June. Farrand I, 134–36, 421–23. See references in Brutus IV, 2.9.45 n.31

6. Cf. George Mason's speech on the Executive in the Constitutional Convention, Farrand I, 101–2, 110–14 (4 June); Brutus VII, 2.9.86 and n.58.

7. Thorpe, *Federal and State Constitutions* VII, 3813.

8. Edmund Pendleton, Elliot III, 37. Mr. Pendleton was elected president of the convention, but most of the debate took place in the committee of the whole, with George Wyth in the chair.

9. Elliot III, 37.

10. Elliot regards this sentence as an interpolation of the compiler of the debates; but there is no such indication in the original edition. It is more likely that Henry is referring to a part of Pendleton's discussion that was only partly reported. Elliot III, 53, 38–39.

11. Edmund Randolph replied: "But it is insinuated by the honorable gentleman, that we want to be a grand, splendid, and magnificent people: we wish not to become so: the magnificence of a royal court is not our object. We want a government, sir—a government that will have stability, and give us security; for our present government is destitute of the one and incapable of producing the other. It cannot, perhaps, with propriety, be denominated a government, being void of that energy requisite to enforce sanctions. I wish my country not to be contemptible in the eyes of foreign nations. A well-regulated community is always respected. It is the internal situation,

the defects of government, that attract foreign contempt; that contempt, sir, is too often followed by subjugation." Elliot III, 81. Not all of the Federalists were so modest, and Henry was right in thinking that some friends of the Constitution had visions of glory. See McMaster and Stone 127–29 (A Pennsylvania Farmer); Northampton, Massachusetts *Hampshire Gazette* 17 October 1787 (Anon. "Observe . . ."); *Virginia Independent Chronicle* 28 November 1787 ("Extract of a letter from a well informed correspondent . . ."); New Hampshire *Freeman's Oracle* 6 June 1788 (A Patriotic Citizen); Herbert J. Storing, "The 'Other' Federalist Papers: A Preliminary Sketch," *Political Science Reviewer* VI (1976), 215–47.

12. Elliot III, 65–66. For Anti-Federalist views of the circumstances of the United States see Federal Farmer I, 2.8.1 n. 4; Plebeian 6.11.5 n. 6.

13. Randolph charged that the Virginia legislature had frequently violated the constitution, giving as an example the following: "A man, who was then a citizen, was deprived of his life thus: from a mere reliance on general reports, a gentleman in the House of Delegates informed the house, that a certain man (Josiah Philips) had committed several crimes, and was running at large, perpetrating other crimes. He therefore moved for leave to attaint him; he obtained that leave instantly; no sooner did he obtain it, than he drew from his pocket a bill ready written for that effect; it was read three times in one day, and carried to the Senate. I will not say that it passed the same day through the Senate; but he was attainted very speedily and precipitately, without any proof better than vague reports. Without being confronted with his accusers and witnesses, without the privilege of calling for evidence in his behalf, he was sentenced to death, and was afterwards actually executed." Elliot III, 66–67. Henry's reply here left him open to severe criticism, which was administered by John Marshall. Elliot III, 223. It appears, however, that Henry's conduct was open to a better defense than he provided himself. See Wirt, *Sketches of Patrick Henry* 234–41; and the full discussion by William W. Crosskey, *Politics and the Constitution* II, 944 ff. Philips was executed not under the attainder but on trial for highway robbery—the indictment having been brought by the attorney general, Edmund Randolph.

14. Elliot III, 66–67.

15. Thorpe, *Federal and State Constitutions* VII, 3813.

16. Ibid.

17. Ibid.

18. Cf. below Mason (Virginia) 5.17.1; Smith 6.12.2. The Federalist contention was that rejection of the Constitution meant destruction of the Union. See, for example, Ford, *Pamphlets* 46 (A Citizen of America), 122 (A Citizen of Philadelphia); McMaster and Stone 386 (Wilson). On claims that the Anti-Federalists preferred separate confederacies, see below, n. 25; Centinel XI, 2.7.142 n. 75; Henry 5.16.11 n.25. It was a concern for Union that finally reconciled many Anti-Federalists to the Constitution. See, for example, Randolph 2.5, Turner 4.18.

19. The reference is probably to Pendleton, Elliot III, 39. Elliot, incidentally, changes Henry's remarks here to "a judiciary which will correct all . . ."

20. The original text does not begin a new paragraph at this point.

21. See Federal Farmer X, 2.8.110 n. 72. On responsibility see Centinel I, 2.7.7 n. 4.

22. Randolph used this term, but upon being criticized by Henry, he explained (according to the reporter) "that he did not use that word to excite any odium, but merely to convey an idea of a multitude." Elliot III, 148.

23. To this argument John Marshall replied: "That economy and industry are essential to our happiness, will be denied by no man. But the present government will not add to our industry. It takes away the incitements to industry, by rendering property insecure and unprotected. It is the paper on your table that will promote and encourage industry." Elliot III, 231. See Candidus 4.9.18 and n. 6.

24. Randolph, Elliot III, 79.

25. Ibid. 79–80; see Randolph 2.5.26 Henry was thought by some Federalists to favor separate confederacies. See *Virginia Independent Chronicle*, 6 February 1788

(An Old State Soldier) 9 April 1788 (A Freeholder); C. Griffin to Thomas Fitzsimons, 15 February 1788, Bancroft, *History of the Formation of the Constitution* II, 461; Edward Carrington to Thomas Jefferson, 24 April 1788, *Proceedings of the Massachusetts Historical Society*, 2d ser. 17 (1903): 497; James McClurg to James Madison, 5 August 1787, ibid. 471. See Centinel XI, 2.7.142 n. 75; James Madison to Thomas Jefferson, 6 June 1787, *Documentary History of the Constitution* IV, 184. On the general question of separate confederacies, see above, vol. 1, ch. 4 n. 2.

26. See Mason on the small republic, (5.17.1) and Randolph's reply, Elliot III, 84–85.

27. Above, 5.16.10.

28. Elliot III, 104–6.

29. Randolph, Elliot III, 84–85; cf. Corbin, ibid. 107; see references in Agrippa IV, 4.6.16 n. 10.

30. For other expressions of this theme see Federal Farmer IV, 2.8.58 n. 44.

31. Montesquieu, *Considerations on the Greatness of the Romans and Their Decline* XI.

32. For other comparisons of the British king and the proposed presidency, see Philadelphiensis XII, 3.9.96 n. 37.

33. Articles of Confederation, Art. 9, para. 7: "The Congress of the United States . . . shall publish the journal of their proceedings monthly, except such parts thereof, relating to treaties, alliances or military operations, as in their judgment, require secrecy . . ." See 5.16.20.

34. Randolph, Elliot III, 114–20.

35. Cf. Alexander Hamilton's remarks to the same effect: Farrand I, 286 (18 June); *The Federalist* no. 15, 93, 97–98; Elliot II, 231. Cf. Brutus X, 2.9.128 and n. 84.

36. Randolph: "Money is the nerve—the life and soul of a government." Elliot III 115. Cf. *The Federalist* no. 30, p. 188: "Money is, with propriety, considered as the vital principle of the body politic; as that which sustains its life and motion and enables it to perform its most essential functions."

37. Corbin, Elliot III, 110.

38. See Corbin, Elliot III, 107–8; Randolph, ibid. 125–26.

39. Regarding military and taxing powers, Madison argued: "The means ought to be commensurate to the end. The end is general protection. This cannot be effected without a general power to use the strength of the Union." Elliot III, 394. Cf. Madison at ibid. 96 (". . . no government can exist unless its powers extend to make provisions for every contingency") and *The Federalist* nos. 23, 31. See Brutus VII, 2.9.88–90.

40. Madison: "In order to judge properly of the question before us, we must consider it minutely in its principal parts. I conceive myself that it is of a mixed nature; it is in a manner unprecedented; we cannot find one express example in the experience of the world. It stands by itself. In some respects it is a government of a federal nature; in others, it is of a consolidated nature. Even if we attend to the manner in which the Constitution is investigated, ratified, and made the act of the people of America, I can say, notwithstanding what the honorable gentleman has alleged, that this government is not completely consolidated, nor is it entirely federal." Elliot III, 94. Cf. *The Federalist* no. 39, 253–57.

41. Madison did not give it a name. Corbin suggested "a representative federal republic, as contradistinguished from a confederacy." Elliot III, 107. On the question of names see above Martin 2.4.43 n. 12. Federal Farmer I, 2.8.10 n. 9.

New York: Introduction

Two weeks after Virginia began her deliberations, the New York delegates convened in Poughkeepsie. As in Pennsylvania, but in sharp contrast to Virginia, two opposing parties existed whose prior differences carried over to the question of ratification. The New York Federalists were the party of the commercial and professional classes of New York City, allied through background, interest and marriage with the large landholders of upper New York State. The Clintonian party, forerunner of the Anti-Federalists, drew its leadership from the radical Whigs and was solidly based on the small farmers.[1]

Always fearful of any relinquishment of state authority, Governor Clinton acquiesced to the growing pressure for a constitutional convention. However the Clintonians showed greater political understanding than the Pennsylvania Constitutionalists and deliberately sent two opponents of greater central powers, John Lansing, Jr., and Robert Yates, to bracket Alexander Hamilton, who was warmly supported by the many Federalists in the Senate and was known for his advocacy of a stronger central government. With the publication of the proposed Constitution, the Anti-Federalists produced a stream of criticism. An Albany Anti-Federalist Committee circulated an address of its own as well as Mercy Warren's Columbian Patriot. General John Lamb, the customs inspector of the port of New York, headed an Anti-Federal group which called itself the Federal Republicans and attempted, unsuccessfully, to concert the plans of Anti-Federalists throughout the country, incidentally providing historians with valuable materials on the ratifying controversy.[2]

The Clinton strategy during the ratification debate remains obscure, and it is difficult to avoid the conclusion that Clinton's normally sure hand in local affairs deserted him on this broader scene. The New York Legislature, in the control of the Clintonians, issued a call for a ratifying convention to be elected by universal manhood suffrage to meet on 17 June, rejecting a proposed preamble to the effect that the Constitutional Convention had exceeded its powers. The Anti-Federalists secured an overwhelming success, electing 46 delegates to the Federalists' 19. Had Clinton arranged to hold the Convention early in the year, a rejection by New York would have been likely, with its inevitable effect on the other states. Clinton appears not to have felt certain that he could carry his party for rejection, if that was indeed what he wanted.[3] He chose to delay. By mid-June, however, eight states had ratified, and mid-way in New York's deliberations New Hampshire and Virginia joined them. New York's unpopular economic policies might now bring retaliation backed by a strong union. There were rumors of secession by the southern counties if the state rejected the Constitution. Many Clintonians, including Melancton Smith, the dominant Anti-Federalist figure in the debate, were anxious to find grounds of agreement. Various compromises were suggested, and unconditional ratification together with explanatory provisions and recommendatory amendments was finally agreed to by the narrow margin of 30 to 25.[4] Accompanying the ratification was a circular letter from Clinton to the other governors urging a second convention to draft amendments to the Constitution.

1. On background and ratification in New York see Spaulding, *New York in the Critical Period;* Thomas Childs Cochran, *New York in the Confederation: An Economic Study* (Philadelphia 1932); Clarence Miner, *The Ratification of the Federal Constitution by the State of New York* (New York 1921); and especially DePauw, *The Eleventh Pillar.*

2. For a discussion of the activities of the Federal Republicans see Isaac Q. Leake, *Memoir of the Life and Times of General John Lamb* ch. 23, and DePauw, *The Eleventh Pillar.*

3. Edward Carrington wrote to Jefferson on 23 October 1787 that "the Governor holds himself in perfect silence, wishing, it is suspected, for a miscarriage, but is not confident enough to commit himself to an open opposition." Curtis, *Documentary History* IV, 345.

4. See DePauw, *The Eleventh Pillar* chs. 18, 19, who regards the ratification as in substance conditional.

Speeches by
Melancton Smith

Delivered in the Course of Debate
by the Convention of the State of New York
on the Adoption of the Federal Constitution

June 1788

The debates of the New York ratifying convention rival those in Virginia for the excellence of their discussion of the Constitution. Perhaps the questions were publicly *debated* more fully here than anywhere else, and in none of the conventions is the essential question of representation so thoroughly discussed on both sides. On the Federalist side the main argument was carried, easily and brilliantly, by Alexander Hamilton. He was met by the solid, often deep, and scarcely less able objections of Melancton Smith. A prominent businessman of New York City and Poughkeepsie, Smith had served in the first Provincial Congress of New York, in the Continental Congress, and as sheriff of Dutchess County.[1]

The five speeches of Smith printed here fall into three parts: the constitution of the House of Representatives, the constitution of the Senate, and the congressional power to tax. The speeches were given on 20, 21, 23, 25 and 27 June, and are taken here from the original 1788 publication.[2]

Smith begins with a series of general introductory remarks, including an affirmation of attachment to both Union and liberty (6.12.1–2), an acknowledgment of the defects of the Articles of Confederation (6.12.3–4), a re-emphasis of his opponent's admission that the new Constitution was a radical change in the Articles (6.12.5–6), and a warning against innovations, especially in a government resting on the opinion of the people (6.12.7). He then proceeds to his objections to the constitution of the House of Representatives, especially that the representation is too small. This leads Smith into a discussion of the origin and true principles of representation, which is one of the major Anti-Federalist statements on this subject (see esp. 6.12.8–25). It is interesting and important to compare Smith's theoretical aim (a representative body that "resembles" the body of the people) and his practical aim (a representative body that will include a due proportion of the middling classes, along with the natural aristocracy, which will inevitably make up a large part of the representation). Like Lee, Smith is concerned that the spirit of liberty, on which the Federalists profess to rely, should be supported and maintained by congenial laws. And, like Lee, Smith concedes that an adequate representation is not possible in any government for the whole United States and that therefore, while the representation must be improved, the powers of the federal government must be carefully limited and checked.

In his discussion of the Senate, Smith admits the need for such a body to stabilize the government; but he insists that a system of rotation and recall is both feasible and consistent with republican principles and that the Federalists exaggerate the danger of state influence (6.12.27–32). It is interesting, in view of the previous argument on representation, that here Smith relies on the argument that the state legislatures are not mere reflectors of the whims of the people but "select bodies" (6.12.30).

The last speech (6.12.36–40) contains Smith's major argument regarding the unlimited power of federal taxation. Here Smith is supporting a limitation on the federal taxing power, without which he believes that the states will ultimately be destroyed as significant parts of the system. Against the Hamiltonian argument that the means must be proportionate to the end and that the end of the federal government is unlimitable, Smith attempts to set the substantial accomplishments of the state and federal governments under the Confederation and the imprudence of radical change.

1. There is no biography of Smith. See Julian P. Boyd, "Melancton Smith," *Dictionary of American Biography* XVII, 319–20. Smith is traditionally identified as the author of the Plebeian essays, see 6.11.

2. *The Debates and Proceedings of the Convention of the State of New York,* Assembled at Poughkeepsie, on the 17th June 1788 (New York: Francis Childs, 1788). Footnote references to these debates are made, as usual, to the more accessible Elliot.

[*The debate having been opened by Chancellor Robert R. Livingston and John Lansing, on the 19th and 20th of June 1788, the Convention turned, at Melancton Smith's suggestion, to a paragraph-by-paragraph consideration of the proposed Constitution. Article I, section 1, was read and passed by without discussion. Section 2, providing for the constitution of the House of Representatives, was discussed at length. The discussion consisted largely in a debate between Smith and Alexander Hamilton, a debate which is one of the high points of the controversy over the Constitution.*]

20 June 1788

6.12.1   Mr. *Smith* again rose—He most heartily concurred in sentiment with the honorable gentleman who opened the debate yesterday, that the discussion of the important question now before them ought to be entered on with a spirit of patriotism; with minds open to conviction; with a determination to form opinions only on the merits of the question, from those evidences which should appear in the course of the investigation.

How far the general observations made by the honorable gentleman accorded with these principles, he left to the House to determine.

It was not, he said, his intention to follow that gentleman through all his remarks—he should only observe, that what had been advanced did not appear to him to apply to the subject under consideration.

He was as strongly impressed with the necessity of a Union, as any one could be: He would seek it with as much ardor. In the discussion of this subject, he was disposed to make every reasonable concession, and indeed to sacrifice every thing for a Union, except the liberties of his country, than which he could contemplate no greater misfortune.[1] But he hoped we were not reduced to the necessity of sacrificing or even endangering our liberties to preserve the Union. If that was the case, the alternative was dreadful. But he would not now say that the adoption of the Constitution would endanger our liberties; because that was the point to be debated, and the premises should be laid down previously to the drawing of any conclusion. He wished that all observations might be confined to this point; and that declamation and appeals to the passions might be omitted.

6.12.2

Why, said he, are we told of our weaknesses?[2] Of the defenceless condition of the southern parts of our state? Of the exposed situation of our capital? Of Long-Island surrounded by water, and exposed to the incursions of our neighbours in Connecticut? Of Vermont having separated from us and assumed the powers of a distinct government; And of the North-West part of our state being in the hands of a foreign enemy?—Why are we to be alarmed with apprehensions that the Eastern states are inimical, and disinclined to form alliances with us? He was sorry to find that such suspicions were entertained. He believed that no such disposition existed in the Eastern states. Surely it could not be supposed that those states would make war upon us for exercising the rights of freemen, deliberating and judging for ourselves, on a subject the most interesting that ever came before any assembly. If a war with our neighbour was to be the result of not acceding, there was no use in debating here; we had better receive their dictates, if we were unable to resist them. The defects of the Old Confederation needed as little proof as the necessity of an Union: But there was no proof in all this, that the proposed Constitution was a good one. Defective as the Old Confederation is, he said, no one could deny but it was possible we might have a worse government. But the question was not whether the present Confederation be a bad one; but whether the proposed Constitution be a good one.[3]

6.12.3

It had been observed, that no examples of Federal Republics had succeeded.[4] It was true that the ancient confederated Republics were all destroyed—so were those which were not confederated; and all antient

6.12.4

Governments of every form had shared the same fate. Holland had undoubtedly experienced many evils from the defects in her government; but
with all these defects, she yet existed; she had under her Confederacy made
a principal figure among the nations of Europe, and he believed few countries had experienced a greater share of internal peace and prosperity. The
Germanic Confederacy was not the most pertinent example to produce on
this occasion:—Among a number of absolute Princes who consider their
subjects as their property, whose will is law, and to whose ambition there
are no bounds, it was no difficult task to discover other causes from which
the convulsions in that country rose, than the defects of their Confederation. Whether a Confederacy of States under any form be a practicable
Government, was a question to be discussed in the course of investigating
this Constitution.

6.12.5 He was pleased that thus early in the debate, the honorable gentleman had
himself shewn, that the intent of the Constitution was not a Confederacy,
but a reduction of all the states into a consolidated government.[5] He hoped
the gentleman would be complaisant enough to exchange names with those
who disliked the Constitution, as it appeared from his own concession that
they were Federalists, and those who advocated it Anti-Federalists.[6] He
begged leave, however, to remind the gentleman, that Montesquieu, with all
the examples of modern and antient Republics in view, gives it as his opinion, that a confederated Republic has all the internal advantages of a Republic, with the external force of a Monarchical Government.[7] He was
happy to find an officer of such high rank recommending to the other officers
of Government, and to those who are members of the Legislature, to be
unbiassed by any motives of interest or state importance.[8] Fortunately for
himself, he was out of the verge of temptations of this kind, not having the
honor to hold any office under the state. But then he was exposed, in
common with other gentlemen of the Convention, to another temptation,
against which he thought it necessary that we should be equally guarded:—If, said he, this constitution is adopted, there will be a number of
honorable and lucrative offices to be filled, and we ought to be cautious lest
an expectancy of some of them should influence us to adopt without due
consideration.

6.12.6 We may wander, said he, in the fields of fancy without end, and gather
flowers as we go: It may be entertaining—but it is of little service to the
discovery of truth:—We may on one side compare the scheme advocated by
our opponents to *golden images, with feet part of iron and part of clay;* and
on the other, *to a beast dreadful and terrible, and strong exceedingly,
having great iron teeth, which devours, breaks in pieces, and stamps the
residue with his feet:* And after all, said he, we shall find that both these
allusions are taken from the same *vision;* and their true meaning must be
discovered by sober reasoning.

6.12.7 He would agree with the honorable gentleman, that perfection in any system of government was not to be looked for. If that was the object, the debates on the one before them might soon be closed.—But he would observe that this observation applied with equal force against changing any systems—especially against material and radical changes.—Fickleness and inconstancy, he said, was characteristic of a free people; and in framing a Constitution for them, it was, perhaps the most difficult thing to correct this spirit, and guard against the evil effects of it—he was persuaded it could not be altogether prevented without destroying their freedom—it would be like attempting to correct a small indisposition in the habit of the body, by fixing the patient in a confirmed consumption.—This fickle and inconstant spirit was the more dangerous in bringing about changes in the government.[9] The instance that had been adduced by the gentleman from sacred history, was an example in point to prove this: The nation of Israel having received a form of civil government from Heaven, enjoyed it for a considerable period; but at length labouring under pressures, which were brought upon them by their own misconduct and imprudence, instead of imputing their misfortunes to their true causes, and making a proper improvement of their calamities, by a correction of their errors, they imputed them to a defect in their constitution; they rejected their Divine Ruler, and asked Samuel to make them a King to judge them, like other nations. Samuel was grieved at their folly; but still, by the command of God, he hearkened to their voice; tho' not until he had solemnly declared unto them the manner in which the King should reign over them. "This, (says Samuel) shall be the manner of the King that shall reign over you. He will take your sons and appoint them for himself, for his chariots, and for his horsemen, and some shall run before his chariots; and he will appoint him captains over thousands, and captains over fifties, and will set them to ear his ground, and to reap his harvest, and to make his instruments of war, and instruments of his chariots. And he will take your daughters to be confectionaries, and to be cooks, and to be bakers. And he will take your fields, and your vine yards, and your olive yards, even the best of them, and give them to his servants. And he will take the tenth of your seed, and of your vineyards, and give to his officers and to his servants. And he will take your men servants and your maid servants, and your goodliest young men, and your asses, and put them to his work. He will take the tenth of your sheep: And ye shall be his servants. And ye shall cry out in that day, because of your King which ye have chosen you; and the Lord will not hear you in that day."[10]—How far this was applicable to the subject he would not now say; it could be better judged of when they had gone through it.—On the whole he wished to take up this matter with candor and deliberation.

He would now proceed to state his objections to the clause just read, (section 2 of article I, clause 3.) His objections were comprised under three heads: 1st the rule of apportionment is unjust; 2d. there is no precise number fixed on below which the house shall not be reduced; 3d. it is inadequate. In

6.12.8

the first place the rule of apportionment of the representatives is to be
according to the whole number of the white inhabitants, with three fifths of
all others; that is in plain English, each state is to send Representatives in
proportion to the number of freemen, and three fifths of the slaves it contains. He could not see any rule by which slaves are to be included in the
ratio of representation: The principle of a representation, being that every
free agent should be concerned in governing himself, it was absurd to give
that power to a man who could not exercise it—slaves have no will of their
own: The very operation of it was to give certain privileges to those people
who were so wicked as to keep slaves. He knew it would be admitted that
this rule of apportionment was founded on unjust principles, but that it was
the result of accommodation; which he supposed we should be under the
necessity of admitting, if we meant to be in union with the Southern States,
though utterly repugnant to his feelings. In the second place, the number
was not fixed by the Constitution, but left at the discretion of the Legislature; perhaps he was mistaken; it was his wish to be informed. He understood from the Constitution, that sixty-five Members were to compose the
House of Representatives for three years; that after that time a census was
to be taken, and the numbers to be ascertained by the Legislature on the
following principles: 1st, they shall be apportioned to the respective States
according to numbers; 2d, each State shall have one at least; 3d, they shall
never exceed one to every thirty thousand. If this was the case, the first
Congress that met might reduce the number below what it now is; a power
inconsistent with every principle of a free government, to leave it to the
discretion of the rulers to determine the number of the representatives of the
people. There was no kind of security except in the integrity of the men who
were entrusted; and if you have no other security, it is idle to contend about
Constitutions. In the third place, supposing Congress should declare that
there should be one representative for every thirty thousand of the people,
in his opinion it would be incompetent to the great purposes of representation. It was, he said, the fundamental principle of a free government, that
the people should make the laws by which they were to be governed: He
who is controlled by another is a slave; and that government which is
directed by the will of any one or a few, or any number less than is the will of
the community, is a government for slaves.

6.12.9   The next point was, how was the will of the community to be expressed?
It was not possible for them to come together; the multitude would be too
great: In order, therefore to provide against this inconvenience, the scheme
of representation had been adopted, by which the people deputed others to
represent them. Individuals entering into society became one body, and that
body ought to be animated by one mind; and he conceived that every form
of government should have that complexion. It was true that notwithstanding all the experience we had from others, it had not appeared that the
experiment of representation had been fairly tried: there was something like

it in the ancient republics, in which, being of small extent, the people could easily meet together, though instead of deliberating, they only considered of those things which were submitted to them by their magistrates. In Great Britain representation had been carried much farther than in any government we knew of, except our own; but in that country it now had only a name. America was the only country, in which the first fair opportunity had been offered. When we were Colonies, our representation was better than any that was then known: Since the revolution we had advanced still nearer to perfection. He considered it as an object, of all others the most important, to have it fixed on its true principle; yet he was convinced that it was impracticable to have such a representation in a consolidated government. However, said he, we may approach a great way towards perfection by encreasing the representation and limiting the powers of Congress.[11] He considered that the great interests and liberties of the people could only be secured by the State Governments. He admitted, that if the new government was only confined to great national objects, it would be less exceptionable; but it extended to every thing dear to human nature. That this was the case could be proved without any long chain of reasoning:—for that power which had both the purse and the sword, had the government of the whole country, and might extend its powers to any and to every object. He had already observed, that by the true doctrine of representation, this principle was established—that the representative must be chosen by the free will of the majority of his constituents: It therefore followed that the representative should be chosen from small districts. This being admitted, he would ask, could 65 men, for 3,000,000, or 1 for 30,000, be chosen in this manner? Would they be possessed of the requisite information to make happy the great number of souls that were spread over this extensive country?—There was another objection to the clause: If great affairs of government were trusted to a few men, they would be more liable to corruption. Corruption, he knew, was unfashionable amongst us, but he supposed that Americans were like other men; and tho' they had hitherto displayed great virtues, still they were men; and therefore such steps should be taken as to prevent the possibility of corruption. We were now in that stage of society, in which we could deliberate with freedom;—how long it might continue, God only knew! Twenty years hence, perhaps, these maxims might become unfashionable; we already hear, said he, in all parts of the country, gentlemen ridiculing that spirit of patriotism and love of liberty, which carried us through all our difficulties in times of danger.—When patriotism was already nearly hooted out of society, ought we not to take some precautions against the progress of corruption?[12]

He had one more observation to make, to shew that the representation was insufficient—Government, he said, must rest for its execution, on the good opinion of the people, for if it was made in heaven, and had not the confidence of the people, it could not be executed:[13] that this was proved,

6.12.10

by the example given by the gentleman, of the Jewish theocracy. It must have a good setting out, or the instant it takes place there is an end of liberty. He believed that the inefficacy of the old Confederation, had arisen from that want of confidence; and this caused in a great degree by the continual declamation of gentlemen of importance against it from one end of the continent to the other, who had frequently compared it to a rope of sand. It had pervaded every class of citizens, and their misfortunes, the consequences of idleness and extravagance, were attributed to the defects of that system. At the close of the war, our country had been left in distress; and it was impossible that any government on earth could immediately retrieve it; it must be time and industry alone that could effect it. He said he would pursue these observations no further at present,—And concluded with making the following motion:

"*Resolved*, That it is proper that the number of representatives be fixed at the rate of one for every twenty thousand inhabitants, to be ascertained on the principles mentioned in the second section of the first article of the Constitution, until they amount to three hundred; after which they shall be apportioned among the States, in proportion to the number of inhabitants of the States respectively: And that before the first enumeration shall be made, the several States shall be entitled to chuse double the number of representatives for that purpose, mentioned in the Constitution."

21 June 1788

6.12.11   Mr. *M. Smith*. I had the honor yesterday of submitting an amendment to the clause under consideration, with some observations in support of it. I hope I shall be indulged in making some additional remarks in reply to what has been offered by the honorable gentleman from New-York [Alexander Hamilton].

He has taken up much time in endeavouring to prove that the great defect in the old confederation was, that it operated upon states instead of individuals. It is needless to dispute concerning points on which we do not disagree: It is admitted that the powers of the general government ought to operate upon individuals to a certain degree. How far the powers should extend, and in what cases to individuals is the question. As the different parts of the system will come into view in the course of our investigation, an opportunity will be afforded to consider this question; I wish at present to confine myself to the subject immediately under the consideration of the committee. I shall make no reply to the arguments offered by the hon. gentleman to justify the rule of apportionment fixed by this clause: For though I am confident they might be easily refuted, yet I am persuaded we must yield this point, in accommodation to the southern states. The amendment therefore proposes no alteration to the clause in this respect.

The honorable gentleman says, that the clause by obvious construction fixes the representation.[14] I wish not to torture words or sentences. I perceive no such obvious construction. I see clearly, that on the one hand the representatives cannot exceed one for thirty thousand inhabitants; and on the other, that whatever larger number of inhabitants may be taken for the rule of apportionment, each state shall be entitled to send one representative. Every thing else appears to me in the discretion of the legislature. If there be any other limitation, it is certainly implied. Matters of such moment should not be left to doubtful construction. It is urged that the number of representatives will be fixed at one for 30,000, because it will be the interest of the larger states to do it.[15] I cannot discern the force of this argument.—To me it appears clear, that the relative weight of influence of the different states will be the same, with the number of representatives at 65 as at 600, and that of the individual members greater. For each member's share of power will decrease as the number of the house of representatives increases.—If therefore this maxim be true, that men are unwilling to relinquish powers which they once possess, we are not to expect that the house of representatives will be inclined to enlarge the numbers. The same motive will operate to influence the president and senate to oppose the increase of the number of representatives; for in proportion as the weight of the house of representatives is augmented, they will feel their own diminished: It is therefore of the highest importance that a suitable number of representatives should be established by the constitution.

6.12.12

It has been observed by an honorable member, that the eastern states insisted upon a small representation on the principles of œconomy.—This argument must have no weight in the mind of a considerate person. The difference of expence, between supporting a house of representatives sufficiently numerous, and the present proposed one would be about 20 or 30,000 dollars per annum. The man who would seriously object to this expence, to secure his liberties, does not deserve to enjoy them. Besides, by increasing the number of representatives, we open a door for the admission of the substantial yeomanry of your country; who, being possessed of the habits of œconomy, will be cautious of imprudent expenditures, by which means a much greater saving will be made of public money than is sufficient to support them. A reduction of the number of the state legislatures might also be made, by which means there might be a saving of expence much more than sufficient for the purpose of supporting the general legislature.—For, as under this system all the powers of legislation relating to our general concerns, are vested in the general government, the powers of the state legislatures will be so curtailed, as to render it less necessary to have them so numerous as they now are.

6.12.13

But an honorable gentleman has observed that it is a problem that cannot

6.12.14

be solved, what the proper number is which ought to compose the house of representatives, and calls upon me to fix the number. I admit this is a question that will not admit of a solution with mathematical certainty—few political questions will—yet we may determine with certainty that certain numbers are too small or too large. We may be sure that ten is too small and a thousand too large a number—every one will allow that the first number is too small to possess the sentiments, be influenced by the interests of the people, or secure against corruption: A thousand would be too numerous to be capable of deliberating.

6.12.15   To determine whether the number of representatives proposed by this Constitution is sufficient, it is proper to examine the qualifications which this house ought to possess, in order to exercise their powers discreetly for the happiness of the people. The idea that naturally suggests itself to our minds, when we speak of representatives is, that they resemble those they represent; they should be a true picture of the people; possess the knowledge of their circumstances and their wants; sympathize in all their distresses, and be disposed to seek their true interests.[16] The knowledge necessary for the representatives of a free people, not only comprehends extensive political and commercial information, such as is acquired by men of refined education, who have leisure to attain to high degrees of improvement, but it should also comprehend that kind of acquaintance with the common concerns and occupations of the people, which men of the middling class of life are in general much better competent to, than those of a superior class. To understand the true commercial interests of a country, not only requires just ideas of the general commerce of the world, but also, and principally, a knowledge of the productions of your own country and their value, what your soil is capable of producing[,] the nature of your manufactures, and the capacity of the country to increase both. To exercise the power of laying taxes, duties and excises with discretion, requires something more than an acquaintance with the abstruse parts of the system of finance. It calls for a knowledge of the circumstances and ability of the people in general, a discernment how the burdens imposed will bear upon the different classes.

6.12.16   From these observations results this conclusion that the number of representatives should be so large, as that while it embraces men of the first class, it should admit those of the middling class of life. I am convinced that this Government is so constituted, that the representatives will generally be composed of the first class in the community, which I shall distinguish by the name of the natural aristocracy of the country.[17] I do not mean to give offence by using this term. I am sensible this idea is treated by many gentlemen as chimerical. I shall be asked what is meant by the natural aristocracy—and told that no such distinction of classes of men exists among us. It is true it is our singular felicity that we have no legal or hereditary distinctions of this kind; but still there are real differences: Every society naturally divides itself into classes. The author of nature has bestowed on some greater capacities than on others—birth, education, talents and wealth, create distinctions among men as visible and of as much influence as titles, stars and garters. In every society, men of this class will command a superior degree of respect—and if the government is so constituted as to admit but few to exercise the powers of it, it will, according to the natural course of things, be in their hands. Men in the middling class, who are qualified as representatives, will not be so anxious to be chosen as those of the first. When the number is so small the office will be highly elevated and distinguished—the stile in which the members live will probably be high—circumstances of this kind, will render the place of a representative not a desirable one to sensible, substantial men, who have been used to walk in the plain and frugal paths of life.

Besides, the influence of the great will generally enable them to succeed in elections—it will be difficult to combine a district of country containing 30 or 40,000 inhabitants, frame your election laws as you please, in any one character; unless it be in one of conspicuous, military, popular, civil or legal talents. The great easily form associations; the poor and middling class form them with difficulty. If the elections be by plurality, as probably will be the case in this state, it is almost certain, none but the great will be chosen—for they easily unite their interest—The common people will divide, and their divisions will be promoted by the others. There will be scarcely a chance of their uniting, in any other but some great man, unless in some popular demagogue, who will probably be destitute of principle. A substantial yeoman of sense and discernment, will hardly ever be chosen. From these remarks it appears that the government will fall into the hands of the few and the great. This will be a government of oppression. I do not mean to declaim against the great, and charge them indiscriminately with want of principle and honesty.—The same passions and prejudices govern all men. The circumstances in which men are placed in a great measure give a cast to the human character. Those in middling circumstances, have less temptation—they are inclined by habit and the company with whom they associate, to set bounds to their passions and appetites—if this is not sufficient, the want of means to gratify them will be a restraint—they are obliged to employ their time in their respective callings—hence the substantial yeomanry of the country are more temperate, of better morals and less ambition than the great.[18] The latter do not feel for the poor and middling class; the reasons are obvious—they are not obliged to use the pains and labour to procure property as the other.—They feel not the inconveniences arising from the payment of small sums. The great consider themselves above the common people—entitled to more respect—do not associate with them—they fancy themselves to have a right of pre-eminence in every thing. In short, they possess the same feelings, and are under the influence of the same motives, as an hereditary nobility. I know the idea that

6.12.17

such a distinction exists in this country is ridiculed by some—But I am not the less apprehensive of danger from their influence on this account—Such distinctions exist all the world over—have been taken notice of by all writers on free government—and are founded in the nature of things. It has been the principal care of free governments to guard against the encroachments of the great. Common observation and experience prove the existence of such distinctions. Will any one say, that there does not exist in this country the pride of family, of wealth, of talents; and that they do not command influence and respect among the common people? Congress, in their address to the inhabitants of the province of Quebec, in 1775, state this distinction in the following forcible words quoted from the Marquis Beccaria. "In every human society, there is an essay continually tending to confer on one part the height of power and happiness, and to reduce the other to the extreme of weakness and misery. The intent of good laws is to oppose this effort, and to diffuse their influence universally and equally."[19] We ought to guard against the government being placed in the hands of this class—They cannot have that sympathy with their constituents which is necessary to connect them closely to their interest: Being in the habit of profuse living, they will be profuse in the public expences. They find no difficulty in paying their taxes, and therefore do not feel public burthens: Besides if they govern, they will enjoy the emoluments of the government. The middling class, from their frugal habits, and feeling themselves the public burdens, will be careful how they increase them.

6.12.18   But I may be asked, would you exclude the first class in the community, from any share in legislation? I answer by no means—they would be more dangerous out of power than in it—they would be factious—discontented and constantly disturbing the government—it would also be unjust—they have their liberties to protect as well as others—and the largest share of property. But my idea is, that the Constitution should be so framed as to admit this class, together with a sufficient number of the middling class to controul them. You will then combine the abilities and honesty of the community—a proper degree of information, and a disposition to pursue the public good. A representative body, composed principally of respectable yeomanry is the best possible security to liberty.—When the interest of this part of the community is pursued, the public good is pursued; because the body of every nation consists of this class. And because the interest of both the rich and the poor are involved in that of the middling class. No burden can be laid on the poor, but what will sensibly affect the middling class. Any law rendering property insecure, would be injurious to them.—When therefore this class in society pursue their own interest, they promote that of the public, for it is involved in it.

6.12.19   In so small a number of representatives, there is great danger from corruption and combination. A great politician has said that every man has his price:[20] I hope this is not true in all its extent—But I ask the gentlemen to inform, what government there is, in which it has not been practised? Notwithstanding all that has been said of the defects in the Constitution of the antient Confederacies of the Grecian Republics, their destruction is to be imputed more to this cause than to any imperfection in their forms of government. This was the deadly poison that effected their dissolution. This is an extensive country, increasing in population and growing in consequence. Very many lucrative offices will be in the grant of the government, which will be the object of avarice and ambition. How easy will it be to gain over a sufficient number, in the bestowment of these offices, to promote the views and purposes of those who grant them! Foreign corruption is also to be guarded against. A system of corruption is known to be the system of government in Europe. It is practised without blushing. And we may lay it to our account it will be attempted amongst us. The most effectual as well as natural security against this, is a strong democratic branch in the legislature frequently chosen, including in it a number of the substantial, sensible yeomanry of the country. Does the house of representatives answer this description? I confess, to me they hardly wear the complexion of a democratic branch—they appear the mere shadow of representation. The whole number in both houses amounts to 91—Of these 46 make a quorum; and 24 of those being secured, may carry any point. Can the liberties of three millions of people be securely trusted in the hands of 24 men? Is it prudent to commit to so small a number the decision of the great questions which will come before them? Reason revolts at the idea.

The honorable gentleman from New York has said that 65 members in the house of representatives are sufficient for the present situation of the country, and taking it for granted that they will increase as one for 30,000, in 25 years they will amount to 200. It is admitted by this observation that the number fixed in the Constitution, is not sufficient without it is augmented. It is not declared that an increase shall be made, but is left at the discretion of the legislature, by the gentleman's own concession; therefore the Constitution is imperfect. We certainly ought to fix in the Constitution those things which are essential to liberty. If any thing falls under this description, it is the number of the legislature. To say, as this gentleman does, that our security is to depend upon the spirit of the people, who will be watchful of their liberties, and not suffer them to be infringed, is absurd. It would equally prove that we might adopt any form of government. I believe were we to create a despot, he would not immediately dare to act the tyrant; but it would not be long before he would destroy the spirit of the people, or the people would destroy him. If our people have a high sense of liberty, the government should be congenial to this spirit—calculated to cherish the love of liberty, while yet it had sufficient force to restrain licentiousness. Government operates upon the spirit of the people, as well as the spirit of the people operates upon it—and if they are not conformable to each other, the one or the other will prevail.[21] In a less time than 25 years, the government

6.12.20

343

will receive its tone. What the spirit of the country may be at the end of that period, it is impossible to foretell: Our duty is to frame a government friendly to liberty and the rights of mankind, which will tend to cherish and cultivate a love of liberty among our citizens. If this government becomes oppressive it will be by degrees: It will aim at its end by disseminating sentiments of government opposite to republicanism; and proceed from step to step in depriving the people of a share in the government. A recollection of the change that has taken place in the minds of many in this country in the course of a few years, ought to put us upon our guard. Many who are ardent advocates for the new system, reprobate republican principles as chimerical and such as ought to be expelled from society. Who would have thought ten years ago, that the very men who risqued their lives and fortunes in support of republican principles, would now treat them as the fictions of fancy?—A few years ago we fought for liberty—We framed a general government on free principles—We placed the state legislatures, in whom the people have a full and fair representation, between Congress and the people. We were then, it is true, too cautious; and too much restricted the powers of the general government. But now it is proposed to go into the contrary, and a more dangerous extreme; to remove all barriers; to give the New Government free access to our pockets, and ample command of our persons; and that without providing for a genuine and fair representation of the people. No one can say what the progress of the change of sentiment may be in 25 years. The same men who now cry up the necessity of an energetic government, to induce a compliance with this system, may in much less time reprobate this in as severe terms as they now do the confederation, and may as strongly urge the necessity of going as far beyond this, as this is beyond the Confederation.—Men of this class are increasing—they have influence, talents and industry—It is time to form a barrier against them. And while we are willing to establish a government adequate to the purposes of the union, let us be careful to establish it on the broad basis of equal liberty.

23 June 1788

6.12.21   Honorable Mr. *Smith*. I did not intend to make any more observations on this article. Indeed, I have heard nothing to day, which has not been suggested before, except the polite reprimand I have received for my declamation. I should not have risen again, but to examine who has proved himself the greatest declaimer. The gentleman wishes me to describe what I meant, by representing the feelings of the people.[22] If I recollect right, I said the representative ought to understand, and govern his conduct by the true interest of the people.—I believe I stated this idea precisely. When he attempts to explain my ideas, he explains them away to nothing; and instead of answering, he distorts, and then sports with them. But he may rest assured, that in the present spirit of the Convention, to irritate is not the way to conciliate. The gentleman, by the false gloss he has given to my argument, makes me an enemy to the rich: This is not true. All I said, was, that mankind were influenced, in a great degree, by interests and prejudices:—That men, in different ranks of life, were exposed to different temptations—and that ambition was more peculiarly the passion of the rich and great. The gentleman supposes the poor have less sympathy with the sufferings of their fellow creatures; for that those who feel most distress themselves, have the least regard to the misfortunes of others:—Whether this be reasoning or declamation, let all who hear us determine. I observed that the rich were more exposed to those temptations, which rank and power hold out to view; that they were more luxurious and intemperate, because they had more fully the means of enjoyment; that they were more ambitious, because more in the hope of success. The gentleman says my principle is not true; for that a poor man will be as ambitious to be a constable, as a rich man to be a governor:—But he will not injure his country so much by the party he creates to support his ambition.

The next object of the gentleman's ridicule is my idea of an aristocracy; and he indeed has done me the honor, to rank me in the order.[23] If then I am an aristocrat, and yet publicly caution my countrymen against the encroachments of the aristocrats, they will surely consider me as one of their most disinterested friends. My idea of aristocracy is not new:—It is embraced by many writers on government:—I would refer the gentleman for a definition of it to the honorable *John Adams,* one of our natural aristocrats.[24] This writer will give him a description the most ample and satisfactory. But I by no means intended to carry my idea of it to such a ridiculous length as the gentleman would have me; nor will any of my expressions warrant the construction he imposes on them. My argument was, that in order to have a true and genuine representation, you must receive the middling class of people into your government—such as compose the body of this assembly. I observed, that a representation from the United States could not be so constituted, as to represent completely the feelings and interests of the people; but that we ought to come as near this object as possible. The gentlemen say, that the exactly proper number of representatives is so indeterminate and vague, that it is impossible for them to ascertain it with any precision. But surely, they are able to see the distinction between twenty and thirty. I acknowledged that a complete representation would make the legislature too numerous; and therefore, it is our duty to limit the powers, and form checks on the government, in proportion to the smallness of the number.

The honorable gentleman next animadverts on my apprehensions of corruption, and instances the present Congress, to prove an absurdity in my

6.12.22

6.12.23

argument. But is this fair reasoning? There are many material checks to the operations of that body, which the future Congress will not have. In the first place, they are chosen annually:—What more powerful check! They are subject to recal: Nine states must agree to any important resolution, which will not be carried into execution, till it meets the approbation of the people in the state legislatures. Admitting what he says, that they have pledged their faith to support the acts of Congress; yet, if these be contrary to the essential interests of the people, they ought not to be acceded to; for they are not bound to obey any law, which tends to destroy them.

6.12.24   It appears to me, that had œconomy been a motive for making the representation small; it might have operated more properly in leaving out some of the offices which this constitution requires. I am sensible that a great many of the common people, who do not reflect, imagine that a numerous representation involves a great expence:—But they are not aware of the real security it gives to an œconomical management in all the departments of government.

6.12.25   The gentleman further declared, that as far his acquaintance extended, the people thought sixty-five a number fully large enough for our State Assembly; and hence inferred, that sixty-five is to two hundred and forty thousand, as sixty five is to three millions.—This is curious reasoning.

I feel that I have troubled the committee too long. I should not indeed have risen again upon this subject, had not my ideas been grossly misrepresented.

[*The Convention turned, on 24 June, to a consideration of Article I, section 3, the constitution of the Senate. Mr. George Livingston moved the following amendment: "Resolved, That no person shall be eligible as a senator for more than six years in any term of twelve years, and that it shall be in the power of the legislatures of the several states to recall their senators, or either of them, and to elect others in their stead, to serve for the remainder of the time for which such senator or senators, so recalled, were appointed."*]

6.12.26   The honorable Mr. *Smith* observed, that when he had the honor to address the committee on the preceding question of the representation, he stated to them his idea, that it would be impossible, under the constitution as it stands, to have such a genuine representation of the people, as would itself form a check in the government: That therefore it became our duty to provide checks of another nature. The honorable gentleman from New-York had made many pertinent observations on the propriety of giving stability to the senate. The general principles laid down, he thought were just. He only disputed the inferences drawn from them, and their application to the proposed amendment. The only question was, whether the checks attempted in the amendment were incompatible with that stability which he acknowledged was essential to good government. Mr. *Smith* said he did not rise to enter at present into the debate at large. Indisposition obliged him to beg leave of the committee to defer what he had to offer to them till the succeeding day.

Convention adjourned.

Wednesday, 25 June

Section third was again read—when

Mr. *Smith* resumed his argument as follows. The amendment embraces two objects: First, that the senators shall be eligible for only six years in any term of twelve years; Second, that they shall be subject to the recall of the legislatures of their several states. It is proper that we take up these points separately. I concur with the honorable gentleman, that there is a necessity for giving this branch a greater stability than the house of representatives. I think his reasons are conclusive on this point. But, Sir, it does not follow from this position that the senators ought to hold their places during life. Declaring them ineligible during a certain term after six years, is far from rendering them less stable than is necessary. We think the amendment will place the senate in a proper medium between a fluctuating and a perpetual body. As the clause now stands, there is no doubt that the senators will hold their office perpetually; and in this situation, they must of necessity lose their dependence and attachment to the people. It is certainly inconsistent with the established principles of republicanism, that the senate should be a fixed and unchangeable body of men. There should be then some constitutional provision against this evil. A rotation I consider as the best possible mode of affecting a remedy. The amendment will not only have a tendency to defeat any plots, which may be formed against the liberty and authority of the state governments, but will be the best means to extinguish the factions which often prevail, and which are sometimes so fatal in legislative bodies. This appears to me an important consideration. We have generally found, that perpetual bodies have either combined in some scheme of usurpation, or have been torn and distracted with cabals—Both have been the source of misfortunes to the state. Most people acquainted with history will acknowledge these facts. Our Congress would have been a fine field for party spirit to act in—That body would undoubtedly have suffered all the evils of faction, had it not been secured by the rotation

6.12.27

established by the articles of the confederation. I think a rotation in the government is a very important and truly republican institution. All good republicans, I presume to say, will treat it with respect.[25]

6.12.28

It is a circumstance strongly in favor of rotation, that it will have a tendency to diffuse a more general spirit of emulation, and to bring forward into office the genius and abilities of the continent—The ambition of gaining the qualifications necessary to govern, will be in some proportion to the chance of success. If the office is to be perpetually confined to a few, other men of equal talents and virtue, but not possessed of so extensive an influence, may be discouraged from aspiring to it. The more perfectly we are versed in the political science, the more firmly will the happy principles of republicanism be supported. The true policy of constitutions will be to increase the information of the country, and disseminate the knowledge of government as universally as possible. If this be done, we shall have, in any dangerous emergency, a numerous body of enlightened citizens, ready for the call of their country. As the constitution now is, you only give an opportunity to two men to be acquainted with the public affairs. It is a maxim with me, that every man employed in a high office by the people, should from time to time return to them, that he may be in a situation to satisfy them with respect to his conduct and the measures of administration. If I recollect right, it was observed by an honorable member from New-York, that this amendment would be an infringement of the natural rights of the people.[26] I humbly conceive, if the gentleman reflects maturely on the nature of his argument, he will acknowledge its weakness. What is government itself, but a restraint upon the natural rights of the people? What constitution was ever devised, that did not operate as a restraint on their original liberties? What is the whole system of qualifications, which take place in all free governments, but a restraint? Why is a certain age made necessary? Why a certain term of citizenship? This constitution itself, Sir, has restraints innumerable.—The amendment, it is true, may exclude two of the best men: but it can rarely happen, that the state will sustain any material loss by this. I hope and believe that we shall always have more than two men, who are capable of discharging the duty of a senator. But if it should so happen that the state possessed only two capable men, it will be necessary that they should return home, from time to time, to inspect and regulate our domestic affairs. I do not conceive the state can suffer any inconvenience. The argument indeed might have some weight were the representation very large: But as the power is to be exercised upon only two men, the apprehensions of the gentlemen are entirely without foundation.

6.12.29

With respect to the second part of the amendment, I would observe that as the senators are the representatives of the state legislatures, it is reasonable and proper that they should be under their controul. When a state sends an agent commissioned to transact any business, or perform any service, it certainly ought to have a power to recall him. These are plain principles, and so far as they apply to the case under examination, they ought to be adopted by us. Form this government as you please, you must at all events lodge in it very important powers: These powers must be in the hands of a few men, so situated as to produce a small degree of responsibility. These circumstances ought to put us upon our guard; and the inconvenience of this necessary delegation of power should be corrected, by providing some suitable checks.

Against this part of the amendment a great deal of argument has been used, and with considerable plausibility. It is said if the amendment takes place, the senators will hold their office only during the pleasure of the state legislatures, and consequently will not possess the necessary firmness and stability. I conceive, Sir, there is a fallacy in this argument, founded upon the suspicion that the legislature of a state will possess the qualities of a mob, and be incapable of any regular conduct. I know that the impulses of the multitude are inconsistent with systematic government. The people are frequently incompetent to deliberate discussion, and subject to errors and imprudencies. Is this the complexion of the state legislatures? I presume it is not. I presume that they are never actuated by blind impulses—that they rarely do things hastily and without consideration. [The state legislatures were select bodies of men, chosen for their superior wisdom, and so organized as to be capable of calm and regular conduct.][27] My apprehension is, that the power of recall would not be exercised as often as it ought. It is highly improbable that a man, in whom the state has confided, and who has an established influence, will be recalled, unless his conduct has been notoriously wicked.—The arguments of the gentleman therefore, do not apply in this case. It is further observed, that it would be improper to give the legislatures this power, because the local interests and prejudices of the states ought not to be admitted into the general government; and that if the senator is rendered too independent of his constituents,[28] he will sacrifice the interests of the Union to the policy of his state. Sir, the senate has been generally held up by all parties as a safe guard to the rights of the several states. In this view, the closest connection between them has been considered as necessary. But now it seems we speak a different language—We now look upon the least attachment to their states as dangerous—We are now for separating them, and rendering them entirely independent, that we may root out the last vestige of state sovereignty.

An honorable gentleman from New-York observed yesterday, that the states would always maintain their importance and authority, on account of their superior influence over the people.[29] To prove this influence, he mentioned the aggregate number of the state representatives throughout the continent. But I ask him, how long the people will retain their confidence for two thousand representatives, who shall meet once in a year to make laws for regulating the heighth of your fences and the repairing of your roads? Will they not by and by be saying,—Here, we are paying a great number of

6.12.30

6.12.31

men for doing nothing: We had better give up all the civil business of our state with its powers to congress, who are sitting all the year round: We had better get rid of the useless burthen. That matters will come to this at last, I have no more doubt than I have of my existence. The state governments, without object or authority, will soon dwindle into insignificance, and be despised by the people themselves. I am, sir, at a loss to know how the state legislatures will spend their time. Will they make laws to regulate agriculture? I imagine this will be best regulated by the sagacity and industry of those who practise it. Another reason offered by the gentleman is, that the states will have a greater number of officers than the general government. I doubt this. Let us make a comparison. In the first place, the federal government must have a compleat set of judicial officers of different ranks throughout the continent: Then, a numerous train of executive officers, in all the branches of the revenue, both internal and external, and all the civil and military departments. Add to this, their salaries will probably be larger and better secured than those of any state officers. If these numerous offices are not at once established, they are in the power of congress, and will all in time be created. Very few offices will be objects of ambition in the states. They will have no establishments at all to correspond with some of those I have mentioned—In other branches, they will have the same as congress. But I ask, what will be their comparative influence and importance? I will leave it, sir, to any man of candour, to determine whether there will not probably be more lucrative and honorable places in the gift of congress than in the disposal of the states all together. But the whole reasoning of the gentlemen rests upon the principle that the states will be able to check the general government, by exciting the people to opposition: It only goes to prove, that the state officers will have such an influence over the people, as to impell them to hostility and rebellion. This kind of check, I contend, would be a pernicious one; and certainly ought to be prevented. Checks in government ought to act silently, and without public commotion.[30] I think that the harmony of the two powers should by all means be maintained: If it be not, the operation of government will be baneful—One or the other of the parties must finally be destroyed in the conflict. The constitutional line between the authority of each should be so obvious, as to leave no room for jealous apprehensions or violent contests.[31]

6.12.32   It is further said, that the operation of local interests should be counteracted; for which purpose, the senate should be rendered permanent. I conceive that the true interest of every state is the interest of the whole; and that if we should have a well regulated government, this idea will prevail. We shall indeed have few local interests to pursue, under the new constitution: because it limits the claims of the states by so close a line, that on their part there can be little dispute, and little worth disputing about. But, sir, I conceive that partial interests will grow continually weaker, because there are not those fundamental differences between the real interests of the several states, which will long prevent their coming together and becoming uniform.

Another argument advanced by the gentlemen is, that our amendment would be the means of producing factions among the electors: That aspiring men would misrepresent the conduct of a faithful senator; and by intrigue, procure a recall, upon false grounds, in order to make room for themselves. But, sir, men who are ambitious for places will rarely be disposed to render those places unstable. A truly ambitious man will never do this, unless he is mad. It is not to be supposed that a state will recall a man once in twenty years, to make way for another. Dangers of this kind are very remote: I think they ought not to be brought seriously into view.

6.12.33

More than one of the gentlemen have ridiculed my apprehensions of corruption. How, say they, are the people to be corrupted? By their own money? Sir, in many countries, the people pay money to corrupt themselves: why should it not happen in this? Certainly, the congress will be as liable to corruption as other bodies of men. Have they not the same frailties, and the same temptations? With respect to the corruption arising from the disposal of offices, the gentlemen have treated the argument as insignificant. But let any one make a calculation, and see whether there will not be good offices enough, to dispose of to every man who goes there, who will then freely resign his seat: for, can any one suppose, that a member of congress would not go out and relinquish his four dollars a day, for two or three thousand pounds a year? It is here objected that no man can hold an office created during the time he is in Congress—But it will be easy for a man of influence, who has in his eye a favorite office previously created and already filled, to say to his friend, who holds it—Here—I will procure you another place of more emolument, provided you will relinquish yours in favor of me. The constitution appears to be a restraint, when in fact it is none at all. I presume, sir, there is not a government in the world in which there is greater scope for influence and corruption in the disposal of offices. Sir, I will not declaim, and say all men are dishonest; but I think that, in forming a constitution, if we presume this, we shall be on the safest side.[32] This extreme is certainly less dangerous than the other. It is wise to multiply checks to a greater degree than the present state of things requires. It is said that corruption has never taken place under the old government—I believe, gentlemen hazard this assertion without proofs. That it has taken place in some degree is very probable. Many millions of money have been put into the hands of government, which have never yet been accounted for: The accounts are not yet settled, and Heaven only knows when they will be.

6.12.34

I have frequently observed a restraint upon the state governments, which Congress never can be under, construct that body as you please. It is a truth, capable of demonstration, that the nearer the representative is to his constituent, the more attached and dependent he will be—In the states, the elections are frequent, and the representatives numerous: They transact

6.12.35

business in the midst of their constituents, and every man may be called upon to account for his conduct. In this state the council of appointment are elected for one year.—The proposed constitution establishes a council of appointment who will be perpetual—Is there any comparison between the two governments in point of security? It is said that the governor of this state is always eligible: But this is not in point. The governor of this state is limited in his powers—Indeed his authority is small and insignificant, compared to that of the senate of the United States.

[*On 26 June the convention reached section 8 of Article I, dealing with the powers of Congress, and Mr. John Williams moved that Congress should lay no direct taxes except when the impost and excise are insufficient to meet the public exigencies and then only after requisitions on the states have been refused or neglected. The following day, Smith spoke as follows.*]

Friday, 27 June

Section 8, was again read,—and

6.12.36   The hon. Mr. *Smith* rose.—We are now come to a part of the system, which requires our utmost attention, and most careful investigation. It is necessary that the powers vested in government should be precisely defined, that the people may be able to know whether it moves in the circle of the constitution. It is the more necessary in governments like the one under examination; because Congress here is to be considered as only part of a complex system. The state governments are necessary for certain local purposes; The general government for national purposes: The latter ought to rest on the former, not only in its form, but in its operations. It is therefore of the highest importance, that the line of jurisdiction should be accurately drawn. It is necessary, sir, in order to maintain harmony between the governments, and to prevent the constant interference which must either be the cause of perpetual differences, or oblige one to yield, perhaps unjustly, to the other. I conceive the system cannot operate well, unless it is so contrived, as to preserve harmony. If this be not done, in every contest, the weak must submit to the strong. The clause before us is of the greatest importance: It respects the very vital principle of government: The power is the most efficient and comprehensive that can be delegated; and seems in some measure to answer for all others. I believe it will appear evident, that money must be raised for the support of both governments: If therefore you give to one or the other, a power which may in its operation become exclusive; it is obvious, that one can exist only at the will of the other; and must ultimately be sacrificed. The powers of the general government extend to the raising of money, in all possible ways, except by duties on exports; to the laying taxes on imports, lands, buildings, and even on persons. The individual states in time will be allowed to raise no money at all: The United States will have a right to raise money from every quarter. The general government has moreover this advantage. All disputes relative to jurisdiction must be decided in a federal court.

It is a general maxim, that all governments find a use for as much money as they can raise.[33] Indeed they have commonly demands for more: Hence it is, that all, as far as we are acquainted, are in debt. I take this to be a settled truth, that they will all spend as much as their revenue; that is, will live at least up to their income. Congress will ever exercise their powers, to levy as much money as the people can pay. They will not be restrained from direct taxes, by the consideration that necessity does not require them. If they forbear, it will be because the people cannot answer their demands. There will be no possibility of preventing the clashing of jurisdictions, unless some system of accomodation is formed. Suppose taxes are laid by both governments on the same article: It seems to me impossible, that they can operate with harmony. I have no more conception that in taxation two powers can act together; than that two bodies can occupy the same place. They will therefore not only interfere; but they will be hostile to each other. Here are to be two lists of all kinds of officers—supervisors, assessors, constables, &c. imployed in this business. It is unnecessary that I should enter into a minute detail, to prove that these complex powers cannot operate peaceably together, and without one being overpowered by the other. On one day, the continental collector calls for the tax; He seizes a horse: The next day, the state collector comes, procures a replevin and retakes the horse, to satisfy the state tax. I just mention this, to shew that people will not submit to such a government, and that finally it must defeat itself.

It must appear evident, that there will be a constant jarring of claims and interests. Now will the states in this contest stand any chance of success? If they will, there is less necessity for our amendment. But, consider the superior advantages of the general government: Consider their extensive, exclusive revenues; the vast sums of money they can command, and the means they thereby possess of supporting a powerful standing force. The states, on the contrary, will not have the command of a shilling, or a soldier. The two governments will be like two men contending for a certain property: The one has no interest but that which is the subject of the controversy; while the other has money enough to carry on the law-suit for twenty years. By this clause unlimited powers in taxation are given: Another clause declares, that Congress shall have power to make all laws necessary to carry the constitution into effect. Nothing therefore is left to construction; but the powers are most express. How far the state legisla-

6.12.37

6.12.38

tures will be able to command a revenue, every man, on viewing the subject, can determine. If he contemplates the ordinary operation of causes, he will be convinced that the powers of the confederacy will swallow up those of the members. I do not suppose that this effect will be brought about suddenly—As long as the people feel universally and strongly attached to the state governments, Congress will not be able to accomplish it: If they act prudently, their powers will operate and be increased by degrees. The tendency of taxation, tho' it be moderate, is to lessen the attachment of the citizens—If it becomes oppressive, it will certainly destroy their confidence. While the general taxes are sufficiently heavy, every attempt of the states to enhance them, will be considered as a tyrannical act, and the people will lose their respect and affection for a government, which cannot support itself, without the most grievous impositions upon them. If the constitution is accepted as it stands, I am convinced, that in seven years as much will be said against the state governments, as is now said in favour of the proposed system.

6.12.39　　Sir, I contemplate the abolition of the state constitutions as an event fatal to the liberties of America. These liberties will not be violently wrested from the people; they will be undermined and gradually consumed. On subjects of this kind we cannot be too critical. The investigation is difficult, because we have no examples to serve as guides. The world has never seen such a government over such a country. If we consult authorities in this matter, they will declare the impracticability of governing a free people, on such an extensive plan.[34] In a country, where a portion of the people live more than twelve hundred miles from the center, I think that one body cannot possibly legislate for the whole. Can the legislature frame a system of taxation that will operate with uniform advantages? Can they carry any system into execution? Will it not give occasion for an innumerable swarm of officers, to infest our country and consume our substance? People will be subject to impositions, which they cannot support, and of which their complaints can never reach the government.

6.12.40　　Another idea is in my mind, which I think conclusive against a simple government for the United States. It is not possible to collect a set of representatives, who are acquainted with all parts of the continent. Can you find men in Georgia who are acquainted with the situation of New-Hampshire? who know what taxes will best suit the inhabitants; and how much they are able to bear? Can the best men make laws for a people of whom they are entirely ignorant? Sir, we have no reason to hold our state governments in contempt, or to suppose them incapable of acting wisely. I believe they have operated more beneficially than most people expected, who considered that those governments were erected in a time of war and confusion, when they were very liable to errors in their structure. It will be a matter of astonishment to all unprejudiced men hereafter, who shall reflect upon our situation, to observe to what a great degree good government has prevailed. It is true some bad laws have been passed in most of the states; but they arose more from the difficulty of the times, than from any want of honesty or wisdom. Perhaps there never was a government, which in the course of ten years did not do something to be repented of. As for Rhode-Island, I do not mean to justify her—She deserves to be condemned—If there were in the world but one example of political depravity, it would be her's: And no nation ever merited or suffered a more genuine infamy, than a wicked administration has attached to her character. Massachusetts also has been guilty of errors: and has lately been distracted by an internal convulsion. Great-Britain, notwithstanding her boasted constitution, has been a perpetual scene of revolutions and civil war—Her parliaments have been abolished; her kings have been banished and murdered. I assert that the majority of the governments in the union have operated better than any body had reason to expect: and that nothing but experience and habit is wanting, to give the state laws all the stability and wisdom necessary to make them respectable. If these things be true, I think we ought not to exchange our condition, with a hazard of losing our state constitutions. We all agree that a general government is necessary: But it ought not to go so far, as to destroy the authority of the members. We shall be unwise, to make a new experiment in so important a matter, without some known and sure grounds to go upon. The state constitutions should be the guardians of our domestic rights and interests; and should be both the support and the check of the federal government. The want of the means of raising a general revenue has been the principal cause of our difficulties. I believe no man will doubt that if our present Congress had money enough, there would be few complaints of their weakness. Requisitions have perhaps been too much condemned. What has been their actual operation[?] Let us attend to experience, and see if they are such poor, unproductive things, as is commonly supposed. If I calculate right, the requisitions for the ten years past, have amounted to thirty-six millions of dollars; of which twenty-four millions, or two thirds, have been actually paid. Does not this fact warrant a conclusion that some reliance is to be placed on this mode? Besides, will any gentleman say that the states have generally been able to collect more than two thirds of their taxes from the people? The delinquency of some states has arisen from the fluctuations of paper money, &c. Indeed it is my decided opinion, that no government in the difficult circumstances, which we have passed thro', will be able to realize more than two thirds of the taxes it imposes. I might suggest two other considerations which have weight with me—There has probably been more money called for, than was actually wanted, on the expectation of delinquencies; and it is equally probable, that in a short course of time the increasing ability of the country will render requisitions a much more efficient mode of raising a revenue. The war left the people under very great burthens, and oppressed with both public and private debts. They are now fast emerging from their difficulties.

Many individuals without doubt still feel great inconveniences; but they will find a gradual remedy. Sir, has any country which has suffered distresses like ours, exhibited within a few years, more striking marks of improvement and prosperity? How its population has grown; How its agriculture, commerce and manufactures have been extended and improved! How many forests have been cut down; How many wastes have been cleared and cultivated; How many additions have been made to the extent and beauty of our towns and cities! I think our advancement has been rapid. In a few years, it is to be hoped, that we shall be relieved from our embarrassments; and unless new, calamities come upon us, shall be flourishing and happy. Some difficulties will ever occur in the collection of taxes by any mode whatever. Some states will pay more; some less. If New-York lays a tax, will not one county or district furnish more, another less than its proportion? The same will happen to the United States, as happens in New-York, and in every other country.—Let them impose a duty equal and uniform— those districts, where there is plenty of money, will pay punctually: Those, in which money is scarce, will be in some measure delinquent. The idea that Congress ought to have unlimited powers, is entirely novel; I never heard it, till the meeting of this convention. The general government once called on the states, to invest them with the command of funds adequate to the exigencies of the union: but they did not ask to command all the resources of the states—They did not wish to have a controul over all the property of the people. If we now give them this controul, we may as well give up the state governments with it. I have no notion of setting the two powers at variance; nor would I give a farthing for a government, which could not command a farthing. On the whole, it appears to me probable, that unless some certain, specific source of revenue is reserved to the states, their governments, with their independency will be totally annihilated.

1. Cf. Henry 5.16.6.

2. See Robert Livingston, Elliot II, 212–13; see *The Federalist* nos. 6–8 and references in Centinel IV, 2.7.91 n. 43; Federal Farmer I, 2.8.1 n. 4; Plebeian 6.11.5 n. 6.

3. Hamilton replied, Elliot II, 230–31. Cf. the order of the argument in *The Federalist:* the utility of union; the defects of the present Confederation; the necessity of a government at least as energetic as the one proposed (no. 1, 6–7). Livingston had followed *The Federalist* in beginning with the desirability of union and moving to the fundamental insufficiency of the Articles of Confederation. Elliot II, 208–16.

4. Livingston, Elliot II, 214.

5. Livingston had argued "that the old Confederation was defective in its principle, and impeachable in its execution, as it operated upon states in their political capacity, and not upon individuals; and that it carried with it the seeds of domestic violence, and tended ultimately to its dissolution. . . . [T]he powers which were, by common consent, intended to be vested in the federal head, had either been found deficient, or rendered useless by the impossibility of carrying them into execution, as the principle of a league of states totally separate and independent;—secondly, that if the principle was changed, a change would also be necessary in the form of the government; but if we could no longer retain the old principle of the confederacy, and were compelled to change its form, we were driven to the necessity of creating a new constitution, and

could find no place to rest upon in the old Confederation. . . . " Elliot II, 214–15; cf. *The Federalist* no. 15. On the Anti-Federalist opposition to consolidation, see Plebeian, 6.11.15 n. 9.

6. See Martin 2.4.43 n. 12.

7. Montesquieu, *The Spirit of Laws* IX, ch. 1.

8. Livingston was Chancellor of New York. On the claim that the Anti-Federalists were mainly state officials see Martin 2.4.117 n. 44.

9. Cf. *The Federalist* no. 49. On dangers of innovation, see Republican Federalist 4.13.15 n. 11.

10. I Samuel 8:11–18.

11. See Brutus IV, 2.9.48 n. 34.

12. See Cato IV, 2.6.27 n. 18.

13. Hamilton replied: "It was remarked yesterday, that a numerous representation was necessary to obtain the confidence of the people. This is not generally true. The confidence of the people will easily be gained by a good administration. This is the true touchstone. . . . The popular confidence depends on circumstances very distinct from considerations of number. Probably the public attachment is more strongly secured by a train of prosperous events, which are the result of wise deliberation and vigorous execution, and to which large bodies are much less competent than small ones." Elliot II, 254. Cf. *The Federalist* no. 17, 106–7; no. 27.

14. While acknowledging that there was no direct prohibition, Hamilton had contended "that the true and genuine construction of the clause gives Congress no power whatever to reduce the representation below the number as it now stands. Although they may limit, they can never diminish the number." Elliot II, 238.

15. See *The Federalist* no. 58. Smith continues this argument at 6.12.22.

16. See 6.12.21 ff. Smith's whole discussion of representation and its bearing on the taxing powers should be compared with *The Federalist* nos. 35, 36, and 63. References to the main Anti-Federalist discussions of representation are collected in Federal Farmer II, 2.8.15 n. 11.

17. Hamilton replied: "But who are the aristocracy among us? Where do we find men elevated to a perpetual rank above their fellow-citizens, and possessing powers entirely independent of them? The arguments of the gentleman only go to prove that there are men who are rich, men who are poor, some who are wise, and others who are not; that, indeed, every distinguished man is an aristocrat. This reminds me of a description of the aristocrats I have seen in a late publication styled the Federal Farmer. The author reckons in the aristocracy all governors of states, members of Congress, chief magistrates, and all officers of the militia. This description, I presume to say, is ridiculous. The image is a phantom. Does the new government render a rich man more eligible than a poor one? No. It requires no such qualification. It is bottomed on the broad and equal principle of your state constitution." Elliot II, 256. See Federal Farmer VII, 2.8.97–100. Smith replies 6.12.21–23. For other Anti-Federalist discussions of the natural aristocracy, see Federal Farmer VII, 2.8.97 n. 64.

18. Hamilton replied: "It is a harsh doctrine that men grow wicked in proportion as they improve and enlighten their minds. Experience has by no means justified us in the supposition that there is more virtue in one class of men than in another. Look through the rich and the poor of the community, the learned and the ignorant, where does virtue predominate? The difference indeed consists, not in the quantity, but kind, of vices which are incident to various classes; and here the advantage of character belongs to the wealthy. Their vices are probably more favorable to the prosperity of the state than those of the indigent, and partake less of moral depravity." Elliot II, 257. See below, n. 22.

19. *Journals of the Continental Congress* I, 105–13. The address, published in 1774, quotes from the Introduction to Beccaria's *Essay on Crimes and Punishments*. See Federal Farmer VII, 2.8.97 n. 61.

20. Sir Robert Walpole? William Coxe, *Memoirs of Walpole* IV, 369.

21. For other Anti-Federalist discussions of this practice see Federal Farmer III, 2.8.25 n. 19.

22. See 6.12.15, 21–22. Chancellor Livingston had said: "As to the idea of representing the feelings of the people, I do not entirely understand it, unless by their feelings are meant their interests. They appear to me to be the same thing. But if they have feelings which do not rise out of their interests, I think they ought not to be represented. What! shall the unjust, the selfish, the unsocial feelings, be represented? Shall the vices, the infirmities, the passions, of the people, be represented? Government, sir, would be a monster; laws made to encourage virtue and maintain peace would have a preposterous tendency to subvert the authority and outrage the principles on which they were founded; besides, the feelings of the people are so variable and inconstant, that our rulers should be chosen every day: people have one sort of feeling today, another tomorrow, and the voice of the representative must be incessantly changing in correspondence with these feelings. This would be making him a political weathercock." Elliot II, 275–76.

23. The Chancellor's sarcasm is broad, but he points to a basic difficulty in Smith's position: "The gentleman . . . is obliged to fortify [his reasoning] by having recourse to the phantom aristocracy. I have heard much of this. I always considered it as the bugbear of the party. We are told that, in every country, there is a natural aristocracy, and that this aristocracy consists of the rich and the great: nay, the gentleman goes further, and ranks in this class of men the wise, the learned, and those eminent for their talents or great virtues. Does a man possess the confidence of his fellow-citizens for having done them important services? He is an *aristocrat*. Has he great integrity? Such a man will be greatly trusted: he is an aristocrat. Indeed, to determine that one is an aristocrat, we need only be assured he is a man of merit. But I hope we have many such. I hope, sir, we are all aristocrats. So sensible am I of that gentleman's talents, integrity, and virtue, that we might at once hail him the first of the nobles, the very prince of the Senate. But whom in the name of common sense, will we have to represent us? Not the rich, for they are sheer aristocrats. Not the learned, the wise, the virtuous, for they are all aristocrats. Whom then? Why, those who are not virtuous; those who are not wise; those who are not learned: these are the men to whom alone we can trust our liberties. He says further, we ought not to choose these aristocrats, because the people will not have confidence in them; that is, the people will not have confidence in those who best deserve and most possess their confidence. He would have his government composed of other classes of men: where will we find them? Why, he must go out into the highways, and pick up the rogue and the robber; he must go to the hedges and ditches, and bring in the poor, the blind, and the lame. As the gentleman has thus settled the definition of aristocracy, I trust that no man will think it a term of reproach; for who among us would not be wise? Who would not be virtuous? Who would not be above want? How, again, would he have us to guard against aristocracy? Clearly by doubling the representation, and sending twelve aristocrats instead of six. The truth is, in these republican governments, we know no such ideal distinctions. We are all equally aristocrats. Offices, emoluments, honors, are open to all." Elliot II, 277–78. See above, n. 17.

24. John Adams, *Defence of the Constitutions of the United States* I, letter 25 (*Works* IV, 396–98).

25. See Hamilton's reply, Elliot II, 320–21, and Gouverneur Morris' opposition to any form of rotation: "It formed a political School, in wch. we were always governed by the scholars, and not by the Masters." Farrand II, 112 (25 July). On rotation see Federal Farmer XI, 2.8.147; Georgian 5.9.4–6.

26. Robert R. Livingston: "The people are the best judges who ought to represent them. To dictate and control them, to tell them whom they shall not elect, is to abridge their natural rights." Elliot II, 292–93.

27. Comment by Smith later this day. Elliot II, 324.

28. The original reads, "independent on his constituents."

29. Alexander Hamilton, Elliot II, 304–5. Cf. *The Federalist* no. 17, 106–7; no. 27, 172–74.

30. Hamilton argued: "Sir, the most powerful obstacle to the members of Congress betraying the interest of their constituents, is the state legislatures themselves, who

will be standing bodies of observation, possessing the confidence of the people, jealous of federal encroachments, and armed with every power to check the first essays of treachery. They will institute regular modes of inquiry. The complicated domestic attachments, which subsist between the state legislators and their electors, will ever make them vigilant guardians of the people's rights. Possessed of the means and the disposition of resistance, the spirit of opposition will be easily communicated to the people, and, under the conduct of an organized body of leaders, will act with weight and system. Thus it appears that the very structure of the confederacy affords the surest preventives from error, and the most powerful checks to misconduct.'' Elliot II, 266–67; see also 304–5. To this argument, Lansing answered: "The circumstances the gentleman had enumerated, which seemed to be in favor of the states, only proved that the people would be under some advantages to discern the encroachments of *Congress*, and to take the alarm; but what would this signify? The gentleman did not mean that his principles should encourage rebellion: what other resource had they? None, but to wait patiently till the long terms of their senators were expired, and then elect other men. All the boasted advantages enjoyed by the states were finally reduced to this. The gentleman had spoken of an enmity which would subsist between the general and state governments: what, then, would be the situation of both? His wish, he said, was to prevent any enmity, by giving the states a constitutional and peaceable mode of checking maladministration, by recalling their senators, and not driving them into hostilities, in order to obtain redress.'' Elliot II, 308–9.

31. Cf. Brutus X, 2.9.128 n. 84. See Monroe 5.21.17 n. 8; cf. Hamilton's argument that the division of powers between the general and state governments is a question of convenience, a prudential inquiry. Elliot II, 350.

32. For similar views see Brutus IV, 2.9.54; DeWitt 4.3.17; A Friend to the Rights of the People 4.23.3; Cincinnatus II, 6.1.12; also Elliot IV, 203 (Lenoir). The Federalists repeatedly warned against excessive jealousy of chosen rulers. For examples see Ford, *Pamphlets* 126 (A Citizen of Philadelphia), 364 (Marcus); Ford, *Essays* 191 (A Landholder); Elliot III, 70 (Randolph); Elliot IV, 195, 221 (Iredell); and, the definitive statement, *The Federalist* no. 76, 513–14.

33. Hamilton replied that the resources of the general government ought to extend "as far as possible exigencies can require; that is, without limitation. A constitution cannot set bounds to a nation's wants; it ought not, therefore, to set bounds to its resources.'' Elliot II, 351. In *The Federalist* Hamilton emphatically conceded that *"in the usual progress of things, the necessities of a nation in every stage of its existence will be found at least equal to its resources."* *The Federalist* no. 30, 190; see also no. 23, 147–48; no. 21, 194–95; Symmes 4.5.14 n. 5.

34. For similar views see Cato III, 2.6.13–21 and n. 8. Hamilton argues that "this idea has been taken from a celebrated writer, who, by being misunderstood, has been the occasion of frequent fallacies in our reasoning on political subjects.'' Elliot II, 352; cf. *The Federalist* no. 9; Agrippa IV, 4.6.16 n. 10.

Bibliography

Works Frequently Cited

John Adams, *Works*	*The Works of John Adams*, ed. Charles Francis Adams (Boston 1851)
Blackstone, *Commentaries*	William Blackstone, *Commentaries on the Laws of England* (1765–69)
Crosskey, *Politics and the Constitution*	William W. Crosskey, *Politics and the Constitution in the History of the United States* (Chicago 1953)
Curtis, *Constitutional History*	George Ticknor Curtis, *Constitutional History of the United States: From Their Declaration of Independence to the Close of the Civil War* (New York 1889)
Dall.	Dallas' Pennsylvania and United States Reports, 1790–1800
Documentary History of the Constitution	*A Documentary History of the Constitution of the United States of America, 1786–1870; Derived from the Records, Manuscripts, and Rolls Deposited in the Bureau of Rolls and Library of the Department of State* (Washington, D.C., 1894–1905)
Elliot	*The Debates of the State Conventions on the Adoption of the Federal Constitution, as Recommended by the General Convention at Philadelphia in 1787*, 2d ed., ed. Jonathan Elliot (Philadelphia 1866)
Evans, *Early American Imprints*	Charles Evans, *Early American Imprints, 1639–1800* (Worcester, Mass., 1955–)
Farrand	*The Records of the Federal Convention of 1787*, ed. Max Farrand (New Haven 1911–37)
The Federalist	*The Federalist*, ed. Jacob E. Cooke (Middletown, Conn., 1961)
Ford, *Essays*	*Essays on the Constitution of the United States, Published during Its Discussion by the People, 1787–1788*, ed. Paul Leicester Ford (Brooklyn, N.Y., 1892)

Bibliography

Ford, *Pamphlets*
Pamphlets on the Constitution of the United States, Published during Its Discussion by the People, 1787–1788, ed. Paul Leicester Ford (Brooklyn, N.Y., 1888)

Harding, *Contest over Ratification*
Samuel Bannister Harding, *The Contest over the Ratification of the Federal Constitution in the State of Massachusetts* (New York 1896)

Jensen, *New Nation*
Merrill Jensen, *The New Nation* (New York 1950)

Madison, *Writings* (ed. Hunt)
The Writings of James Madison, ed. Gaillard Hunt (New York 1900–1910)

Main, *Antifederalists*
Jackson Turner Main, *The Antifederalists: Critics of the Constitution* (Chapel Hill, N.C., 1960)

McMaster and Stone
Pennsylvania and the Federal Constitution, 1787–1788, ed. John Bach McMaster and Frederick D. Stone (Published for the Subscribers by the Historical Society of Pennsylvania, 1888)

Thorpe, *Federal and State Constitutions*
The Federal and State Constitutions, Colonial Charters, and Other Organic Laws of the States, Territories, and Colonies Now or Heretofore Forming the United States of America, comp. Francis Newton Thorpe (Washington, D.C., 1931–44)

Wood, *Creation*
Gordon Wood, *The Creation of the American Republic, 1776–1787* (Chapel Hill, N.C., 1969)

Further Readings

Bancroft, George. *History of the Formation of the Constitution of the United States of America.* New York, 1882.

Beard, Charles. *An Economic Interpretation of the Constitution of the United States.* Rev. ed. New York, 1961.

Borden, Morton, ed. *The Antifederalist Papers.* Lansing, Mich., 1965–67.

Boyd, Steven R. *The Politics of Opposition: Antifederalists and the Acceptance of the Constitution.* Millwood, N.Y., 1979.

Crosskey, William Winslow, and William Jeffrey, Jr. *Politics and the Constitution in the History of the United States,* vol. 3: *The Political Background of the Federal Convention.* Chicago, 1980.

DePauw, Linda Grant. *The Eleventh Pillar: New York State and the Federal Constitution.* Ithaca, N.Y., 1966.

Diamond, Ann Stuart. "The Anti-Federalist 'Brutus.'" *Political Science Reviewer* 6 (1976): 249–81.

Documentary History of the Ratification of the Constitution. Vols. 1–3, ed. Merrill Jensen. Vols. 13–14, ed. John P. Kaminski and Gaspare J. Saladino. Madison, Wisc., 1976–.

Douglass, Elisha P. *Rebels and Democrats: The Struggle for Equal Political Rights and Majority During the American Revolution.* Chapel Hill, N.C., 1955.

Dry, Murray. "The Anti-Federalists and the Constitution." In *Principles of the Constitutional Order*, ed. Robert L. Utley, Jr. Washington, D.C., forthcoming.

Goldwin, Robert A., and William A. Schambra, eds. *How Democratic is the Constitution?* Washington, D.C., 1980. (Essays by Gordon S. Wood, Walter Berns, Wilson Carey McWilliams, and Alfred E. Young refer to the Anti-Federalists.)

Hutson, James H. "Country, Court, and Constitution: Antifederalism and the Historians." *William and Mary Quarterly*, 3d ser., 38, no. 3 (1981): 337–68.

Jeffrey, William, Jr., ed. "The Letters of 'Brutus'—a Neglected Element in the Ratification Campaign of 1787." *University of Cincinnati Law Review* 40 (1971): 643–77.

Kenyon, Cecelia M., ed. *The Antifederalists.* Indianapolis 1966. (Selected writings; introductory essay by Kenyon, "The Political Thought of the Antifederalists," originally published as "Men of Little Faith: The Anti-Federalists on the Nature of Representative Government," *William and Mary Quarterly*, 3d ser., 12, no. 1 [1955]: 3–46.)

Levy, Leonard, ed. *Essays on the Making of the Constitution.* New York, 1969.

Lewis, John D., ed. *Anti-Federalists versus Federalists: Selected Documents.* San Francisco, 1972.

Lienesch, Michael. "In Defense of the Antifederalists." *History of Political Thought* (Exeter, England) 4, no. 1 (1983): 65–87.

———. "Interpreting Experience: History, Philosophy, and Science in the American Constitutional Debates." *American Politics Quarterly* 11, no. 4 (1983): 379–401.

Lutz, Donald S. *Popular Consent and Popular Control: Whig Political Theory in the Early State Constitutions.* Baton Rouge, La., 1980. (See especially chapter 8.)

McDonald, Forrest. *We the People: The Economic Origins of the Constitution.* Chicago, 1958.

———. "The Anti-Federalists, 1781–1789." *Wisconsin Magazine of History* 46, no. 3 (1963).

McDonald, Forrest, ed. *Empire and Nation.* Englewood Cliffs, N.J., 1962.

McDowell, Gary. "Richard Henry Lee and the Quest for Constitutional Liberty." In *The American Founding: Politics, Statesmanship, and the Constitution*, ed. Ralph Rossum and Gary McDowell. Port Washington, N.Y., 1981.

———. "Were the Anti-Federalists Right? Judicial Activism and the Problem of Consolidated Government." *Publius* 12, no. 3 (1982): 99–108.

Main, Jackson Turner. *Political Parties before the Constitution*. Chapel Hill, N.C., 1975.

Mason, Alpheus Thomas, ed. *The States Rights Debate: Antifederalism and the Constitution*. 2d ed. New York, 1972.

Rossum, Ralph A. "Representation and Republican Government: Contemporary Court Variations on the Founders' Theme." In *Taking the Constitution Seriously: Essays on the Constitution and Constitutional Law*, ed. Gary McDowell. Dubuque, Iowa, 1981.

Rutland, Robert. *The Ordeal of the Constitution: The Anti-Federalists and the Ratification Struggle of 1787–1788*. Norman, Okla., 1966.

———. "George Mason: The Revolutionist as Conservative." In *The American Founding: Politics, Statesmanship, and the Constitution*, ed. Ralph Rossum and Gary McDowell. Port Washington, N.Y., 1981.

Storing, Herbert J. *What the Anti-Federalists Were For*. Chicago 1981. (Vol. 1 of *The Complete Anti-Federalist* issued separately as a paperback.)

———. "The Constitution and the Bill of Rights." *In Essays on the Constitution of the United States*, ed. M. Judd Harmon. Port Washington, N.Y., 1978. Also in *Taking the Constitution Seriously: Essays on the Constitution and Constitutional Law*, ed. Gary McDowell. Dubuque, Iowa, 1981.

———. "The Constitutional Convention: Toward a More Perfect Union." In *American Political Thought: The Philosophic Dimension of American Statesmanship*, 2d ed., ed. Morton J. Frisch and Richard G. Stevens. Dubuque, Iowa, 1976.

———. "The 'Other' Federalist Papers: A Preliminary Sketch." *Political Science Reviewer* 6 (1976): 215–47.

Storing, Herbert J., ed. *The Complete Anti-Federalist*. 7 vols. Chicago, 1981.

Wood, Gordon. "The Democratization of Mind in the American Revolution." In *The Moral Foundations of the American Republic*, ed. Robert H. Horwitz. Charlottesville, Va., 1977.

Wood, Gordon, ed. *The Confederation and the Constitution: The Critical Issues*. Boston, 1973.

Yarbrough, Jean. "Representation and Republican Government: Two Views." *Publius* 9, no. 2 (1979): 77–78.

Index

Adams, John: balanced government, 8, 15, 21 n. 4; on merchants as advocates for liberty, 77, 100 n. 65; on natural aristocracy, 100 n. 64, 345; on Philadelphia v. Boston, 253 n. 19; on San Marino, 272 n. 53; on the schools hostile to democracy, 100 n. 65
Addison, Joseph, 313
Agrippa (pseud.): on commerce as bond of union, 230, 243; on consolidation, 235–36, 238–39; on freedom, commerce, and tranquillity, 230–32, 252 n. 6; identity of, 227, 229 n. 1; on large republic v. confederacy of smaller states, 235–36; on motives of Federalists, 251–52; outline of letters, 228; replies to, 229 n. 1; resolution to amend Articles of Confederation, 248–49
ale, taxation of, 141
amendment, constitutional, difficulty of, under proposed constitution, 59–60
America (Noah Webster), 201 n. 1, 222 nn. 6 and 7. See also Webster, Noah
American Citizen (Tench Coxe), on standing army, 194 n. 71
American Revolution, principles of, 153
Anti-Federalists: agreement among, 3–4; attitude toward Washington and Franklin, 21 n. 2; Charles Beard on, 1–2; concern over possibility of military enforcement of federal law, 194–95 n. 73; dilemma of, 4; on equal representation of states in Senate, 192 n. 26; on large republic v. confederacy of smaller states, 235–36, 252 n. 10; name, 5 n. 6; negative portrayal of, 1; principles of, 2–4; state officials as, 357 n. 8; traditional view of, 1; as the true Federalists, 276
Aristides (Alexander Contee Hanson), and [Maryland] Farmer, 258
aristocracy
—natural: John Adams on, 100 n. 64, 345; Anti-Federalists on, 100 n. 64;

Brutus on, 125; Federal Farmer on, 76–77; Federalists on, 100 n. 64; Alexander Hamilton on, 357 n. 17; Robert R. Livingston on, 358 n. 23; Melancton Smith on, 340–41
—and Senate, 189
—types of, 76
arms, right to bear, 207
Articles of Confederation
—amendment of: Agrippa on, 245, 248–49; Patrick Henry on, 297; Impartial Examiner on, 276, 289
—benefits of present system: Agrippa on, 231–35, 247; Patrick Henry on, 296–97, 299, 306–7
—general conditions under, 306–7, 326 n. 12, 318, 356
—imperfect system: Agrippa on, 243–45; Centinel on, 9; Patrick Henry on, 306–7; Pennsylvania Convention Minority on, 202–3; Melancton Smith on, 333
—John Jay on, 99 n. 54
—leading features, 70–73
—requisitions under, 88–92
—standing army in states, 156
—violation of, by Constitutional Convention, 205
attainder, bills of prohibition of, 154
Austria, House of, 265

bail, excessive, 207
balanced government: Centinel on John Adams' idea of, 8, 15; Constitution not providing, 47; Federal Farmer on 69, 77–79; and responsibility, 196 n. 112; and taxation, 144–45
bankruptcy laws, Federal Farmer on, 52, 98 n. 32
Beard, Charles, view of Anti-Federalists, 1–2
Beccaria, Cesare (marquis), on tendency toward inequality, 75, 99–100 n. 61, 342